Accountability and democracy in Poland and Spain

STUDIES IN POLITICS, SECURITY AND SOCIETY

Edited by Stanisław Sulowski
Institute of Political Science of the University of Warsaw

VOLUME 8

PETER LANG
EDITION

Anna Sroka

Accountability and democracy in Poland and Spain

PETER LANG
EDITION

Bibliographic Information published by the Deutsche Nationalbibliothek
The Deutsche Nationalbibliothek lists this publication in
the Deutsche Nationalbibliografie; detailed bibliographic
data is available in the internet at http://dnb.d-nb.de.

Library of Congress Cataloging-in-Publication Data
Names: Sroka, Anna, author.
Title: Accountability and democracy in Poland and Spain / Anna Sroka.
Description: Frankfurt am Main : Peter Lang, 2017. | Series: Studies in politics, security and society, 2199-028x ; vol. 8 | Includes bibliographical references and index.
Identifiers: LCCN 2016051007| ISBN 9783631674475 | ISBN 9783653065923 (E-PDF) | ISBN 9783631706527 (EPUB) | ISBN 9783631706534 (MOBI)
Subjects: LCSH: Government accountability--Poland | Government accountability--Spain. | Democracy--Poland. | Democracy--Spain. | Poland--Politics and government--1989- | Spain--Politics and government--1982-
Classification: LCC JN6759.5.A33 S76 2017 | DDC 352.3/509438--dc23 LC record available at https://lccn.loc.gov/2016051007

This publication was financially supported by the
Institute of Political Science of the University of Warsaw.

ISSN 2199-028X
ISBN 978-3-631-67447-5 (Print)
E-ISBN 978-3-653-06592-3 (E-PDF)
E-ISBN 978-3-631-70652-7 (EPUB)
E-ISBN 978-3-631-70653-4 (MOBI)
DOI 10.3726/b10679

Peter Lang – Frankfurt am Main · Bern · Bruxelles · New York ·
Oxford · Warszawa · Wien

This publication has been peer reviewed.

www.peterlang.com

Table of Contents

Introduction

For years, discussions concerning the issue of young democracies centred on the conditions necessary for successful democratic transitions to be conducted. Next, they revolved around the issue of consolidation. In the past decade, a new expression has arisen in studies on democratic systems: the concept of "quality of democracy". One of the primary elements in most conceptions of quality of democracy, whether in the quantitative or the qualitative dimension, is accountability.

This term is eagerly employed not only by researchers focused on quality of democracy, but also by journalists and politicians. In spite of the increasing presence of the concept of "accountability" in both political science analyses and political discourse, there is no generally accepted definition of the concept. It is most frequently used as a sort of "umbrella" term, with a range of definitions underneath. Accountability is constantly intermingled with other concepts: transparency, effectiveness, responsibility and efficiency. Accountability is also applied as a synonym for good governance, both in the public sector and the private one. The multiplicity of meanings assigned to the concept of accountability, which dilutes its analytical value, is a consequence *inter alia* of the absence of a deeper conceptualisation and operationalisation of that idea grounded in global scholarship. The majority of studies concerning quality of democracy (in which accountability plays a role) are of a quantitative character. In their essence, they consist in developing quality of democracy barometers without a detailed conceptualisation of its particular elements. On the other hand, qualitative studies most frequently concern only selected aspects of accountability.[1]

When considering the foregoing, an attempt at conceptualisation and operationalisation of accountability as one of the elements in quality of democracy would seem to be most justified. The results presented in this book are innovative, and contribute to filling a discernible research gap concerning one of the most important elements in quality of democracy: accountability. Accountability is understood according to the definition given by O'Donnel. Horizontal accountability is based on a system of checks and balance. The essence of this system is ensuring a separation of interdependent powers based on the functions they perform within the system, and providing them with autonomy so that they can exercise oversight and control functions in respect of one another's activities. Horizontal

1 A detailed description of the state of research on accountability in studies on quality of democracy will be presented in the first chapter.

accountability also includes public mandate agencies, e.g. those with both legal authority and the operational capacity to engage in activity, running from standard oversight to criminal law sanctions. Vertical accountability consists in ensuring that citizens have not only the potential to select their representatives, but also to observe and to sanction them in situations when selected representatives take decisions inconsistent with the expectations of the voters.

The primary objective of the research is to determine at what moment and in what field the creation occurs of elements of changes which in one country stimulate positive effects, while in another result in the emergence of numerous delays and growth in negative post-transformation phenomena concerning accountability in Poland and Spain. In order to explain the causes of existing differences and similarities, there will be an examination of the link between institutional solutions, policies implemented, and the time that passed from the moment of consolidation of both systems and the impact of these variables on accountability mechanisms.

The book is composed of three parts: I. Theoretical foundations; II. Horizontal accountability; III. Vertical accountability. In Part I, the discussion will centre around the concept of quality of democracy and the primary strands in research on quality of democracy. Next, there will be a presentation of the links between quality of democracy and accountability, including a discussion of selected conceptualisations and operationalisations of quality of democracy and accountability. This will facilitate portrayal of the issue of operationalisation of democracy, as quality of democracy is associated with accountability; it will also draw attention to the types of accountability and manners of operationalisation. At the end of the first chapter a research plan and the main assumptions for empirical analysis to be conducted in further parts of the work are presented.

Part II (Chapter 2) will address the executive authority in the system of horizontal accountability. There will be an examination of the capacity of the government and head of state to shape the legislative and decision agenda of parliament, including a discussion of informal mechanisms influencing the work of parliament. The analysis will take into consideration procedural conditions and the support enjoyed by governments in the lower house of parliament. Additionally, regarding the head of state in Poland and Spain, alongside procedural conditions attention will also be paid to situations of cohabitation. This structure for the chapter will facilitate finding an answer to a range of more detailed research questions. The first regards the strength of the executive in both systems and its capacity to influence the legislative and decision agenda of parliament. The second concerns to what extent the impact of the government on the legislative and decision agenda of parliament is conditioned by institutional architecture and by the "political balance of power" in the parliament. The third is about whether the time that has passed from the moment of consolidation of the political system leads to strengthening of the executive within the system of horizontal accountability or not.

The third chapter is dedicated to the legislative branch within the accountability system. Here as well, procedural conditions will be one of the determinants captured in research on the functioning of the legislature within the system of horizontal accountability. The second determinant will be the support enjoyed by particular governments in successive parliamentary terms, as alongside procedural conditions it is precisely this support which has the largest significance for the dynamics of the accountability tools employed. This will also facilitate the search for answers to the following questions: which of the determinants has the greatest influence on the use of instruments of accountability in Poland and in Spain? To what extent does the time elapsed from the moment of consolidation of the political system affect institutionalisation of the control exercised by the lower chamber of parliament?

The fourth chapter will be dedicated to the judiciary and mandate agencies. Similarly to the case of the executive and legislative powers, in this case as well attention will be paid to procedural conditions and the type of government and support it enjoys in the lower house of parliament. The objective of this chapter is to answer the following questions: are we dealing with a fully independent judiciary and mandate agencies which should work to protect the rule of law and counteract abuses? Is the level of independence enjoyed by the judiciary and mandate agencies more dependent on procedural conditions, or rather political constellations? How does parliamentary support for the government influence the independence of the judiciary and mandate agencies? Does the time that has elapsed from the consolidation of the political system lead to greater independence of the judiciary and mandate agencies?

In Part III (Chapter Five) there is a discussion of the impact of various determinants on the functioning of vertical accountability mechanisms at the level of the electoral decision, both in respect of the procedural dimension and in reference to final effects. These determinants have been divided into two groups. The first includes the type of electoral system and the territorial structures of the state. The second includes the type of party system and government. This structure makes it possible to answer a primary research question: do institutional factors disrupt the functioning of vertical accountability mechanisms in Poland and in Spain?

The sixth chapter contains a study of whether and to what extent economic voting was used by voters as a measure of vertical accountability. In other words – if and how much voters in Poland and Spain are motivated by the desire to reward or punish ruling parties. In this portion of the work a quantitative analysis based on the multinomial logistic regression model. The primary research question that will be answered is: can we speak in Poland and Spain of retrospective economic voting, which is considered the gauge of electoral accountability?

At the end, it is worth adding that the ambition harboured by the proposed strategy is to analyse accountability captured holistically. The phenomenon of accountability will be portrayed in cross-section, in the context of almost the entire political situation of Poland and Spain. This approach requires a synthesis to be performed in respect of each of the discussed issues and the selecting of only those aspects that are significant for the matter of accountability. The difficulty of such a task stems from two aspects. Firstly, the existing scientific literature in this area has not yet seen operationalisation of accountability at the qualitative level. Secondly, analysis of a political system in respect of one of its specific elements, *id est* accountability, requires the adoption of a new perspective on the functioning of that political system. We may take the example of changes in electoral law. From the perspective of effectiveness of a political system, it is well-understood that frequent changes do not contribute to the proper functioning of the political system, as voters can begin to feel "disoriented". Nevertheless, from the perspective of vertical accountability this is a very beneficial arrangement. It works to limit the creation of party and ideological links, which in turn leads to voters applying reward/punishment mechanisms. Therefore, voters do not vote based on ideology, but rather on the basis of assessment of the previous governing group's activities. In spite of these difficulties and limitations resulting from the adopted research strategy, the author retains hope that this work will contribute to the expansion of knowledge and the development of research in the field of quality of democracy, with particular attention paid to accountability.

This book would not have been possible without the assistance of institutions, friends, family, and many others. Support from the Ministry of Science and Higher Education, which awarded funding for the project "Accountability as one of the elements in quality of democracy on the example of Poland and Spain" (no. 1172/B/H03/2010/39), made it possible to engage in the empirical portion of the study. These funds, combined with support from my parent research institution, the Institute of Political Science of the University of Warsaw, made it possible to present particular portions of the work at conferences and seminars both domestically and abroad. This facilitated critical assessment of the theoretical assumptions and the correctness of the methodology employed, as well as the first research results. This is also why I would like to thank the Institute of Political Science of the University of Warsaw, and in particular its director, Professor Stanisław Sulowski. During the conceptualization and operationalization phase of the book I received invaluable assistance from prof. Leonardo Morlino, prof. Fernando Vallespína Oña, prof. Andrzej Antoszewski, prof. Konstanty Adam Wojtaszczyk, prof. Gonzalo Angulo Núñez, prof. Mikołaj Cześnik, and dr. Michał Kotnarowski, for which I would like to extend my sincerest thanks. Thanks to my mother, Grażyna Sroka, who was the first critical reader and editor of this book, as well as my brother Daniel for reviewing one chapter. I would especially like to thank dr. Małgorzata Kaczorowska, dr. Aleksandra Moroska-Bonkiewicz, dr. Marta Witkowska, dr. Marta Żerkowska-Balas and dr. Agnieszka Bejma, who not only provided me with substantive support while writing the book, but also helped me in moments of doubt as to the sense of my work. I would also like to thank Borja Polo de la Morena for his help, patience, and the dignity with which he has borne my frequent absence.

Anna Sroka
Warsaw
June 2016

Part I. Theoretical foundations

Chapter 1. Accountability in studies on quality of democracy

The concept of quality of democracy emerged from studies on transition and processes involved in consolidation of democracy. The results of research on countries engulfed by the third wave of democratisation indicated that the majority of those regimes succeeded in maintaining democratic stability. Scholars conducting research on young democracies within a comparative framework have concluded that their primary dependent variable – i.e. the stability of political regimes, which has previously been the primary plane of conventional studies – has declined in importance. By the same token, this variable has ceased to be attractive. In recent years this situation has made it necessary for these researchers to seek answers to new and more nuanced questions about the conditions of democratic consolidation. They have sought these answers through analysing more detailed institutional characteristics of new democracies. This has led to the development of interest in the quality of democratic experiences. Numerous attempts at conceptualising quality of democracy have been undertaken. Interest in the issue of quality of democracy within political science is attested to by, the number of studies conducted around the world related to this new field of knowledge, which demonstrates the explanatory strength of this new concept. At present, the relevant subject literature contains a rich collection of theoretical conceptualisations and operationalisations of quality of democracy. The majority of authors approach the issue from a quantitative perspective, but there are also quantitative treatments of the issue.

The concept of quality of democracy has doubtlessly become more defined and useful in studies on contemporary democratic systems, particularly when we view quality of democracy as a sort of ideal model or reference point for a ceaselessly imperfect reality. Following this logic, we may establish parameters of "idealness" and propose solutions to improve existing political regimes. Why, then, has the concept of quality of democracy been for decades the subject of intense discussion among researchers from around the world, and what are the reasons a generally accepted operationalisation of the concept which could assist political scientists around the world in comparing the quality of democracy in particular political systems has yet to be developed?

This chapter will present answers to both the questions posed above, as well as to many others that arise in the course of research on accountability in quality of democracy. A broader analysis will be conducted of existing approaches to and conceptualisations of quality of democracy and of accountability. In addition, assessment of selected operationalisations of quality of democracy and accountability will be undertaken. This will facilitate the formulation of answers to the following questions: What generates the greatest difficulties in operationalisation of quality of democracy? How is quality of democracy linked to accountability? What types of accountability can be distinguished? This chapter will ultimately lead to the construction of a model of accountability that will be employed in successive portions of the book for examining accountability in Poland and Spain.

1.1. The conception of quality of democracy

Quality of democracy can be and is studied at various levels of analysis. There is a very large number of manners in which quality of democracy has been conceptualised, and an equal variety of methods for measuring it. Many researchers around the world, either working for their parent research institutions or at the behest of various international and non-governmental organisations, have taken up the challenge of conceptualising and operationalising quality of democracy. It should, however, be kept in mind that political science has proven unable to offer one universal definition of democracy accepted by all at the empirical level. A definition free of value judgments and broad enough to capture the multidimensional nature of contemporary democratic systems. As a result, different definitions of democracy lead to the development of different conceptualisations of quality of democracy. The definition of democracy, in turn, is crucial in defining and operationalising quality of democracy. It essentially constitutes a starting point, as the types of indices to be used are dependent on that definition.

In analysing the conceptualisations of quality of democracy it is easy to observe that the point of reference, particularly in respect of quality of democracy barometers, is most frequently so-called minimal and procedural definitions. This is a result of the significant ease that such definitions offer in operationalising and employing in empirical analyses compared to axiological, teleological, processual or substantial ones. In the case of more in-depth studies on quality of democracy a frequent operation is employment of the Dahlian polyarchy as the general framework for the research. It should be kept in mind that the polyarchy of R. Dahl[2] is derived from the minimalist conception of democracy advanced by J. Schumpeter.[3] The definition of liberal democracy offered by L. Diamond is also

2 R. Dahl, *Polyarchy: participation and opposition*, New Haven 1971.

3 J. Schumpeter, *Capitalism, Socialism and Democracy*, London 1976.

invoked, as an expansion of the concept of polyarchy by three additional conditions referring to protection of individual and collective freedoms.[4] Although the most frequently employed definitions of democracy are products of a procedural understanding of democracy, there is still an absence of one common, generally accepted definition of democracy in the empirical sphere. As a result, there has yet to be developed a unified catalogue of dimensions or elements of quality of democracy which would be accepted by the community of scholars engaged with the issue. And yet, it is on this foundation that barometers of quality of democracy are built, which at present are one of the most frequently-used parameters in classifying political system. Nearly every political scientist has encountered this type of ranking. They are often subjected to criticism. None of the rankings in use is perfect. A brief analysis of the legend of particular rankings allows even an inexperienced political scientist to grasp the conceptual gaps and shortfalls in justifications for the selection of some indices. One may frequently get the impression that some of the indices were chosen only due to the availability of data; this is particularly true in the case of rankings involving a large number of states.

This, in turn, is associated with another problem encountered when analysing studies on quality of democracy: the majority of them are quantitative. The difficulties faced by quality of democracy researchers employing the quantitative approach result primarily from the specificity of individual democracies. The political system of every state is a historical and social construct. The form in which a society defines itself, just as the very role of civil society in the functioning of a political system, is extremely diverse. This is also why it is hard to disagree with P. Schmitter and T. Karl, who state that the form of a democracy depends on the social and economic conditions existing in a given country, as well as ensconced state structures and patterns of political behaviour.[5] One example is that of the states of South America, in which societies have succeeded in consolidation of political and social rights. However, the fact that they are faced with a high level of poverty and social inequality is decisive when attempting to assess these democracies.

In spite of the convolutedness inherent in comparisons of quality of democracy across states, it is precisely the places occupied by states in this type of ranking that has the strongest influence on contemporary opinions about the political system of a given country. These judgements have a direct impact not only on

4 L. Diamond, *Is the Third Wave Over?*, "Journal of Democracy" 1996, no. 7, p. 22.

5 P. Schmitter, T. Karl, *Czym jest demokracja i czym nie jest* in: J. Szczupaczyński (ed.), *Władza i społeczeństwo: antologia tekstów z zakresu socjologii polityki*, Warsaw 1995, pp. 28–29.

the position of a given country in the international sphere, but also play a role in shaping its future. This results from the fact that the decisions of international organisations about providing financing are dependent on places occupied in quality of democracy rankings, and thus of particular importance in developing countries. This is also why criticism of the legitimacy of studies examining quality of democracy, while justified, comes across as unconvincing. One example of such criticism is that offered by C. Cansino, who claims that the operationalisation of quality of democracy and the concomitant assigning of heuristic value to it demonstrating that democracy X is better in quality than democracy Y, ultimately reduces democracy to the category of a product.[6] While this argument is not without a certain degree of merit, studies on quality of democracy are a fact and they will certainly be continued. For this reason also it is very important to precisely define quality of democracy and its reach as one is trying to measure it with the use of various theoretical propositions. The present debate taking place among political theorists concerns the selection of indices and elements that should be taken into consideration when measuring quality of democracy, in order to ensure that measurements are empirically valid and realistic.

Two streams of thought can be distinguished in studies on quality of democracy in respect of the object under study. In the first group, researchers are focused on finding an answer to the question of which states from among those being analysed are more democratic. Those from the second group are seeking an answer to the question of which democracies are better democracies. These questions lead to different types of studies. In respect of the former, quality of democracy is the result of a certain continuum which stretches from ideal totalitarian regimes to perfect democracies. Here the efforts of scholars are focused on applying various techniques and indices to measure the level of democracy, generally on a large number of states. In this case, democracy and quality of democracy is an extension of the same concept. We are therefore dealing with measuring the degree to which states have democratised, but not the condition of their democracy. In addition, the majority of indices employed in this strand of research are not particularly sensitive, and they do not reflect the minor differences among individual democracies concerning quality of democracy. They are generally designed to measure "drastic" changes of regimes, not the delicate differences exhibited across particular democracies. In the main, studies within this strand are focused on institutional determinants of democracy. The criteria for quality of democracy

6 C. Cansino, *Entre la democracia real y democracia ideal. Consideraciones críticas*, "Metapolítica" 2005, Enero/ Febrero, pp. 99–108.

adopted in definitions of that concept refer to normative and descriptive models which can be compared to the idea of rule of law. The second strand, apart from institutional determinants also encompasses social and political determinants capable of impacting quality of democracy. In line with this perspective, a democracy which has achieved a minimal procedural level can also be devoid of the traits characteristic of good democracy. By the same token, only consolidated democracies can be subjected to comparison.

Many of the popular barometers of quality of democracy are aligned with the first of the research trends described above. The best illustration of this approach to studies on quality of democracy is likely the one most frequently cited by researchers, the *Freedom in the World* barometer developed by the non-governmental organisation Freedom House, published since 1972 and presently encompassing 190 states around the world.[7] The *Freedom in the World* barometer is one of a group of barometers based on panel surveys conducted among experts. This group also includes barometers which are based not only on expert opinions, but also on surveys conducted on the general population, such as *The Economist Intelligence Unit* (EIU index)[8], *Índice de Desarrollo Democrático*[9] and *Polity*.[10]

Barometers of quality of democracy aligned with the second trend in research are very frequently based on indices not associated with the perceptions of experts or citizens, but also on numerical factors such as the effective number of parties or proportionality in voting systems. Barometers consistent with this type and approach to conceptualising quality of democracy include Witold Henisz's "Checks and balances",[11] that of M. Bühlmann, W. Merkel, L. Müller, and B. Wessels,

7 Freedom House, Freedom in the World: http://www.freedomhouse.org/report-types/freedom-world#.UtzuqbTdhVc.

8 L. Kckic, *The Economist Intelligence Unit's index of democracy*, "The Economist" 2006, special edition: *The World in 2007*,. http://www.economist.com/media/pdf/DEMOCRACY_INDEX_2007_v3.pdf; *The Economist Intelligence Unit s Index of Democracy 2008*, "The Economist" 2008, special edition: *The World in 2009*, http://graphics.eiu.com/PDF/Democracy%20Index%202008.pdf; *The Economist Intelligence Unit s Index of Democracy 2008*, "The Economist" 2008, special edition: *Democracy index 2010 Democracy in retreat*, http://graphics.eiu.com/PDF/Democracy%20Index%202008.pdf.

9 Índice de Desarrollo Democrático, http://www.idd-lat.org/2013/.

10 Polity IV Project: Political Regime Characteristics and Transitions, 1800–2012, http://www.systemicpeace.org/polity/polity4.htm.

11 W. Henisz, *The Institutional Environment for Economic Growth*, "Economics and Politics" 2000, no. 12 (1), pp. 1–31.

"Democracy Barometer for Established Democracies",[12] and State of Democracy developed by the International Institute for Democracy and Electoral Assistance (International IDEA).[13] One of the more interesting barometers is State of Democracy by International IDEA, which is distinct from the barometers previously described. In this case, a unified methodology is used to develop an in-depth and comprehensive assessment of the level of democracy in studied countries. This is also why only 20 states have been reviewed by the study.

Attempts at conceptualisation and operationalisation of quality of democracy that should be grouped within the second strand of research addressed to a small number of states and/or with the use of qualitative and mixed methods include those of D. Altman and A. Pérez-Liñán,[14] G. O'Donnell, O. Iayyett and J. Vargas Cullell,[15] L. Morlino and L. Diamond,[16] and lastly A. Roberts.[17]

1.2. Accountability as a component of quality of democracy

It is not possible to list all the barometers of quality of democracy, nor attempts at its conceptualisation and operationalisation, as at present practically every important scientific centre engaged in research on democracy is attempting to develop its own, more perfect barometer.[18] This is why the discussion below will only encompass some of the conceptualisations of quality of democracy that are aligned with the second trend in research, which have inspired quality of democracy scholars and, as a result, are the most frequently cited. In addition, the criterion for selection

---

12 M. Bühlmann, W. Merkel, L. Müller, B. Wessels, *The Quality of Democracy: Democracy Barometer for Established Democracies, NCCR Democracy*, 2008, www.hertie-school.org/fileadmin/images/Downloads/working_papers/22.pdf.

13 International Institute for Democracy and Electoral Assistance (International IDEA), http://www.idea.int/sod/.

14 D. Altman, A. Pérez-Liñan, *Assessing the quality of democracy: freedom, competitiveness and participation in eighteen Latin American countries*, "Democratization" 2000, vol. 9, no. 2, pp. 85–100.

15 G. O'Donnell, O. Iazzetta, J. Vargas-Cullell, *The quality of democracy: theory and applications*, Notre Dame 2004.

16 L. Diamond, L. Morlino (eds.), *Assessing the quality of democracy*, Baltimore 2005.

17 A. Roberts, *The quality of democracy in Eastern Europe: public preferences and policy reforms*, New York 2009.

18 A comparison of some of the barometers mentioned above can be found in: G. Munck, J. *Verkuilen, Conceptualizing and Measuring Democracy: Evaluating Alternative Indices*, "Comparative Political Studies" 2002, no. 35 (1), pp. 5–34; W. Szewczak, *Jak zmierzyć demokrację? Skale pomiaru demokracji politycznej stosowane w politologii porównawczej*, „Przegląd Politologiczny" 2011, no. 1, pp. 121–137.

of the following conceptualisations, alongside clarity and detail of the conceptualisation of quality of democracy itself, was the explicit inclusion of accountability as one of the key elements in operationalisation.

Analysing selected conceptualisations of quality of democracy captured in Table 1 below, it can easily be observed that the adopted definitions of democracy can be categorised as procedural definitions. For L. Morlino, the starting point is minimal democracy, while a high-quality democracy is one in which there is "a stable institutional structure that realizes the liberty and equality of citizens through the legitimate and correct functioning of its institutions and mechanisms."[19] For M. Bühlmann, W. Merkel, L. Müller, and B. Wessels, the point of departure is stabilised democracy – although they do not offer a definition of this concept – while the ultimate objective is liberal and participatory democracy.[20] A. Roberts defined democracy in categories of formal (institutional) democracy; this author invokes S. Huntington's definition of democracy. The objective is a democracy defined as one in which rights are universal.[21] D. Levine and J. Molina start from a definition of procedural democracy, and in their opinion a high-quality democracy is one in which well-informed citizens participate in a process of free, independent and regular elections, impacting political decisions and holding their leaders to account.[22]

Table 1 also presents components of the discussed conceptualisations of quality of democracy. It can be observed that all of the discussed conceptualisations contain elements of both horizontal and vertical accountability, with the exception of A. Roberts, which is restricted to the latter form of accountability. The concepts of L. Morlino and of M. Bühlmann, W. Merkel, L. Müller and B. Wessels encompass the greatest range of dimensions. That said, the concept of L. Morlino presents severe difficulties when attempting to apply it at the empirical level; perhaps this is why it has not yet been fully operationalised. Additionally, it concerns

19 L. Morlino, *'Good' and 'Bad' Democracies: How to Conduct Research into the Quality of Democracy*, "Journal of Communist Studies and Transition Politics" 2004, vol. 20 no. 1, p. 7.

20 M. Bühlmann, W.Merkel, L. Müller, B.Wessels, *The Democracy Barometer: A New instrument to Measure the Quality of Democracy and tis Potential for Comparative Research*, "European Political Science" 2011, http://www.democracybarometer.org/Papers/eps201146_AOP.pdf.

21 A. Roberts, *The Quality…*, op. cit.

22 D. Levine, J. Molina, *Calidad de la democracia: Fortzalezas y Debilidades en América Latina*, in: G. Munck, S. Mantilla (eds.), *La calidad de la democracia: perspectivas desde América Latina*, Quito 2012, p. 115.

to a greater extent the conditions that should be met for a given democracy to be a good one, rather than a way of measuring its quality. It is worth mentioning here that the plan for analysis quality of democracy analysis composed of eight dimensions was first presented jointly by L. Diamond and L. Morlino in the book *Assessing the Quality of Democracy*. Initially, L. Diamond and L. Morlino distinguished five procedural dimensions: rule of law, participation, representation, competition, and accountability (both vertical and horizontal). Two substantive dimensions are identified: freedom and equality. The final dimension, responsiveness, is a sort of connection of the procedural dimension with the substantive, as it boils down to examining the extent to which actions by those in power are a response to the expectations and preferences of citizens engaged in the political process.[23] L. Morlino then developed this conception in successive works.[24]

The concept created by M. Bühlmann, W. Merkel, L. Müller, and B. Wessels is elaborated at the operationalisation level, as each of the quality of democracy components is assigned the relevant indices. Frequently, however, one may get the impression that some of the indices have not been chosen due to their explanatory function, but rather with a view to the availability of data. A study conducted on the basis of the proposed concept for quality of democracy encompasses all of the states associated within the OECD. The remaining two concepts were designed for states from two specific regions. The proposal advanced by A. Roberts encompasses the countries of Central and Eastern Europe, while that of D. Levine and J. Molina addresses South America. A. Roberts's proposal is limited only to the electoral dimension and to the capacity of those in power to react to the needs of ordinary citizens (*responsiveness*). On the other hand the concept developed by D. Levine and J. Molina encompasses not only the electoral dimension, but also the institutional one. Furthermore, because of the specificity of democracy in

23 L. Diamond, L. Morlino, *Introduction*, in: L. Diamond, L. Morlino (eds.), *Assessing the Quality of Democracy*, Baltimore 2005, pp. XIV–XXXI.

24 See: L. Morlino, Calidad democrática entre líderes y partidos, 2008, www.democraciaenamericalatina.org/articulos/seminarios/sem_partidos/morlino.pdf; L. Morlino, Qualities of democracy: how to analyze them, 2009, indicatorsinfo.pbworks.com/f/Morlino+Qualities+of+Democracy.pdf; L. Morlino, *Democracias y democratizaciones*, Madryt 2009; L. Morlino, *What is a 'Good' Democracy*?, "Democratization" 2004, vol. 11, no. 5, pp. 10–32; L. Morlino, *Good' and 'Bad' Democracies: How to Conduct Research into the Quality of Democracy*, "Journal of Communist Studies and Transition Politics" 2004, vol. 20, no. 1, pp. 5–27; L. Morlino, *Changes for Democracy: Actors, Structures, Processes*, Oxford University Press 2011.

South America they have included a component addressing social inequality and level of satisfaction with democracy.

Table 1. Selected examples of conceptualizations of quality of democracy

Author(s)	**L. Morlino (2004)**	**M. Bühlmann, W. Merkel, L. Müller, B. Wessels (2011)**	**A. Roberts (2009)**	**D. Levine, J. Molina (2011)**
Starting definition of democracy	Minimal democracy	Stabilized democracy	Formal democracy (institutional)	Procedural democracy (minimal)
Definition of quality of democracy	High-quality democracy	Liberal and participatory democracy	Democracy understood as universality of rules	Democracy
Relation between quality of democracy and fundamental conception of democracy	Quality of democracy refers to procedures, contents and results, while the examined cases must fulfil the starting criteria of democracy.	Quality of democracy is understood in terms of adherence to democratic rules; it is only applicable when the starting criteria are met	Quality of democracy concerns the functioning of democracy (strength of general control), the degree of democratization is not important, only applies in cases when the starting criteria are fulfilled	Quality of democracy refers to the conditions for effective functioning of procedural democracy; level of democratization is not important; only applies in countries which fulfil the starting criteria
Elements of conception (components)	1. Rule of law 2. Accountability 3. Responsiveness 5. Freedom and Equality	1. Freedom: Rule of law, Individual liberty, public voice 2. Equality: governmental power, Mutual constraints, Vertical accountability 3. Control: transparency, Participation, Inclusion	1. Electoral accountability 2. Policy responsiveness; Mandate responsiveness	1. Electoral decision 2. Participation 3. Accountability 4. Responsiveness 5. Sovereignty

Source: own work.

In analysing accountability in the conceptions of quality of democracy presented in Table 1 above, it should be emphasised that each author distinguishes different types. It should be underlined here that the scholar who inspired later research on accountability in the conception of quality of democracy was G. O'Donnell, although his proposal does not include an operationalisation and is limited solely to conceptualisation. However, it would be remiss to not mention the theoretical proposition offered by this Argentinian researcher. G. O'Donnell initially proposed two types of accountability in contemporary democratic systems: horizontal and vertical.[25] Horizontal accountability is understood as the existence of organs and state institutions with both the legal authority and the operational capacity to initiate activities ranging from simple oversight to sanctions of a penal nature, and even impeachment in respect of the activities and omissions of other state organs and institutions. In addition, the author distinguishes two types of institutions: balancing, and mandate agencies. Balancing institutions are ones which engage in the exercise of control functions, by the same token ensuring balance across the different powers. Primarily this concerns mechanisms that place limits on the executive through such means as veto, impeachment, revocation of immunity for individuals exercising public authority, the appointment of investigative commissions, interpellations and queries, the activity of a Constitutional Tribunal and a State Tribunal. The second type of institution is those mandate agencies, which have not been appointed for the purpose of regulating the balance between primary centres of power, but rather with managing threats associated with the abuse of power. Such institutions can be found in practically every democratic system. These are institutions with similar names and objectives, but in different positions depending on their institutional roots, the type of relations among the three traditional powers, the process by which their leaders are appointed, the scope of their authority, or their sources of financing. In consequence, we are dealing with differing degrees of autonomy enjoyed by such institutions. These are such institutions as audit chambers, citizens' rights ombudsmen, or anti-corruption agencies.[26] Vertical accountability, on the other hand, apart from ensuring that citizens have the right to select their representatives, also involves the possibility to observe, hold to account and sanction them. This type of accountability is retrospective in nature. Assessment is offered of decisions already taken, activities already completed, and results already generated. By the same token, elections become a process by which politicians assume responsibility and should be held accountable for the decisions they have taken. Elections are thus a form of periodic accountability realised *ex-post*. The conception of horizontal accountability was then expanded by the author to include such elements as the, participation of

25 G. O'Donnell, *Rendición de cuentas horizontal y neuvas poliarquías*, "Nueva Sociedad" 1997, no. 152 1997, pp. 143–167.

26 G. O'Donnell, *Further Thoughts on Horizontal Accountability*, Conference on Institutions Accountability and Democratic Governance in Latin America, Notre Dame: Kellogg Institute for International Studies, 2000.

non-state actors, such as non-governmental organisations, social groups, and the media; this is referred to as societal accountability.[27]

The impact of the Argentinian researcher's theoretical proposal is best seen in the conception developed by L. Morlino. The difference is one of naming: horizontal accountability is referred to as inter-institutional, while vertical accountability is called electoral. L. Morlino, as in the case of G. O'Donnell, defines electoral accountability as the capacity of voters to hold their rules to account in respect of the degree to which they fulfilled their campaign promises. In the author's opinion, this type of accountability is periodic in nature and dependent on the election cycle. That said, L. Morlino takes into account elections at multiple levels: local, regional, national and supranational. This is also why, in that author's opinion, the frequency with which all types of elections are held – including the possibility of holding referenda – makes the nature of this type of accountability a continual one. On the other hand, the second type of accountability, inter-institutional, is understood as the liability that those in power must bear before other institutions and collective actors possessing the knowledge and authority to assess the activities of those exercising power. This type of accountability is of a continual nature. In practice, this refers to oversight of the government exercised by the opposition in parliament, as well as various evaluations and audits performed by judicial organs, constitutional tribunals, central bank, and other organs appointed for that purpose. The role of the opposition is very important in this type of accountability. The author emphasises that when we are faced with a lasting bipolarism, this type of accountability can be significantly weakened. That said, he does not operationalise the two types of accountability, but rather lists the conditions that must be met at the procedural level for those two forms of accountability to function. In respect of vertical accountability, the author distinguishes the necessary conditions to be fulfilled at the procedural level: 1) free and fair elections held periodically (along with the appropriate procedural safeguards); 2) freedom to establish political parties; 3) existence of (capable of governing) a parliamentary alternative. The primary condition for the emergence of inter-institutional accountability is the existence of a legal system that ensures the presence of the aforementioned institutions exercising oversight functions. They should be characterised by independence and stable structures.

27 The author included the concept of societal accountability as developed by C. Smulovitz, E. Peruzzotti. See: C. Smulovitz, E. Peruzzotti, *Societal accountability in Latin America*, "Journal of Democracy" 2000, vol. 11, no. 14, pp. 147–158; C. Smulovitz, E. Peruzzotti, *Controlando la política.Ciudadanos y medios en las nuevas democracias*, Buenos Aires 2002.

Additionally, the author also includes in this type of accountability: political parties' activity outside of parliament, mass communication, and non-governmental organisations. In L. Morlino's opinion, the role of independent media and networks of active associations and organisations that provide information and accept the task of protecting democratic values is key. By the same token, the author does not distinguish societal accountability, but rather includes it as part of inter-institutional accountability.[28]

The impact of G. O'Donnell on the way in which accountability is understood can clearly be seen in the case of D. Levine and J. Molina as well. These authors distinguish three types of accountability – horizontal, vertical and societal. Their contribution does not consist so much in the introduction of a new definition of accountability, as it does in their interesting conceptualisation. D. Levine and J. Molina are of the opinion that horizontal accountability is directly associated with corruption and the effectiveness of the judiciary. A high level of corruption is indicative of a weak judiciary, unable to effectively enforce accountability towards the executive. The manner of measurement selected by the authors is the use of existing corruption barometers. On the other hand, vertical accountability, in accordance with the assumptions of D. Levine and J. Molina, depends on the quality of electoral processes.[29] In addition, analysis is performed of the level of institutionalisation in the party system and the possibility of re-election. The possibility of re-election is problematic in countries with weak institutions that have no capacity to counter abuses of power, as in consequence they can be neither rewarded nor punished. As for the party system, in the opinion of D. Levine and J. Molina the higher the level of institutionalisation, the greater are citizens capable of assigning accountability and, by the same token, employ carrot/stick mechanisms. The authors in this case use as their index the index

28 L. Morlino, *Calidad democrática…*, op. cit.; L. Morlino, *Qualities of democracy: how…*, op. cit.; L. Morlino, *Democracias y…*, op. cit., pp. 194–195.

29 In the case of electoral decisions associated with vertical accountability, the authors believe that the following dependencies emerge: 1) the shorter the term of office, the greater the level of control exercised by voters, 2) elections should be universal, which also means extending the right to vote to citizens living abroad, as well as residents; 3) elections should be impartial, not only in terms of the law (with or without budgetary financing of political parties), but also in the eyes of public opinion, which can be determined via public opinion polling; 4) freedom and plurality of the press must exist (the greater the number of politically active individuals have access to mechanisms permitting them to receive opinions and information, the greater the possibility of decisions being taken in conditions of quality, which contributed to quality of democracy).

of party system institutionalisation proposed by S. Mainwaring and T. Scully. A second index employed for measuring electoral accountability is Pedersen's Index of Electoral Volatility, which the authors feel to also be a good measure of the institutionalisation of the party system, as the stability of voting in particular elections is generally associated with the organisational level and social penetration of political parties. The greater the stability of the party system, meaning the smaller the flow in the electorate, the easier it becomes for voters to assign responsibility. When volatility is high, combined with parties that appear and disappear between elections, the capability of voters to hold their politicians to account declines, particularly when dealing with closed electoral slates. In these authors' opinion, societal accountability consists in the effective use of the right to assembly and to petition. This is also why the authors employ public opinion polling, in this case the Latinobarometer, which contains questions addressing both the activities of citizens concerning work on solving local problems and their participation levels in non-governmental organisations. At the same time, the engagement of citizens in social issues is assessed. As the authors emphasise, the more active the citizenry is in seeking solutions to problems that emerge in the community or in the promotion of shared interests, the greater the effectiveness of social impact and oversight of the doings of those in power.[30]

Accountability as one of the key elements in quality of democracy has also been used in the conception developed by M. Bühlmann, W. Merkel, L. Müller, and B. Wessels. Concerning the way in which accountability itself is understood, here as well we may observe the influence of G O'Donnell's theoretical proposals, particularly in respect of horizontal accountability. The starting point for the authors of this conceptualisation of quality of democracy is to distinguish three fundamental principles: freedom, equality and control. Within the context of control, three partial regimes are distinguished: the electoral regime, horizontal accountability, and effective power to govern. Each partial regime is assigned a function; in the case of horizontal accountability it is the mutual constraints of constitutional power, while in respect of the electoral regime it is the functions of vertical accountability and representation. Additionally, in respect of horizontal accountability, the authors distinguish three components: 1) checks and balances; 2) independence of the judiciary; 3) Rule of law constraint. Within the framework of the first component, three sub-components are distinguished:

30 D. Levine, J. Molina, *Evaluating the Quality of Democracy in Latin America*, in: D. Levine, J. Molina (eds.), *The Quality of Democracy in Latin America*, Boulder 2011, pp. 1–19; D. Levine, J. Molina, *Measuring the Quality of Democracy*, in: D. Levine, J. Molina (eds.) *The Quality* ..., op. cit., pp. 21–37.

1) strength of parliament and the parliamentary opposition; 2) institutional checks; 3) effective sanctions. In the context of independence of the judicial system, they distinguish: 1) recruitment of judges, 2) honesty and professionalism of judges; 3) transparency of judicial procedures. In the context of limitations resulting from the rule of law, they distinguish two constituent elements: 1) an effective constitutional court, 2) effective administrative jurisdiction. In respect of vertical accountability, the authors distinguish two sub-components: 1) competitiveness of elections; 2) openness of elections. The first of the sub-components is comprised of tree constituent elements: 1) effective opportunities to choose; 2) importance of the offer; 3) transparent offer of alternatives. In respect of the second component – Openness of elections the authors distinguish: 1) straightforward admission of new competitors; 2. equal chances for competitors.[31]

A. Roberts, however, distinguishes only vertical accountability, which he also calls electoral accountability. In spite of the very interesting manner in which he captures the dependency between accountability and the capacity of authorities to react to the needs of citizens, the conception of quality of democracy he proposes is not a multidimensional perspective. Nevertheless, worthy of attention is the manner in which electoral accountability itself is operationalised. In addition, the author focuses his studies on the countries of Central and Eastern Europe, with particular attention paid to Poland, Czechia, and Hungary. A. Roberts feels that the measure of electoral accountability is economic voting. This approach by A. Roberts allows us to determine whether we are dealing with a real settling of accounts, and hence with the application of the carrot/stick approach in the act.[32] Thus, the author does not limit himself to examining whether the conditions necessary for the existence of vertical accountability have been fulfilled, as is the case in other operationalisations of quality of democracy; his operationalisation helps us answer the question of whether voters really do pass judgement on their politicians when they go to the polls.

In summary, while all of the conceptualisations and operationalisations presented above are essentially consistent with the second type of study on quality of democracy, they are significantly different from one another; this is true in respect of the dimensions of quality of democracy examined, as well as operationalisation and the methodology employed. While they are among the most successful, they are not without drawbacks. There are holes in the above conceptualisations and

31 M. Bühlmann, W. Merkel, L. Müller, B. Wessels, *The Democracy Barometer…*, op. cit., pp. 51–53.

32 A. Roberts, *The Quality of….*, op. cit., pp. 51–72.

operationalisations of quality of democracy, concerning both the very definitions of democracy itself and definitions of the quality of democracy. The same holds for individual components, whose definitions are not quite complete. Accountability itself is also only partially defined. Furthermore, there is no explanation given for the dependencies among components in the analysed conceptions of quality of democracy. This is the case, including with respect to accountability, as there is no elaboration of the dependencies existing among particular types of accountability.

1.3. Key concepts and definitions

While the importance of accountability is continually growing in both studies on the quality of democracy and in political discourse, nevertheless the concept of accountability is used as a sort of conceptual umbrella encompassing various expressions and definitions. We can observe the use of the concept in a very broad sense as a synonym for various evaluation mechanisms. Most frequently we can encounter the term "accountability" used in relation to transparency, the capacity of authorities to react, and control. This is also why this subchapter will bring order to the ways in which accountability is defined.

While transparency is frequently equated with accountability, it *de facto* boils down primarily to the obligation of public authorities to make information available and to facilitate its use in specified cases and procedures. It is a sort of mechanism setting a process in motion. Transparency of the activities of public authorities is one of the fundamental assumptions of modern democracy. It facilitates understanding of the rules under which power operates, as well as the participation of citizens in the exercise of it. Transparency is thus another instrument used in a complex system of accountability.

In a similar manner, responsiveness obliges authorities to react to preferences, criticism and demands voiced by citizens.[33] The difference between accountability and responsiveness is that the former is tasked with stimulating the capacity of authorities to act, while they may be capable and responsive without the obligation to give an accounting of their activities[34].

33 B. Manin, A. Przeworski, S.C. Stokes, *Introduction*, in: B. Manin, A. Przeworski, S.C. Stokes (eds.), *Democracy, Accountability and Representation*, Cambridge, 1999; L.C. Ugalde, *Rendición de cuentas y democracia. El caso de México*, 2002, p. 16.

34 J. Fearon, *Electoral Accountability and the Control of Politicians: Selecting Good Types versus Sanctioning Poor Performance*, in: B. Bernard, A. Przeworski, S.C. Stokes (eds.), *Democracy…*, op. cit., p. 55.

The category of control is also at times identified with accountability. However, control is rather a mechanism for oversight of authority, and does not always imply the obligation on the part of officials to periodically provide information about their activities. For example, the legislature sets a control process in motion on its own initiative, and the sole duty of the executive is to provide the information demanded of it. In this case, however, the process is a unidirectional one, in which the parliament has the power to request information and to impose sanctions if it is not received. Thus, control is an element initiating the process of accountability, as the commencement of control itself does not necessarily result in being held to account. This is also why control should be viewed as an instrument in a system of accountability that also encompasses other mechanisms initiated by the authorities themselves.

The next reason for the terminological "mess" is the interchangeable treatment of the definition of accountability with the conditions necessary for its existence, with its types, or its mechanisms. What, then, is this accountability, which is quite frequently confused with or substituted by other concepts or categories? In the opinion of A. Schedler, accountability signifies the duty of politicians and civil servants to inform about and justify their actions (*answerability*); this is associated with the possibility of imposing penalties (*enforcement*). Answerability can be understood as the right of citizens tor receive information, which is accompanies by the duty of public authorities to provide it accompanied by the existence of mechanisms enabling control of the activities of authorities. In turn, following the principle of the rule of law, enforcement demands adherence to the law and punishment of those in power when they do not exercise the mandate entrusted to them. It can also signify the activation of mechanisms of preventative control.

Thus A. Schedler argues that accountability has three primary elements: information, justification, and punishment or reward. The first element, information about e.g. the activities of a politician or of an entire organ such as the government, parliament, etc., is a necessary precondition for assessment or evaluation of responsibility. The second element refers to the motivations for the behaviour of those in power and the decisions they take. The third element is the action of a voter, who employs knowledge – including that of the justifications offered by the ruling class – to reward or to punish them in alignment with his interests and expectations.[35]

---

35 A. Schedler, *Conceptualizing Accountability*, in: A. Schedler, L. Diamond, M. Plattner (eds.), *The selfrestraining state: power and accountability in new Democracies*, Boulder 1999, pp. 17–26.

M. Bovens proposes a more comprehensive definition of accountability, as the association between the actor and the forum in which that actor is obliged to explain and own up to her behaviour, the forum may pose questions and issue verdicts, and the actor must accept their consequences.[36] A similar definition of accountability comes from R.W. Grant and R.O. Koehane, who operate on the assumption that accountability concerns the relationship between two actors (X and Y), in which X has the right to monitor the activities of Y, to evaluate the activities of Y, and to impose sanctions on Y.[37] In order to operationalise the definition proposed by the two authors, the following elements of it should be brought into sharper definition: who is Y, and thus who is being held to account? Who plays the role of X, and thus before whom is Y being held to account? What can Y be held accountable for? What does the process of holding Y accountable consist in? What are the consequences of holding Y accountable?

A an approach to accountability similar to that of R.W. Grant and R.O. Keohane is taken by J. Fearon, who adds that in order for Y to be held accountable by X, two conditions must be fulfilled: first, there must be agreement that Y is obliged to act on behalf of X; second, X must be formally or informally authorised to punish or to reward Y for the tasks Y performs.[38] Undoubtedly, a very important role in the conception of accountability is that of sanctions; as D. Dunn writes, so that the final effect of accountability is "sensitivity" or "responsiveness" on the part of authorities is achieved, there must be a catalogue of sanctions and motivations. Failure to be re-elected is a direct sanction, but elected officials may not only lose elections, but also stand accused and be punished.[39]

The conditions that must be met for accountability to be effective are well-described by R. López-Pintor. In his opinion: first, the borders of responsibility must be clearly set out in the legal, financial, and political spheres; second, precisely drawn borders facilitate effective and transparent performance of the functions of governance; third, the integrity of functionaries of state administration and the judiciary must be maintained. In order for these conditions to be ensured, this author argues that certain measures are necessary: the manifestation of the

36 M. Bovens, *New Forms of Accountability and EU-Governance*, "Comparative European Politics" 2007, no. 5, pp. 7, 450–451.

37 R.W. Grant, R.O. Koehane, *Accountability and Abuses of Power in World Politics*, "American Political Science Review" 2005, no. 99 (01), p. 29.

38 J. Fearon, *Electoral…*, op. cit., p. 56.

39 D. Dunn, *Mixing Elected and Nonelected Officials in Democratic Policy Making: Fundamentals of Accountability and Responsibility*, in: A. Przeworski, S. Stokes, B. Manin (eds.), *Democracy…*, op. cit., p. 299.

law-governed state and division of powers, an independent auditing and control process, legal conditions for effective implementation, and strong parliamentary powers of oversight.[40]

S. Rose-Ackerman, however, proposes a dualistic understanding of accountability. First, accountability means that governmental institutions, both those chosen in elections and those selected by appointment, are held accountable by their superiors via a system of monitoring and oversight. This type of accountability is referred to as "performance accountability", and it encompasses the potential for control of the professional administrative apparatus by elected politicians, while they themselves are subordinated to the electorate. In order for this type of accountability to exist, both transparency and freedom of the media must be guaranteed. The author also adds that in the case of this type of accountability, decisions are assumed to be made, while the focus is placed on their execution. The second understanding of accountability consists in "policy-making accountability", which is associated with the previously described concept of responsiveness. In Rose-Ackerman's opinion, accountability for making policy requires that political actions and decisions constitute a response to the interests and the needs of citizens. A necessary condition for the existence of this type of accountability is electoral competition and a competent legislative authority.[41]

1.4. Research strategy

This portion of the subchapter presents the applied methodological approach, choice of cases, timeframe for research and the model of accountability that will be used in subsequent portions of the work. This work is consistent with the neo-positivist line of scientific inquiry, in accordance with which the empirical search for causal links between social phenomena are based on a critical analysis of the following theoretical approaches: empirical neo-institutionalism and rational choice theory.[42] In line with the adopted research perspective, the primary

40 R. López-Pintor, *Para que la democracia crezca. Diagnosticao z propuesta*, in: M. Beltrán Villalva (ed.), *La sociedad: teoría e investigación empírica. Libro homenaje a José Jiménez Blanco*, Madrid, 2002, pp. 649–670.

41 S. Rose-Ackerman, *Od wyborów do demokracji. Budowa państwa odpowiedzialnego przed społeczeństwem*, Warsaw 2008, pp. 19–21.

42 V. Lowndes follows G.B. Petersen in holding that empirical institutionalism is so closely associated with rational choice theory as to adopt the assumption that the creators of institutions can select with almost total freedom from among institutional forms, V. Lowndes, *Instytucjonalizm*, in: D. Marsh, G. Stoker (eds.), *Teorie i metody w naukach politycznych*, Kraków 2006, p. 95.

method applied in the work is the comparative approach, both in quantitative and qualitative aspects. A significant role is played in the work by institutional and legal analysis, historical analysis, and statistical analysis.[43] In accordance with the neo-positivist paradigm, both quantitative and qualitative methods will be applied;, however, qualitative analysis will be the dominant approach in the work.

Empirical neo-institutionalism, alongside normative, historical and rational choice neo-institutionalism, is one of the primary strands of thought in contemporary neo-institutionalism[44]. It is derived from studies addressing the third wave of democratisation and the need to constitute formal governments which would prevent a crisis of legitimacy in new democratic systems. Studies on empirical neo-institutionalism consists in evaluating the effects of an institution's functioning on the basis of empirical research. The impact of broadly-understood institutions on political behaviours, as well as on the general social and political sphere (within the framework of traditional institutionalism and various forms of neo-institutionalism) has become the object of many studies in both Poland and Spain. However, there are very few works which have applied an empirical neo-institutional approach, but without empirical analysis there is no way of determining to what extent – if at all – a given institution has influenced individual behaviours, leading to such results as limitations on formal and informal behaviours. It is worth emphasising that, in line with this strand of thought, it is institutions which determine individual behaviours and not the other way around; nonetheless, individuals, in this case political elites, can select and modify various institutional forms. In accordance with the adopted approach of empirical neo-institutionalism, the primary point of emphasis has been placed on the shape and the nature of a formal structure, *id est* well-designed and effective institutions within the accountability systems of Poland and Spain. Modifications to this approach in comparison with classic institutionalism will accent the reciprocal influences of structures (institutions) and individuals. The effects of activities by such institutions will be examined on the basis of analysed empirical data.

The use of rational choice theory and associated statistical methodology is limited to examining the factual extent in Poland and Spain of electoral

43 For more: R.A. Rhodes, *El institucionalismo*, in: D. Marsh, G. Stoker (eds.), *Teoría y métodos de la ciencia política*, Madrid 1997.

44 For more: B.G. Peters, *Institutional theory: problems and prospects*, in: J. Pierre, B.G. Peters, G. Stoker (eds.), *Debating Institutionalism*, Manchester 2013, pp. 1–21, B.G. Peters, *El nuevo institucionalismo: Teoría institucional en ciencias políticas*, Barcelona 2003, pp. 121–146, V. Lowndes, *Instytucjonalizm*, in: D. Marsh, G. Stoker (eds.), *Teorie i metody…*, op. cit., pp. 89–107.

accountability. Rational choice theory invokes methodology applied in economics. One of the fathers of the use of this theory in studies on electoral behaviours was A. Downs.[45] The starting point for this scholar is the assumption that voters are rational in their choices. This means they are capable of comparing the proposals of particular political parties and candidates, and select those which serve their particular interests to the greatest extent. This approach is linked with the so-called "responsibility hypothesis", which assumes that citizens hold their government to account for the state's economic circumstances.[46] This means that in their opinion the macroeconomic situation which the state finds itself in is a derivative of the decisions made by politicians in power. In consequence, if the economic situation is good then, voters reward the governing party through re-election, while if it is poor, the voters punish the ruling party by supporting one of the opposition parties. The use of economic voting as a measure of satisfaction or dissatisfaction at the moment electoral decisions are taken is supported in the results of existing research.[47] As it turns out, in comparison with other public policy the greatest interest is aroused by economic policy. It is constantly present in the media, and it has an impact on the lives of all citizens regardless of age, gender, education, profession or wealth. This is also why economic policy is, for the general public, a sort of "informational short-cut" when assessing the activities of the government. The use of the so-called economic vote in researching electoral behaviours would therefore seem to be the best means of examining whether citizens employ the reward/punishment when voting. Among researchers there is general agreement as to the correctness of applying the economic voting model, used in the present work as well, in which an examination is made of the responsibility hypothesis in measuring vertical accountability.[48] A precise

45 A. Downs, *An Economic Theory of Democracy*, New York 1957, A. Downs, *Social Values and Democracy*, in: K.R. Monroe (ed.), *The Economic Approach to Democracy*, New York 1991.

46 V.O. Key, The responsible electorate: Rationality in presidential voting, 1936-1960, New York 1968; M.P. Fiorina, *Retrospective Voting in American National Elections*, New Haven 1981

47 H. Dorussen, M. Taylor, *Group economic voting A comparison of the Netherlands and Germany*, in: H. Dorussen, M. Taylor (eds.), *Economic Voting*, New York 2002, pp. 92–120; H. Dorussen, H. Palmer, *The context of economic voting*, in: H. Dorussen, M. Taylor (eds.), *Economic…*, op. cit., pp. 1–14.

48 For more: J.E. Mueller, *Presidential Popularity from Truman to Johnson*, "American Political Science Review" 1970, no 64, pp. 18–34; Jr. V.O. Key, *The responsible electorate… op.cit.*; C.A.E. Goodhert, R.J. Bhansali, *Political Economy*, Political Studies" 1970, no. 18, pp. 43–106.48 B.S. Frey, F. Schneider, *A Politico-Economic Model of the United Kingdom*,

description of the economic voting model and justification for the variables used is presented in chapter six.

Connecting empirical neo-institutionalism and rational choice theory facilitates balancing the importance of institutional structures and the role of political actors, and it enables analysis of accountability mechanisms captured dynamically. Additionally, it makes it possible to emphasise the importance of the institutional factor in relation to the role of political actors in order to explain the differences and similarities between Poland and Spain.

The present work is based on a case study of two countries—Poland and Spain—with an explorative comparison of these two cases of democratization. Even though the findings allow for conclusions related mainly to Poland and Spain, some explorative generalizations are formulated as bases for future research. The comparative method will be used in order to formulate empirical generalities and to verify hypotheses. Based on an individual analysis of each case - individual terms of office in Poland and in Spain - induction will be employed to develop medium-range generalisations through the application of institutional and legal analysis, historical analysis, and statistical analysis. In doing so, excessive generalisation in the results generated by the research can be minimised. The problem of limitations associated with the small number of cases analysed has been overcome by applying periodisation in respect of each country, as a result of comparing particular terms of office separately for each case. The choice of cases was based on the consent method developed by J.S. Mill, as well as of the most different systems

---

"Economic Journal" 1978, no. 88, pp. 243–253; D.A. Hibbs, *The Mass Public and Macroeconomic Performance: The Dynamics of Public Opinion Toward Unemployment and inflation*, "American Journal of Political Science" 1979, no. 23, pp. 705–462; M.P. Fiorina, *Retrospective Voting...op.cit.*; D.R. Kinder, R.D. Kiewiet, *Sociotopic Politics: The American Case*, "British Journal of Political Science" 1981, vol. 11 no. 2, pp. 129–161; P. Nannestad, P.M. Paldam, *From the Pocketbook of the Welfare Man: A Pooled Cross-Section Study of Economic Voting in Denmark*, 1986–92, "British Journal of Political Science" 1997, no. 27, pp. 119–137; M.S. Lewis-Beck, *Economics and Elections: The Major Western Democracies*, Ann Arbor, 1988; M.S. Lewis-Beck, M. Celeste Ratto, *Economic voting in Latin America: A general model*, "Electoral Studies" 2013, vol. 32 no. 3, pp. 489–493; M. Kanji, K. Tannahill, *What are the current preoccupations of economic voting research?*, "Electoral Studies" 2013, vol. 32 no. 3, pp. 391–392; S. Weschle, *Two Types of Economic Voting: How Economic Conditions Jointly Affect Vote Choice and Turnout*, "Electoral Studies", available online from 7 November 2013.

approach of A. Przeworski and H. Teune.[49] They adopt the rule that the analysed cases should be distinct in all measures apart from the analysed variables.

Poland and Spain represent two groups of states (Southern Europe and Central and Eastern Europe) which underwent the process of democratisation at different times. In Spain, this process was initiated in the mid-1970s. At present, the country is one with a consolidated democratic system. Poland, however, began its move towards democratisation at the beginning of the 1990s and is one of Central and Eastern Europe's most advanced states in respect of forming stable democratic structures. A strong stimulus on the road to democratisation and consolidation of democracy in both cases was the European Union. It exerted influence on such aspect as the effectiveness and transparency of how state structures in Member States function. During the pre-accession phase this is primarily related to adapting national law to EU law. After accession, it involves efforts towards implementing general European standards of transparency and accountability, expressed inter alia in the 2001 White Paper on European Governance. On the other hand, membership in structures which have been assigned a portion of the powers enjoyed by nation-states leads to a diffusion of accountability at the domestic level. Thus, in the cases of both Spain and Poland, we are dealing with the impact of similar external factors on accountability.

Doubtlessly there is also a great deal of differences between Poland and Spain. Spain is a monarchy, while Poland a republic. The territorial structures of the two states also differ. Poland is a classic example of a unitary decentralised state, while Spain is held to be a quasi-federal one. Nevertheless, in respect of the most important constitutional solutions regarding horizontal and vertical accountability, they are similar. In both Poland and Spain we may speak of a parliamentary-cabinet form of government and proportional electoral system, and it is these very elements responsible for similarities in horizontal and vertical accountability mechanisms in given political systems.

The research will employ diverse types of data: documents from state institutions as well as the results of research conducted by non-governmental organisations and international bodies (reports, papers), legislative activity of MPs, semi-structured face-to-face interviews (with politicians and experts in the reviewed material who have participated in the analysed processes, as well as with scholars in Poland and abroad), media content (press articles, television programmes, radio interviews), statistical data (public opinion polling, expert research results), political

49 For more: J. Hopkin, *Metody porównawcze*, in: D. Marsh, G. Stoker (eds.), *Teorie i metody…*, op. cit., pp. 251–271.

science literature (articles and other publications). The use of differentiated analytical methods and sources of information – triangulation – will make it possible to achieve a comprehensive picture of accountability in Poland and Spain, which will facilitate not only a more in-depth understanding of the issue under investigation, but also will generate high-quality research and, in turn, reliable results.

Analysis of accountability in Poland encompasses the period 1997–2011, and thus four terms of office, while in Spain it runs 1982–2011, and thus eight terms. The temporal boundaries result from the assumption that quality of democracy, and therefore also accountability, can only be analysed in countries where the political systems have undergone consolidation. There is general agreement among Polish researchers that the date which marks the moment of consolidation in Poland is the adoption of the 1997 Constitution. Spanish political scientists are also in agreement that the moment of consolidation in the Spanish system is the year 1982, when power was handed over following the electoral victory of PSOE, the leading opposition force against the post-Franco establishment.

The point of departure of the model used for studying accountability as one of the elements of quality of democracy, using the examples of Poland and Spain, consists of the elements in the operationalisation of quality of democracy presented in the previous section of this chapter. It should be mentioned here that the selection has been limited to those elements in the operationalisation of accountability which facilitate the real study of how effectively accountability functions in Poland and Spain. However, there are no discussions of the criteria and conditions necessary for the existence of accountability. It is accepted that a necessary condition for the existence of accountability is the requirement to meet the criteria of Dahlian polyarchy. It is thus assumed, essentially *a priori*, that both in Poland and in Spain the conditions of polyarchy vital for the proper functioning of accountability have been met. In respect of horizontal accountability, these are: a legal system containing independent organs of control; independent media aware of its social role; a network of organisations and associations with awareness of democratic values. Similarly, in the case of vertical accountability such necessary preconditions have been met as: functional mechanisms of political competition, distribution of political power; electoral openness, real choice, and also equal chances for entities competing for power, and the existence of independent media.

This does not mean, however, that the institutional architecture of the two systems will not be taken into account. Quite the opposite – for the purposes of this work, a differentiation into two dimensions has been made in accordance with the logic proposed by L. Morlino, i.e. the procedural dimension and the final result dimension (result of political practice). However, it should again be emphasised that both dimensions – the procedural and the final result – refer not to conditions for the existence of accountability in the two countries, but rather to its functioning. This way of capturing the subject results from the conviction that studies on accountability cannot be limited only to the institutional architecture written into the constitution, as from the perspective of political science the practical dimension, and thus the implementation of that architecture, is of far greater importance.

There is also no discussion of the indices used in the operationalisations previously described, which are rather determinants impacting the effectiveness of accountability and not means of measuring it. An example depicting the interchangeable use of determinants with the manner of measuring the use of accountability tools may be that of the way in which the strength of parliament and parliamentary opposition are measured in the conception developed by M. Bühlmann, W. Merkel, L. Müller, and B. Wessels. These authors propose measuring the strength of parliament and the parliamentary opposition using the percentage of mandates held by the governing party, the type of majority held in the chamber of parliament that is responsible for making law, and the level of fractionalisation. At the same time, they do not link the type of majority and type of opposition or fractionalisation with the use of instrument of accountability which parliament enjoys. This means that they do not measure, for example, how particular compositions of parliament impact the frequency with which tools are used.

The proposals of L. Morlino, of M. Bühlmann, W. Merkel, L. Müller, and B. Wessels, and also D. Levine and J. Molina concerning measurement of vertical accountability also concern determinants. It should be emphasised that there is no closed catalogue of determinants in existence for consolidated democracies. An entire range of studies can be found concerning individual factors, without situating them in a comprehensive model of vertical accountability. Among them, those most frequently referred to in the context of vertical accountability include the electoral system in place and its consequences for vertical accountability, difficulties associated with assigning responsibility in the case of coalition governments, federal states, and also the type of party system itself.[50]

---

50 More on the effect of proportional electoral systems, limitations of mandate and problems with assigning responsibility: G.B. Powell, *Wybory jako narzązdzie demokracji. Koncepcje większościowe i proporcjonalne*, Warsaw 2006; G.B Powell, G.D. Whitten, *A Cross-National Analysis of Economic Voting: Taking Account of the Political Context*, "American Journal of Political Science, 1993 no. 37(2), p. 414; S. Przeworski, S. Stokes, B.Manin (eds.), *Democracy, Accountability…*, op. cit.; P. Aguillar, I. Sánchez –Cuenca, *Performance or Representation? The Determinants of Voting in Complex Political Contexts*, in: J.M.Maravall,

This is also why the proposed model for studying accountability will first define the determinants of horizontal and vertical accountability, then present the means of measurement. Discussion of the model of accountability applied in the work has been preceded by an outline of the various manners in which accountability is understood and defined.

The work has adopted the definition of accountability proposed by M. Bovens, and the distinction first introduced by G. O'Donnell of horizontal and vertical accountability. It is assumed that an uncomplicated typology will be easier to employ in operationalisation of the study, and in consequence it will be more useful analytically.

The primary dependency between horizontal and vertical accountability consists in the generation of information by the former. In the opinion of G. O'Donnell, when horizontal accountability falters we experience what is referred to as a *democracia delegative*, and thus a type of democracy in which the activities of institutions is a sham, and there is no information about the activities of the government; this all leads to the impossibility of voters holding their elected officials to account.[51] Thus, a product of the proper functioning of accountability instruments – both those contained in checks and balances mechanisms as well

I.Sánchez-Cuenca (eds.), *Controlling Governments: Voters, Institutions and Accountability*, Cambridge 2008, p. 105; A. Bosh, A. Díaz, C. Riba, *Las funciones de popularidad: estado de la cuestión y principales debaes*, "Revista de Investigaciones Sociólogicas" 1999, no. 85, pp. 171–197; J. Font, *El pez grande se come al chico: las consecuencias electorales de gobernar en las CC.AA. y municipios españoles*, "Revsita española de Investigaciones Sociológicas" 1999, no. 87, pp. 145–176; I. Urquizu, *Gobiernos de coalición y gobirnos unipartidista: ¿es posible la asignación de responsabilidades?*, M. Sánchez de Dios, La accountability democrática en Europa: el trabajo de los parlamentos, Paper presented at the VI Congreso de la Asociación Española de Ciencias Política y de la Administración (AECPA), Barcelona 18–20 September 2003; H. Pitkin, *El conepto de representación polítca*, Madrid 1985, pp. 60–65; H.D. Clarke, C. Marianne, P.F. Whitley, *Emotions, expectations and the dynamics of party support in Britain*, in: H. Dorussen, M. Taylor (eds.), *Economic Voting*, London 2002, pp. 235–260; R.M. Duch, R.T. Stevenson, *The Economic Vote: How Political and Economic Institutions Condition Election Results*, Cambridge 2008; T.J. Rudolph, *Who's responsible for the economy? The formation and consequences of responsibility attributions*, "American Journal of Political Science" 2003, vol. 47 no. 4, pp. 698–713; J.A. Cheibub, *Presidentialism, Parliamentarism, and Democracy*, Cambridge 2007; C.J. Anderson, *The end of economic voting? Contingency dilemmas and the limits of democratic accountability*, "Annual Review of Political Science" 2007, no. 10, pp. 271–296.

51 G. O'Donnell, *Estado de derecho y Democracia en América Latina*, X Seminario Eduardo García Máynez, Meksyk 2000, pp. 24–26; G. O'Donnell, *Hacia un estado de y para Democracia*, PNUD 2006, pp. 38–40.

as those of a special mandate – is information, which then becomes made public. The generation and publication of information counters so-called information asymmetry, which to a large extent renders vertical accountability impossible.[52]

Doubtlessly, the politicians of ruling parties enjoy a significant information advantage over citizens, and this refers not only to confidential information. Not infrequently it is politicians who decide whether a given piece of information becomes a subject for public debate or not. Imbalances in the distribution of information between the government and voters can, in consequence, lead to the government's activities being viewed by the public as less than transparent. At the same time, those in power can manipulate the information provided to citizens in order to avoid being punished at the voting booth. Indeed, we may frequently observe situations in which politicians do not hesitate to ascribe guilt for poor economic or political performance to external factors, such as the International Monetary Fund or the European Union, while always taking credit for their successes.[53] This asymmetry of information between citizens and politicians makes

---

52 More about the probloems associated with the lack of access to information for voters, or distortions of information: B. Manin, *Los principios del gobierno representativo*, Madrid 1998; J.M. Maravall, *Surviving Accountabilty*, in: S. Przeworski, S. Stokes, B. Manin (eds.), *Democracy, Accountability...*, op. cit.; J.M. Maravall, *El control de los politicos*, Madrid 2003; G. Montero, I. Lago, *The 2004 Election in Spain: Terrorism, Accountability, and Voting*, Working Paper 253, Insitut de Ciénces Polítiques I Socials, Barcelona 2006; S. Stokes, *Public Opinion and Market Reforms: The limits of Economic Voting*, "Comparative Political Studies" 1996, no. 29, pp. 499–519.

53 Undoubtedly, the main actor in contemporary political systems "demystifying" the situation as portrayed by politicians is the media. This is also why, in order to go beyond the intuitive understanding of the limitations associated with asymmetry of information, research should account for the role and the impact of the media on mechanisms of vertical accountability. There is no doubt that the media can perform a "monitoring" function towards various institutions and organs, and this depends largely on the model of media that exists in a given country. Under the classification proposed by D. Hallin and P. Mancini, in Poland we have a Democratic Corporatist Model, characterised by the existence of media linked with social and political groups; the state also plays an active role, yet one that is limited by the law. In Spain, however, a Polarised Pluralist Model, defined as a model with strong ties between the media and politics, while at the same time the media market is not commercialised and is dominated by state intervention. This would indicate that in Poland, the control exercised by the media should be more effective. In other words, the existence in Spain of a polarised pluralist model could contribute to the election of the same party, while in Poland the democratic corporatist model could contribute to more frequent changes in power. Confirmation of these hypotheses would require in-depth studies focused on the model of media in both

control more difficult, as it is linked with access to information. If citizens do not possess knowledge about policies implemented, they can end up punishing and rewarding politicians at random. In this situation the "mechanism for exchanging rogues" ceases to operate, which, in G.B. Powell's view, is the primary mechanism in the relation between the represented and the representative. This is also why the use of horizontal accountability instruments is of such importance, and does not refer only to the effectiveness of the justice system or mandate agencies. Of equal importance are properly functioning checks and balances.

For this reason also, in operationalising a conception of accountability the components of the accountability system included balancing institutions, mandate agencies, and elections. However, institutions and organs comprising the body of balancing institutions and those of a special mandate, along with citizens, are classified as the object of accountability (Figure 1). In the case of Poland, balancing institutions include: the president, the government, parliament, and the judiciary (along with the constitutional tribunal). In Spain's case, they are: the monarchy, the government, the parliament equipped with instruments for control of the executive, and the judiciary (along with constitutional tribunal). Among institutions with a special mandate created to prevent abuses and corruption, those in Poland that have been subjected to analysis include the Commissioner for Human Rights, Supreme Audit Chamber, and Central Anticorruption Bureau. In the case of Spain, however, these include the Commissioner for Human Rights and the Audit Office. Only elections held at the national level are taken into consideration.

Each of these entities possesses appropriate instruments; in the case of institutions, these are balancing instruments and oversight instruments (such as presidential veto, presidential legislative initiative, application to the constitutional tribunal, capacity of the executive to shape the legislative and decision agenda of parliament; the potential to initiate a vote of confidence, vote of no confidence, instruments of parliamentary control, judicial oversight, measures for resolving various types of conflicts, investigative powers, authority to punish, the power to file a report to the prosecutorial service about suspicion of the commission of a crime). The tool available to citizens is their vote in elections.

---

countries. Finding an answer to the question of to what extent the model of media has an effect on voters would also require comprehensive studies on citizens' perceived levels of knowledge, which is not a simple task. As it turns out, the available research generally addresses citizens' levels of knowledge, not the degree to which they are informed, which are not the same things. This is also why the influence of the media on accountability will not be analysed; although it is doubtlessly of great significance in the context of accountability, such a deep analysis goes beyond the scope of this work.

Figure 1. Conceptualisation of accountability

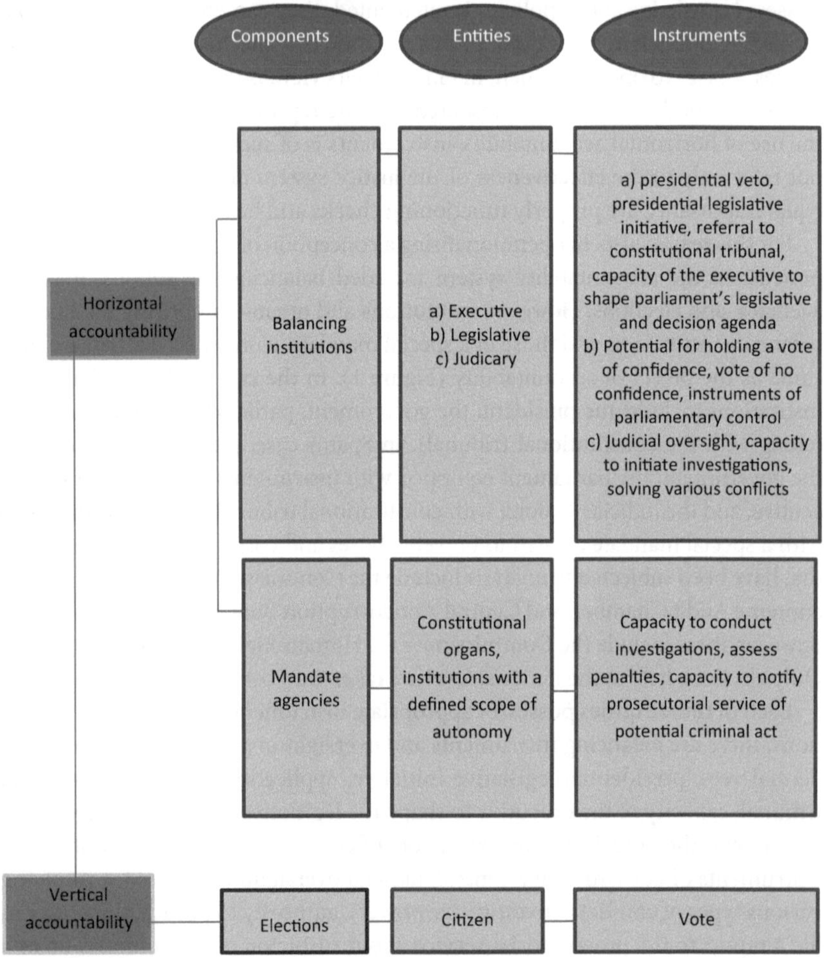

Source: own work.

The starting point for this operationalisation is distinguishing the determinants that impact the functioning of accountability. It is accepted that effectiveness of horizontal accountability is, among other things, a result of institutional architecture. This is also why formal conditions studied at the procedural level will be one of the determinants taken into account in examining the effectiveness of the executive, legislative and judicial branches, as well as mandate agencies in the system of horizontal accountability. Regarding the final result, in the case of the executive and the legislative branches, attention has been paid to the scope of support enjoyed by individual governments during successive terms of parliament *versus* the other parties in the parliament as one of the determinants. It is assumed that alongside procedural conditions, this particular determinant has the largest impact on the dynamics of the use of accountability instruments. In the case of the judiciary, the second determinant, alongside procedural conditions, is the level of politicisation, as it is precisely politicisation that impacts the effectiveness of the use of accountability instruments, as it either facilitates or hampers effective protection against abuses. In the case of mandate agencies the second determinant will also be the level of politicisation (Figure 2).

Figure 2. Determinants of horizontal accountability at the procedural level and the final results level

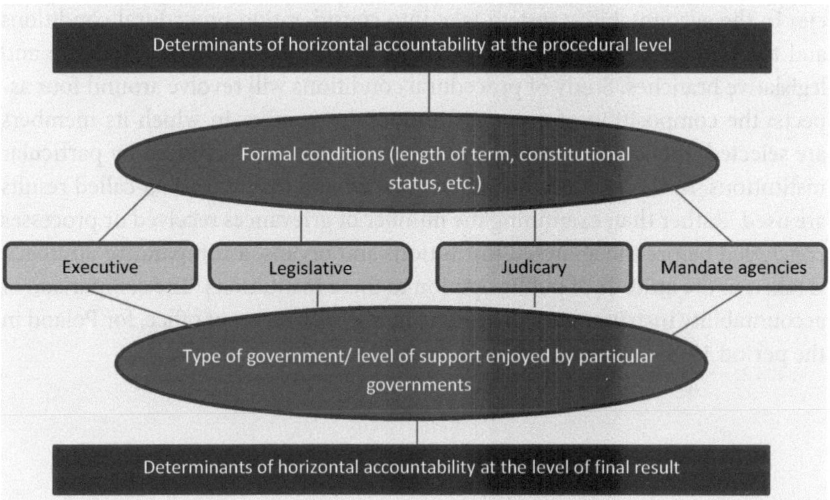

Source: own work.

In order to examine the position of the executive power in the system of horizontal accountability, an analysis is made of the capacity of the government to shape the legislative and decision agenda of parliament. This is measured by the relation between the number of bills proposed by the government in comparison to those offered by non-governmental entities, the number of government bills adopted compared to others, and analysis of informal mechanisms used by government to influence the work of parliament. There is also an examination of the impact of cohabitation situations on the use of instruments available to the president, measured by the number of bills submitted, the number of vetoes used and the number of bills referred to the Constitutional Tribunal. With regard to the exceptional position of the monarchy in the accountability system, the activity of the monarchy during a given period will serve as the basis for examining the degree to which the consolidation of the Spanish political system weakens or strengthens its role and position in the system of horizontal accountability. In the case of the legislature, there is an examination of the dynamics visible in the use of instruments available to the two parliaments. These instruments are a form of *ex post* control, expanded to include instruments associated with combating the information asymmetry which exists between members of the government and parliamentarians. A measurement is taken on the basis of the number of times which particular instruments are used in the lower chambers of both parliaments. Examination of the role of the judiciary and mandate agencies in the accountability system take into consideration procedural conditions and the type of government and majority, as in the case of the executive and legislative branches. Study of procedural conditions will revolve around four aspects: the composition of every institution, the manner in which its members are selected, the length of term, and the scope of powers enjoyed by particular institutions. In research on the judicial branch and institutions so-called results are used. Rather than examining the number of grievances received or processes concluded before the analysed institutions and organs, a comparative approach is taken to the attitude of public opinion to these institutions. The comparison of accountability instruments will be done in line with terms of office, for Poland in the period 1997–2011 and for Spain in 1982–2011.

Figure 3. Determinants of vertical accountability at the procedural level and the final results level

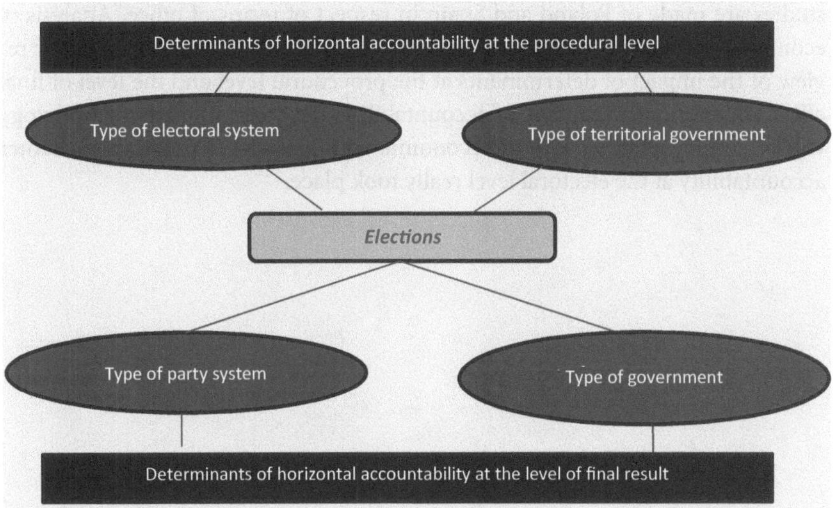

Source: own work.

In the case of vertical accountability, it is also assumed that analysis of the political and institutional context is key in studying this type of accountability, as institutional factors play an important role in the process of taking electoral decisions. However, they do not make it possible to answer the question of whether citizens really hold political parties to account during elections. This is also why the starting point for research on the extent to which during elections in Poland and Spain the mechanism of vertical accountability is analysis of the political and institutional context. Assessment will be made of the factors limiting the functioning of vertical control mechanisms at the level of the electoral decision. Also, a division of factors will be made into those which impact electoral accountability in the procedural dimension (and thus the adopted institutional architecture), and those in respect of the final effect, a result of the practice of politics. Among the former, those subjected to analysis include the electoral system and the territorial structure of the country, while among the latter they are the type of party system and type of government. This allows for examination of the dependencies between the level of proportionality in the electoral system, the level of decentralisation in the territorial structure, the level of institutionalisation in the party system, the type of government, and the responsibility assigned to it at the electoral level. The measure of vertical accountability, however, is essentially the use of the economic voting model, the tool A. Roberts proposed for this purpose. That said, similarly to the case of horizontal accountability, separate studies are made of Poland and Spain in respect of terms of office. Analysis of economic voting, the measure of vertical accountability, will be preceded by review of the impact of determinants at the procedural level and the level of final effect which impact that sort of accountability; next, quantitative methodology will be employed along with the economic voting model to determine whether accountability at the electoral level really took place.

Part II. Horizontal accountability: balancing institutions and mandate agencies

Chapter 2. The executive

Elements differentiating the mechanisms of horizontal accountability in Poland and Spain can easily be found. Spain is a monarchy, whilst Poland is a republic. This fact leads to substantial differences in the powers, role and position of the head of state in both systems. That said, in terms of one of the most important constitutional distinctions for the state system, the type of political regime, both Poland and Spain have a parliamentary-cabinet form of government. This issue is of key significance for the effectiveness of horizontal accountability, as this form of government limits the functioning of horizontal accountability mechanisms to the greatest extent: in a parliamentary-cabinet system there is no clear division between the legislative and executive power. There is cooperation between the two branches, which need each other in order to govern; this, in turn, means that the effectiveness of accountability tools is the result of procedural conditions on one hand, while on the other it stems primarily from the existing party system and the effectiveness of the opposition, dependent precisely on that party system.

When analysing the position of the executive branch in accountability structures, the relations between the executive and legislative branches of government should be taken into account. In their work titled *Delegation and Accountability in Parliamentary Democracies*, T. Bergman, W.C. Müller, K. Strom, and M. Blomgren propose the following factors of analysis of relations between the executive and legislative branches: first, the ability of the legislative to analyse the actions of the executive, primarily through parliamentary opposition; second, the cabinet's ability to shape the decision agenda of the parliament; third, the existence or absence of parliamentary enquiries, written and spoken enquiries, enquiries concerning documents, the requirement to prepare and send to parliament detailed reports on the activities of the executive and other administrative institutions; fourth, the possibility to hold a vote of confidence or no confidence on individual ministers or the cabinet as a whole; fifth, the ability of bodies such as commissions and committees to pose questions regarding the activities of members of the executive, as well as the actual use of these powers.[54]

L. Morlino, however, in analysing relations and dependencies between the legislative and executive branches of government, mentions three additional

54 T. Bergman, W.C. Müller, K. Strom, M. Blomgren, *Democratic Delegation and Accountability: Cross-national Patterns*, in: K. Strom, W.C. Müller, T. Bergman (eds.), *Delegation and Accountability in Parliamentary Democracies*, Oxford 2003, pp. 109–220.

elements associated with the legislative function: first, the right of initiative, i.e. the number of bills proposed by the government, as opposed to those proposed by the parliament; second, the output of the legislative branch – laws adopted in line with the proposals of the legislative and executive branches; third, the effectiveness of the executive, i.e. the number of government initiatives adopted compared to those of the parliament.[55] It would seem that combining these two proposals for examination of the interdependencies between the executive and legislative branches will facilitate their exhaustive analysis in the context of horizontal accountability.

Analysis of the position of the executive in Poland and Spain within the system of horizontal accountability, which is the subject of the research presented in this chapter, will be conducted partly based on the proposals of T. Bergman, W. C. Müller, K. Strom, M. Blomgren, and L. Morlino. In this chapter, only the position of the executive branch in the system of accountability will be analysed, while the next chapter will review the position of the legislative branch within the system of accountability. Therefore, this chapter will present an examination of the government's ability to shape the legislative and decision agenda of the parliament, measured by the ratio of government draft bills compared to those proposed by non-governmental entities, and the number of passed legislative initiatives coming from the government compared to the remaining ones. Informal mechanisms of the government's influence on the work of the parliament will also be examined. Determinants to be taken into consideration in the course of analysis of the head of state will be procedural conditions, and in the case of the President of Poland, circumstances of co-habitation. As for analysis addressing both governments, procedural determinants and the support they enjoyed in the lower house of parliament will be taken into account.

This composition of the chapter will make it possible to capture the main tendencies specific for both political systems. It will also facilitate finding answers to a number of detailed research questions, as well as verification of hypotheses offered in this part of the work. First, how strong the position of the executive branch in both systems is and whether it exerts real influence on the legislative and decision agenda of the parliament. Second, to what extent the government's influence on the legislative and decision agenda is conditioned by the institutional architecture, and to what extent by the "political configuration" of the parliament. Third, whether the time elapsed since political transformation has led to the

55 L. Morlino, *Democracy Between Consolidation and Crisis: Parties, Groups, and Citizens in Southern Europe*, Oxford 1998, p. 63.

strengthening of the executive branch within the system of horizontal accountability or not. The following hypotheses will be verified: Hypothesis 1: *The weaker and less stable parliamentary support for the government in Poland and Spain is, the weaker is the government's ability to impose a legislative and decision agenda on the parliament.* Hypothesis 2: *The absence of co-habitation strengthens the position of the President as an active entity in the accountability system, while the level of consolidation of the Spanish political system weakens the position of the monarch.* Hypothesis 3: *The longer the time from the moment of consolidation, the stronger the position of the government within the accountability system; therefore in Spain it is stronger than in Poland.*

2.1. Poland

Poland's executive branch is distinguished by its duality. This means that within the executive branch there is a government headed by the prime minister, along with a president elected by popular vote. When analysing the position of the president of Poland in the years 1997–2011, we may conclude that this position is much stronger not only in comparison with that of the Spanish monarch, but also compared to the powers of other presidents in parliamentary-cabinet systems. This holds true even though the 1997 Constitution substantially limits the president's prerogatives compared to those granted under the so-called Little Constitution, which was in effect during the transformation period.[56] The president's

56 When analysing the most important changes from the point of view of accountability, undoubtedly some that should be noted are abandoning in the 1997 Constitution the president's right to veto the budget bill and constitutional amendment bills, lowering the parliamentary majority needed to repeal the veto from 2/3 to 3/5, abandoning the requirement for appointments to three of the ministries to be opined by the president, the presumption of competence of the Council of Ministers in regards to executive power, abandoning the president's right to dissolve the parliament, the alternative of either invoking the legislative veto or requesting that the Constitutional Tribunal verify a bill. It should also be mentioned that, according to many scholars, the president's prerogatives were limited in the 1997 Constitution mostly because of Lech Wałęsa's tempestuous presidency in the years 1990–1995. For more about the change of presidential powers after 1989, see: R. Mojak, *Pozycja ustrojowa Prezydenta RP w świetle nowej Konstytucji*, "Państwo i Prawo" 1997, no. 11–12, pp. 54–70; J. Ciapała, Udział Prezydenta Rzeczypospolitej Polskiej w ustawodawstwie, "Przegląd Sejmowy" 1997, no. 3, pp. 34–51; T. Borkowski, *System rządów w nowej Konstytucji*, "Państwo i Prawo" 1997, no. 11–12, pp. 71–85, T. Słomka, *Prezydent Rzeczypospolitej Polskiej – moderator systemu konstytucyjnego państwa*, in: W. Jakubowski, T. Słomka (eds.), *Porządek konstytucyjny w Polsce*, Warsaw-Pułtusk 2008, pp. 130–135; T. Mołdawa, J. Szymanek (eds.)

position is definitely strengthened by the power of the legislative veto and the ability to refer bills to the Constitutional Tribunal for review of their compliance with the Constitution. Furthermore, the president also enjoys the right of legislative initiative. Additionally, the system for electing the president in Poland, i.e. via direct popular elections for a 5-year term of office, with the right to one re-election, gives the president a stronger mandate than in the case of presidents elected by parliaments. The president is not accountable before the parliament, and has only constitutional liability.[57] The mandate resulting from direct elections and a five-year instead of a four-year term of office mean that the president is perceived as an independent entity, overseeing other state institutions. Both the legislative veto and the ability to send a bill to the Constitutional Tribunal are part of the role of arbiter assigned to the President of the Republic of Poland.[58]

In the light of the 1997 Constitution, the position of the Council of Ministers was strengthened from the perspective of horizontal accountability, unlike the role of the president.[59] A. Antoszewski writes thusly about what led to this strengthening of the government's role: "In order to strengthen its position, and at the same time make the process of governing more stable, it was decided that additional instruments should be adopted protecting the government from a capricious parliamentary majority and – possibly – from an unwanted president."[60] The

---

Instytucja Prezydenta. Zagadnienia teorii i praktyki na tle doświadczeń polskich oraz wybranych państwa obcych, Warsaw 2010; R. Glajcar, *Instytucja Prezydenta w Polsce, Czechach i Słowacji w latach 1989–2000*, Toruń 2004; T. Słomka, *Prezydent Rzeczypospolitej po 1989 r. Studium porównawcze*, Warsaw 2005; J. Szymanek, *Arbitraż polityczny głowy państwa*, Warsaw 2009.

57 The president can be charged at the motion of 140 members of the National Assembly and sentenced by the State Tribunal; the basis of the motion can only be a violation of the constitution, of the law, the perpetration of a crime. See: H. Zięba-Załucka, *Formy odpowiedzialności konstytucyjnej w Rzeczypospolitej Polskiej*, in: S. Grabowska, R. Grabowski (eds.), *Formy odpowiedzialności konstytucyjnej w państwach europejskich*, Toruń 2010, pp. 224–226.

58 In the literature there exists a distinction between "arbitration of power" and "arbitration of authority". According to Z. Witkowski, in Poland the second kind of arbitration is being used, *per* Z. Witkowski, *Model prezydentury polskiej w Konstytucji z 1997 r. w porównaniu z rozwiązaniami Francji, Niemiec i Włoch*, in: E. Gdulewicz, H. Zięba-Załucka (eds.), *Dziesięć lat Konstytucji Rzeczypospolitej Polskiej*, Rzeszów 2007, pp. 332–333.

59 For more: J. Wiatr, p. 123, M. Grzybowski, *Premier jako podmiot kierujący polityką państwa w systemie parlamentarnym*, in: Z. Kiełmiński, J. Szymanek (eds.), *Instytucje prawa konstytucyjnego…*, op. cit., pp. 243–256.

60 A. Antoszewski, *System polityczny RP*, Warsaw 2012, pp. 83–84.

Constitution of the Republic of Poland places the government within the orbit of a parliamentary regime. This is partly due to management of internal and foreign policy being assigned to the government rather than the prime minister, and partly because of the existence of both collective liability of the entire government and individual liability of individual ministers. However, as was previously mentioned, the president also has some powers in the areas of foreign policy and security.[61] Nevertheless, two aspects of the manner in which the government is appointed gives the Prime Minister a privileged position in the Polish political system: a vote of confidence from the parliamentary majority for the Prime Minister, and not the government itself, along with the constructive vote of no confidence.

Owing to the aforementioned duality of the executive branch, which can be described as both parliamentarism and semi-presidentialism, the Polish system of government tends to be classified differently across various typologies. The president being elected via popular vote and enjoying the ability to block some decisions of the government often leads to the Polish political regime being classified as semi-presidential, although studies by Polish scholars more frequently describe it as a parliamentary-cabinet system.[62] The question of classifying Poland

61 The competences of the government and the president concerning foreign affairs were not clearly delineated in the 1997 Constitution. This is why in the face of conflicts between the government and the president regarding Poland's representation in the European Council, then-Prime Minister D. Tusk requested the Constitutional Tribunal to adjudicate a constitutional dispute regarding the central institution authorised to represent Poland at sessions of the European Council. On 20 May 2009 the Constitutional Tribunal decided that the Prime Minister represents the Republic of Poland at Council of Europe sessions and presents the country's position, "Monitor Polski" 2009, no. 32, item 478.

62 For more on typologies of political regimes and Poland's place within them: A. Antoszewski, *Konflikty w obrębie władzy wykonawczej na tle doświadczeń państw Europy Środkowej i Wschodniej*, in: Z. Kiełmiński, J. Szymanek (eds.), *Instytucje prawa konstytucyjnego w perspektywie politologicznej*, Warsaw 2013, pp. 256–258; J. Szymanek, *"Premierowska" odmiana systemu parlamentarnego*, in: T. Mołdawa, J. Szymanek, M. Mistygacz (eds.), *Parlamentarny system rządów. Teoria i praktyka*, Warsaw 212, pp. 124–159; J. Raciborski, *System polski między semiprezdencjalizmem a systemem parlamentarno-gabinetowym*, in: J.J. Wiatr, J. Raciborski, J. Bartkowski, B. Frątczak-Rudnicka, J. Kilias, *Demokracja polska. 1989–2003*, Warsaw 2003, pp. 75–97; S. Gebethner, *System rządów w Rzeczypospolitej Polskiej: model konstytucyjny a praktyka*, in: Z. Maciąg (ed.), *Stosowanie Konstytucji RP z 1997 roku. Doświadczenia i perspektywy*, Warsaw 2003, pp. 211–231, R. Piotrowski, *Relacje między parlamentem, prezydentem a rządem: model konstytucyjny i praktyka ustrojowa*, in: W. Jakubowski, T. Słomka, *Porządek konstytucyjny w Polsce*, Warsaw-Pułtusk 2008, pp. 63–84. For more on the

as a specific type of political regime aside, it should be stressed that from the point of view of horizontal accountability, the duality of the Polish executive enriches the system of checks and balances. That said, it also leads inevitably to conflicts between the Council of Ministers and the Prime Minister with the President.

2.1.1. The President

From the point of view of horizontal accountability, the two most important instruments at the president's disposal in Poland are the legislative veto and the ability to refer a bill to the Constitutional Tribunal for review of its compliance with the Constitution. Both are among the classic collection of instruments used for balancing the legislative by the executive through oversight of bills adopted. It should also be noted that the president is only forbidden from vetoing the budget act and bills containing constitutional amendments. A. Chorążewska distinguished three main reasons for employing the legislative veto: 1) the bill violates basic constitutional principles; 2) the bill was passed in violation of constitutional procedures; 3) the bill carries with it the danger of undesirable legal, economic or social consequences.[63] The model of the veto implemented in the 1997 Constitution is a suspending veto, not an absolute veto, although of a total rather than selective character. According to Art. 122(5) of the Constitution, a veto must be accompanied by a justification. Additionally, the veto can be rejected by a 3/5 majority assuming a quorum of at least half of the total number of MPs.[64] This last mentioned property of the veto means that it is really effective only in the case of a government with weak support in the parliament. It also means that the possibility of forcing through the rejection of a bill is a predictable measure.

The situation is different in the case referring a bill to the Constitutional Tribunal. The Tribunal may rule that the bill is 1) complaint with the Constitution; 2) unconstitutional as a whole; 3) unconstitutional only in part. Constitutional Tribunal rulings are final and universally binding. It should also be noted that the president cannot use both tools in respect of the same bill, but must choose

position of the parliament and government in the constitutional order see: J. Szymanek, *Zmiany pozycji ustrojowej parlamentu w państwach demokratycznych*, in: T. Mołdawa, J. Zaleśny (eds.), *Parlamentaryzm w świecie współczesnym. Między ideą a rzeczywistością*, Warsaw 2011, pp. 9–28; J. Szymanek, *Sejm i Senat w porządku konstytucyjnym RP*, in: T. Mołdawa, J. Zaleśny (eds.) *Parlamentaryzm w świecie…*, op. cit., pp. 172–206.

63 See.: A. Chorążewska, *Model prezydentury w praktyce politycznej po wejściu w życie Konstytucji RP z 1997 r.*, Warsaw 2008, p. 238.

64 A. Więckowska, *Weto Prezydenta Rzeczypospolitej Polskiej w praktyce politycznej po wejściu w życie nowej konstytucji*, "Przegląd Sejmowy" 2003, no. 6(59), pp. 35–39.

one of them. Despite the unpredictability of Constitutional Court rulings, this tool can be more effective than a legislative veto in situations where the president hails from a different political camp than the one enjoying a parliamentary majority. Even though presidents must resign from membership in a party, there is no doubt that informal ties with the previous party remain.

Without doubt, aside from party affiliation, the style in which the office of president is exercised can be influenced by the personality traits of individual presidents or simply the vision of the presidency by its holder. In politics, however, there are often situations in which official declarations are not entirely consistent with political practice. Therefore, an analysis of the use of accountability tools depending on the existence of co-habitation[65] can serve to answer the question of whether the declarative character of subsequent presidencies is reflected by political practice, and to what extent the party affiliation of the president influences the use of accountability instruments.

In the analysed period (1997–2011), the office of president was held twice by A. Kwaśniewski (1995–2000 and 2000–2005), who came from the party known as the Left Democratic Alliance (SLD). President Kwaśniewski declared belief in the principle of negotiation and dialogue, which was especially notable following the tempestuous presidency of L. Wałęsa. In the period of 2005–2010 the presidency was held by L. Kaczyński, whose original political formation was Law and Justice (PiS). Kaczyński's vision of the presidency was very different from that of his predecessor. From the beginning he declared that he would actively engage in state politics. The president was killed in an airplane crash several months before the end of his term, on 10 April 2010, which triggered early presidential elections. On 6 August 2010, B. Komorowski, from Civic Platform (PO), was elected President of the Republic of Poland. Komorowski from the beginning spoke of his presidency in a similar tone to that of Kwaśniewski, rejecting the confrontational style demonstrated by L. Kaczyński.

---

65 Co-habitation is understood as a situation in which the President is associated with a different political formation than the parliamentary majority that formed the government. More about this: T. Słomka, *Prezydent…*., op. cit., pp. 240–259.

Table 2. Co-habitation situations in the years 1997–2011

Presidents (party affiliation, inauguration)	**Political parties in government coalitions in subsequent terms***			
	3rd Term 31.10.1997–19.10.2001	**4th Term 19.10.2001–31.10.2005**	**5th Term 31.10.2005–16.11.2007**	**6th Term 17.11.2007–08.11.2007**
A. Kwaśniewski (SLD) 1st term *23.12.1995*	AWS/UW	-	-	-
A. Kwaśniewski (SLD) 2nd term *23.12.2000*	-	SLD/PSL	-	-
L. Kaczyński (PiS) *23.12. 2005 r.–10.04. 2010 r.*	-	-	PiS/Sam./LPR	-
B. Komorowski (PO) *6.08.2010-*	-	-	-	PO/PSL

Source: own work.

* In the years 1997–2001, 2001–2005 and 2005–2007 the coalitions did not survive until the end of the term. More information on this can be found in Chapter 4.

When analysing the practice of the use of the legislative veto, it should be stressed that in the years 1997–2001 President Kwaśniewski, originally from SLD, vetoed as many as 28 bills, of which 19 were initiated by a government formed by rival parties, i.e. AWS and UW. Only once did the parliament manage to repeal his veto. In this case, the government coalition was able to gain the support of PSL. However, it should also be added that these 19 bills accounted for little more than 2.5% of all bills passed in the years 1997–2001. The influence of the president's party affiliation on the use of the veto was especially visible in the 4th term of the Parliament (2001–2005), when the country was governed by a coalition consisting of SLD and PSL. The president then used the legislative veto in only five cases, accounting for 0.5% of all bills passed.

President L. Kaczyński used the legislative veto even more rarely in the years 2005–2007, when Poland was governed by PiS, Kaczyński's party of origin. During the 5th term of parliament, L. Kaczyński only once motioned for a bill to be reconsidered, accounting for merely 0.26% of all bills passed. However, during the next term, L. Kaczyński's activity increased significantly, which was correlated with the formation of a government by PO-PSL. President Kaczyński used the veto as many as 17 times, 10 of which were for bills proposed by the government. President Komorowski exercised his right of veto twice. During that term of parliament nearly 2% of bills were vetoed, and in five cases the veto was overridden.

Chart 1. The practice of legislative veto use in the years 1997–2011

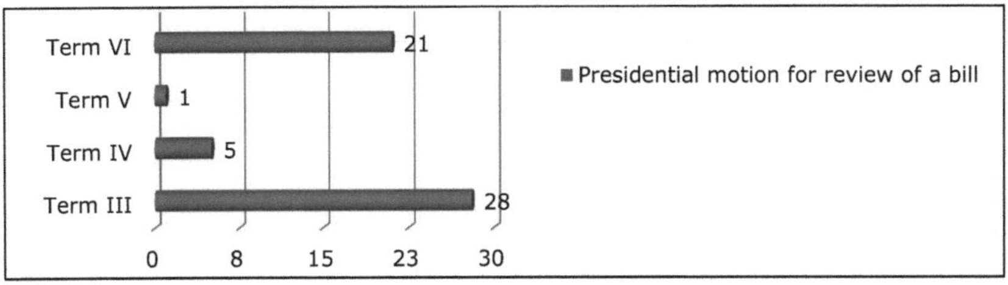

Source: own work, based on: Sejm Rzeczypospolitej Polskiej, *III Kadencja. Informacja o działalności (20 października 1997 r.–18 października 2001 r,)*, Kancelaria Sejmu, Wydawnictwo Sejmowe, Warsaw 2002, p. 27 and 30; Sejm Rzeczypospolitej Polskiej, *IV Kadencja. Informacja o działalności (19 października 2001 r.–18 października 2005 r,)*, Kancelaria Sejmu, Wydawnictwo Sejmowe, Warsaw 2006, p. 30, 33; Sejm Rzeczypospolitej Polskiej, *V Kadencja. Informacja o działalności (19 października 2005 r.–4 listopada 2007 r.)*, Kancelaria Sejmu, Wydawnictwo Sejmowe, Warsaw 2008, p. 64; Sejm Rzeczypospolitej Polskiej, *VI Kadencja. Informacja o działalności (5 listopada 2007 r.–7 listopada 2011 r.)*, Kancelaria Sejmu, Wydawnictwo Sejmowe, Warsaw 2012, pp. 66–67.

A similar relation exists in the case of presidential applications for preventive control of legislation to the Constitutional Tribunal. What may come as a surprise is the number of such motions made by A. Kwaśniewski during the 4th term of parliament, when the government was formed by his party of origin, SLD. When comparing the parliamentary terms during which A. Kwaśniewski held the office of president (1997–2001 and 2001–2005), it should be stressed that in both cases a large number of applications was made to the Constitutional Tribunal. During the 3rd term the president made 13 such motions, out of which the Constitutional Tribunal only once decided that the bill concerned was unconstitutional, while six bills were deemed only partially constitutional. During the 4th term the number of motions did not significantly decrease, as there were nine of them. Five of the bills were deemed partially constitutional, and three were deemed unconstitutional. The situation was different in the case of L. Kaczyński's presidency. During the 5th term, the president did not refer any bills to the Constitutional Tribunal, while during the 6th term he did so as many as 19 times. In the years 2010–2011, President Komorowski twice referred legislation for review by the Constitutional Tribunal.

Chart 2. The practice of referring legislation to the Constitutional Tribunal by presidents in the years 1997–2011

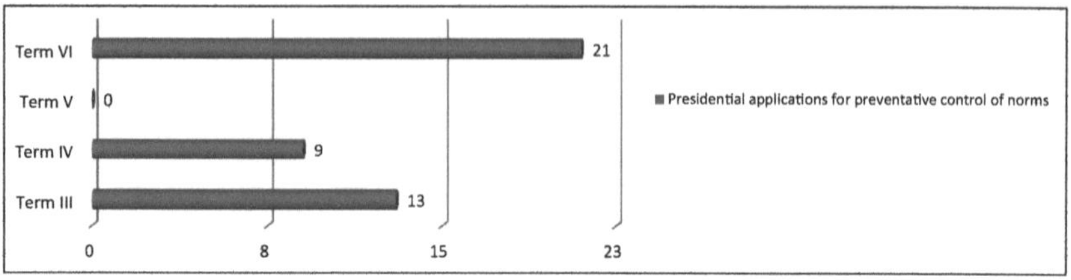

Source: official website of the President of the Republic of Poland: www.prezydent.pl/; *Informacja o istotnych problemach wynikających z działalności i orzecznictwa Trybunału Konstytucyjnego w 2012 roku*, Warsaw 2013, p. 80.

A look at the number of bills proposed by the president also proves interesting. While the legislative initiative is not an accountability instrument, it is part of the president's role as an arbiter. In analysing the use of the legislative initiative, it should be clearly stated that the same dependency as in the case of legislative veto and applications to the Constitutional Tribunal does not occur. The ratio of draft bills proposed in the years 1997–2011 was 1.39% in the 3rd term, 1.67% in the 2nd term, 3.25% in the 5th term, and 1.85% in the 6th term. President Kwaśniewski proposed slightly more bills during his second term – there were only 16 during the first one, and 21 during the second one. The opposite was true during the presidency of L. Kaczyński, who proposed 23 bills under the PiS government, and 28 under the PO government, thus proposing proportionally more of them in 2005–2007 than in 2007–2010. B. Komorowski did not propose any bills until the end of the 6th term of parliament.

Chart 3. Presidential draft bills compared to all bills proposed in the Sejm during the 3rd–6th terms

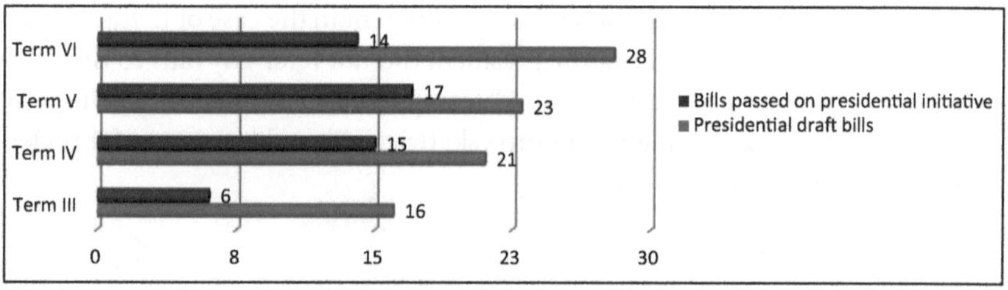

Source: own work, based on: Sejm Rzeczypospolitej Polskiej, *III Kadencja…*, op. cit., p. 27; Sejm Rzeczypospolitej Polskiej, *IV Kadencja…*, op. cit., p. 29; Sejm Rzeczypospolitej Polskiej, *V Kadencja…*, op. cit., p. 62, Sejm Rzeczypospolitej Polskiej, *VI Kadencja…*, op. cit., p. 63.

This analysis should also be supplemented by the presidential prerogatives granted under Art. 144(3) of the Constitution, as it transpires that official acts of the president which do not require a countersignature are not purely formal.[66] From the viewpoint of accountability, the most important element, alongside the previously-discussed legislative veto, right of referral of legislation to the Constitutional Tribunal, and right of legislative initiative, is the president's right to make appointments to various important positions. The proposed candidates do not have to be approved by a parliamentary majority. Although this is not always effective, it does serve to strengthen the president's position in the Polish political system.

In summary, the above comparisons clearly point to the fact that usage of the available instruments increases when there is no co-habitation, regardless of the style of presidency declared by the office's holder. This was the case with President A. Kwaśniewski after parties in opposition to SLD came into power. It became

66 According to Art. 144 Par. 3 of the Constitution of the Republic of Poland, the following official acts of the President do not require a countersignature: 1) proclaiming elections to the Sejm and to the Senate; 2) summoning the first sitting of a newly elected Sejm and Senate; 3) shortening of the term of office of the Sejm in the instances specified in the Constitution; 4) introducing legislation; 5) proclaiming the holding of a nationwide referendum; 6) signing or refusing to sign a bill; 7) ordering the promulgation of a statute or an international agreement in the Journal of Laws of the Republic of Poland (Dziennik Ustaw); 8) delivering a Message to the Sejm, to the Senate or to the National Assembly; 9) making a referral to the Constitutional Tribunal; 10) requesting the Supreme Chamber of Control to carry out an audit; 11) nominating and appointing the Prime Minister; 12) accepting resignation of the Council of Ministers and obliging it to temporarily continue with its duties; 13) applying to the Sejm to bring a member of the Council of Ministers to responsibility before the Tribunal of State; 14) dismissing a minister in whom the Sejm has passed a vote of no confidence; 15) convening the Cabinet Council; 16) conferring orders and decorations; 17) appointing judges; 18) exercising the power of pardon; 19) granting Polish citizenship and giving consent for renunciation of Polish citizenship; 20) appointing the First President of the Supreme Court; 21) appointing the President and Vice-President of the Constitutional Tribunal; 22) appointing the President of the Supreme Administrative Court; 23) appointing the presidents of the Supreme Court and vice-presidents of the Supreme Administrative Court; 24) requesting the Sejm to appoint the President of the National Bank of Poland; 25) appointing the members of the Council for Monetary Policy; 26) appointing and dismissing members of the National Security Council; 27) appointing members of the National Council of Radio Broadcasting and Television; 28) establishing the statute of the Presidential Chancellery and appointing or dismissing the Chief of the Presidential Chancellery. 29) issuing orders in accordance with the principles specified in Article 93; 30) resigning from the office of President of the Republic.

even more visible in the case of President L. Kaczyński, who did not make use of accountability instruments in the years 2005–2007 when PiS was in power, while in 2007–2010, with a government formed by a PO-PSL coalition, he used them frequently. This demonstrates that the system of checks and balances works differently in the absence of co-habitation. The president, with substantial instruments of accountability at his disposal, becomes to some extent the exponent of the will of the opposition. The situation in Poland is thus not only one of the executive being controlled by the legislative branch, which will be discussed later in the chapter. The president also performs the role of an arbiter, which is expressed by the head of state's influence on the legislative system. However, the scale of this role depends on the balance of powers among parties.

2.1.2. The Council of Ministers and the Prime Minister

In accordance with the adopted plan for examining the position of the government from the point of view of accountability, the effectiveness of the government measured by the number of government draft bills passed compared to ones proposed by extra-governmental entities, and therefore the ability to impose a legislative agenda, will be analysed. The influence of informal mechanisms on the shaping of the parliament's decision agenda will also be examined. However, before the position of the government in relation to parliament is analysed, a short description of the cabinets that existed in Poland during the years 1997–2011 and the support they enjoyed in the parliament should be presented.

The first of the cabinets in the analysed period was headed by J. Buzek.[67] It was a coalition government formed by AWS,[68] which had 33.83% of the popular vote, and UW[69] with 13.37%. Together, the coalition controlled 261 of the 460 seats in the Sejm. By the same token, following a government formed by SLD and PSL, the right wing came into power.[70] J. Buzek, who was appointed as Prime Minister, was not a well-known politician at the time. M. Krzaklewski, the real leader of AWS, assumed the role of the "*eminence grise* of the new government". A tense relationship with UW, as well as strife within AWS itself, led to a breakup of the governing

67 For more on the criteria of distinction of individual cabinets, see Chapter 5.

68 Akcja Wyborcza Solidarność (AWS) was a coalition of the Solidarity Trade Union and right-wing parties. AWS was formed on the 8th of June 1996 and was a centre-right political formation.

69 Unia Wolności (UW) was created from the merger of two parties: Unia Demokratyczna (UD) and Kongres Liberalno-Demokratyczny (KLD). It was founded on 23 April 1994 and was a centrist party.

70 See.: G. Rydlewski, *Rządzenie koalicyjne w Polsce*, Warsaw 2000, pp. 45–64.

coalition. The cabinet of J. Buzek became a minority government. It should be mentioned here that the formation of a minority government was a novelty in Poland's political history. This became possible with new regulations addressing the formation of the government contained in the 1997 Constitution, specifically the constructive vote of no confidence.[71] The minority government of J. Buzek not only had to seek support through *ad hoc* alliances in the Sejm, but was also hit by a lack of firm backing from AWS which itself had begun breaking up, a process hastened by the party's defeat in the presidential election. Additionally, AWS failed to transform itself into a cohesive political party. In the wake of the group's demise, new political formations came into being, including PO and PiS. At that time Poland was additionally being shaken by corruption scandals, which led to poor popular support for the government. These factors all contributed to the absence of reforms being introduced during J. Buzek's minority government. However, it should also be noted that he was the first Prime Minister in the history of democratic Poland who was able to remain in office throughout the entire term of the parliament, although with changes to his cabinet.

The 2001 elections resulted in the return to power of post-communist parties. The government was formed by SLD-UP and PSL. SLD-UP received 41.04% of the vote, which resulted in 216 seats (out of which 200 went to SLD and 16 to UP), while PSL received 8.98% of the vote and 42 seats. The coalition government led by L. Miller was characterised by strong leadership. SLD was unquestionably the leader of a coalition that was strong during the initial period of its government, which was necessary in the course of negotiations regarding Poland's membership in the European Union. However, in the spring of 2003 a major conflict took place that resulted in PSL being "expelled" from the coalition. The proximate cause of the coalition's breakup was to be found in the issues of vignettes and biofuels. The next cabinet was also led by L. Miller, but this time it was a minority government. However, it should be stressed that Miller, as the Prime Minister of a minority government, was in a much better situation than his predecessor Buzek, as he could count on over 200 votes of MPs from SLD-UP. The two minority governments differed not only in the number of seats held in the parliament, but also the capacity to form *ad hoc* alliances that SLD enjoyed during that term of the Sejm. That said, Miller's leadership style within SLD led to internal party dissent. Additionally, public opinion, as in the case of J. Buzek's minority government, was shaken by corruption scandals involving members of the government. A major conflict between Miller and then-President A. Kwaśniewski also occurred. The split within

71 See: W. Jednaka, *Gabinety koalicyjne w III RP*, Wrocław 2004, p. 182–197.

SLD resulted in the formation of a new party, SDPL, headed by M. Borowski. As promised, L. Miller resigned from office after Poland's accession to the European Union on 1 May 2004. The new government was headed by M. Belka, while the composition of the cabinet went largely unchanged. From the beginning Belka had the support of President Kwaśniewski, although he was not fully backed by SLD. This was the result of M. Belka's distancing himself from "partisanship", which went down poorly with many members of his party. In summary, Belka led a minority government without the full support of its party, which in turn resulted in the lack of party backing for the government in the Sejm. Additionally, in May 2005, the Prime Minister declared that he would engage in the formation of a new party descended from UW, further distancing himself from SLD.

The next cabinet was formed following the 2005 election, although it was from the beginning a minority government, which was a result of the collapse of coalition negotiations between PiS and PO. Eventually PiS, which received 26.99% of the vote (155 seats), formed a minority cabinet with the support of a parliamentary coalition comprised of PiS-Samoobrona-LPR-PSL. The government was headed by K. Marcinkiewicz. As a result of a parliamentary crisis caused by the inability to pass a budgetary bill in February 2006, a so-called "stabilisation pact" was signed by J. Kaczyński (leader of PiS), R. Giertych (leader of LPR) and A. Lepper (leader of Samoobrona). It allowed the minority government to continue to function. In consequence, on 27 April 2006, Samoobrona and the National Parliamentary Circle signed a coalition agreement with PiS, while 8 days later LPR joined the agreement as well. Samoobrona held 56 seats in the Sejm, and LPR had 34; together, the coalition had 242 seats. As a result of these manoeuvres, the government achieved a parliamentary majority. Despite this, K. Marcinkiewicz resigned as Prime Minister on 10 July 2006,. There are several possible explanations for hit move. Most analysts, however, agree that J. Kaczyński, the leader of PiS, did not need his "bumper Prime Minister" anymore. The next government, supported by LPR, Samoobrona and the National Parliamentary Circle, was headed by J. Kaczyński. However, tensions soon appeared among the groups supporting Kaczyński's government. Already in September 2006, A. Lepper was dismissed from his posts as Deputy Prime Minister and Minister of Agriculture and Rural Development. Samoobrona thus joined the opposition. However, only a month later Samoobrona returned to the coalition. The coalition survived the next nine months, proceeding to dissolve in 2007, which, among other issues, was associated with a scandal involving an attempt to bring some Samoobrona PMs into PiS. Journalists referred to this process as J. Kaczyński "gobbling up the appetisers."[72] The final PiS government took on the form of a minority cabinet which survived for four and a half months.

The next government was formed after the 2007 election by a coalition of PO-PSL. PO received 41.51% of the vote and 209 seats, while PSL took 8.91% of the vote and 31 seats. The government was headed by D. Tusk. What was distinctive about the D. Tusk cabinet compared to all previous governments in the so-called Third Republic was the fact that the parliamentary majority survived for the entire term of the parliament. Additionally, for the first time a coalition between a post-Solidarity and post-communist party was formed. In 2011, PO received 39.18% of the vote and 207 seats, which allowed it to form another government. PSL was again invited into the coalition, having achieved a similar result in the election (8.36% of the vote and 28 seats). This was another unique moment in the history of democratic Poland, as for the first time the same party managed to form a government in two subsequent terms of the parliament.

Table 3. Types of governments in the years 1997–2011

Sejm term	Government	Parties forming the government (% of seats)	Type of government
3rd 1997–2001	**J. Buzek** I (AWS/UW)	56.74	Majority with strong support
	J. Buzek II (AWS)	40.43	Minority with weak support
4th 2001–2005	**L. Miller** I (SLD-UP/PSL)	56.09	Majority with strong support
	L. Miller II (SLD)	45.43	Minority with weak support
	M. Belka (SLD)	37.39	Minority with weak support

72 W. Szacki, *PiS zjada przystawki: Samoobrona i LPR przegrały wybory*, "Gazeta Wyborcza", 14.11.2006.

Sejm term	Government	Parties forming the government (% of seats)	Type of government
5th 2005–2007	**K. Marcinkiewicz** I (PiS)	33.48	Minority with very weak support
	K. Marcinkiewicz II (PiS/ Samoobrona/LPR)	52.61	Majority with strong support
	J. Kaczyński I (PiS)	51.96	Majority with strong support
	J. Kaczyński II (PiS/ LPR)	43.04	Minority with very weak support
	J. Kaczyński III (PiS/ Samob./ LPR)	48.70	Minority with weak support
	J. Kaczyński IV (PiS)	32.83	Minority with very weak support
6th 2007–2011	**D. Tusk** (PO/PSL)	52.17	Majority with strong support

Source: own work, based on: www.sejm.gov.pl/Sejm7.nsf/page/archiwum.

When examining the position of the previously characterised governments in the political system, as well as their influence on the legislative and decision agenda, first the list of governmental legislative projects will be presented against a list of projects by extra-governmental entities.[73] When analysing projects proposed in the years 1997–2001, it can easily be noticed that the government is the main initiator of the legislative process in Poland. As many as 52.11% of all bills were submitted by the Council of Ministers, while members' bills accounted for 34.26%, those of parliamentary commissions were 6.82%, Senate bills 3.94%, presidential bills 1.91%, and citizens' bills only 0.97%. It should also be added that some initiatives proposed by MPs may constitute camouflaged government initiatives. According to M. Mistygacz, such initiatives are justified by the

73 More about the opposition in the process of creating lain: K. Sobolewska-Myślik, D. Kasprowicz, *Opozycja parlamentarna w III kadencji Sejmu (1997–2001)*, in: K. Łabędź (ed.), *Opozycja parlamentarna w Polsce w latach 1997–2010*, Kraków 2012, pp. 46–68; M. Simlat, *Struktura i funkcjonowanie opozycji w IV kadencji Sejmu (2001–2005)*, in: K. Łabędź (ed.), *Opozycja parlamentarna*, op. cit., pp. 108, 121; G. Foryś, *Wielokierunkowa opozycja parlamentarna w okresie rządów Kazimierza Marcinkiewicza i Jarosława Kaczyńskiego (2005–2007)*, in: K. Łabędź (ed.), *Opozycja parlamentarna*, op. cit., pp. 140–147; K. Łabędź, *Funkcjonowanie opozycji w VI kadencji Sejmu (2007–2010)*, in: K. Łabędź (ed.), *Opozycja parlamentarna*, op. cit., pp. 178–201.

lengthened procedures concerning international agreements or agreements with representatives of interested parties.[74] In the subsequent terms of the parliament, members' bills made up 28.02%, 18.28%, 27.56% and 19.41% of all legislative initiatives.[75]

Chart 4. Proponents of draft bills voted upon in the Sejm in the years 1997–2011 (in %)

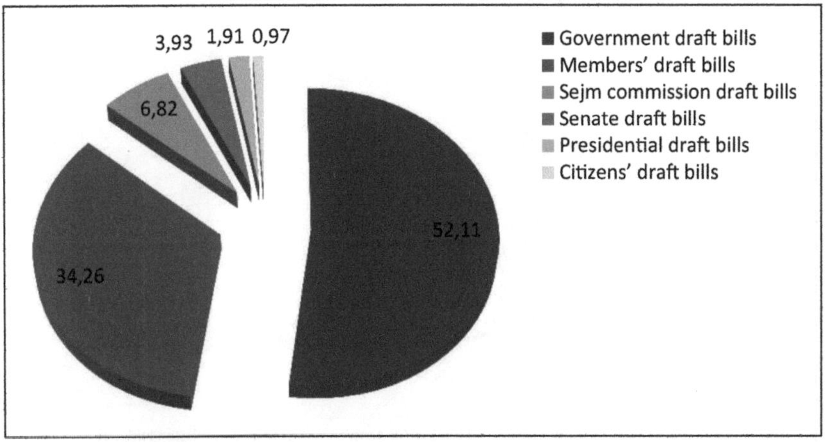

Source: own work, based on: Sejm Rzeczypospolitej Polskiej, *III Kadencja...*, op. cit., pp. 27–28; Sejm Rzeczypospolitej Polskiej, *IV Kadencja...*, op. cit., p. 30; Sejm Rzeczypospolitej Polskiej, *V Kadencja...*, op. cit., p. 62, Sejm Rzeczypospolitej Polskiej, *VI Kadencja...*, op. cit., p. 63.

As can be concluded from the following chart, the proportions in individual terms do not differ significantly from the average, although it is hard to identify any consistent trend. In the years 1997-2001, bills proposed by the Council of Ministers accounted for 48% of all legislative initiatives, while in the years 2001-2005 for 64.5%, in 2005-2007 for 53.25%, and in 2007-2011 for 44.61%. The highest number of governmental legislative projects was proposed in the 4th term, which could indicate that stable parliamentary support is correlated with a higher number of legislative initiatives. However, the data from the 6th term does not confirm that, and the number of initiatives in the 5th term is also relatively high. Therefore, based only on the number of governmental legislative

74 M. Mistygacz, *Rząd w procesie ustawodawczym w Polsce*, Warsaw 2012, p. 359.

75 Sejm Rzeczypospolitej Polskiej, *III Kadencja...*, op. cit., p. 27; Sejm Rzeczypospolitej Polskiej, *IV Kadencja...*, op. cit., p. 29; Sejm Rzeczypospolitej Polskiej, *V Kadencja...*, op. cit., p. 62; Sejm Rzeczypospolitej Polskiej, *VI Kadencja...*, op. cit., p. 63.

initiatives advanced in subsequent terms of the parliament, it is hard to draw any firm conclusions regarding the influence of the type of government and the support it has in the parliament on the legislative agenda.

Chart 5. Legislative initiatives based on the entity initiating the legislative process in subsequent terms of the Sejm (in %)

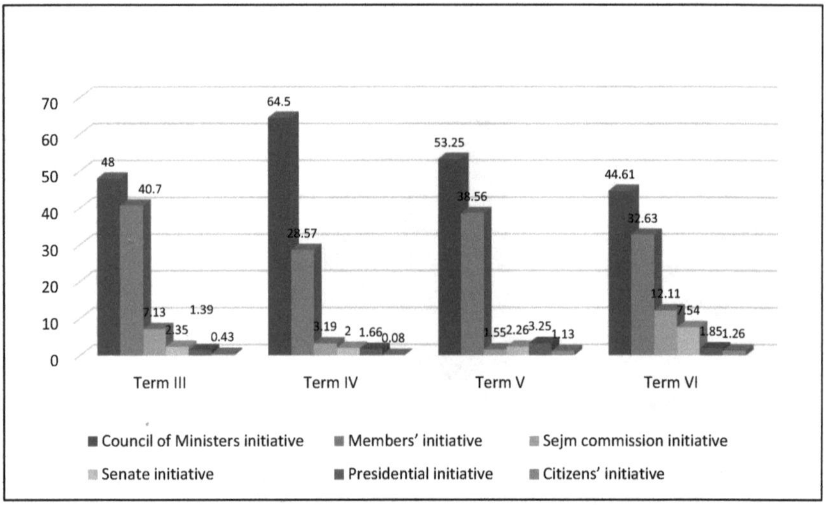

Source: own work, based on: Sejm Rzeczypospolitej Polskiej, *III Kadencja…*, op. cit., p. 28; Sejm Rzeczypospolitej Polskiej, *IV Kadencja…*, op. cit., p. 30; Sejm Rzeczypospolitej Polskiej, *V Kadencja…*, op. cit., p. 62; Sejm Rzeczypospolitej Polskiej, *VI Kadencja…*, op. cit., p. 63.

However, if we compare the number of proposed governmental legislative drafts with the number of bills passed, it turns out that some regularities can be discerned. Changing the numbers shown in Chart 6 to percentages makes it easier to observe the influence of the support individual governments had in the parliament on the number of bills passed. Therefore, in the 2005–2007 term we can note the lowest percentage of government bills passed compared to the number of drafts submitted by the government, as it was only 77.98%; however, in the case of other proponents the percentage of passed bills was also low, only 43.81%. It can, however, be assumed that this may have been related to the shortened term of the parliament. In the 1997–2001 term as well there was a relatively low number of governmental bills passed, 82.46%, while for other proponents this number was 53.13%. In the 2001–2004 and 2007–2011 terms, the proportions of bills passed which were submitted by the government was similar, at 91.71% and 96.35% respectively. In the case of other proponents it was 55.96% and 51.37%.

Therefore, based on the above data a regularity can be noticed: the weaker and less stable the parliamentary support for the government, the lesser the government's ability to impose a legislative agenda on the parliament.

Chart 6. Bills passed according to the entity initiating the legislative process in subsequent terms of the Sejm

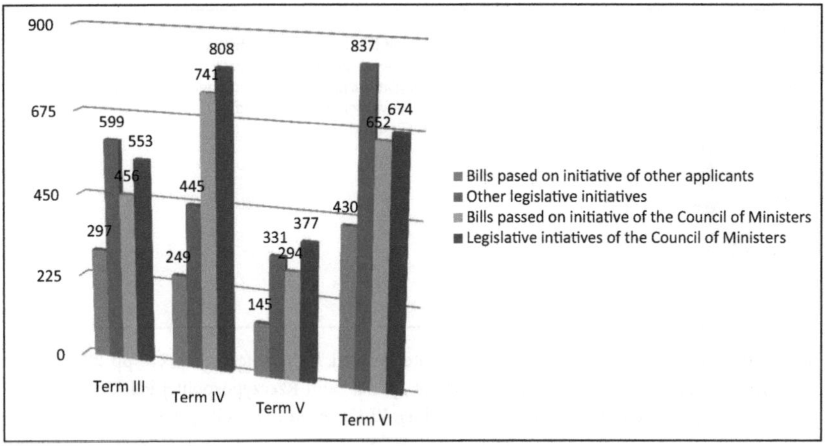

Source: own work, based on: Sejm Rzeczypospolitej Polskiej, *III Kadencja…*, op. cit., p. 27; Sejm Rzeczypospolitej Polskiej, *IV Kadencja…*, op. cit., p. 29; Sejm Rzeczypospolitej Polskiej, *V Kadencja…*, op. cit., p. 62; Sejm Rzeczypospolitej Polskiej, *VI Kadencja…*, op. cit., p. 63.

Remarks on the roots of the government's reduced effectiveness in imposing its legislative agenda on the parliament may be interesting. The main reason is the end of the Sejm's term of office.[76] In the years 1997–2001, these projects comprised 54.64%, while in the years 2001–2005 65.66%. In turn, during the shortened 5th term of 2005–2007 the percentage of bills that were not passed because of the term coming to an end was as high as 91.76% of all government-proposed bills that were not passed, while in the years 2007–2011 this percentage was 72.72%. The next reason was the withdrawal or rejection of draft bills. In the subsequent terms, the percentages of bills that were not passed for that reason were, respectively, 36.08%, 26.87%, 7.06%, and 4.55%. It can also be clearly seen, as previously

76 For more about the principle of discontinuation of parliamentary work, see: *Zasada dyskontynuacji prac Sejmu*, "Ekspertyzy i opinie prawne" 2001, no. 4(45), biurose.sejm.gov.pl/teksty_pdf_01/biul45.pdf; M. Mistygacz, *Rząd w procesie…*, op. cit., pp. 264–269.

mentioned, that the highest percentages of government legislative initiatives failing to pass after a presidential veto were recorded in the absence of cohabitation, i.e. in the 3rd and 6th terms. They comprised 8.25% and 18.18% respectively, while in the 4th and 5th terms these percentages were only 2.99% and 1.18%.

Chart 7. Governmental draft bills submitted in the Sejm in terms 3–6

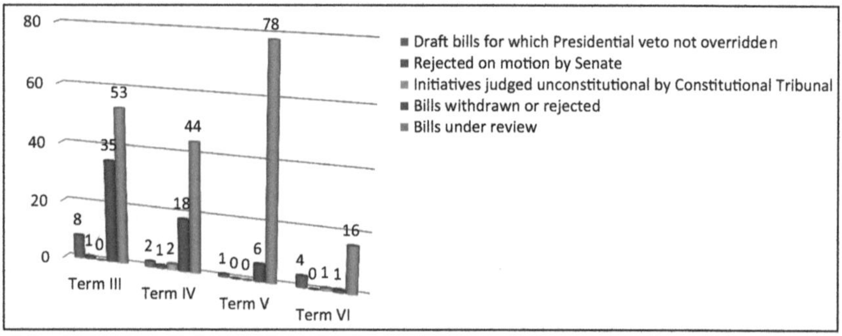

Source: own work, based on: Sejm Rzeczypospolitej Polskiej, *III Kadencja…*, op. cit., pp. 27–28; Sejm Rzeczypospolitej Polskiej, *IV Kadencja…*, op. cit., p. 30; Sejm Rzeczypospolitej Polskiej, *V Kadencja…*, op. cit., p. 62; Sejm Rzeczypospolitej Polskiej, *VI Kadencja…*, op. cit., p. 63.

There are also informal ways for the government to influence the parliamentary legislative process, which are unrelated to the type of government and the support it has in the parliament. The press has reported widely on the mechanisms of the "freezer" and "shredder". Both of these instruments depend on the will of the Marshal (speaker) of the Sejm. The accepted practice in Polish politics is to elect a person politically close to the Prime Minister as Marshal.[77] The ability to influence the legislative agenda of the Sejm is connected with putting legislative initiatives in motion, a power which was delegated to the Marshal in an amendment to the Statute of the Sejm of 28 October 1997. Before that, activation of the legislative process was a matter for the Presidium of the Sejm, which reflects the configuration of forces in the parliament.[78]

The first of the aforementioned mechanisms, the so called "freezer", consists in the Marshal of the Sejm blocking the opposition's draft bills by not directing them for a first reading to have them opined by the lower house. However, one should distinguish the initial procedure concerning draft bills, which is required

77 E. Milewicz, *Syf – do wenerologa, Sejm – dla polityków*, "Gazeta Wyborcza", 6 July 2012.
78 Uchwała Sejmu Rzeczypospolitej Polskiej z dnia 28 października 1997 r. w sprawie zmiany Regulaminu Sejmu Rzeczypospolitej Polskiej, "Monitor Polski" no. 80 item 779.

under Art. 34(2) of the Statute of the Sejm, from the wait for the motion to add an item to the Sejm's agenda to be tabled, which is called the "freezer". Pursuant to a resolution of the Sejm of 19 December 2008, the period in which the Marshal of the Sejm mush present a motion to supplement the agenda of the Sejm was shortened from six to four months.[79] However, the mechanism makes it possible for a draft bill to "disappear", particularly at the end of a term.

The second mechanism, the so called "shredder", is used by sending selected drafts to the legislative committee, the composition of which reflects the composition of the Sejm and is part of the initial procedure regarding draft bills set out in Art. 34 of the Statute of the Sejm. The Marshal of the Sejm may decide to refer a draft bill to the legislative committee if there are doubts about its constitutionality.[80] Sending a draft to the legislative committee entails not assigning it a bill number and not placing it on the Sejm's agenda. Although the committee's opinion is not binding on the Marshal, it can be used as an excuse for rejecting a bill. This mechanism of selection leads to evasion of responsibility and renders accountability by the voters harder. It can lead to the Marshal rejecting a bill out of alleged concern for compliance with the constitution, while in reality the cause is political. Since the 5th term of parliament it has been used very frequently. In the 5th term of the Sejm, the committee adopted 268 opinions, of which 20 were sent to the committee via the procedure described in Art. 34(8) of the Statute of the Sejm, while in the 6th term this was 58 out of 571 accepted opinions.[81] And although it is not formally associated with the government, just like the "freezer" mechanism, it is beyond doubt that there are still connections between the will of the government and the Marshal's decision to refer a project to the legislative committee. To visualise the scale of this phenomenon, it should be added that in

---

79 Uchwała Sejmu Rzeczypospolitej Polskiej z dnia 19 grudnia 2008 r. w sprawie zmiany Regulaminu Sejmu Rzeczypospolitej Polskiej, "Monitor Polski"2009, no. 2, item 9.

80 The Legislative Committee was created in 2001. Before that matters of legislative problems and consistency of the law were considered by the Justice Committee. Bill and resolution projects of which there are doubts as to whether they are inconsistent with the existing law, including European Union law, are being opinionated at the motion of the Marshal of the Sejm (after seeking the opinion of the Presidium of the Sejm) on the basis of Art. 34 Par. 8 of the Sejm Statute. The Committee acquaints itself with legal opinions about the projects, listens to the representatives of movers and representatives of the government, discusses the project, and in a vote by 3/5 majority, opines on whether they are legally admissible or inadmissible.

81 Sprawozdanie Komisji Ustawodawczej z działalności w V kadencji Sejmu (2005–2007), Warsaw 2007, p. 8; Sprawozdanie Komisji Ustawodawczej z działalności w V kadencji Sejmu (2007–20011), Warsaw 2011, pp. 7–8.

the 4th term drafts sent on their first reading to a session of the Sejm comprised only 33%, while drafts sent on their first reading to the committee comprised 65%, while 2% (27 projects) were left without a decision.[82]

In summary, the above comparisons confirm the hypothesis that in Poland the Council of Ministers' ability to influence the legislative and decision agenda of the Sejm is directly proportional to the support it has in the parliament. This can be confirmed through data regarding first and foremost the ratio of draft bills proposed by the Council of Ministers to the number of bills passed compared to other entities enjoying legislative initiative. It should also be added that in studies published in Polish scholarly literature, the weakness of legislation created in Poland is often stressed. The organisation of legislative work on draft bills and the absence of assessment of the results of new regulations are often criticised; this also concerns governmental initiatives.[83] W. Staśkiewicz additionally stresses the weakness of the government in imposing a legislative and decision agenda on the parliament, postulating the reversal of the roles of the government and parliament. He writes: "The parliament should put more emphasis on substantive discussions of the challenges facing Polish society and focus less on legislative work regarding draft bills projects, which should be the domain of lawyers and the government."[84] The presented data confirms the relatively weak position of the government as an

82 J. Lipski, R. Tymiński, *Analiza ustaw wniesionych do Sejmu w toku całej IV kadencji*, in: *Ustawy 2001–2005, Sejm IV kadencji*, Biuro Studiów i Ekspertyz, Warsaw 2006, pp. 35–36.

83 The government, as legislative initiator, was criticized for: 1) a departmental model of law creation and lack of coordination 2) excessive readiness to initiate the legislative process 3) lack of influence by the Government Legislative Centre on the government's legislative process 4) treating consultations in the process of law creation as a formality 5) the lack of assessment of the effects of regulations, failure to take into account rulings by the Constitutional Tribunal, the Supreme Administrative Court and the Supreme Court in its legislative works, not appreciating the work of the Legislative Council and its output. For more: S. Wronkowska, *Tworzenie prawa w Polsce – ocena i proponowane kierunki zmian. Raport Rady Legislacyjnej przy Prezesie Rady Ministrów*, "Przegląd Legislacyjny" 2006, no. 1, pp. 7–21; R. Zubek, *Jak i dlaczego reformować ocenę skutków regulacji w Polsce?*, opracowanie przygotowane na zlecenie Rzecznika Praw Obywatelskich (final version 26/01/2007), www.rpo.gov.pl/pliki/12180262910.pdf; R. Zubek, K.H. Goetz, M. Lodge, *Planowanie legislacyjne w Europie Środkowej. O strategicznym zarządzaniu legislacją rządową*, Warsaw 2007, pp. 1–44; K.H. Goetz, R. Zubek, *Stanowienie prawa w Polsce. Reguły legislacyjne a jakość ustawodawstwa*, Warsaw 2005, pp. 1–62.

84 W. Staśkiewicz, *Stanowienie prawa*, in: L. Kolarska-Bobińska (ed.), *Co warto, co należy zmienić. Poprawa jakości demokracji w Polsce*, Warsaw 2008, p. 52.

entity entitled to submit legislation. The effectiveness of the government measured by the ratio of proposed legislative drafts to ones passed in the years 1997–2011 was 96.74%, while for extra-governmental entities it was 51.37%, in which for parliamentary groups and Sejm committees it was 55%. While the government's effectiveness seems very high, it should be noted that bills passed at the motion of the government comprised only 65.65%, while for extra-governmental entities the percentage was 34.35%, with parliamentary groups and Sejm committees accounting for 32.17%. The number of urgent bills passed in each term is also low, which could be seen as a measure of the government's effectiveness.[85]

2.2. Spain

Under the Constitution of 1978, Spain is a constitutional monarchy. The monarch in the Spanish political system is equipped with the traditional functions of a Head of State. Unlike the President of the Republic of Poland, the monarch was not given a legislative veto, nor the capacity to file a motion with the Spanish Constitutional Tribunal to decide whether a piece of legislation is constitutional or not. The monarch also does not enjoy the legislative initiative. Moreover, all official acts, apart from the appointments of civilian and military members of the royal court, are required to be countersigned by the Prime Minister, the chair of the Congress of Deputies, or the appropriate minister, depending on the type of government act.[86] Additionally, the monarch cannot be held accountable, neither under the constitution nor in any political sense. According to Art. 56(1) of the Spanish Constitution, the role of the Spanish monarch is to be an arbiter and a supervisor of the proper functioning of governmental institutions. Furthermore, the monarch is a symbol of the nation's unity and permanence. In reality, the monarch does not function as an arbiter, and his role is reduced to serving a symbol of the nation's unity and representing the state in international relations.

The weak position of the monarch in the Spanish political system is contrasted with the strong position of the government and the prime minister in particular. According to I. Van Biezen and J. Hopkin, Spain has been an example of the so called "Moncloa Complex" from the moment of consolidation, and one which has gradually extended. In practice, this means strengthening of the

85 In the 3rd term, out of the 473 proposed government projects, 80 were classified as urgent, in the 4th term – 32 out of 776, in the 5th term – 11 out of 336, and in the 6th term - 32 out of 642, after M. Mistygacz, *Rząd w procesie*..., op. cit., pp. 206–207.

86 P. Uziębło, *Formy odpowiedzialności konstytucyjnej w Królestwie Hiszpanii*, in: S. Grabowska, R. Grabowski, *Formy odpowiedzialności*..., op. cit., pp. 408–410.

presidential character of the government system.[87] According to the definition proposed by T. Pogunte and P. Webb, presidentiality of a government system is a process in which some states function as presidential states, at times without changes in their formal structure. One of the symptoms of Spain's presidentiality is the 'absorption' of the government by the Prime Minister. This has occurred even though the Constitution clearly establishes the position of the government as one of a classic parliamentary regime when considering that it is the government, rather than the Prime Minister, which is given authority to pursue internal and external political objectives. However, the sole responsibility of the PM before the government, a vote of confidence given to the PM rather than to the government, the PM's ability to dissolve the government, and the constructive vote of no confidence all place the PM in a position of authority.[88] That position is further strengthened by the possibility of forming a minority government rather than only a coalition government in the event a parliamentary majority cannot be achieved.[89] Moreover, the PM's leadership in the party holding the parliamentary majority leads to further reinforcement of that person's autonomy.[90]

---

87 I. Van Biezen, J. Hopkin, *The Presidentialization of Spanish Democracy: Sources of Prime Ministerial Power in Post Franco Spain*, in: T. Poguntke, P. Webb (eds.), *The presidentialization of politics. A comparative study of modern democracies*, Oxford 2004, p. 114.

88 For more: Ó.I. Mateos De Cabo, *El Presidente del Gobierno en España: status y funciones,* Madrid 2006, J. Montabes, *El Gobierno*, in: M. Alcántara, A. Martínez (eds.), *Política y Gobierno en España,* Valencia 1997, pp. 151–189; J.L. Paniagua Soto, *El modelo parlamentario en la Constitución Española de 1978*, in: R. Cotarelo (ed.), *Transición política y consolidación democrática. España (1975-1986)*, Madrid 1992, pp. 201–217; A. Bar Cendón, *El Gobierno en la Constitución y en la Ley del Gobierno de 1997: ¿Colegialidad o Presidencialismo?*, "Teoría y Realidad Constitucional" 2004, no. 14, pp. 64–84; J. Capo Giol, *The Spanish Parliament in a triangular relationship*, 1982–2000, "Journal of Legislative Studies" 2003, vol. 9 no. 2, pp. 107–129; G. Rico, *Candidatos y Electores. La popularidad de los líderes políticos y su impacto en el comportamiento electoral*, Barcelona 2002, G. Rico, *Los factores de la personalización del voto en las elecciones generales en España, 1979–2004*, Trabajo presentado en el VII Congreso Español de Ciencia Política y de la Administración, Madrid, 21–23 September 2005; M. Myśliwiec, *Cechy hiszpańskiego systemu rządów*, "Przegląd prawa konstytucyjnego" 2010, no. 2/3, pp. 131–145.

89 More about types of governments in Spain in Chapter 5.

90 It is also worth mentioning that also during election campaigns attention is first and foremost focused on the candidates for the office of Prime Minister, their charisma and style, and to a lesser extent on the parties and electoral platforms. However, this tendency is connected more with the personalization of power than with the presidentialization of the political system. See more: L. Picarella, *Presidencialización y*

2.2.1. The monarch

Under Art. 57(1), the Spanish monarchy is a hereditary monarchy in the person of the successors of King of Spain Juan Carlos Bourbon. Juan Carlos Bourbon took the throne under the fundamental law on 22 November 1975, during the Franco regime. However, as observed by T. Mołdawa, Spanish society's support for political reform in the referendum of 15 December 1976 also signified its acceptance of monarchy. This was much like the referendum held on 6 December 1978, which sanctioned the introduction of the new constitution upholding the monarchical character of the political system.[91]

As previously mentioned, constitutional regulations allow us to distinguish three functions fulfilled by the monarch. Firstly, the monarch symbolises the unity and permanence of the state; secondly, the monarch fulfils the function of moderator; and thirdly, the monarch performs the role of an arbiter. A. Łabno-Jabłońska points out that the location of those functions in the constitution can indicate either a constitutional monarchy or a parliamentary one.[92] This dilemma can be resolved by analysing the real position of the monarch in Spain. When we examine not only the legislative but also political role of the monarch in Spain's political system, it is certain that we are dealing with a wholly neutral power. In the monarch's relations with the *Cortes Generales*, the most important powers are the right to sanction and promulgate acts of parliament pursuant to Art. 62(a and b), as well as the right to dissolve the parliament. The right to sanction and promulgate the acts of parliament does not encompass the right to veto them, and is performed in a somewhat automatic manner. This means that the monarch has no influence on the parliament's legislative agenda. J. Iwanek describes the role of the monarch in the legislative process by saying "The monarch's participation in the legislative process and in passing the government's normative acts is not the act of his willpower. Its character is purely formal and ceremonial, and to which action the King is duty-bound."[93] The situation in the event of dissolution of the parliament is similar. The monarch's decision to shorten the Parliament's term

---

personalización en el Sistema Político Español, 1975–2008, "Revista Enfoques" 2009, vol. 7 no. 11, pp. 518–519.

91 See: T. Mołdawa, *System konstytucyjny Hiszpanii*, Warsaw 2013, p. 70; J. Solé Tura, M. A. Aparicio Pérez, *Kortezy Generalne w systemie konstytucyjnym Hiszpanii*, Warsaw 2003, pp. 9–13.

92 A. Łabno-Jabłońska, *Iberyjska droga do demokracji. Studium prawnokonstytucyjne*, Warsaw 1996, p. 79.

93 J. Iwanek, *Postępowanie ustawodawcze w Hiszpanii*, in: E. Zwierzchowski (ed.), *Postępowanie ustawodawcze*, Warsaw 1993, p. 129.

is purely formal, as according to Art. 115(1) it is the PM who can appeal to the monarch to do so, asking for the dissolution of the Congress of Deputies, the Senate, or the Cortes Generales. All of this implies that the monarch does not hold the actual power to dissolve the parliament, which means that the monarch's moderation of the normal functioning of this institution is only symbolic and not dependent on the political winds of the day. When analysing the relations between the monarch and the government, it must be emphasised that, according to Article 62, it is the monarch who proposes a candidate for the role of PM following prior consultations with political groups represented in the parliament; in practice, the parties' opinions must be taken into consideration. The same applies for deposing a PM, an action that is purely formal as well. Moreover, it must be stressed that neither the constitution nor any other legislative act provides a role for the monarch in establishing the course of state policy in any direct manner. A thorough analysis requires that we should also mention the remaining powers of the monarch. He is the leader of the Armed Forces, although in reality this is an honorary title. In terms of international affairs the monarch enjoys only representational rights, which means that he cannot enter into legally binding agreements with other states, although the Spanish press and literature highlights the King's accomplishments in his efforts to boost Spain's foreign trade.

In summary, the constitutional powers granted to him do not give the Spanish monarch the potential to have any influence on politics, neither to serve as its de facto arbiter nor moderator. The requirement for almost all royal political acts to be countersigned makes it impossible for the monarch to pursue any independent course of action. A. Łabno-Jabłońska states that "The real significance of the monarch is dependent on his moral and political authority."[94] However, when we analyse the role of the monarch from the beginning of the transformation of the Spanish political system, we may observe a different tendency. The more stable the Spanish political system is, the smaller the role played by the monarch in politics. In the years 1989–2011, the role of the king in the Spanish political system was reduced to the performance of representative functions. Nonetheless, it is worth mentioning that during the transformation period of 1975–1982 the king was one of the most important political actors owing to the weaknesses of the newly-established democratic system. The king's vote of confidence played a major part during the establishment of the new government by A. Suarez in 1979, who was a key politician during the period of political transformation in Spain. It was also the king's lack of confidence that influenced his dismissal in 1981.

94 A. Łabno-Jabłońska, *Iberyjska droga…*, op. cit., p. 99.

Juan Carlos Bourbon additionally took part in stifling the military revolt led by Colonel Tejero in 1981. In doing so, the king played an important role in the process of Spain's democratic transformation, which brought him the respect and support of Spanish society, something reflected in the results of public opinion polling as seen in the chart below.[95]

Chart 8. Spanish society's opinions on the role of the monarch in the political system

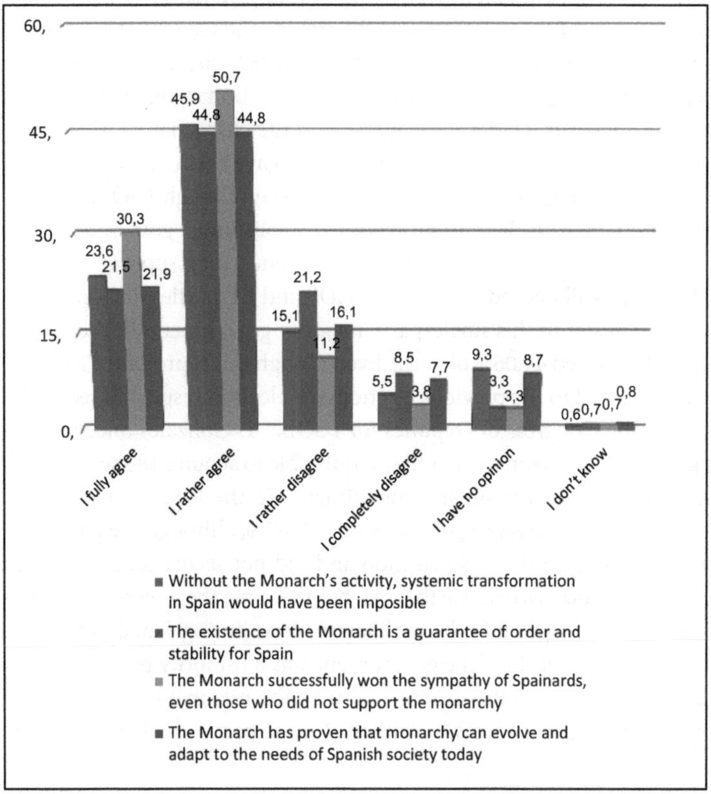

Source: CiS, Barómetro no 2778, Listopad 2008, www.cis.es/cis/opencm/ES/1_encuestas/estudios/ver.jsp?estudio=8920.

95 On the role played by the monarch in the process of systemic political transformation see: W.L. Berncecker, *El papel político del Rey Juan Carlos en la trasición*, "Revista de Estudios Políticos" 1996, no. 92, pp. 113–135, M. Myśliwiec, *Hiszpania*, in: M. Myśliwiec, K. Krysieniel (eds.), *Systemy polityczne wybranych państw basenu Morza Śródziemnego*, Poznań-Chorzów 2011, p. 141.

However, it should be added here that the Spanish monarchy has lost popularity in opinion polls conducted in recent years. This is mostly the result of personal scandals relating to the king, as well as a corruption scandal in which some members of the royal family were involved.

2.2.2. The Government and the Prime Minister

The role of government and its leader will be analysed here using the same methods as in the case of Poland. First, we will provide the reader with a short description of Spanish governments during the years 1982–2011, as well as the support they had in the Congress of Deputies. The 1982 election resulted in a historical victory for the Socialists. Under the leadership of the charismatic F. Gonzalez, PSOE received as much as 48.11% of the vote, which gave them an opportunity to create an independent government. Nonetheless, even though PSOE, with 202 seats in a 350-seat Congress, had no problem in establishing a government, nor did it need to negotiate with the remaining parties concerning support for the investiture, they were still backed by the PCE, CDS and EE parties. F Gonzalez became the Prime Minister in this single-party majority government. In the next election 1986, PSOE received 44.06% of votes. Even though this represented a loss of 4.05% of votes compared to the previous election, the election result still secured a stable majority in the Congress of Deputies for PSOE.[96] F. Gonzales once more became the leader of the government. PSOE was only able to acquire 180 seats, which again allowed them to rule without any impediments. In the 1989 election, PSOE again won enough votes to create a government – 39.87%, although the party lost 4.46% of votes compared to the 1986 election and did not secure an absolute majority. Once again F. Gonzales became the PM, but this time the government had a mere 175 seats at their disposal in the parliament, constituting exactly half of the total number of seats. Therefore, the government was a minority government and was only able to exist due to the support given by the regional parties CiU and PNV during the investiture process.[97] Neither of these parties had any representatives

96 PSOE is a federal structure, comprised of regional departments. The only exception is the Catalonian Partit Socialista de Catalunya (PSC-PSOE), registered as a separate party. Currently, PSC takes part in practically all internal activity, like the other regional PSOE departments. Additionally, since 1982 it has formed a common parliamentary club with PSOE in the Cortes. Therefore, votes acquired by PSC-PSOE in the years 1986–2011 were included as PSOE votes.

97 For the purpose of this work, the term "regional party" was accepted for both regional and nationalist parties. In the Spanish-language literature, the term "non-nationwide parties" is in use for parties that were created as an effect of the division into centre

in the government. As it transpired, the unfettered socialist reign was secured owing to the Basque nationalist party Herri Batasuna, which refused to accept their parliamentary seats as a form of protest. All this meant that the party headed by F. Gonzalez was able to secure a *de facto* absolute majority with 175 seats compared to the 173 seats held by their opposition. In 1993, PSOE nearly repeated their electoral success of 1989, achieving a result of 39.1%, which again allowed them to form a government. However, they held only 159 seats, thus the party needed support during the investiture process; the parties providing that support to the fourth consecutive government of F. Gonzalez were CiU, PNV and CC. Even though PSOE could have formed a coalition with IU-IC, they decided to turn to the regional parties for support. In the end they formed a minority government, however, they were not able to retain power to the end of the parliamentary term due to the growing number of corruption scandals involving PSOE politicians, as well as the GAL case coming to light. Early elections had to be called.

The People's Party (PP) won the elections in 1996, although the electoral result of 37.19% did not allow the PP to form a majority government. As a result, the PP and the regional parties PAR and UPN, which secured two seats each, had a total of 154 seats at their disposal in the Congress of Deputies. This situation forced the PP leader, J.M. Aznar, to negotiate with the rest of the regional parties. After two months of negotiations, Aznar was able to secure the support of CiU leader J. Pujol, which was necessary for PP to carry out the investiture process. At the same time, negotiations with representatives from PNV and CC were being held. With the support he was given by the Catalonians, Aznar did not need the support of the remaining regional parties. However, the PP leader worked towards achieving some form of compromise with both CC and PNV. In the end, both parties gave their support to the government during the investiture process, providing PP with 179 seats in total. During the 2000 elections, the PP achieved a majority

---

and the peripheries, i.e. regional and nationalist parties. A division into regional and nationwide parties was also proposed by K. Deschouwer. The author introduces two variables, on the basis of which he determines the character of a given party in a multi-level system. The first of these is the degree of *territorial penetration*, which allows one to distinguish between parties active only in one region, in several regions and in all regions. The other variable is the kind of elections given parties take part in – nationwide elections, regional elections or all of them. Based on these two variables, in Spain in the examined period, 5 nationwide parties can be distinguished: PSOE, PP, IU, CDS and UPiD, while the other parties were classified as regional parties. See K. Deschouwer, *Political Parties as multi-level organizations*, in: R.S. Katz, W. Crotty (eds.), *Handbook of party politics*, London 2006, pp. 291–300.

in the parliament by winning 45.24% of votes, which again saw J.M Aznar take the office of PM. This was seen as an historic victory, as it was the first time since the establishment of democracy that a Francoist successor party, as PP was perceived by many, succeeded in achieving an absolute majority. The PP did not need the support of nationalists in the new parliament, as they had 183 votes at their disposal. Nevertheless, the unstable agreement with CC remained in place.

The 2004 election drastically changed the political scene in Spain. PSOE returned to government again after eight years, receiving 43.27% of votes. However, many analysts highlighted the fact that the socialists were helped by a lie perpetrated during the electoral campaign lie by the People's Party, who claimed that 11 March 2004 attacks were supposedly committed by the ETA rather than by Islamic extremists.[98] With 164 seats at their disposal, PSOE did not gain an absolute majority, which in Spanish conditions meant the formation of a minority government. The cabinet was led by the new head of PSOE, J.L. Rodríguez Zapatero. The parties that gave PSOE their support during the investiture process were CC, IU, BNG and ERC. The next elections of 2008 were also won by PSOE, with a 46.5% share of votes, which allowed Zapatero to again form a minority government. This time, none of the other parties supported the socialists. The new prime minister was elected in a second vote by a simple majority. With fierce criticism of the government's inaction in the face of a deepening economic crisis an early election was called, in which the winner was PP, receiving 41.89% of the vote and 170 seats.

Table 4. Types of governments in Spain in the period 1982–2011

Term of the Congress of Deputies	Government	Parties forming the government (% of seats in the parliament)	Type of government
2nd 1982–1986	F. González I (PSOE)	57.71	Majority government with very strong support
3rd 1986–1989	F. González II (PSOE)	52.57	Majority government with strong support
4th 1989–1993	F. Gonzaléz III (PSOE)	50	Minority government with very strong support
5th 1993–1996	F. González IV (PSOE)	45.43	Minority government with weak support

98 More about this in Chapter 5.

Term of the Congress of Deputies	Government	Parties forming the government (% of seats in the parliament)	Type of government
6th 1996–2000	J. M. Aznar I (PP)	44.57	Minority government with weak support
7th 2000–2004	J. M. Aznar II (PP)	52.29	Majority government with strong support
8th 2004–2008	J.L. Rodríguez Zapatero I (PSOE)	46.86	Minority government with weak support
8th 2008–2011	J.L. Rodríguez Zapatero II (PSOE)	48.29	Minority government with weak support

Source: own work, based on: Congress of Deputies website: www.congreso.es.

By examining the role of the government in mechanisms of horizontal accountability, as was previously done in the case of Poland, one may easily conclude that the government is one of the main initiators of new law. According to Chart no. 9, in the years 1982–2011 draft bills proposed by the government accounted for 33.34% of all proposed legislative initiatives, while those proposed by parliamentary groups comprised 45.13%. In Spain, there are three types of government legislative initiatives – aside from draft bills there are also decree-laws and legislative decrees. Decree-laws are used based on Art. 86(1) of the Constitution in situations of exceptional and urgent need. Only then can the government adopt this kind of temporary legislative act. Additionally, a decree-law cannot concern the organisation of the fundamental institutions of the state nor the rights and freedoms of citizens, as well as the autonomous communities and electoral law. Decree-laws are presented directly before the Congress of Deputies to be voted upon, without the possibility of introducing amendments. The second type of decree, i.e. legislative decree, results from the so-called delegated legislative authority, and consists in assigning to the government the power to establish new laws with the power of legislative acts, with the exception of fundamental laws. With all the legislative initiatives of the government taken together, the percentage of government bills compared to all others would be 44.71%.

Chart 9. Sponsors of draft bills submitted in the Congress of Deputies in the years 1982–2011 (%)

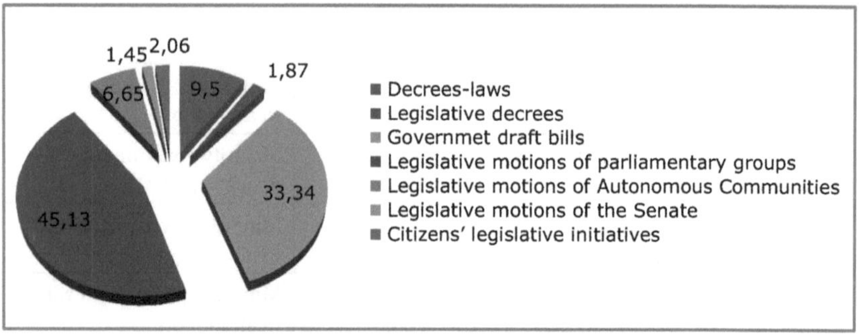

Source: own work based on www.congreso.es.

When comparing the number of governmental legislative initiatives in subsequent terms, a downward trend can be noticed regardless of the type of the government. The percentage of all types of government initiatives in subsequent terms was: 2nd term – 66.16%, 3rd term – 49.70%, 4th term – 45.53%, 5th term – 47.95%, 6th term – 44.36%, 7th term – 37.48%, 8th term – 39.85%, 9th term – 36.88%. On the other hand, the percentage of legislative initiatives of parliamentary groups grew, as in the 2nd term they constituted only 28.54%, in the 3rd term – 43.60%, in the 4th term – 43.9%, in the 5th term – 40%, in the 6th term – 47.69%, in the 7th term – 52.70%, in the 8th term – 44.59%, and in the 9th term – 51.77%. The share of other legislative entities stayed at a similar level, aside from the 8th term in which the percentage of Senate projects increased significantly, and in the 9th term, when the percentage of citizens' legislative projects increased.

Chart 10. Sponsors of draft bills and legislative motions proposed in the Congress of Deputies in terms 2–9

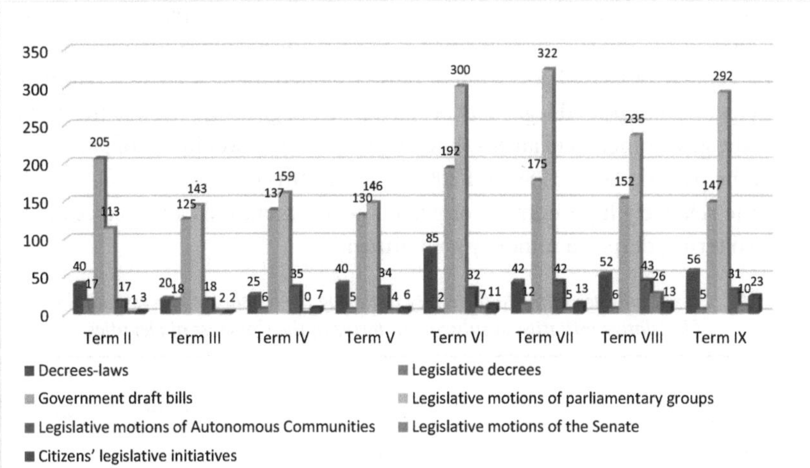

Source: own work, based on: www.congreso.es.

On the other hand, when analysing the number of acts of law passed by the Congress of Deputies it is clear that, despite the decreasing number of governmental legislative initiatives, the number of bills passed has remained at a relatively constant level. When converting the numbers in Chart 11 to percentages, it is noticeable that with a decreasing number of government legislative initiatives the percentage of laws passed upon government initiative is high compared to bills initiated by other entities. In the analysed period the percentage of passed government bill projects, decree-laws and legislative decrees fluctuated between 82.20% and 92.21%. When observing the share of passed acts of law proposed by the government in subsequent terms, we may easily observe the influence of the type of government and the support it had in the Congress of Deputies on the legislative agenda. In the 2nd term, during the period 1982–1986, as many as 92.12% of all passed legal acts were initiated by the government. In that term, the socialists enjoyed the highest support in the Congress of Deputies in the analysed period. A high percentage of government drafts was also passed in the years 1986–1989, in total 91.82%. In the next term, during the period 1989–1993 the share of government drafts passed decreased to 83.85%, which was connected with the government's minority status; this was similar to 1993–1996, when the number was 82.2%. In the next term, 1996–2000, as the People's Party came into power and formed a minority government, the share of passed government bills was similar at 84.37%. As the party improved its electoral performance, acquiring an absolute majority in the years 2000–2004, the percentage of passed bills also rose to 92.21%. In the next two terms, during the periods 2004–2008 and 2008–2011, the socialists formed minority governments; despite this fact, the percentage of passed government bills remained high, at 88.34%. Therefore, the percentage of passed legal acts proposed by the government was the highest when the government had an absolute majority in the lower house of parliament, i.e. in the periods 1982–1989 and 2000–2004. In this context, it is interesting to note the relatively high number of passed government bills and decrees in the last two terms, despite a minority government.

Chart 11. Passed bills according to the entity initiating the legislative process and the type of legislative initiative in subsequent terms of the Congress of Deputies

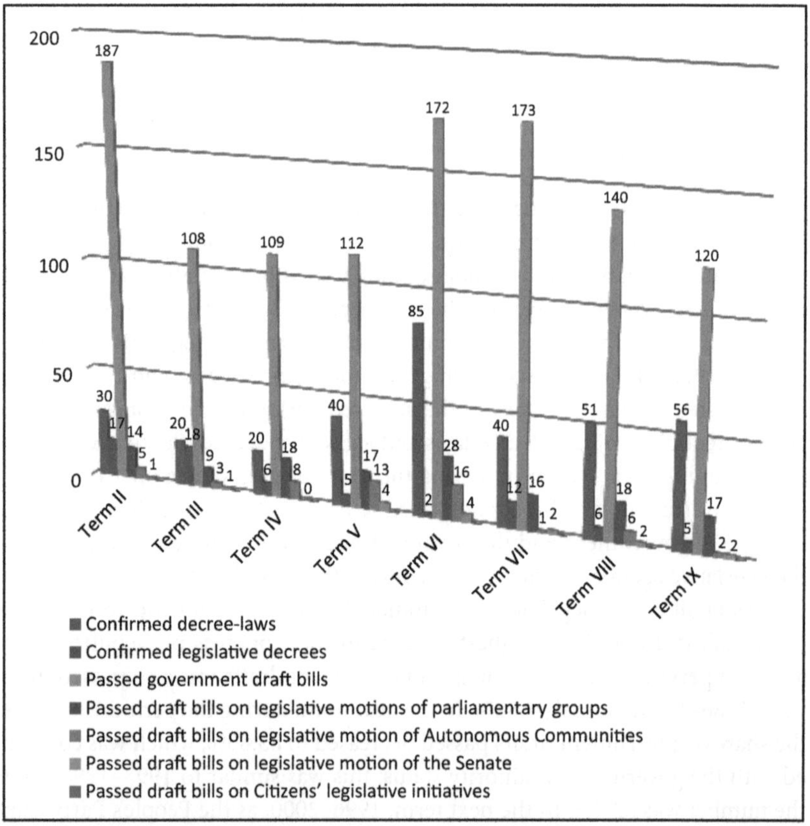

Source: own work, based on: www.congreso.es.

Therefore, the number of legal acts passed at the behest of the government is very high. This indicates the government is highly effective, which results mainly from the privileged position of the governmental legislative initiative pursuant to Art. 89 of the Constitution, under which government draft bills have priority in the parliamentary agenda.[99] Additionally, all governments used the right to propose decree-laws and legislative decrees. The former type of legal act has been used much more often in recent years. Also, in practice governments have used this formula on various occasions to present acts of dubious urgency, in order to quickly pass their own legislative initiatives and avoid debate with the opposition parties. As many as a quarter of all legal acts passed were decree-laws and legislative decrees. That said, some of them were eventually adopted in the form of legislative motions, and not decree-laws. In the 2nd term this was the case with 27.50% of all decree-laws, in the 3rd term - 10%, in the 4th term - 30%, in the 5th term - 25%, in the 6th term - 22.35%, in the 7th term 21.43%, in the 8th term - 9.80%, and in the 9th term - 19.64%. It should also be noted that only once in the 4th term was a decree-law repealed. The most common cause of legal acts not being passed was, like in Poland, the expiration of parliament's term of office.

99 More about the objective and subjective character of legislation in Spain: T. Mołdawa, *System konstytucyjny...*, op. cit., pp. 102–105.

Chart 12. Governmental bills proposed in the Congress of Deputies during terms 2–9

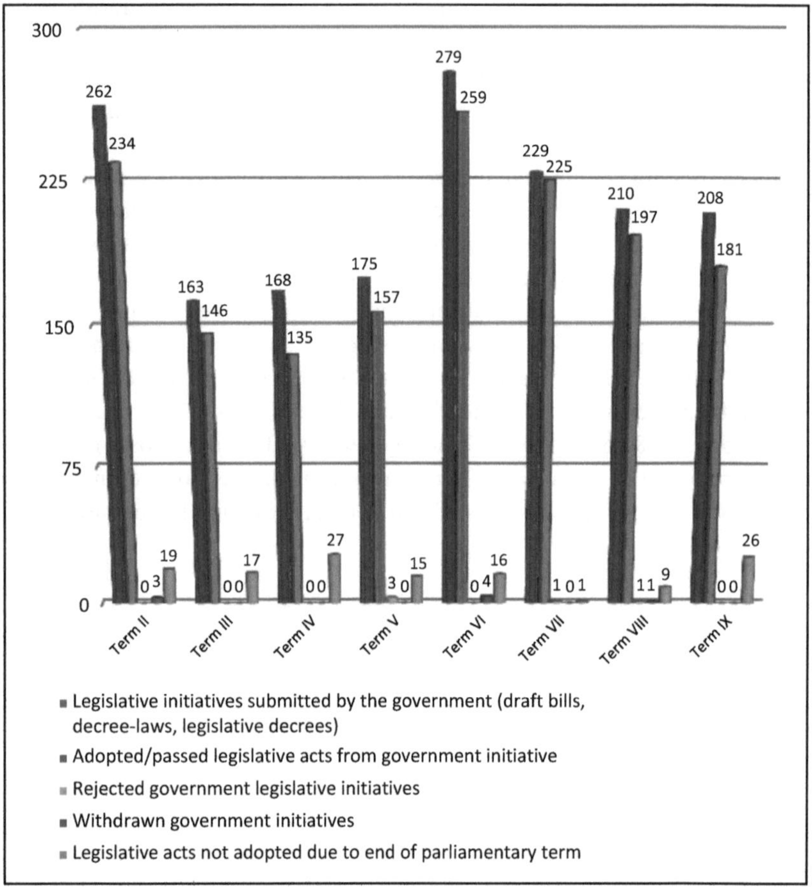

Source: own work, based on: www.congreso.es.

Spain lacks an equivalent of the Polish "freezer", although the "procedure of accepting for consideration" in some ways can be compared to the Polish "shredder". Projects that are subject to this procedure include all legislative initiatives except for government projects, which are exempt from this, and Senate motions, for which an analogous procedure exists[100]. This procedure is meant to protect the Congress

100 For more about the legislative procedure in Spain, see: J. Iwanek, *Postępowanie ustawodawcze w Hiszpanii*, in: E. Zwierzchowski (ed.), *Postępowanie ustawodawcze,*

of Deputies from being flooded with legislative initiatives that have no chance of being realised. The plenum of the Congress of Deputies decides on whether a legislative motion should be accepted by simple majority. In this initial review of acceptability of projects proposed by extra-governmental entities, the government is also permitted to participate. The government can oppose the acceptance of a legislative motion which would result in a decrease in budgetary income and increase in public spending, or is contradictory to the standing legislative delegation. The government's opposition is synonymous with preventing a legislative motion from being considered. Therefore, a mechanism allowing the government to influence the decision agenda of the parliament exists, although it is very transparent. Additionally, given the small number of bills passed at the motion of parliamentary groups, this is not of key significance for horizontal accountability.

In summary, the government in Spain, as a constitutional institution, enjoys a strong position. This is expressed mainly in the ratio of legislative projects proposed by the government to those that are eventually passed. In the examined period, i.e. in the years 1982–2011, 88.11% of bills and decree-laws proposed by the government were passed, while in the case of extra-governmental entities this number amounted to only 11.89%, of which ones passed at the motion of parliamentary groups were only 8.01%. It is worth mentioning that according to J. Calvet Crespo, the dominance of the government is not just quantitative, but also qualitative. According to Crespo, it is the government that proposes and leads to the enactment of the most important laws for the functioning of the state, while legislative motions proposed by parliamentary groups are of little significance.[101] Therefore, the legislative function of the Congress of Deputies is limited, as few acts are enacted via the initiative of parliamentary parties. It is the Spanish government that decides first and foremost on the legislative and decision agenda of the parliament. Its influence is slightly weakened in the case of minority governments, but it still remains at a high level.

***

Comparing the position of the Polish president with that of the Spanish monarch is difficult, given the very different range of competences at their disposal. During the period of systemic transformation, i.e. in the years 1975–1982, Juan

---

Warsaw 1993, pp. 105–136, T. Mołdawa, *Procedura Legislacyjna w Hiszpanii*, "Przegląd Sejmowy" 1993, no. 4, pp. 66–80.

101 J. Calvet Crespo, *Gobiernos minoritarios, pactos parlamentarios y producción legislativa*, "Política y Sociedad" 2003, vol. 40, no. 40, p. 91.

Carlos Bourbon was one of the main political actors and played a major role in the process of democratisation. However, in the period under review, i.e. 1982–2011, the role of the monarch in the political system of Spain has been limited to merely a representative function. The constitution does not give the Spanish monarch the ability to genuinely influence day-to-day politics, and therefore the monarch does not play an important role in the system of horizontal accountability, as there are no significant mechanisms to facilitate such. This is very different from the case of the Polish president, although here the use of available instruments depends on whether the president comes from the same political formation as the government. Based on empirical analyses shown in Charts 1 and 2, it can be stated categorically that the role of the President as an active player in the system of horizontal accountability increases in the absence of cohabitation. The absence of cohabitation was directly linked to increased use of available instruments, i.e. the legislative veto and applications made by the head of state to the Constitutional Tribunal for the preventive review of new laws; the declared style of presidency was not very significant. Therefore, the first of the hypotheses stated is confirmed: *The absence of co-habitation strengthens the position of the president as an active player in the system of accountability; the level of consolidation of the Spanish political system weakens the position of the monarch.*

When comparing the position of the executive in the accountability system, it can be concluded that its position in Spain is slightly stronger than in Poland, even though in Poland as many as 52.11% of all legislative drafts were proposed by the Council of Ministers, while in Spain, when accounting for all types of initiatives the percentage of government drafts was 44.71%. However, when comparing the percentage of legislative drafts submitted by the government to those eventually passed with the ratio for extra-governmental entities, the greater strength of the Spanish government's position is visible. In Spain, in the years 1982–2011, 88.11% of all bills and other legal acts proposed by the government were passed, while in the case of extra-governmental entities the percentage was only 11.89%. In Poland it was 87.12% and 51.05% respectively.[102] Therefore, in the case of Spain the legislative function of the Congress of Deputies is limited, as few bills are enacted at the initiative of parliamentary groups. It is the government of Spain that exercises decisive influence over the legislative and decision

102 For comparison, it should be noted that in Western Europe, the percentage of bills enacted through the initative of governments fluctuates between 68% and 95%, and therefore is very high. More: T. Bräuninger, M. Debus, *Legislative Agenda-Setting in Parliamentary Democracies*, "European Journal of Political Research" 2009, no. 48, pp. 804–839.

agenda, and does so in a transparent manner – through decree-laws and legislative decrees on the one hand, and on the other thanks to the privileged position of the governmental legislative initiative, granted under Art. 9 of the Constitution of the Kingdom of Spain. In Poland, despite the existence of informal channels for the government to influence the legislative process through the use of the "freezer" and "shredder", the effectiveness of the government is much lower.

When comparing the ability of the Polish and Spanish governments to influence the legislative and decision agenda of the parliament, it can be concluded that in both cases it was proportional to the support the governments enjoyed in their respective terms of parliament. This is confirmed by the data presented in Charts 6 and 11. In Poland, in the 2005–2007 term, when governments enjoyed the weakest parliamentary support, the lowest number of bills proposed by the government was passed (77.98%) compared to the number of all legislative drafts proposed. In addition, during the 1997–2001 term the number of passed bills proposed by the Council of Ministers was also proportionally low (82.46%). In the 2001–2004 and 2007–2011 terms, the percentage of government-initiated bills passed was similar and also high (91.71% and 96.35%). The situation in Spain was comparable – the highest percentage of legal acts was enacted at the motion of the government in the periods when it had an absolute majority in the lower house of parliament, i.e. in the years 1982–1989 (92.12% and 91.82%) and 2000–2004 (92.21%). In the 1989–1993, 1993–1996 and 1996–2000 terms, the percentage of governmental projects passed was much lower, which was associated with the fact of minority governments (respectively: 83.85%, 82.2%, and 84.37%). In the two subsequent terms, i.e. in the years 2004–2008 and 2008–2011, when minority governments were also formed, the percentage of legal acts enacted at the motion of the government was slightly higher compared to the aforementioned terms with minority governments, although not as high as in the 1982–1989 and 2000–2004 terms. Therefore, the results of the empirical research presented in the second chapter confirm the second hypothesis – *the weaker and less stable the parliamentary support for the government in Poland and Spain, the lower its ability to impose a legislative and decision agenda on the parliament.*

In relation to the influence of the time from the moment of consolidation of the political system in Poland and Spain on the position of the government in the system of accountability, the results of the analyses are not without ambiguity. However, the fact that the minority governments' ability to influence the legislative and decision agenda of the government in the last two terms of the parliament in Spain was higher than that of the minority governments in the years 1993–2000 may indicate that not only the level of support for the government in the parliament is significant. The analyses conducted do not seem to confirm, however, that the time elapsed from the consolidation of the political system is of key significance for the stronger position of the Spanish government compared to that of the Polish Council of Ministers. Therefore, the third hypothesis cannot be confirmed: *The longer the time from the moment of consolidation, the stronger the position of the government in the accountability system – in Spain it is stronger than in Poland.*

Chapter 3. The legislative

Both Poland and Spain feature a system of rationalised parliamentarism, under which the government must have the support of a parliamentary majority, while also guaranteeing a decisive role for the Prime Minister in the parliament. As stated by M. Kruk, rationalised parliamentarism allows for the "effectiveness and stabilisation of the government without undemocratic limitations on the parliament's rights."[103] At the same time, a number of researchers note that in many modern democracies, parliaments are far less autonomous as legislative bodies than before.[104] One of the reasons for the limitation of the role of parliaments is the rationalisation of parliamentarism. This is expressed in such ways as the limited role of the so-called negative control of the parliament in the legislative process, which was discussed in Chapter 2. Undoubtedly, from the perspective of horizontal accountability, negative control by parliament of bills submitted by the government is very important. However, limiting the role of the parliament to merely a law-making machine inhibits assessment of its role in the horizontal accountability system.[105] Therefore, the control function of the parliament is also very important. In the concept of accountability, the distinction in constitutional law of instruments of political responsibility and of control is not applied.[106] Both the former and the latter are considered to be accountability instruments. The most important division of control functions is into *ex ante* instruments, connected with the appointment of public officials, and *ex post*, connected with

---

103 M. Kruk, *Idea stabilności i efektywności rządów w Konstytucji RP z 1997*, in: W. Czapliński (ed.), *Prawo w XXI wieku*, Warsaw 2006, p. 411.

104 See: H. Döring (ed.), *Parliaments and Majority Rule in Western Europe*, Frankfurt 1995; D.H. Kim, G. Loewenberg, *The Role of Parliamentary Committees in Coalition Governments. Keeping Tabs on Coalition Partners in the German Bundestag*, "Comparative Political Studies" 2005, vol. 38, no. 9, pp. 1104–1129; K. Strøm, *Minority Government and Majority Rule*, Cambridge 1990.

105 Scholars examining modern parliaments from the comparative perspective usually concentrate on the legislative function of the parliament, somewhat routinely forgetting about its control function. See: M. Gallagher, M. Laver, P. Mair, *Representative Government in Modern Europe*, Boston 2006; P. Norton (ed.), *Parliaments and Governments in Western Europe*, London 1998.

106 A. Antoszewski, *Funkcje parlamentów państw Europy Środkowej i Wschodniej jako przedmiot badań politologicznych*, in: S. Sulowski, J. Szymanek (eds.), *Ustrój polityczny państwa. Polska, Europa, Świat*, Warsaw 2013, pp. 213–214.

dismissal of the government.[107] This chapter will focus on *ex post* control, including instruments associated with preventing asymmetry of information between members of government and the parliament.[108] According to M. McCubbins and T. Schwarz, the primary tool preventing abuses of power by the executive is *ex post* parliamentary control, which they call "police patrol oversight", i.e. the procedures of invigilation and control of decisions made and policies carried out by the government.[109] Therefore, this work will employ the classification proposed by M. Kruk,[110] itself practically identical to the typology used by Spanish researchers such as E. Guerrero and M. Sánchez de Dios.[111] The cited authors classify instruments of control based on the criterion of the entity authorised to use a given instrument, which means they divide them into instruments used by the lower houses of parliament in the plenary forum and those at the disposal of parliamentary committees, counting control mechanisms of individual MPs among the former group.[112] This classification will be used to analyse the

---

107 U. Sieberer, *The institutional Power of Western European Parliaments: A Multidimensional Analysis*, "West European Politics" 2011, vol. 34, no. 3, p. 732.

108 According to K. Strom, one of the main problems of the parliamentary regime, from the point of view of the principal-agent theory, is preventing the asymmetry of information, which favours the government. A. Lupia is of similar opinion, stating that loss of "agency" increases if parliaments have both limited information and limited means. See: K. Strom, *Parliamentary Democracy and Delegation*, in: K. Strom, W. Mueller, T. Bergman (eds.), *Delegation…*, op. cit., p. 86; A. Lupia, *Delegation and its perils*, in: K. Strom, W. Mueller y T. Bergman (eds.), *Delegation…*, op. cit., p. 35.

109 M. McCubbins, T. Schwartz, *Congressional Oversight Overlooked: Police Patrols versus Fire Alarms*, "American Journal of Political Science" 1984, no. 28, pp. 165–179.

110 M. Kruk, *Funkcja kontrolna sejmu*, Warsaw 2008.

111 M. Sánchez de Dios, *The accountability game in parliamentary democracy*, 22nd World Congress of Political Science, Madrid 8–12 June 2012, pp. 1–27; E. Guerrero, *Responsabilidad y control: rendición de cuentas del gobierno*, w: A. Martínez (ed.), *Representación y calidad de la democracia en España*, Madryt 2006, pp. 165–178.

112 On the basis of constitutional law, a common classification is one proposed by L. Garlicki. When describing the control functions of the Sejm he divides instruments of control into four groups. The first is connected with the right to demand information, and here the author lists: presentations of reports, submitting information, participating in the works of committees. The second group, connected with the right to demand a hearing, includes: desiderata, opinions and resolutions. The third group includes general instruments employed with the cooperation of appropriate organisational units, e.g. the Supreme Audit Office, based on the plans of Sejm committees. The fourth group includes special control procedures, such as: forming investigative committees, interpellation procedures, control over the execution of the

instruments of parliamentary control in Poland and Spain, which comprise part of the horizontal accountability system.[113]

As with the executive, also in the case of the legislative branch the effectiveness of horizontal accountability tools is, among other things, a product of the institutional architecture. Therefore, procedural conditions will be one of the determinants taken into consideration in this analysis when examining the functioning of the legislative branch in the system of horizontal accountability. The second determinant will be the range of support that each government had in subsequent parliamentary terms, as alongside procedural conditions this is the factor that determines the dynamics of the use of accountability tools to the greatest extent. Taking these determinants into consideration will allow us to answer the following questions: Which of the determinants influences the use of accountability instruments more in Poland and Spain? To what extent does the time elapsed since consolidation of the political system in both countries influence the institutionalisation of control performed by both houses of the parliament? Accordingly, two theses will be verified. Hypothesis 1: *In Poland and in Spain, the dynamics of the use of accountability tools is more dependent on procedural conditions than on the balance of forces in the lower houses of parliament.* Hypothesis 2: *Control of Spain's Congress of Deputies is more institutionalised than control of Poland's Sejm, which results from the longer time elapsed since the moment of consolidation of democracy.*

It should be added that while both Poland and Spain have a bicameral system, the analysis focuses on the lower houses of both parliaments.[114] In each of the two countries, the role of the Senate is that of the house of the second reading, and in both countries its role in the system of accountability is secondary. In Poland, pursuant to Art. 95(2) of the Constitution, the Senate does not have a control role at all, although in practice some instruments of control used by the upper house

---

budget. See: L. Garlicki, *Polskie prawo konstytucyjne zarys wykładu*, Warsaw 2006, pp. 248–254.

113 Out of the tools proposed by M. Kruk, the exposé will be excluded, as other authors do not include this instrument.

114 The Polish parliament is composed of two chambers – the Sejm, with 460 MPs, and the Senate, with 100 senators. According to Art. 96(2) of the Constitution of Poland, the Sejm electoral system is proportional; the specifics of the Polish electoral system in the lower house of the parliament are described in detail in Chapter 5. Elections to the Senate, since 2011, are held under a first-past-the-post system in single-seat districts. Elections to both houses take place every four years.

have emerged.[115] In Spain, although the Senate does have control functions, similarly to Poland it does not take part in the process of giving a vote of confidence nor a vote of no confidence.[116] This is why the data regarding the control function of the Spanish Senate has only been included in the annex to this analysis.[117]

3.1. Poland

Undoubtedly, one of the most important tools for accountability that can be utilised in the plenary forum is the constructive vote of no confidence. Since the 1997 Constitution came into effect, the only formula available for holding the government politically responsible is the vote of no confidence. A motion for a vote of no confidence for the Council of Ministers can be made by at least 46 MPs, and the same motion should also include the name of the candidate to assume the post of Prime Minister. For the motion to pass, an absolute majority of the total constitutional number of MPs is needed, i.e. 231 votes. If the motion for a vote of no confidence passes, the Prime Minister is obliged to tender his/her resignation to the President. During the analysed period of 1997–2011, only one motion for a vote of no confidence for a government was submitted, during the 5th term. Votes of no confidence for individual ministers were used much more frequently. For a vote of no confidence towards individual ministers to pass, 231 votes are needed on a motion of at least 69 MPs. If the motion passes, the minister is dismissed by the President. A special form of control is the vote of confidence as another instrument of control exercised in the plenary forum of the Sejm. In Poland, two forms of vote of confidence exist. The first to be discussed is not part of the system of accountability, and at most can be treated as *ex ante* control. This is, of course, the vote of confidence following the swearing in of a government, pursuant to Art. 155 of the Constitution of Poland, which is an expression of the acceptance of the program and the composition of the government by the Sejm. In order for a vote

115 L. Garlicki notes that senatorial declarations can also include remarks and motions for members of the Council of Ministers, and the addressee is required to reply within 30 days. However, he also observes that the requirement to reply might be based only on the Senate's authority. See: L. Garlicki, *Polskie prawo...*, op. cit., p. 254.

116 Parliaments in both Poland and in Spain are bicameral. The lower house of the Spanish parliament, the Congress of Deputies, is composed of 350 deputies, while the Senate has 208 senators. The electoral system in the case of the Congress of Deputies is proportional, with the dominating effects of the majority system. The specifics of the Spanish electoral system in the lower house of the parliament are described in detail in Chapter 5. In the case of the Senate, the majority formula and open lists are used.

117 See annex.

of confidence to pass, an absolute majority is needed in the presence of at least half the statutory number of MPs. However, there also exists another formula for a vote of confidence, pursuant to Art. 160 of the Constitution. This form can be applied to an incumbent government. For it to pass, a simple majority is needed. This form of vote of confidence stabilises the position of the government. In this way, the government confirms its position and support for its programme, a move associated with assessment of the government's previous activity, and therefore constitutes a form of *ex post* control. It should be noted that if the vote fails, the government is required to resign.

The next accountability tool, the issue debate, is conducted through a hearing of the government or an organ of governmental administration by the Sejm. These debates are comprised of a first stage involving the presentation of specific information, followed by statements detailing the positions of the relevant committees. The debate then commences, during which MPs can present their own opinions and assessments, and formulate questions. The next stage usually involves responses to those questions. In recent years, a custom has emerged of the government presenting the results of its activities after the first 100 days of its term, but it is difficult to say whether this tradition will continue. Similarly, regular debates on issues surrounding foreign, social and economic policy take place, in the presence of the relevant ministers. There are also parliamentary debates of a "purely" control character, which usually follow presentations of reports on the activities of such institutions as the Supreme Audit Office, the Commissioner for Human Rights, the Constitutional Tribunal, the National Broadcasting Council and the Polish National Bank. Although such information is usually reviewed by committees and the presidium of the Sejm, it is also frequently presented in plenary sessions during issue debates. Such debates may also take place following reports on the control activities of the Sejm's committees and reports of the committees themselves. At the end of a debate, the Sejm can adopt a resolution expressing the position of the chamber, but this is not obligatory.

The next instrument of accountability used during plenary sessions are resolutions. Here it should be noted that under Art. 69 of the Statute of the Sejm, there are four types of resolutions. The first are declarations positing a duty to undertake specific actions; the second are appeals for an initiative or task to be undertaken; the third type are statements that are nothing more than expressions of the sense of the Sejm on a specific matter; the final type are resolutions proper. This last category is probably the most important from the point of view of horizontal accountability, as resolutions are calls for concrete, one-off actions by a state organ towards the Sejm (Art. 55(1)(1) of the Statute of the Sejm). Resolutions are not legally binding, but custom requires that the addressee respond officially to them. Debates, associated with the right to demand a hearing, are another tool in the accountability system, but unlike the previously mentioned issue debates, these debates are regulated by the Statute of the Sejm. Under Art. 174 of the Statute of the Sejm, the Marshal of the Sejm can lodge a request with the appropriate state organs and organisations to present its position on the remarks and motions made during the session.

Questions on current affairs are another instrument employed during plenary sessions (Art. 196 of the Statute of the Sejm). They were introduced under the 1997 Constitution, supplementing the so-called interpellatory procedures, which also include interpellations and queries. The addressees of interpellatory procedures are members of the Council of Ministers as defined under Art. 147 of the Constitution of Poland. Questions on current affairs are submitted verbally and are formulated during every session. The Marshal of the Sejm must be given notice not later than 9:00 PM of the day preceding the plenary session by the MP about the general subject matter and content of the question, as well as its addressee. This is because the daily agenda cannot include more than 11 questions. An oral response is not grounds for a debate, although it creates the possibility of asking several further questions. Two minutes for a question, six minutes for an answer, one minute for a follow-up question and three minutes for an answer to that question are provided. The accepted practice is to allow questions from all parliamentary clubs and circles.

Requests for current information are another instrument used in parliamentary practice (Art. 194 of the Statute of the Sejm). Such a request can also be addressed to a member of the Council of Ministers; however, a request for information cannot be made by an individual MP, but by a parliamentary club or a group composed of at least 15 MPs. The motion is considered and either accepted or rejected by the Presidium of the Sejm, after receiving the opinion of the Council of Elders. If the decision of the Presidium is not unanimous, the request is considered at a session of the Sejm. Presentation of justification for the request by an MP selected by the applicants cannot be longer than five minutes, and the reply is limited to ten minutes. During the discussion following presentation of the information, statements by MPs cannot exceed two minutes. At the conclusion of the discussion, the applicant is given five minutes to speak, and then a representative of the Council of Ministers may speak for ten minutes. The time allotted for consideration of current information cannot be longer than 90 minutes total.

Individual MPs may also submit interpellations and parliamentary queries, to which members of the government must reply within 21 days (Art. 192 and 195 of the Statute of the Sejm). Interpellations are submitted regarding fundamental issues and broad issues connected with state policy, while queries address individual cases, often of a local character. Both interpellations and queries are submitted in written form via the Marshal of the Sejm. In the event of an unsatisfactory answer or the absence of an answer altogether, an MP can, in the case of an interpellation, renew the demand for a response. The use of these tools does not lead to a debate in the Sejm.

A special accountability tool functioning in the plenary forum of the parliament is the vote of discharge and passage of the budget. The legislative procedure regarding the budget takes the form of a legislative bill. The bill lists the state income and expenses in a given budgetary year (identical to the calendar year). Unlike the regular legislative procedure, only the Council of Ministers has the right of initiative in respect of the budget. The draft bill should be submitted not later than three months prior to the start of a budgetary year, thus before 1 October. In special circumstances, when a draft bill cannot be submitted, the government must offer a provisional budget, which is a provisional act regulating state finances. In the case of the budgetary bill, the procedure for accelerated consideration of legislature cannot be used, and there must always be a first reading. Next, the draft is sent to the Public Finances Committee, and the Senate must consider the bill within 20 days. In this case, the President does not have the right to veto the bill, and must sign it within seven days. In regards to oversight of performance of the budget, not later than within five months of the end of a budgetary year the Council of Ministers must present the Sejm with a report on the execution of the budget and information on the state of the public debt. The Sejm has 90 days to consider the report following a procedure analogous to that used for the budgetary bill. Alongside the report of the Council of Ministers, the Sejm also receives an analysis of the execution of the budget and the foundations of monetary policy drafted by the Supreme Audit Office, together with an opinion from the Committee of Public Finances regarding the vote of discharge for the Council of Ministers. On this basis, the Sejm enacts a resolution regarding the vote of discharge for the government.

When analysing the legal and formal conditions of the accountability tools at the level of Sejm committees, it should be emphasised that one of the basic instruments of control exercised by those committees is the right to demand information under Art. 153 of the Statute of the Sejm. This means that committees have the right to obligate ministers, directors of administrative organs and other state offices and institutions to present reports, supply information and take part in proceedings. Another instrument is that of the so-called desiderata, used as part of the right to demand a hearing according to Art. 159 of the Statute of the Sejm. Desiderata are a type of postulate formulated by committees, and then served to the addressee by the Marshal. The addressee can be the Council of Ministers, a minister, but also the director of the Supreme Audit Office, the National Bank of Poland or the Chief Labor Inspector. The aforementioned entities have a duty to respond to the postulates within 30 days, although it should be noted that the postulates are not legally binding. If a given committee considers a reply to be unsatisfactory, it can submit a motion to the Marshal of the Sejm to consider a resolution in the plenary forum of the Sejm. The next tool are opinions, which under Art. 164 of the Statute of the Sejm comprise the position of a committee on a specific issue. They can be addressed to all central organs and institutions in the government administration system. The addressee must respond within 30 days, while the committee can take the same actions as in the case of desiderata. There are also two other tools available to committees: control of the enactment of legal acts and resolutions (Art. 161 of the Statute), as well as visitations and auditing the activities of companies owned wholly or in part by the State Treasury and state institutions (Art. 167 of the Statute).

A special tool within the system of accountability for scrutiny of the executive by the legislature is the ability to form investigative committees. This institution was established in Poland in 1999.[118] Pursuant to the relevant act, an investigative committee is formed by the Sejm through a resolution, by an absolute majority vote. This can be proposed by the Presidium of the Sejm, a Sejm committee or at least 46 MPs. The composition of the committee should reflect the representation of parliamentary clubs and circles that are represented in the Council of Elders. An investigative committee can have up to 11 members. Committees are granted powers similar to those enjoyed by prosecutors, and therefore members of a committee have the right to question witnesses based on the Code of Criminal Procedure, although the only outcome of a committee's activities, aside from submitting the case to the public prosecutor, is referral to the State Tribunal (this requires a 2/3 majority of votes in the presence of at least a half of the members of the committee).

In summary, we may say that there are many accountability tools in Poland following the systemic solutions introduced on the basis of the 1997 Constitution

118 The Sejm Investigative Commisson Act of 21 January 1999, OJ L 2010 No. 182, item 1228 with amedments.

and specified in the 1992 Statute of the Sejm.[119] To answer the question to what extent they are an effective weapon in the hands of the opposition, an analysis of the dynamics of their use is given in the following subchapter.

3.1.1. The plenary forum of the Sejm

When analysing the use of the vote of no confidence, it should first be noted that with the enactment of the Constitution of the Republic of Poland in 1997 and the introduction of a constructive vote of no confidence, this instrument became less attractive in the eyes of the opposition. During the analysed period, only once, at the end of the J. Kaczyński government, was a motion for a vote of no confidence submitted. The parliamentary club that made a motion on 13 July 2007 for a vote of no confidence in the Council of Ministers led by J. Kaczyński, designating J. K. Kaczmarek as candidate for Prime Minister, was the club formed by SLD. Eventually, the government collapsed as a result of the shortened term of the parliament. However, this situation was the result of the inability of PiS to form a coalition with other parliamentary groups, and therefore the incapacity to continue governing, not the motion for a vote of no confidence itself as it was never put to a vote. The vote of no confidence against individual ministers was used much more often, as frequently as 67 times. Motions for a vote of no confidence were submitted most often in the 2005–2007 parliamentary term (27 times). Such attempts were also made frequently by the opposition in the years 2001–2005 (20 times). The number of votes of no confidence against ministers in the 1997–2001 and 2007–2011 terms was comparable, at 10 and 11 respectively. Neither of these motions was successful: in the years 1997–2011 not a single vote of no confidence against a minister was passed. However, the motions themselves often led to discussion about the activities of a given ministry, and in the case of a minority government, such motions constituted a real threat to the shape of the government. On the other hand, a vote of confidence based on Art. 160 was used twice, both of which were passed in the same term of 2001–2005. The first motion was made by L. Miller on 10 June 2003, three months after the minority government was formed (236 MPs voted for, 213 against, 0 abstained, 11 did not vote). Also, the

119 After the enactment of the Constitution of Poland in 1997, a new Statute of the Sejm was not enacted. In the analyzed period, i.e. in the years 1997–2011, the Statute of the Sejm enacted on the 30th of July 1992 was in effect. The Statute was amended numerous times. The current text of the statute was enacted on 29 May 2002, and more amendments have since been passed. See: Regulamin Sejmu, www.sejm.gov.pl/prawo/regulamin/kon7.htm.

next Prime Minister, M. Belka, motioned for a vote of confidence on 15 October 2004, just over a month after the formation of the government (234 votes for, 218 against, 0 abstained, 8 did not vote). Therefore, the support given to both prime ministers was comparable. The votes of confidence put a stop to discussions about the lack of both governments' legitimacy. However, this did give those governments the capacity to enact more ambitious legislative projects.[120]

*Chart 13. Use of votes of confidence and no confidence in 1997–2011**

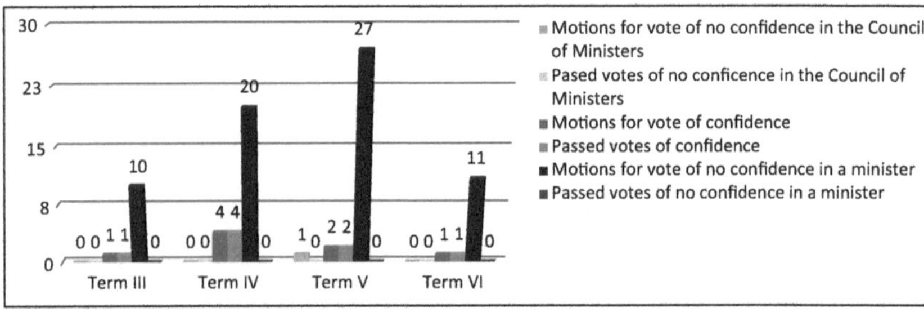

Source: Sejm website: www.sejm.gov.pl.
*The table includes votes of confidence held under Art. 155 and 160 of the Constitution.

The presence of members of the government and high-ranking officials serving as secretaries and undersecretaries of state was quite frequent in all the terms, including in the 5th term when taking into consideration its shorter duration. Prime Ministers were most frequently present in the 4th term, and least frequently in the 3rd term (Table 5). What is characteristic is the presence of secretaries and undersecretaries during Sejm sessions. It is hard, however, to determine whether control was being institutionalised in this period, as the accessible data is consolidated and does not specify how many issue debates took place in a given term with the participation of members of the government, nor whether any resolutions were passed as a result. Individual examples can, however, be found, indicating that some attempts at influencing the government in the parliamentary forum were made, although they were not always successful. One such example can be a resolution cited by M. Kruk regarding the signing of the Constitutional Treaty by the Belka government, which went ignored by the Prime Minister[121].

---

120 See: B. Michalak, M.S. Wincławska, *Rząd Leszka Millera (19 X 2001–2 V 2004)*, in: M. Chmaj (ed.), *Rządy koalicyjne…*, op. cit., pp. 247–255; G. Rydlewski, *Rząd Marka…*, op. cit., pp. 269–272.

121 M. Kruk, *Funkcja…*, op. cit., p. 42.

Scholars generally agree, however, that questions on current affairs are one of the most attractive forms of control in parliamentary practice, similarly to requests for information on current events, although this is not synonymous with their effectiveness.[122] Questions about current affairs are important in the system of horizontal accountability, as they make it possible to force the government to publicly address some inconvenient issues without waiting for a debate on a similar issue. Their attractiveness is attested to by the data included in Chart 1 and Table 5. Although the number of questions does not seem impressive compared to interpellations and queries, it should be noted that this results from the aforementioned statutory limitations regarding the number of questions. Additionally, interest in this tool can be better measured not by the number of questions asked, but the number of questions submitted. It should also be noted that the number of submitted questions in subsequent terms decreases, while the number of responses to questions increases.

When analysing government information on current affairs it is also clear that this tool is frequently used in the Sejm. When comparing the number of requests for government information on current affairs with the number of requests granted, this tool appears even more attractive than questions on current affairs. There is no data about the number of submitted requests for the 1997–2001 term, but in the years 2001–2005, 22.8% of them resulted in information being presented in plenary sessions. In the periods 2005–2007 and 2007–2011 it was 10.44% and 30.19% respectively. The significant interest in this tool is likely due to the fact that the time at the disposal of the applicant and the addressee is much longer than in the case of questions on current affairs. Additionally, this is associated with the reduced importance of interpellations as accountability tools, itself the result of an amendment to the Statute of the Sejm in 2003. Previously it had been possible to place interpellations on the daily agenda of a session. Currently, interpellations are reduced in the Statute of the Sejm to MP-minister relations, and the Marshal is now free to decide whether they should be admitted or not. M. Kruk assesses this change thusly: "an interpellation in the current version of the Statute does not become the subject of debate in the Sejm, even though this should be its greatest strength. In this way interpellations were "defanged", and instead of a political instrument bringing an important issue into the public eye, it has become an exchange of correspondence between an

---

122 R. Małajny, *Funkcja parlamentarnej kontroli działalności rządu*, in: Z. Jarosz (ed.), *Parlament. Model konstytucyjny a praktyka ustrojowa*, Warsaw 2006, p. 141; L. Garlicki, *Polskie prawo…*, op. cit., p. 253, M. Kruk, *Funkcja kontrolna…*, op. cit., p. 73.

MP and a member of the government. (…) In this way, the entire value of the interpellation as an instrument of control over the government was discarded, leaving it with the importance of a mere collectible."[123] However, an increase in the number of interpellations in the analysed period can be noted (Table 5). In practice, three kinds of interpellations can be distinguished based on subject matter. The vast majority of interpellations involve acquiring information about the activities of the government, while the second category is connected with interventions in the MPs' own constituencies, and only the third type of interpellation, the least frequently used, relates to critical assessments of government policy.[124]

What characterises interpellations and parliamentary queries in Poland is the fact that this instrument is used not only by members of the opposition, but also of the governing majority (Chart 14). According to R. Małajny, this is an effect of interpellations being used as a tool for correcting government policy by various factions of the majority in order to protect their particular interests, and this phenomenon is observed not only in Poland.[125] Questions and requests for information are also instruments employed not only by opposition parties, but also by MPs belonging to the parliamentary majority forming the government. According to J. Zaleśny, this is due to the fact that opposition MPs try to prove the government's ineffectiveness through these instruments, while MPs from groups forming the government ask questions and request information in a manner allowing the government to present its position on issues where it can show its achievements.[126]

---

123 M. Kruk, *Funkcja kontrolna…*, op. cit., p. 67.

124 R. Małajny, *Rozdział władzy w systemie parlamentarnym*, in: T. Mołdawa, J. Szymanek, M. Mistygacz (eds.), *Parlamentarny system rządów. Teoria i praktyka*, Warsaw 2012, p. 88.

125 Ibid. pp. 87–88.

126 J. Zaleśny, *Interpelacja poselska. Uwagi na tle praktyki polskiej*, in: M. Zubik (ed.), *Dwadzieścia lat transformacji ustrojowej w Polsce*, Warsaw 2010, p. 474.

Chart 14. The use of accountability tools by the parliamentary majority forming the government and by the opposition in the years 1997–2011

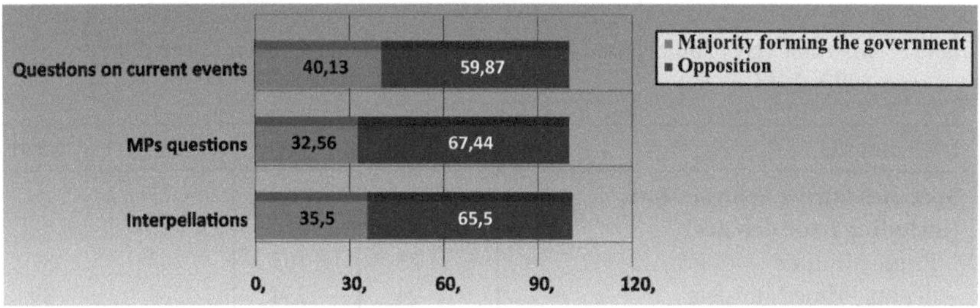

Source: own work, based on data from www.sejm.gov.pl.

Ex post budgetary control in Poland is primarily a political assessment of the government's activities. Each yeah the opposition uses the annual debate over the report on the execution of the budget as an opportunity to criticise government policy.[127] A negative assessment of the execution of the budget can lead to a resolution denying the Council of Ministers a vote of discharge, although this does not lead to a constitutionally obligatory dismissal of the government. Nevertheless, in the years 1997–2011 no such resolution was enacted, even though it could have been done in the case of minority governments. How to explain the fact that despite the increasing public debt, the government received a vote of discharge each year? According to the authors of a report on corruption-preventing mechanisms in Poland, this is mainly because of the MPs being insufficiently prepared, in conjunction with the very complicated methodology used in drafting the budget, which results in the opposition being unable to control its execution. Therefore, it is left with a "total" critique of the government's activities of a political nature. Additionally, the approach of particular MPs is significant,

127 For more, see: K. Sobolwska-Myślik, D. Kasprowicz, *Opozycja parlamentarna w III kadencji Sejmu (1997–2001)*, in: K. Łabędź (ed.), *Opozycja parlamentarna w Polsce w latach 1997–2010*, Kraków 2012, pp. 69–70; M. Simlat, *Struktura i funkcjonowanie opozycji w IV kadencji Sejmu (2001–2005)*, in: K. Łabędź (ed.), *Opozycja parlamentarna*, op. cit., pp. 124–128; G. Foryś, *Wielokierunkowa opozycja parlamentarna w okresie rządów Kazimierza Marcinkiewicza i Jarosława Kaczyńskiego (2005–2007)*, in: K. Łabędź (ed.), *Opozycja parlamentarna*, op. cit., pp. 153–157; K. Łabędź, *Funkcjonowanie opozycji w VI kadencji Sejmu (2007–2010)*, in: K. Łabędź (ed.), *Opozycja parlamentarna*, op. cit., pp. 202–206.

as they defend expenses for the benefit of their constituencies regardless of the global situation of public finances.[128]

Table 5. Instruments of control used in the Sejm in the plenary forum in the years 1997–2011

Instruments	3rd term	4th term	5th term	6th term
Speeches during Sejm sessions (including issue debates)				
– Prime Minister	25	103	43	87
– deputy Prime Ministers	94	254	174	89
– Ministers	680	967	420	913
– Secretaries and Undersecretaries	3260	3775	2049	4834
Government reports and information	37	50	33	66
Reports on the activities of organs	22	39	14	40
Resolutions				
– motioned for (all)	225	310	173	248
– passed (all)	190	256	203	289
– passed (in connection with the hearing of information)	10	3	2	4
Questions on current affairs				
– submitted	1757	1285	628	1082
– answered	311	710	439	947
Government information on current affairs				
– motioned for	No data	250	182	159
– acquired	50	57	19	48
Interpellation (spoken and written)				
– submitted (and resubmitted)	7444	10884	9691	24665
– answered	7551	11199	9883	25279
MP inquiries (individual and collective)				
– submitted	4247	4386	3495	10598
– answered	4337	4508	3585	10836

Source: own work, based on: Sejm Rzeczypospolitej Polskiej, *III Kadencja…*, op. cit., pp. 27–36, 40, Sejm Rzeczypospolitej Polskiej, *IV Kadencja…*, op. cit., pp. 29–40, 44–45, Sejm Rzeczypospolitej Polskiej, *V Kadencja…*, op. cit., pp. 59–75, Sejm Rzeczypospolitej Polskiej, *VI Kadencja…*, op. cit., pp. 60–82, 85–86 and www. sejm.gov.pl.

128 A. Kobylińska, G. Makowski, M. Solana-Lipiński (eds.), *Mechanizmy przeciwdziałania korupcji w Polsce. Raport z monitoringu*, Warsaw 2012, www.isp.org.pl/uploads/filemanager/Mechanizmyprzeciwdziaaniakorupcji.PDF, p. 71.

3.1.2. Parliamentary committees

When discussing the role of parliamentary committees, it is hard to disagree with M. Kruk that "parliamentary committees are the machinery of parliamentary work."[129] When analysing data from Table 6, it can easily be observed that parliamentary committees in each of the analysed terms were very active, as attested to by the number of desiderata, opinions and visitations. It should also be noted, however, that the personal composition of committees reflects the political composition of the Sejm. Therefore, this instrument of horizontal accountability is limited in effectiveness, as the governing majority has control over parliamentary committees, which limits their ability to engage in real oversight.[130]

Table 6. Instruments of control used in Sejm committees in the period 1997–2011

Instruments	3rd term	4th term	5th term	6th term
Number of desiderata (all types of committees)	338	230	134	220
Number of opinions	1096	1507	886	1675
Visitations and examinations of activities	126	138	67	120

Source: own work, based on: Sejm Rzeczypospolitej Polskiej, *III Kadencja...*, op. cit., pp. 27–36, Sejm Rzeczypospolitej Polskiej, *IV Kadencja...*, op. cit., pp. 29–40, Sejm Rzeczypospolitej Polskiej, *V Kadencja...*, op. cit., pp. 59–73, Sejm Rzeczypospolitej Polskiej, *VI Kadencja...*, op. cit., pp. 60–82.

The situation is somewhat different in the case of investigative committees. Although the committee as an institution has existed for over a decade, it is hard to form an unambiguous opinion regarding its influence on the Polish system of accountability. Eight investigative committees were formed in the analysed period (1997–2011) - three during the SLD government, one during the PiS government, and four during governments formed by PO. Out of these eight committees, three can be assessed positively from the point of view of effective accountability. The first, active in the years 2003–2004 (the so-called Rywin Committee), led to the correction of systemic problems affecting the legislative

129 M. Kruk, *Funkcja kontrolna...*, op. cit., p. 77.

130 For more, see: K. Sobolewska -Myślik, D. Kasprowicz, *Opozycja parlamentarna w III...*, op. cit., pp. 44–66, M. Simlat, *Struktura i funkcjonowanie...*, op. cit., pp. 97–102; G. Foryś, *Wielokierunkowa opozycja....*, op. cit., pp. 138–140, K. Łabędź, *Funkcjonowanie opozycji...*, op. cit., pp. 172–178.

process.[131] The investigative committee formed for the purposes of solving the case of the death of J. Olwenik is also viewed by most specialists as an important and necessary committee; although it did not lead to any improvements in the political system, it did demonstrate the weakness of the Polish law enforcement system. The third committee that contributed to strengthening the system of accountability was the so-called Gambling Committee. Although none of the corruption charges were proven, this committee did lead to Grzegorz Schetyna quitting his post as the second most important politician in the government in the role of the minister exercising oversight over special services. Mariusz Kamiński, the chief of the Central Anticorruption Bureau, also lost his office, but from the accountability perspective the dismissal of G. Schetyna was more important. Although some still argue that it was entirely undeserved, it gave society and party members a clear signal that in the face of corruption charges even the highest-ranking politicians will face consequences. Apart from "media buzz", the elimination of political rivals and scoring cheap political points, the remaining five committees failed to contribute to improvements in the accountability system in Poland. This is why investigative committees are increasingly perceived as arenas for political combat. It should also be added that no motions have been brought to place anyone before the State Tribunal. A side effect of investigative committees is lowered prestige of the state and its institutions.

131 For more on the Rywin affair: A. Bagieńska-Masiota, *Sejmowa komisja śledcza w systemie politycznym Rzeczypospolitej Polskiej*, Warsaw 2010, pp. 194–209.

Figure 4. Investigative committees in the years 2001–2011[132]

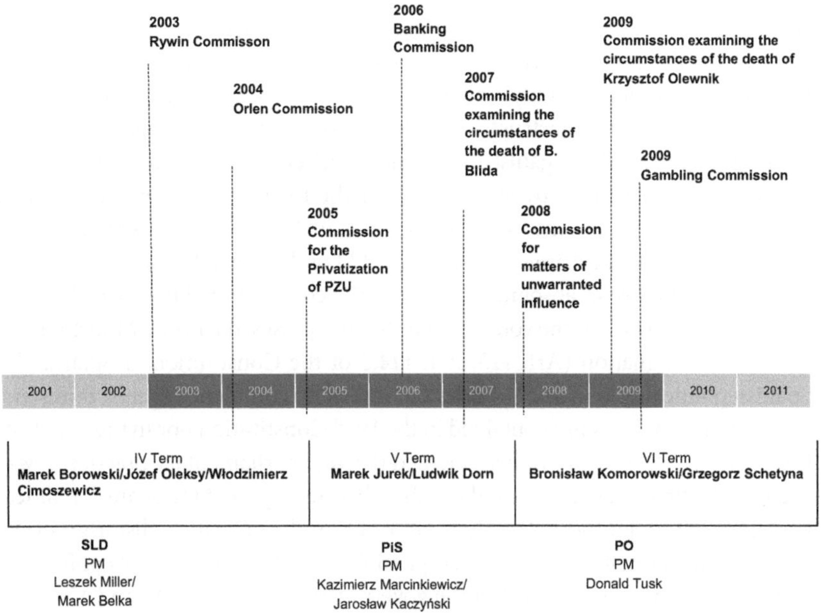

Source: own work, based on the Sejm website www.sejm.gov.pl.

To summarise the dynamics of the use of accountability tools, it can be concluded that from the quantitative perspective there are no major differences to be observed across particular terms of the Sejm. The only exception is the 2005–2007 term, in which the vote of no confidence against individual ministers was used much more often than in other terms, as well as the vote of no confidence against the government. As far as the effectiveness of the instruments is concerned, those that do not require a parliamentary majority are effective, i.e. questions on current affairs and current information, as with amendments to the Statute of the Sejm the role of interpellations as an accountability tool was diminished. However, the investigative committee constituted an exception during the analysed period, although this was mostly a result of the role played by the media, especially during the activities of the Rywin Committee.

132 The names of the committees shown in the chart were those used by the media.

3.2. Spain

Among the control tools available for use in the plenum, one of the most important ones is the constructive vote of no confidence. In Spain, unlike in Poland, the Prime Minister is the only member of the government directly accountable to the parliament, as the constructive vote of no confidence is not made against the entire government, but against the Prime Minister. A motion for a vote of no confidence can be made by at least 1/10 of the total constitutional number of MPs, i.e. at least 36, and the same motion must include the name of the new candidate for the office of Prime Minister (Art. 133 of the Constitution of Spain). For the motion to pass, an absolute majority of the constitutional number of MPs is needed, i.e. 181 votes. If the vote of no confidence passes, the Prime Minister must submit his resignation (Art. 113, Art. 114.2 of the Constitution of Spain). The Spanish political system also includes the vote of no confidence against ministers, although this tool was not contained in the 1978 Constitution nor in the Statute of the Cortes Generales, but rather emerged through parliamentary practice. It was used for the first time in 1981, and has since became a part of the Spanish political landscape, although formally it does not result in the obligatory dismissal of the minister. However, like in Poland, it is possible to motion for a vote of confidence, which is an expression of trust in the government, under Art. 112 and 114(1) of the Constitution of Spain as well as Art. 173 and 174 of the Statute of the Congress of Deputies. The motion for a vote of confidence is made by the Prime Minister, and requires a simple majority to pass.

The annual debate on the state of the nation is another tool that emerged through parliamentary practice. The first such debate took place in 1983, during F. González's second term. It is not addressed by any specific regulations in the Constitution nor the Statue of the Congress of Deputies. The debate on the state of the nation, like other general debates that take place after statements of the government, proceeds pursuant to Art. 196 of the Statute of the Congress of Deputies. The debates are concluded with resolutions. Based on Art. 111 of the Constitution of Spain and Art. 185–190 of the Statute of the Congress of Deputies, other accountability tools are available in the form of verbal and written queries. Spoken queries are characterised by periodicity, as they are formed during each plenary session, and are presented with little advance notice. They are also characterised by the small amount of time at the disposal of the MP tabling the query and the addressee – five minutes total. Questions are asked by the heads of parliamentary groups, and are answered by members of the government, including the Prime Minister. The Prime Minister is obliged to answer three questions chosen from among the 24 questions asked during the session. The Prime Minister decides which questions to answer. Written queries, or rather queries with a written response, can be made by individual deputies, and the government is required to answer them within 20 days, although this period can be extended. When a deputy submitting a written query does not receive an answer, it automatically transforms into a verbal query posed in a committee. It should be added that the right to submit queries and interpellations is given proportionally to the number of deputies in each parliamentary club (1 for every 10 deputies), although in practice parliamentary control is exercised by parliamentary minorities.

Interpellations, according to Art. 111 of the Constitution and Art. 180–184 of the Statute of the Congress of Deputies, are another tool in the hands of the deputies, similarly to queries submitted in the plenum. Unlike the former, however, they address general issues, and therefore the time allocated for them is longer, i.e. 10 minutes. Interpellations can be drafted by both individual deputies and parliamentary groups in written form and submitted to the presidium. Three interpellations are debated weekly. Additionally, unlike queries, other parliamentary groups that do not submit interpellations can also express their position. The plenum can enact a resolution following every interpellation, another accountability tool alongside non-legislative motions. Resolutions and non-legislative motions differ in form from queries and interpellations, but not in their goal. In theory, they are designed to facilitate parliamentary intervention in the political course of the state, which according to Art. 97 of the Constitution of Spain is determined by the government. Resolutions are presented after interpellations and allow for a re-evaluation and debate regarding government policy, although resolutions differ from interpellations in that they are put to a vote. Adopted resolutions become non-legislative motions (Art. 193 of the Statute of the Congress of Deputies), which comprise recommendations for the government regarding its political line. However, if the parliament's recommendations expressed in resolutions are not taken into consideration, there is no way of holding the government to account. The role of parliament in this situation is reduced to reminding and demanding that the government take action. The next tool is the motion for government reports. To some extent these motions are a response to the weakness of written queries, as they concern information used by the government to take decisions or information based on which it decided not to take a given decision.

The accountability system would be incomplete if financial and budgetary control were not taken into account. In Spain, the government has the exclusive right of initiative in this matter; it must propose a draft budget for the next calendar year by 1 October. Unlike Poland, in the case of failure to propose a draft, the previous year's bill is automatically put to a vote. According to Art. 133 of the

Statute of the Congress of Deputies, the draft budgetary bill has priority during proceedings over other workings of the Houses. The enactment of the budget requires a simple majority. In Spain there is no budgetary vote of discharge, although in this case the Court of Accounts, the equivalent of the Polish Supreme Audit Office, makes a report to parliament on the formal execution of the budget. Parliamentary control in the area of economy and finances is done through amendments, discussions and the enactment of the budgetary bill proposed by the government. Aside from the aforementioned annual state of the nation debate, this is the second most important debate in the parliamentary calendar.

Within committees, one of the tools of accountability are verbal queries; these are limited to 15 minutes, divided between the MP tabling the query and the addressee. Questions can be answered by ministers, secretaries of state and vice-secretaries of state. Non-legislative motions should once again be mentioned, as they may also be adopted by committees. According to Art. 194 of the Statute of the Congress of Deputies, the Presidium of the Congress decides on whether they should be considered by the plenum or the appropriate committee, depending on the will of the parliamentary group and the importance of the issue at hand. Such motions are also formed within the committee forums themselves.

The next tool in the system of accountability is the investigative committee, regulated by Art. 76(1) of the Constitution of Spain. In most parliamentary-cabinet regimes, including Spain, a parliamentary majority is needed for an investigative committee to be formed. According to Art. 52 of the Statute of the Congress of Deputies, the motion itself can be made by the government, two parliamentary groups or 1/5 of the deputies. The effect of the committee's work are conclusions which must be approved by the plenum in the form of opinions, and only then are published in the Official Journal of the Cortes Generales. Conclusions are of a purely political character, although if the presidium considers it appropriate they can be submitted to the public prosecutor.

3.2.1. The plenary forum of the Congress of Deputies

In Spain, during the analysed period of 1982–2011, the vote of no confidence was an instrument rarely employed. Only once, on 23 March 1987, during the González government, was a motion for a constructive vote of no confidence made. The motion was tabled by the opposition party AP, which transformed into the PP in 1989. The Socialists, enjoying an absolute majority, easily defeated the motion, while none of the other groups in the parliament supported it. In the vote conducted on 30 March, there were 67 votes for the motion to be passed (PP and the Union of Valencia), 195 against (PSOE, IU, PNV, EE), and 70 deputies abstained (CDS, CiU, PDP, PL, PSR, AIC, CG).[133] A vote of confidence has also been used only once, during the 4th term of parliament, in April 1990. Then, at the initiative of Prime Minister F. González, a vote of confidence in the government was passed. It allowed the government to complete painful economic reforms associated with adjustments necessary in light of Spain's accession to the European Union, as well as to reform the country's territorial system. As previously explained, the vote of no confidence against particular ministers was first used in 1981, during the UCD government. PSOE proposed a vote of no confidence against five ministers responsible for a 1981 scandal regarding the consumption of poisoned olive oil, which resulted in the deaths of 700 people and the hospitalisation of 20,000. This new initiative sparked a very lively argument regarding the possibility of including this formula in the existing constitutional model. Eventually, the presidium of the Congress of Deputies allowed for the vote to take place, although the result was to be non-binding. In the years 1982–2011 only once was a vote of no confidence passed, against M. Álvarez, the Minister of Promotion in J. Rodriguez Zapatero's first government, although this was done not by the Congress of Deputies but in the Senate, when the opposition PP had the necessary majority. The vote of no confidence did not cause any action to be taken against the minister, as it was not legally binding.[134]

133 For more, see: M. Sánchez de Dios, *La moción de censura. Un estudio comparado*, Madrid 1992, pp. 318–336; *Así fueron las cuestiones de confianza y mociones de censura de la Democracia*, "El Mundo", 25 May 2011, www.elmundo.es/elmundo/2011/05/24/espana/1306235420.html.

134 P. Mellado Prado, *La responsabilidad política del gobierno*, "Revista de Derecho Político" 1992, no. 37, pp. 139–147.

Chart 15. Use of the vote of no confidence and vote of confidence in the years 1982–2011

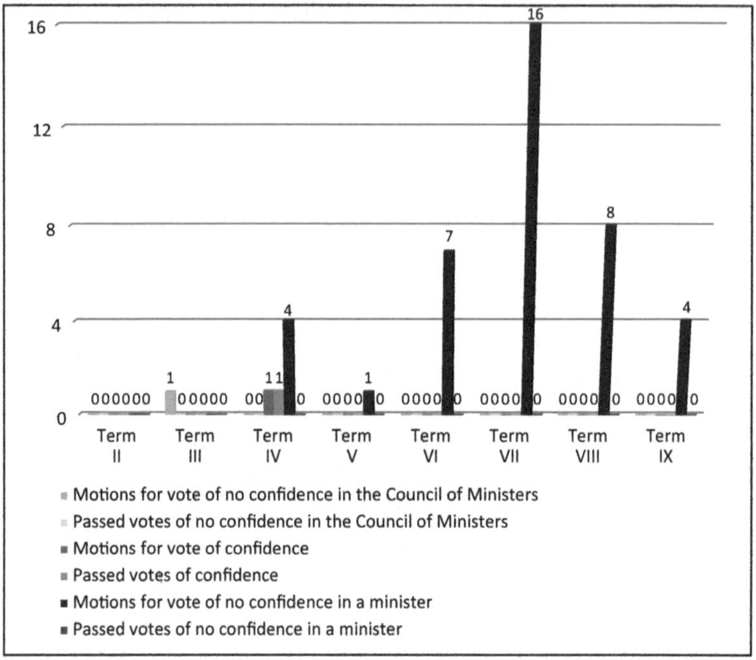

Source: own work, based on the Congress of Deputies website, www.congreso.es.

In Spain, scholars generally agree that initiatives of oversight and control over the executive have gained in importance with time. Control was not only institutionalised, but was increasingly noticed by public opinion.[135] In Spain this was undoubtedly facilitated by the institutionalisation of the annual debate on the state of the nation. This debate has usually been focused on the issue of the Spanish territorial system, although there have also been debates revolving around other issues, such as political scandals during the 5th term, or the Iraq War during the 7th term. The debate is one of the most important events in Spain's political life, as it lasts for two days and captures the attention of virtually all media outlets.

The presence of members of government and high-ranking officials in the parliament in order to supply information is increasingly frequent (Tab. 7). This is a result of the popularity of verbal queries as tools of accountability. Verbal queries

135 J. Capo, *The Spanish parliament in a Triangular Relationship, 1982–2000*, "Journal of Legislative Studies" 2003, no. 9/2, p. 124.

attract media attention and are one of the most effective mechanisms of control. The Spanish *question time* takes place each Wednesday and lasts four hours. According to J. Xuclà i Costa, in practice members of the government often give evasive answers or do not answer at all, claiming that they are unable to provide a response due to official secrecy. Additionally, the government may provide information about its activities each week, even if there is no query in the daily agenda about a given issue, while deputies' inquiries are submitted one week in advance, although they may be amended up to 24 hours before the question time starts.[136] Despite these weaknesses, given that they are televised, verbal queries are among the most important instruments of control in use; this has made them quite numerous, with an observable increase in the number of questions answered compared to those submitted. (Tab. 7).

As previously mentioned, verbal queries are the perfect instruments of control for current and local issues, while interpellations are more adequate for debating issues associated with the government's general policies. The effectiveness of interpellations as an instrument is, however, limited, as, like in the case of inquiries, the government can refuse to answer or try to evade the question. Interpellations, however, do not lead to as many repercussions in the media as queries. It seems that the sequence associated with the use of the two instruments is important. Interpellations are answered after queries, which become the subject of debate. Therefore, interpellations are given less attention than queries. A similar mechanism exists in the case of queries: the government may refuse to answer, although the instrument of the resolution is very helpful in this situation, as it can be debated in the plenum even if the government fails to provide a substantive answer.[137] The data in Table 7 indicate an increase in the number of interpellations submitted over the last three terms, which shows the popularity of this tool despite its aforementioned weaknesses. Resolutions and non-legislative motions, however, are ineffective tools according to E. Guerrero, as they require an absolute majority to be passed. In Guerrero's view the only repercussions they can cause is to shift the discussion into the forum of public opinion through the use of the media.[138] Despite this, the number of proposed and enacted resolutions and non-legislative motions is also increasing. The Congress of Deputies was especially active in this

136 J. Xuclà i Costa, *El control parlamentario del Ejecutivo en España:instrumentos y propuestas de mejora*, „Revista de Economía y Derecho" 2011, vol. 8, no. 29, p. 40.

137 For more, see: E. Guerrero, *Responsabilidad y rendición de cuentas del gobierno*, in: A. Martínez (ed.), *Representación y caliad de la Democracia en España*, Madrid 2006, pp. 174–175.

138 Ibid. p. 177.

regard over its last three terms (Table 7). Nevertheless, as stressed by M. Sanchez de Dios, resolutions enacted after interpellations in particular allow for a second assessment and debate over government policy.[139]

The number of written queries is also increasing annually (Tab. 7), yet this has not rendered them a more effective tool. Responses are usually vague and do not lead to a better functioning of the accountability system. Nevertheless, according to E. Guerrero this instrument has both a regional and sectoral character, as it allows deputies to obtain information important in overseeing a specific government policy or a policy important to their constituencies.[140] Government reports also have similar weaknesses (Tab. 7).

Table 7. Instruments of control used in the Congress of Deputies in the plenary forum in the years 1982–2011

Instruments	**2nd term**	**3rd term**	**4th term**	**5th term**	**6th term**	**7th term**	**8th term**	**9th term**
Demand of presence								
– demanded	10	26	58	34	46	77	101	91
– realized	3	14	24	19	21	24	26	43
Resolutions								
– proposed	33	102	145	108	175	242	232	236
– debated	7	23	40	50	59	71	116	161
Non-legislative motions								
– proposed	96	214	272	261	439	849	648	905
– voted	16	31	44	83	125	113	89	120
Verbal queries								
submitted/answered	1583	1510	2003	1610	2112	2280	2227	1669
	953	1085	1509	1196	1732	1952	1916	1504
Interpellations								
– submitted	210	214	225	142	203	338	320	297
– debated	60	115	151	110	180	245	231	239
Written queries								
– submitted	9200	19458	15309	14886	32721	75326	140322	104314
– answered	8401	17982	14224	12976	30866	71165	130077	98064

139 M. Sánchez de Dios, *La accountability democrática en Europa: el trabajo de los parlamentos*, Paper presented at the X Congreso de la Asociación Española de Ciencia Política (AECPA), 7–9 September 2011, Murcia, p. 12.

140 E. Guerrero, *Responsabilidad…*, op. cit., p. 176.

Government reports – proposed – realized	No data	No data	4716 4146	3026 2690	2504 2249	4636 4487	2479 2168	3126 2796
Government declarations	8	6	3	9	7	4	4	3

Source: own work based on the Congress of Deputies website: www.congreso.es.

Inquiries and interpellations are used usually only by deputies from parties that do not form the government – this includes opposition parties, as well as parties that did not form the government but did support it during the investiture process and in selected votes. This is especially visible in the case of interpellations and written queries (Chart 16). Similarly to Poland, deputies from governing parties do submit verbal queries in order to help the government present its position on issues where it can show its achievements, although this happens much less frequently than in the case of the Sejm.

Chart 16. The use of accountability instruments by the parliamentary majority and the opposition in the years 1982–2011

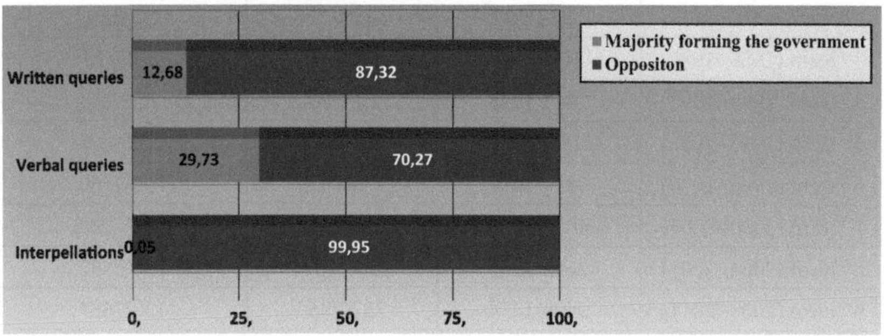

Source: own work, based on the Congress of Deputies website, www.congreso.es.

In the last three months of the year, deputies are concentrated on the numerous budgetary debates (central administration, regional and local budgets). Stormy discussions, votes on amendments, and vetoes by the Senate last for three months. However, due to the lack of actual control over the execution of the budget by the government, the control of the Congress of Deputies seems even more illusory than in Poland. The parliament tends to merely ratify decisions of the executive.

3.2.2. Parliamentary committees

When analysing the dynamics of the use of accountability instruments in the committee forum, the lack of replies to verbal queries seems to be a particularly pressing problem. Therefore, written queries have become the primary tool used, which is a consequence of the instrument's construction. As noted by M. Sánchez de Dios, approximately 50% of those appearing before the committees are ministers, and only 5% of the time is the requested presence connected with legislative debates.[141] As for non-legislative motions, the situation is similar to that concerning motions undertaken by the plenum. However, the data shown in Table 8 indicate that parliamentary committees in Spain are very active, yet the party quotas determining the composition of the committees yields a similar effect to that in Poland.

Table 8. Instruments of control used in the Congress of Deputies in the committees in the years 1982–2011

Term	Spoken inquiries submitted/ answered	Non-legislative motions proposed/voted	Demand of presence demanded/granted
2nd term (1982–1986)	244/96	128/25	No data
3rd term (1986–1989)	1593/907	287/43	350/225
4th term (1989–1993)	2464/1248	514/76	722/397
5th term (1993–1996)	1865/969	692/221	859/485
6th term (1996–2000)	2829/1090	1800/675	1508/760
7th term (2000–2004)	4016/1063	2396/510	3257/2592
8th term (2004–2008)	2692/1207	2504/1074	1309/592
9th term (2008–2011)	3508/1338	2329/860	1391/667

Source: own work, based on the Congress of Deputies website, www.congreso.es.

As for investigative committees, in the period 1982–2011 as many as 16 were formed, 12 coming during PSOE governments and 4 during PP governments. It should also be noted that in the years 1979–1982, three investigative committees were formed during UCD government as well. As in Poland, opinions regarding the role of this instrument in the accountability system are mixed.[142] On the one

141 M. Sánchez de Dios, *La accountability democrática…*, op. cit., p. 15.

142 J.M. Irujo, *El partidismo ciega las comisiones de investigación*, "El País" 2 July 2012, sociedad.elpais.com/sociedad/2012/07/02/actualidad/1341255394_001443.html.

hand, investigative committees are a very strong instrument of control over the executive branch, as they compel even the highest ranking officials to attend hearings and provide information. They also generate significant interest from public opinion. In Spain, since 1994, representatives of the media have enjoyed the right to be present during committee proceedings. The decision on making them public resulted from the fact that the media were receiving "leaks" from committee sessions, which subsequently led to speculation over the committees' activities. On the other hand, in Spain the effectiveness of this instrument relies on the support enjoyed by the government in the parliament, or rather the lack thereof. Given that they require a parliamentary majority to be appointed, only in the case of minority governments are they a real instrument of accountability. The list of rejected proposals for investigative committees to be formed is quite extensive, from ones connected with the functioning of the monarchy, through GAL, to secret CIA flights in Spanish territory (Figure 5).

When assessing the activities of individual committees, it should be stressed that, like in Poland, the first investigative committee, addressing human rights violations in Basque Country prisons, is best regarded. However, this committee functioned during the UCD government, and thus not in the period analysed here. Among the committees active in the years 1982–2011, those assessed positively are the 1983 Rumas company group expropriation committee, the 1983 Barajas airport plane crash committee, the 1999 EU funds embezzlement committee, and the 2001 committee investigating the case of Gescarter, a road management company charged with embezzlement.[143] They all resulted in strengthening of the rule of law in Spain. From the perspective of the functioning of the Spanish political system, the Roldán committee, investigating corruption in the Civil Guard, is also important. The Roldán case, as well as allegations of GAL "Spanish death squads" executing members of the ETA, resulted in the 1996 electoral defeat of PSOE, which had previously ruled Spain for 14 years

143 There have been investigative committees formed by the Senate as well, but unlike the ones in the Congress of Deputies, they did not concern major issues but were of specialised character. The only investigative committee formed in the Senate to elicit a heated discussion was a committee formed during the 5th term in 1995, during the first J.M. Aznar government, and concerned the political responsibility for the formation and activities of GAL. Witnesses that testified before the committee included José Barrionuevo, the minister of interior in the F. González government. Eventually, PP dissolved the committee.

without interruption. The other 11 investigative committees, aside from politicians generating political capital through "media noise", did not result in any improvement of the accountability system in Spain. Therefore, like in Poland, investigative committees are increasingly perceived as merely a tool of political combat. It should also be added that so far, out of all the committees to have finished their investigations, only two – the 11 March 2001 terrorist attack committee and the 1997 committee investigating the validity of the enactment of fiscal amnesty - were concluded with accusations of neglect towards previous governments, respectively those of F. Gonzalez and J.M. Aznar.

Figure 5. Investigative committees in Spain in the years 1982–2010

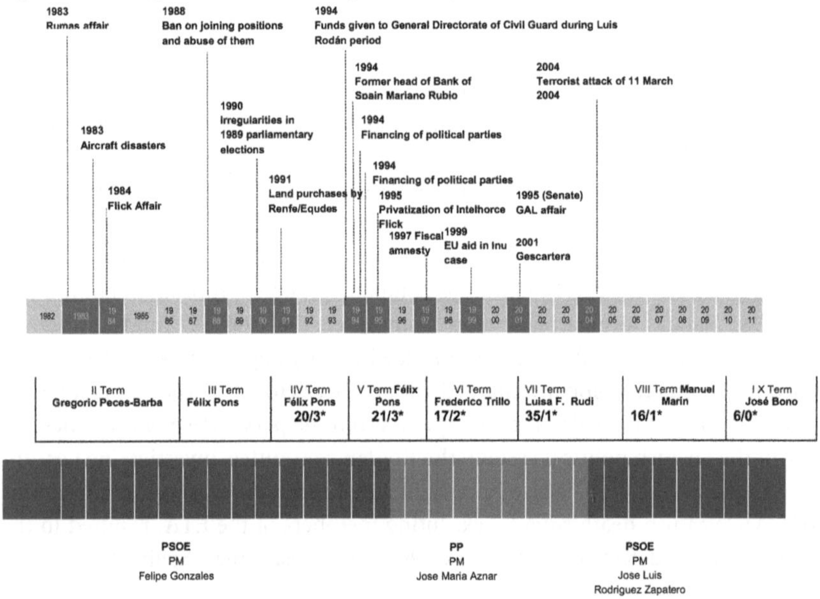

Source: own work, based on the Congress of Deputies website, www.congreso.es.
*Number of motions for the formation of investigative committees/number of investigative committees formed.

To summarize the analysis of the use of horizontal accountability tools by the Cortes Generales, it can be surmised that quantitatively they have become more prevalent in the last three terms of parliament. How can this be explained? The type of government is a major source of influence on the dynamics of the use of these tools in Spain, as has already been noted. This is how the increase in their use can be explained in the last two terms, in which the J.L. Rodríguez Zapatero administration formed a minority government. On the other hand, in the years 2000–2004, when the PP was in power, it achieved an absolute majority in the Cortes Generales for the first time. This influenced changes in the policies of the J.M Aznar government in comparison with the previous term, during which the PP under the same Prime Minister had formed a minority government. A total lack of cooperation with other groups in the Cortes Generales on the part of the PP government led to intensified use of accountability tools during this term. As for the effectiveness of the described instruments, regardless of the type of government, the tools that do not require a majority in the Congress of Deputies, i.e. verbal queries and interpellations, are more effective, and to a certain extent investigative committees.

***

When comparing the position of the legislative in Poland and Spain, it should be emphasised that in both cases the lower houses of parliament have a similar set of instruments at their disposal. Based on empirical data presented in Chapter 3, it can be concluded that in Poland there are no major quantitative differences between individual terms, with the exception of the 5th term (Tables 5 and 6). In the years 2005–2007 all instruments of control used in the Sejm in the plenary forum (speeches at Sejm sessions; government information and reports; reports on the activities of various organs; resolutions, declarations; questions on current affairs, information on current affairs, interpellations, queries), as well as instruments of control used in the committees (desiderata; opinions; visitations and investigations of activities) were used more rarely. At the same time, more often than in other terms the vote of no confidence against ministers was used, and this represented the vote of no confidence against the government that passed during the analysed period (Chart 13). Without doubt, the lower number of instruments of control used in the plenary forum and Sejm committees of the 5th term of the Sejm was connected with its shorter duration, but the number of votes of no confidence can be an effect of the very weak parliamentary support that the minority governments formed in the years 2005–2007 enjoyed. To summarise the dynamics of the use of accountability tools in the Congress of Deputies, an increase in the use of instruments of control in the last three terms can be noted, particularly tools used in the plenary forum: demands of presence, resolutions, non-legislative motions, interpellations, written queries and, to a lesser extent, government reports (Table 7). The situation was similar in the case of instruments of control used in the committees – the number of verbal queries, non-legislative motions and demands of presence also rose (Table 8). The 2000–2004 term in particular stands out. Unlike the 5th term in Poland, the 7th term in Spain saw the formation of a majority government, as PP had an absolute majority in the Congress of Deputies. In this term as well, motions for a vote of no confidence against ministers were most frequent, while the only motion for a vote of no confidence against a prime minister was in the 3rd term (Chart 15). The increase in the use of control tools during the 7th term can be explained by the fact that, for the first time since the transformation of the political system, PP, a party perceived as the heir to Francoism, won an absolute majority. The style of government employed by the same prime minister who ruled in the 6th term, J.M. Aznar, was based to a lesser extent on compromise than in the previous term, when PP had formed a minority government. During the last two analysed terms, on the other hand, the PSOE governments were minority governments.

When analysing the effectiveness of the tools described herein, both in Poland and in Spain the instruments that do not require a parliamentary majority are more effective. Neither in Poland nor in Spain has a constructive vote of no confidence ever passed. Accountability for performance of the budget also leaves much to be desired, although in Poland there is the mechanism involving the vote of discharge. However, in neither term was this vote denied, despite the growing public debt. In Spain there have been many more investigative committees than in Poland, a fact associated with the length of the analyzed period. Their importance in the system of accountability in both countries is similar, given the similar formula involved in their formation (Figure 4 and 5). Effective instruments of accountability in the Sejm include questions on current affairs, current information and interpellations (with their limited importance as an accountability tool after amendments to the Statute of the Sejm). In the Congress of Deputies, however, regardless of the type of government and support it had, effective instruments include verbal queries and interpellations. What differentiates Spain from Poland is a higher level of institutionalisation of accountability tools. Initiatives of oversight and control of the executive gained in importance over time and were more noticeable to the public. From the point of view of horizontal accountability, the annual state of the nation debate is especially significant as a tool that emerged through parliamentary practice, an event lasting for two days and focusing the attention of nearly all media outlets. This is similar to the Spanish *question time* which takes place every Wednesday and lasts four hours. While a custom has emerged in Poland of presenting the results of policies implemented after the first 100 days of the government in the recent years, similarly to questions about current events and issue debates it has not become an event as widely commented on by the media.

Based on the empirical data presented, the second hypothesis can confidently be confirmed: *Control of the Congress of Deputies is more institutionalised than control of the Sejm, which is a result of the longer time elapsed since the moment of consolidation of democracy*. The results of analyses regarding the influence of procedural conditions and the support of the composition of the lower houses of parliament on the dynamics of use of accountability tools are more ambiguous. It is difficult to unambiguously determine which factor influences the use of these tools more, as neither in Poland nor in Spain are there repeating regularities. Therefore, the first of the hypotheses remains not fully confirmed: *In Poland and in Spain, the dynamics of the use of accountability tools is more dependent on the procedural conditions than on the balance of forces in the lower houses of parliament.*

Chapter 4. The judicial and mandate agencies

The special character of the judicial branch within the separation of powers is reflected well in P. Winczorek's statement that "the judicial power is somewhat distant from the main connections between the legislative and executive. It allows for the independence of courts and judges to be protected."[144] The judicial branch therefore plays a very important role within the separation of powers. According to J. Garlicki, it "plays the role of an apolitical balancing factor",[145] and is thus a procedural guarantee of the other branches' independence and their mutual balancing. However, the independence of the judicial branch is at times limited, which disturbs the functioning of democracy by leading to a situation where power is concentrated in the hands of a small group of people. One of the conditions necessary for an independent judiciary to function is the absence of influence of the other branches on the decisions of judges, which is a consequence of *inter alia* a clear division of powers among political actors. If we accept that constitutions are a tool for defending citizens from abuses of power by politicians, then the objective of the institutional architecture should be defending institutions from political arbitrariness.

Therefore, the separation of powers and constitutional control are among the basic mechanisms ensuring the protection and realisation of citizens' interests. Constitutional control is one of the most important attributes of the judicial branch, as it guarantees that the laws enacted by the legislative and executive branches comply with a given country's constitution. Therefore, the performance of constitutional control is one of the fundamental pillars of the system of checks and balances. Accordingly, the judicial branch is a guarantee of democratic stability without which accountability is impossible. The existence of mandate agencies, which E. Peruzzotti calls the "institutionalisation of the lack of trust in the government",[146] is an additional defence against abuses of power. It is generally assumed that the effectiveness of both the judicial branch and mandate agencies

---

144 P. Winczorek, *Wstęp do nauki o państwie*, 1996, p. 143.

145 L. Garlicki, Polskie prawo…, op. cit. p. 341.

146 E. Peruzzotti, *Rendición de cuentas, participación ciudadana y agencias de control en America Latina*, Paper presented at the at the 17th Asamblea General Ordinaria OLACEFS, 1–6 October 2007, Santo Domingo, acij.org.ar/wp-content/uploads/2010/12/peruzzotti-rendicion-de-cuentas-participacion-ciudadana-y-agencias-de-control-en-america-latina.pdf, p. 7.

is based on procedural conditions on the one hand, while on the other their actual independence, determined by the extent of political influence on the judiciary and mandate agencies.[147]

In order to examine the role of the judicial branch and mandate agencies in the system of accountability, two determinants will be considered – procedural conditions and the influence of the type of government and the support each government had on the judiciary and mandate agencies. Examination of procedural conditions will focus on four aspects: the composition of each institution, the method for appointing its members, the length of their term, and the range of powers enjoyed by each institution. It should be emphasised that the scope of authority will only be analysed in the context of horizontal accountability, and

147 In the subject literature one can find various interpretations of the independence of the judicial branch. A. Binder distinguishes between "independence" and "autonomy", while M. Cappelletti, J.J. Toharia, and J. Sharman differentiate "impartiality" and "independence". J.E. Méndez, in turn, distinguishes "formal" and "material" independence, E.M. Salzberger "material" and "structural", and J.M. Rico, L. Salas differentiate between "external" and "internal" independence. Ch. Larkins introduces the separation of "insularity" and "neutrality", while P. Karlan as well as G. Negretto and M. Ungar refer to positive and negative aspects of independence. Different terms are frequently used for the same thing. For example, structural independence, formal independence and autonomy refer to exerting pressure on the activities of the judicial branch. The opposite situation also occurs: the same terms are sometimes used for different phenomena. In this work, the independence of the judicial branch and mandate agencies is understood as the lack of interference in the work of the judicial branch and mandate agencies on the part of the legislative, the executive, parties to any court case or other actors connected with the administration of the judiciary. See: A. Binder, *Introducción al libro Imagen de la justicia: independencia y asociacionismo en el sector judicial nicaragüense*, Managua 2001; M. Cappelletti, *La responsabilidad de los jueces*, La Plata 1999; J.J. Toharia, *La independencia judicial y la buena Justicia*, Justicia y Sociedad, PNUD 1999, no. 3; J. Sharman, *Ética judicial: independencia, imparcialidad e integridad*, Washington 1996; J.E. Méndez, *Legislatures, judiciaries and innovations in horizontal accountability*, Paper presented at the conference *Accountability, and Democratic Governance in Latin America*, Kellog Institute, Notre Dame 2000; E.M. Salzberger, *The Independence of the Judiciary an Economic Analysis of Law Perspective*, Budapest 2001, www.ceu.hu/legal/Salzberger.htm; J.M. Rico, L. Salas, *Independencia judicial en América Latina, replanteamiento de un tema tradicional*, Florida 1989; Ch. Larkins, *Judicial independence and Democratization: A Theoretical and Conceptual Analysis*, "The American Journal of Comparative Law" 1996, no XLIV; G. Negretto, M. Ungar, *Independencia del poder judicial y Estado de derecho en América Latina: los casos de Argentina y Venezuela*, "Política y gobierno" 1997, no. IV; P. Karlan, *Two Concepts of Judicial Independence*, 1992, www.usc.edu/dept/law/symposia/judicial/pdf/karlan.pdf.

not in its entirety – from the perspective of the institutions' functioning in the political system. The issue of guarantees of judges' independence will also not be analysed in detail. This results from the fact that both countries are considered to be consolidated democracies. Therefore it is assumed *a priori* that the conditions of judicial independence, understood in terms of stabilisation of the office of a judge, their irremovability, judicial immunity, incompatibility of mandates, the requirement of apoliticism, and the adequate salaries of judges, are met.[148]

Therefore, as concerns procedural conditions, the formal aspects of the functioning of the judicial branch and mandate agencies in the system of horizontal accountability in Poland and Spain will be presented. The main organs of the judicial branch will be analysed, i.e. courts and tribunals. In the case of mandate agencies, following the classification created by F. Carillo Flórez, three types of institutions

148 Issues of judiciary independence have been widely examined in comparative studies. The works of L. Campa Keith, F.A. Hanssen, L. Hammergen, Sh. Smithey and J. Ishyam, E. Herron, K. Randazzo, R. La Porta, F. López de Silanes, C. Pop-Eleches, A. Shleifer or L. Feld and S. Voigt are worth mentioning here. The issue of judiciary independence is also examined in reports prepared by the Group of States Against Corruption-GRECO, including reports on Greece and Spain. It should be noted that the reports use the same methodology, so their conclusions can be compared. More: L. Camp Keith, *Writing Constitutions that Protects against Human Rights Abuse. How Important Are Provisions for Judicial Independence and Judicial Review?*, 1999, www.artsci.wustl.edu/~polisci/epstein/conference/archive99/Keith.pdf; F.A. Hanssen, *Is there a Politically Optimal Level of Judicial Independence?*, 2002, www.2.montana.edu/ahanssen/Papers/optimal%20level.pdf; L. Hammergen, *Diagnosing Judicial Performance: toward a tool to help guide judicial reform programs*, 2001, www.transparency.org/iacc/9th_iacc/papers/day4/ws1/d4ws1_lhammergren.html; Sh. Smithey, J. Ishyama, *Judicious Choices: Designing Courts in Post-Communist Politics*, "Communist and Post-Communist Studies" 2002, no. 33. E. Herron, K. Randazzo, *Judicial Institutions and the Evolution of Independent Courts in New Democracies*, 2002, www.isp.msu.edu/CERS/randazz.htm; L. Feld, S. Voigt, *Economic Growth and Judicial Independence: Cross Country Evidence Using a New Set of Indicators*, 2002, in: http://www.wirtschaft.uni-kassel.de/Voigt/PDF/GroningenRevstv.pdf; R. La Porta, F. López de Silanes, C. Pop-Eleches, A. Shleifer, *The Guarantees of Freedom*, 2002, post.economics.harvard.edu/faculty/laporta/papers/freedom.pdf; Group of States Against Corruption (GRECO), Corruption prevention in respect of members of parliament, judges and prosecutor. Evaluation Report Poland, 25 January 2013, www.coe.int/t/dghl/monitoring/greco/evaluations/round4/GrecoEval4%282012%294_Poland_EN.pdf; Group of States against corruption (GRECO), Corruption prevention in respect of members of parliament, judges and prosecutor. Evaluation Report Spain, 15 January 2014. www.coe.int/t/dghl/monitoring/greco/evaluations/round4/GrecoEval4%282013%295_Spain_EN.pdf.

will be distinguished: supreme audit institutions (e.g. courts of accounts), prosecutorial/investigative agencies (e.g. prosecutors) and agencies for the defence of citizens' rights (e.g. human rights ombudsman).[149] The division made by the cited author is partially synonymous with the division present in constitutional law into organs of state control and law enforcement.[150] The examination of the influence of the type of government/parliamentary majority on the judicial branch and mandate agencies will be based on analysis of the relationship between types of governments/parliamentary majority and changes in both procedural conditions and personnel policy regarding those entities. In the examination of the judicial branch and mandate agencies, the so-called "soft" results will be used rather than "hard" ones. For example, instead of examining the number of cases brought before the institutions compared to how many were resolved, attitudes towards these institutions in public opinion polls will be examined. This results from the fact that a purely quantitative comparison of the activities of the judicial branch and special mandate activities would yield very little useful information. Even if the numbers were compared to the expenses incurred by these institutions, it would only answer the question of effectiveness, and not whether they actually function as instruments of accountability. Therefore, instead of "hard" data, "soft" results will be presented from the results of public opinion polls in which these institutions have been assessed. The analysis of the aforementioned aspects of the functioning of the judicial branch and mandate agencies will therefore allow us to answer the following questions: To what extent do institutional rules influence the independence of the judicial branch and mandate agencies? Are there fully independent judicial authorities and mandate agencies which should protect the rule of law and prevent abuses of power? Is the extent of the independence enjoyed by the judicial branch and mandate agencies more dependent on procedural conditions or political constellations? How does the government's support in the parliament influence the independence of the judicial branch and mandate agencies? Does the time since the consolidation of the political system lead to a greater independence of the judiciary and mandate agencies? The following hypotheses will be verified: hypothesis 1: *In Poland and Spain, the independence of the judicial branch and mandate agencies is more dependent on procedural conditions than on the power configuration in*

149 F. Carrillo Flórez, *Instituciones democráticas de rendición de cuentas en América Latina: diseño legal y desempeño real*, w: J.M. Payene, D. G. Zovatto, M. Mateo Díaz (eds.), *La politica importa. Democracia y desarrollo en América Latina*, Washington 2006, p. 135.

150 More: M. Kruk, *Wprowadzenie: prawa i wolności – przedmiotem ochrony prawnej*, in: M. Kruk (ed.), *System ochrony prawnej w Polsce*, Warsaw 2008, pp. 9–10.

the lower houses of parliament. Hypothesis 2: *The weaker and less stable the parliamentary support for a given government in Poland and Spain, the lower its ability to limit the independence of the judicial branch and mandate agencies.* Hypothesis 3: *The longer the time since political transformation, the greater the independence of the judicial branch and mandate agencies in the system of accountability; therefore, in Spain it is stronger than in Poland.*

4.1. Poland

The process of transforming the judicial branch was initiated during the Round Table talks. With the enactment of a new constitution in 1997, the institutional transformation of the organs of judicial power was completed. In the years 1997–2002 a number of bills were passed that concluded the process of adjusting the law concerning the judiciary to the new constitution. The foundations for the Polish judicial system were placed in the chapter of the Constitution titled *Courts and Tribunals* (Art. 173–197). Even though tribunals are not part of the judicature, according to the adopted model of accountability the Constitutional Tribunal (*Trybunał Konstytucyjny*) will be analysed together with the main organs of the judicial system, i.e. the Supreme Court (*Sąd Najwyższy*), the Supreme Administrative Court (*Najwyższy Sąd Administracyjny*) and the National Council of the Judiciary (*Krajowa Rada Sądownictwa*). The Tribunal of State (*Trybunał Stanu*) will not be analysed, as according to some researchers it is an institution that does not function properly, or even a façade institution.[151] The Public Prosecutor's Office (*Prokuratura*), alongside the Central Anti-Corruption Bureau (*Centralne Biuro Antykorupcyjne*), will be analyzed pursuant to the division of mandate agencies proposed by F. Carillo Flórez among prosecuting and investigative institutions. Additionally, the Supreme Audit Office (*Najwyższa Izba Kontroli*, NIK) will be analysed as a supervisory institution. The activities of the Commissioner for Human Rights (*Rzecznik Praw Obywatelskich*) will also be scrutinised as an example of an institution formed to defend the rights of citizens.

4.1.1. The normative dimension

The structure of the administration of justice in Poland, according to Art. 175(1) of the Constitution of the Republic of Poland, is comprised of the Supreme Court, the common courts, administrative courts, and military courts. The Supreme Court exercises supervision over common and military courts in respect

151 More: K. Zuba, *Polska scena...*, op. cit., p. 173.

of judgments. The Supreme Court is a special and final instance of appeal, allowing for the cassation of binding rulings issued by courts of the second instance. It also undertakes resolutions explaining specific legal questions, analyses electoral complaints, approves the results of national and constitutional referendums, elections to the Sejm, Senate and presidential elections. According to the Supreme Court Act of 23 November 2002, it is comprised of four chambers: the civil chamber, criminal chamber, military chamber, and the social security and public matters chamber.[152] Common courts include District Courts, Regional Courts, and Appellate Courts. Administrative courts have a separate place in the judiciary's structure.[153] Provincial Administrative Courts and the Supreme Administrative Court are a separate, two-instance system. The Supreme Administrative Court is comprised of three chambers: the financial chamber, the economic chamber, and the general administrative chamber. They control the legality of the actions of public administration and resolve competence conflicts. The constitution also makes mention of military courts: Military District Courts and Garrison Courts, which administer justice in the Polish armed forces. Like the administrative courts, they comprise a separate judicative system, independent from the common courts. All judges are part of the same judiciary corps.

According to Art. 186 Par. 1 of the Constitution, the National Council of the Judiciary safeguards the independence of courts and judges, and was created as a result of the 1989 Round Table talks. It has a wide range of powers, including verification of candidates for Supreme Court judges and for positions in the common, administrative and military courts, presenting motions for the appointment of judges to the president, as well as enacting and enforcing a professional ethics code for judges. In specified cases, one can appeal against resolutions by the National Council of the Judiciary to the Supreme Court when they are not in compliance with the law. The method under which resolutions are enacted by the National Council of the Judiciary is important: they are voted on in a public vote and need an absolute majority.[154]

---

152 Act of 23 November 2002 on the Supreme Court, OJ L 2002 no. 240 item 2052 with amendments; Act of 27 July 2001: Law of the System of Common Courts, OJ L 2001 no. 98 item 1070 with amendments.

153 Act of 25 July 2002: Law of the System of Administrative Courts, OJ L no., 153, item 1269 with amendments; Act of 30 August 2002: Law on Proceedings before Administrative Courts, OJ L 02.153.1270 with amendments.

154 Act of 20 December 1989 on the National Council of the Judiciary, OJ L no 73, item 435; Act of 27 July 2001 on the National Council of the Judiciary, OJ L 2001 no. 100, item 1082 with amendments.

The Constitutional Tribunal was created in 1986, alongside other institutions such as the Commissioner for Human Rights, as an attempt at boosting credibility and legitimacy in the face of growing criticism of the communist establishment of the time. Initially the Tribunal's rulings could be rejected by a 2/3 majority of members of parliament. The Constitutional Tribunal gained more independence only as a result of systemic transformation. Ruling on the constitutionality of parliamentary acts is the exclusive right of the Constitutional Tribunal, and since the enactment of the constitution in 1997, its rulings are final – there is no mechanism for the legislative to quash them.[155] In Poland, the following institutions have the right to make applications to the Constitutional Tribunal: the President, the Commissioner for Human Rights, the president of the Supreme Administrative Court, the Public Prosecutor-General, the Supreme Audit Office, the National Council of the Judiciary, and a group of 50 MPs. Additionally, under Art. 191 and 193 of the Constitution any court can file a motion to the Tribunal to examine the constitutionality of the law regarding a given case. Also, citizens whose rights have been violated and who have exhausted other ways of pursuing the matter legally can make a motion to the Tribunal under Art. 79. This article is invoked by around 200 citizens per year. Qualified to be a judge of the Constitutional Tribunal is anyone who meets the qualifications for the position of a Supreme Court or Supreme Administrative Court judge, which in practice means having been a judge for at least 10 years and holding the title of professor or a post-doctoral title in law.

As in the case of the Constitutional Tribunal, the duties, functions and regulations regarding the Public Prosecutor's Office, as well as the duties, rights and guaranties of prosecutors were defined in the 1980s in the Public Prosecutor's Office Act of 20 June 1985, which, with some amendments, is still in force today.[156] The main goal of the Public Prosecutor's Office is the protection of law and order, as well as the supervision of criminal prosecution. There are three departments in the Prosecutor's Office: general, military and the Institute of National Remembrance – the Commission for the Prosecution of Crimes against the Polish Nation. All these departments are subject to the Prosecutor-General. The Prosecutor's Office is divided into four hierarchical organisational levels: the General Prosecutor's Office, appellate prosecutors' offices, regional prosecutors' offices and district prosecutors' offices. To replace the previous Prosecutors' Council, the National

155 Act of 1 August 1997 on the Constitutional Tribunal, OJ L no. 102, item 643 with amendments.

156 Act of 20 June 1985 on the Prosecutorial Service of the People's Republic of Poland, OJ L no. 102, item 643 with amendments.

Prosecution Council was created, with similar competences regarding prosecutors as the ones the National Council of the Judiciary has regarding judges.

The creation of the Central Anti-Corruption Bureau (Centralne Biuro Antykorupcyjne, CBA) in 2006 was a certain novelty in the Polish institutional system. Like the Public Prosecutor's Office, the CBA is an institution of special mandate that investigates and prosecutes crimes. The main task of the bureau is the investigation and prosecution of crimes connected with corruption.[157] The duties of the CBA include operational intelligence in order to prevent, discover and detect crime, as well as investigative activities if there is reasonable suspicion of a crime being committed in order to apprehend the perpetrators. They also involve control activities in order to uncover cases of corruption in state institutions and the local government as well as abuses by public officials and activities against the economic interest of the state. Additionally, the CBA engages in operational, investigative and analytical activities in order to acquire and process information necessary to combat corruption in public institutions and local government, as well as activities against the economic interest of the state. This wide range of powers leads the CBA to be classified as one of the special forces. The CBA has regional offices around the country, and is run by the Head of the CBA. The Prime Minister is accountable for the activities of the CBA. The Head of the CBA can be recalled by the Prime Minister, following consultation with the President, the Special Services Committee and the Parliamentary Committee for Special Services. This statutory connection results in this institution being highly politicised.

The Supreme Audit Office (Najwyższa Izba Kontroli, NIK) is a supervisory institution. According to Art. 203 of the Constitution, the NIK controls the activities of the organs of government administration, the National Bank of Poland, State legal persons and other State organisational units in respect of legality, economic prudence, efficacy and diligence. It also audits the activities of the organs of local government, communal legal persons and other communal organisational units in respect of legality, economic prudence and diligence. It may also audit the activity of other organisational units and economic subjects regarding legality and economic prudence, to the extent to which they utilise state or communal property or resources or satisfy financial obligations to the state. The NIK is comprised of the Council of NIK and departments (21) and regional branches (16). The Council of NIK is headed by the President. The position of the NIK President,

157 Act of 9 June 2006 on the Central Anti-Corruption Bureau, OJ L no. 104 item 708.

like in the case of the CBA, is strong. The President of the NIK is responsible for the activities of the NIK before the Sejm.[158]

The Commissioner of Human Rights (Rzecznik Praw Obywatelskich, RPO) is the final institution discussed here. The Constitution guarantees the Commissioner's independence from other organs. The Commissioner is responsible only before the Sejm, according to regulations specified in the relevant statute.[159] The primary responsibility of the RPO is to defend human and civil rights and liberties that arise out of the Constitution of Poland and other normative acts. The RPO's activities consist in examining the legality of the activities of state institutions obligated to uphold the law, and making sure that the principles of social coexistence and social justice are upheld. The RPO initiates proceedings if it is determined that the liberties and rights of a person are being violated systemically, or at the motion of a potentially aggrieved party. Since 1997, the RPO is obliged to present information once per year on its most important activities and their results to the Sejm and the Senate, and to present information on the state of observance of human and civil rights and liberties. This information does not take the form of a report and does not need to be accepted by the Sejm through a vote.

Table 9. The composition, method of selection and terms of the organs and institutions of judicial power in Poland (state for 2011)

Organ	Number of members selected by the executive branch	Number of members selected by the legislative branch	Number of members selected by the judicial branch	Term length
Supreme Court	The First President of the Supreme Court is appointed by the President of Poland from among 2 candidates proposed by the General Assembly of the Supreme Court	-		6 years (First President of the Supreme Court)

158 Act of 23 December 1994 on the Supreme Audit Office, OJ L 1995 no 13 item 59 with amendments.

159 Act of 15 July 1987 on the Commissioner for Human Rights, OJ L 1987 no 21 item 123 with amendments.

Organ	Number of members selected by the executive branch	Number of members selected by the legislative branch	Number of members selected by the judicial branch	Term length
Supreme Administrative Court	The President of the Supreme Administrative Court is appointed by the President of Poland from among 2 candidates proposed by the General Assembly of the Supreme Administrative Court	-		6 years (First President of the Supreme Administrative Court)
National Council of the Judiciary	1 representative of the President The Minister of Justice is automatically a member of the Council	4 members selected by the Sejm from among MPs 2 members selected by the Senate from among senators	First President of the Supreme Court, President of the Supreme Administrative Court, 15 members elected from out of the judges: Supreme Court, general courts and military courts	4 years, with the possibility of one-time extension
Constitutional Tribunal	The President and Vice-President of the Tribunal are appointed by the President of Poland from among 2 candidates proposed by the General Assembly of the Tribunal	15 judges elected by the Sejm by absolute majority with the consent of the Senate, at the motion of 50 MPs or the Presidium of the Sejm		9 years without the right to re-election
Public Prosecutor's Office	The Prosecutor General is appointed by the President of Poland from among 2 candidates – one proposed by the General Council of the Judiciary and one by the National Prosecutors' Council			6 years (Prosecutor General)

Organ	Number of members selected by the executive branch	Number of members selected by the legislative branch	Number of members selected by the judicial branch	Term length
National Prosecutors' Council	1 representative of the President The Minister of Justice is automatically a member of the Council	4 members selected by the Sejm from among MPs 2 members selected by the Senate from among senators	Prosecutor General, 1 prosecutor elected by the Chief Military Prosecutor Office, 1 prosecutor elected by the Institute of National Remembrance – Commission for the Prosecution of Crimes against the Polish Nation, 3 prosecutors elected by the General Prosecutors' Office 11 prosecutors elected by prosecutors' assemblies in the appellate prosecutors' offices	4 years, with the possibility of one-time extension
Central Anti-Corruption Bureau	The Bureau's Head is appointed by the Prime Minister, after consulting the President and the Special Services Board and the Sejm Committee for Special Services			4-year term
President of the National Audit Office		The Sejm with Senate's consent at the motion of the Marshal of the Senate or a group of 35 MPs, through absolute majority vote		6-year term, with the right to re-election
Commissioner for Human Rights		The Sejm with Senate's consent at the motion of the Marshal of the Senate or a group of 35 MPs, through absolute majority vote		6-year term, with the right to re-election

Source: own work.

When analysing the composition, method of selection and terms of various judicial organs and mandate agencies, it should be concluded that they differ substantially. The procedure for the selection and appointment of judges to the main organs of judicial power in Poland remains almost entirely in the hands of the judiciary. Therefore, the influence of individual governments on the selection of judges is minimal, which is a result of the legal framework. In the case of the presidents of the Supreme Court and the Supreme Administrative Court, the President of Poland can choose from between two candidates, who nevertheless are proposed by the General Assembly of the Judges of the Supreme Court and the General Assembly of the Judges of the Supreme Administrative Court, respectively.[160] In the case of the National Council of the Judiciary, as many as 17 out of 25 members are chosen from among judges by judges (save for the aforementioned presidents of the Supreme Court and Supreme Administrative Court). The situation is different in the case of the Constitutional Tribunal, where the judges are selected by the legislature, which makes this organ more politicised. In the case of the Commissioner for Human Rights and the President of the Supreme Audit Office, these organs are also selected by the first house of the parliament. In each case, their appointment requires an absolute majority, which in practice means that they must be chosen through the votes of the parliamentary majority which forms the government.

4.1.2. Political practice

Under the law as of 2011, aside from the judiciary and the prosecutor's office, the composition of each of the institutions described here depended on the legislative or the executive. In the case of the Prosecutor's Office, in the years 1997–2011 there was a dispute regarding the shape of the office, which ended with the separation of the functions of Minister of Justice and Prosecutor General and the creation of the National Prosecution Council. In the analysed period it was sometimes the case that Ministers of Justice were more concentrated on their authority as Prosecutor General than on the functions of Minister of Justice. This is what happened during Jerzy Buzek's minority government, when the Minister of Justice was Lech Kaczyński. During his term, guidelines for prosecutors were issued demanding more frequent use of preventive measures, including temporary arrest. This led to an increase in the number of judgements against Poland in the European Tribunal of Human Rights, which perceived a systemic problem in the abuse of this

160 Act of 18 August 2011 on the system of common courts, no. 203 item 1192 with amendments.

instrument in Poland.[161] The situation was similar in the years 2005–2007, when Zbigniew Ziobro served as the Minister of Justice, and the minister's supervision over the prosecution service was strengthened. In March 2007, major changes to the Public Prosecutor's Office Act were passed. The supervision of prosecutors' superiors over their activities was strengthened at the cost of the independence of prosecutors in their investigations. The PiS government also caused widespread media tempestuousness, as issues concerning corruption were widely commented on by minister Ziobro himself. Particularly significant was his statement following the arrest of cardiac surgeon Mirosław G. by the Central Anti-Corruption Bureau in which – disregarding the principle of presumption of innocence – the minister supported the charges against the detainee. During that period it was also not uncommon for investigation materials to be disclosed during press conferences, e.g. in the case of National Prosecutor J. Engelking. After PO came to power in 2007, work began on changes to the Public Prosecutor's Office Act, with a view to depoliticising it. In 2010, after 20 years, the positions of Minister of Justice and Prosecutor General were again separated. This change in the law does not, however, guarantee the Prosecutor General's complete independence from the executive, as he or she must present an annual report to the Prime Minister on the Office's activities. Additionally, the Prime Minister can reject the report and, after consulting with the National Prosecution Council, can motion for the Sejm to dismiss the Prosecutor General before the end of his or her term. It should be noted that the changes made, including the separation of positions of Prosecutor General and Minister of Justice, and the creation of the Prosecutors' Council, tasked with guarding prosecutors' independence, have obviously reduced the influence of the executive on the prosecution.

Despite the above changes, the prosecution and the courts are the most poorly regarded institutions in Poland, although since 2006 an increase in positive opinions can be noted. In 2007, for the first time there were more positive opinions about the courts and prosecution than negative ones. In the years 2008–2011, opinions of the Polish justice system worsened again, especially in the case of the prosecutorial service. G. Skąpska and G. Bryda note, however, that when interpreting evaluations of the justice system in Poland, one should take into consideration the historical legacy and social experiences connected with the depth and character of the reforms made in Poland after 1989. According to these authors, opinion polls conducted within Polish society about the justice system should be

161 For more, see: *Biuletyn Programu Spraw Precedensowych Helsińskiej Fundacji Praw Człowieka*, February 2009.

interpreted through the lens of the "transformation trauma" and not politicisation of the institutions.[162] It remains a fact that polls from 2011 recorded the smallest number of negative responses since 1997, which can be associated with the institution's depoliticisation in 2010.

Chart 17. The evaluation of the functioning of courts and the prosecution in Poland (in %)

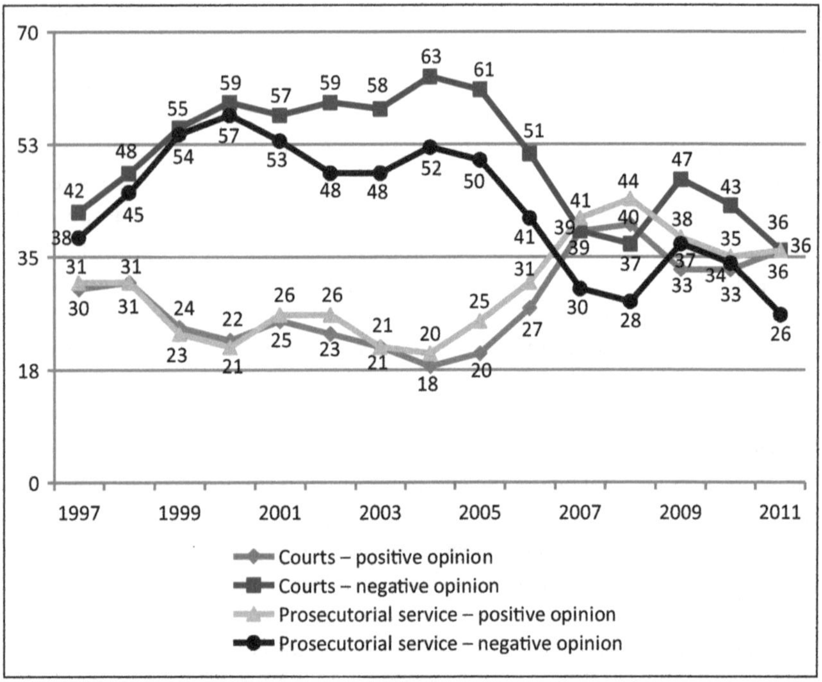

Source: own work based on CBOS data[163].

162 G. Skąpska, G. Bryda, *Apolityczność czy sprawiedliwość proceduralna? Zaufanie do sądowego wymiaru sprawiedliwości na tle innych instytucji publicznych w Polsce*, "Studia Socjologiczne" 2013, no. 1(208), pp. 77–94.

163 All charts in this sub-chapter regarding the public opinion ratings of Polish institutions were based on the following CBOS reports: Ocena działalności wybranych instytucji politycznych. Communique no. 2026 from CBOS study, S/157/157/98 Warsaw, November 1998, pp. 8, 10; Działalność instytucji publicznych w ocenie społecznej. Communique no. 2207 from CBOS study, BS/153/99 Warsaw, October 1999, pp. 8, 10; Oceny działalności instytucji publicznej. Communique no. 22–80 from CBOS study, BS/23/2000, Warsaw, February 2000, pp. 8, 16; Instytucje publiczne w opinii społecznej. Communique no. 2361 from CBOS study, BS/104/2000, Warsaw, July

The selection of Constitutional Tribunal members is dependent on the legislative branch, which makes it likely to be politicised. Under the 1997 Constitution several mechanisms were included in order to limit the politicisation of the Tribunal. They are: the requirement of a qualified majority – judges are elected by an absolute majority of the Sejm; a long, 9-year term of office for judges, much longer than a parliamentary term, which allows for continuity; partial renewal of the Tribunal's composition – every three years 1/3 of the Tribunal is replaced, which prevents problems associated with replacing them all at the same time and situations in which a change of ruling party could directly influence the functioning of the Tribunal. Despite these safeguards, in the years 1997–2011 the selection of judges was highly politicised regardless of the type of government. In the 1997–2001 term 9 new judges were sworn in, including 7 recommended by the main coalition partner (AWS) and 2 recommended by UW. As a result of these changes, 2/3 of the judges were nominated by parties that were in power. The situation was similar in the 2001–2005 term, during which 6 new judges were sworn in. All of them were recommended by the ruling party (SLD). At the end of the 4th term, the composition of the Tribunal was: 6 judges recommended by SLD, 6 by AWS, and 2 by UW. In the next term (2005–2007), the situation was analogous – among the 6 newly appointed judges, 4 were recommended by the main coalition member (PiS) and 2 by its coalition partners (LPR and

2000, pp. 8, 16; Instytucje publiczne w opinii społecznej. Communique no. 2629 from CBOS study, BS/6/2002,Warsaw, January 2002, pp. 2, 8, 16; Opinie o działalności instytucji publicznych. Communique no. 3013 from CBOS study, BS/167/2003, Warsaw, October 2003, pp. 4, 9; Opinie o działalności instytucji publicznych. Communique no. 3083 from CBOS study, BS/36/2004, Warsaw February 2004, pp. 4, 9; Opinie o działalności instytucji publicznych. Communique no. 3285 from CBOS study, BS/35/2005, Warsaw, February 2005, pp. 5, 8, 10; Opinie o działalności instytucji publicznych. Communique no. 3488 from CBOS study, BS/32/2006/B, Warsaw, February 2006, pp. 6, 8, 9; Opinie o działalności instytucji publicznych. Communique no. 3672 from CBOS study, BS/17/2007, Warsaw, February 2007, pp. 7, 10, 14; Opinie o działalności instytucji publicznych. Communique no. 3866 from CBOS study, BS/16/2008, Warsaw, January 2008, pp. 7, 8, 11; Oceny instytucji publicznych. Communique no. 4107 from CBOS study, BS/42/2009, Warsaw, March 2009, pp. 8, 10, 12; Oceny instytucji publicznych. Communique no. 4278 from CBOS study, BS/39/2010, Warsaw, March 2010, pp. 11, 13, 16; Oceny instytucji publicznych. Communique no. 4442 from CBOS study, BS/30/2011, Warsaw, March 2011, pp. 10, 13, 14; Oceny instytucji publicznych. Communique no. 4619 from CBOS study, BS/39/201, Warsaw, March 2012, pp. 10, 13, 15, Opinia publiczna o korupcji i lobbingu w Polsce, Communique no. 4302 z badań CBOS BS/63/2010, Warsaw, May 2010, p. 12.

Samoobrona). In the next term, during the years 2007–2011, the only difference was the recommendation of a judge together by the ruling party (PO) and an opposition party (SLD), although the candidate had already been recommended by SLD before. The other judges were recommended by the ruling coalition: 6 by PO and 1 by PSL[164].

According to R. Alberski, given that after the enactment of the Constitution, parties came to pay more attention to the process of appointing judges, qualifications began to matter less while party affiliation started to matter more. In this author's view, although it is extremely hard to prove to which extent this influences judges' rulings, it can be used to undermine their impartiality[165]. Despite this, the Constitutional Tribunal is one of the most highly rated institutions in Poland according to opinion polls. The percentage of respondents with a positive view oscillated during the examined period between 56% and 37%, while only from 11% to 17% of respondents held a negative opinion about the Tribunal.

Chart 18. Evaluation of the functioning of the Constitutional Tribunal (in %)

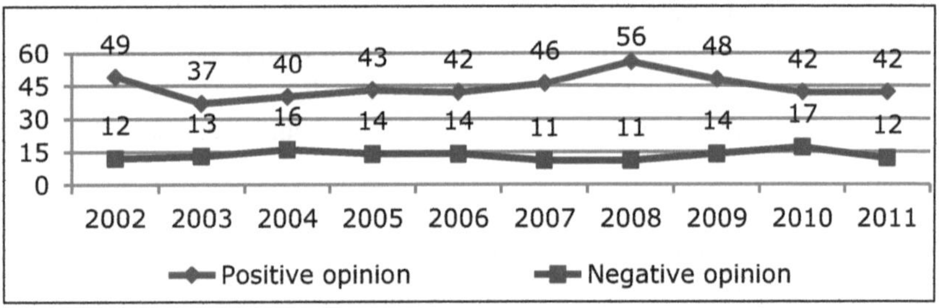

Source: own work based on CBOS data.

The Anti-Corruption Bureau was also formed during the 2005–2007 parliamentary term. Since its creation in 2006 it has been a subject of public debate. Ambiguous opinions about this institution are connected with the fact that, on the one hand, many anti-corruption investigations have been initiated by the bureau,[166]

---

164 More about Constitutional Tribunal candidates: Projekt OMX TK, www.inpris.pl/wazne/omx-monitoring/omx-tk-poprzednie-wybory/; R. Alberski, *Trybunał Konstytucyjny w polskich systemach Politycznych*, Wrocław 2010, pp. 187–199.

165 R. Alberski, op. cit., p. 198.

166 Only in 2011, according to the data presented in the report, as part of operative and prosecution activities in Central Anti-Corruption Bureau units, 256 operative cases were started, and 227 were concluded. The total number of cases was 511. Also in 2011, 248 preliminary proceedings were being conducted, and 205 were concluded.

but on the other hand, the fact that the CBA head is appointed and supervised by the Prime Minister has led it to be used as a tool in political combat. The first CBA head, Mariusz Kamiński, appointed to this position in 2006 during the PiS government, resigned from his party membership in order to fulfil the formal requirements. The activities of the CBA during his term were very controversial, raising many doubts about the politicisation of this organ. Such activities definitely included the 2007 arrest of an MP from the main opposition party before parliamentary elections, which generated substantial media coverage in no small part due to a media campaign by the CBA itself. The bureau also initiated many anti-corruption investigations against representatives of the executive branch, including former president Aleksander Kwaśniewski and his wife. These investigations were often fiascoes, which has been widely commented on in the media. Eventually, after exposing an attempt at illegal lobbying at the highest echelons of government during the so-called "Gambling Affair", which involved a then-incumbent Deputy Prime Minister in the D. Tusk government, the CBA Head M. Kamiński and 90% of all upper management of the bureau were dismissed. The new CBA head was Paweł Wojtunik, who was not affiliated with any party. However, the highly political activities of the bureau in the years 2005–2007 and the 2009 dismissals show controversies regarding this institutions' activities. Evaluations of this institution in opinion polls are comparable to those of the courts and the prosecution service, and therefore relatively low. Even at the moment of its formation the institution was not highly regarded. In 2007, almost as many respondents judged its activities negatively as positively, and in the following years there was no major change in this regard, although 2009 is the year in which the most respondents perceived it positively. Undoubtedly, society's low opinion of this institution was connected with the disclosure of the behind-the-scenes activities of the CBA and major criticism of this institution.

Additionally, 419 investigations were ongoing. From out of the cases started that year, 75 were referred to the Bureau by the Prosecutor's Office. The Bureau also resumed 7 previously suspended cases. More: Centralne Biuro Antykorupcyjne, *Informacja o wynikach działalności Centralnego Biura Antykorupcyjnego w 2011 roku*, Warsaw 2012, p. 4.

Chart 19. Evaluation of the functioning of the Central Anti-Corruption Bureau (in %)

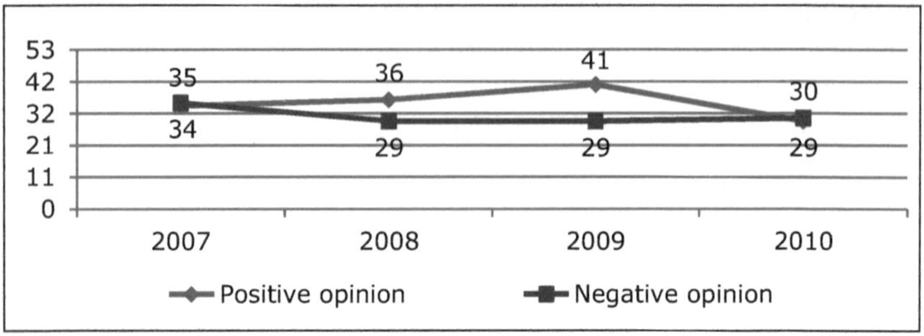

Source: own work based on CBOS data.

In the case of the President of the Supreme Audit Office (NIK) and the institution itself, as in the case of the Commissioner for Human Rights, there is a lack of meaningful and reliable signals from the media and researchers about the possibilities of and attempts at direct political influence on the decisions and activities of these institutions. However, appointments to both of these positions are usually associated with specific political groups. NIK Presidents Janusz Wojciechowski (1995–2001) from PSL and Mirosław Sekuła (2001–2007) from AWS resigned from political activity for the time of their work at this position. On the other hand, Jacek Jezierski, appointed in 2007, was a longtime NIK employee and had not been an active politician before that. This is one of the most highly-rated state institutions. However, since 2003 the assessment of NIK has worsened; the number of respondents that assessed its activity negatively increased by 8% compared to 1997, and the number of respondents assessing it positively decreased by 15%.

Chart 20. Evaluation of the functioning of the Supreme Audit Office (in %)

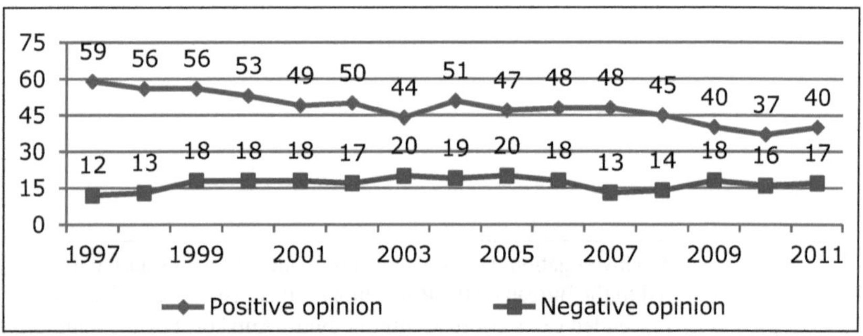

Source: own work based on CBOS data.

It is also hard to put direct political pressure on the Commissioner for Human Rights, although, as in the case of the Supreme Audit Office, people appointed to this position were also associated with various political groups. Adam Zieliński (1996–2000) was recommended by MPs from SLD, PSL and UP, while Adam Zoll (2000–2005), associated with UW, was recommended by AWS and UW. Jan Kochanowski (2006–2010) was recommended by PiS, while Irena Lipowicz, who began her term in 2010, was recommended by PO. Jan Kochanowski was probably the most controversial Commissioner in the history of democratic Poland, and was often said to openly sympathise with PiS.[167] When analysing public opinion on the activities of the Commissioner for Human Rights (Chart 2) it can easily be observed that at the end of Jan Kochanowski's term respondents rated it the lowest. It is also worth noting that, although it is the most highly rated institution in Poland, the number of positive opinions during the examined period systematically decreased.

Chart 21: Evaluation of the functioning of the Commissioner for Human Rights (w %)

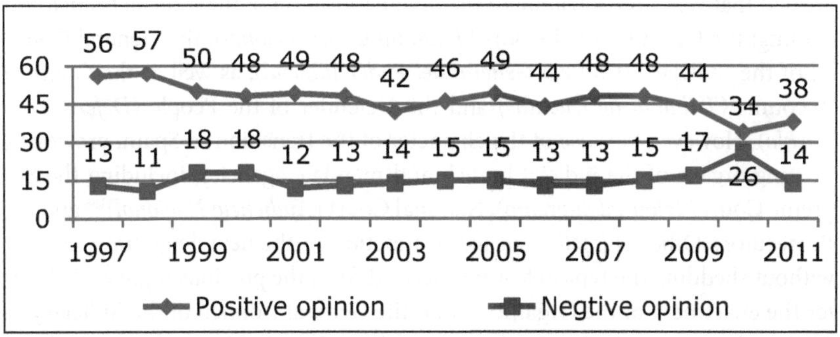

Source: own work based on CBOS data.

In summary, one can observe a relationship between respondents' perceptions and attempts at influencing institutions and organs predominately by the executive branch. The lowest-rated institutions of the judicial branch and mandate agencies in the examined period were the courts, the Prosecutor's Office and the Central Anti-Corruption Bureau. If poll results are to be considered in connection with such data as statistics of the activities of the Ministry of Justice, which

167 M. Gurtowski, *Rzecznik Praw Obywatelskich*, w: A. Kobylińska, G. Makowski, M. Solana-Lipiński (eds.), *Mechanizmy przeciwdziałania korupcji w Polsce. Raport z monitoringu*, Transparency International, Warsaw 2012, p. 165.

show a dynamic increase in the number of cases referred to courts, the low ratings can be connected with the low effectiveness of courts or the phenomenon which G. Skąpska and G. Bryda call the "transformation trauma". It is, however, not necessarily well-founded in the case of the Prosecutor's Office and the Central Anti-Corruption Bureau. It rather seems that the low opinion of these institutions results from their high degree of politicisation. One exception is the evaluation of the Constitutional Tribunal, which, despite its politicisation, is one of the highest-rated institutions in Poland during the whole period. The Supreme Audit Office and the Commissioner for Human Rights are two institutions that as a rule should not be influenced by party configurations and should uphold the law regardless of who is in power, and their high ratings in polls prove they are perceived as such by Polish society.

4.2. Spain

With the enactment of the 1978 Constitution, new institutions and organs were created that were to contribute to the democratisation of the judicial branch, including: the Constitutional Court (*Tribunal Constitucional*), the General Council of the Judiciary (*Consejo General del Poder Judicial*), as well as the Court of Accounts (*Tribunal de Cuentas*) and the Defender of the People (*Defensor del Pueblo*). However, because of the character of the transition in Spain, previously existing organs of the judicial branch and mandate agencies, including the Supreme Court (*Tribunal Supremo*), National Court (*Audiencia Nacional*)[168] and the Prosecutor's Office (*Fiscalía*) started to function in the new democratic context without shedding the typical features derived from the previous regime. Only after the enactment of the Organic Act on the General Council of the Judiciary in 1981 and the Organic Act on the Judicial Branch in 1985 was the institutional reconstruction of the judicial system finished. At the same time, the rulings of the Constitutional Court were immensely important, especially in the years 1981–1985. It was the Constitutional Court, as an organ formally independent from the judicial branch, which democratised the Spanish political system. In the years 1981–1985, the Constitutional Court's rulings limited the military's authority,

168 The National Court was formed based on a January 4 1977 Decree. More about the circumstances of the creation of the National Court: J.M. Olarieta Alberdi, *El origen de la Audiencia Nacional*, "Jueces para la Democracia. Información y debate" 1997, no. 29, pp. 29–33.

introduced guarantees of the rule of law and oversight of the executive, and consolidated the position of the new territorial system.[169]

As in the case of Poland, aside from the main organs of the judicial branch and the Constitutional Court, mandate agencies will be analysed, following the typology proposed by F. Carillo Flórez. The Prosecutor's Office will be analysed among prosecuting and investigative institutions; in Spain, there is no equivalent of the Polish Central Anti-Corruption Bureau. Only at the regional level, in Catalonia, is there the Anti-Fraud Office of Catalonia, but its jurisdiction is limited to that autonomous community. Additionally, the Court of Accounts will be analysed as a supervisory institution, while the Defender of the People will be analysed as an institution formed to defend the rights of citizens.

4.2.1. The normative dimension

The structure of the judiciary in Spain consists of the Supreme Court, the National Court, and courts of each autonomous community, including the Upper Courts of Justice (*Tribunales Superiores de Justicia*). The Provincial Courts (*Audiencias Provinciales*) are subject to the Upper Courts. In court districts comprised of one or more municipality, there are courts of first instance (*Juzgados de Primera Instancia e Instrucción*). In municipalities in which there are no courts of first instance, there are the so-called justices of the peace (*juzgados de paz*). Justices of the peace are elected by the municipal government and are not professional judges. They also do not have to be lawyers.[170] The jurisdiction of the Supreme Court and the National Court encompasses the entire country. The Supreme Court is the court of the highest instance according to Art. 123(1) of the Constitution. It is the highest judicial organ for all kinds of cases, save for constitutional ones, in which the Constitutional Court is the highest authority. The Supreme Court is divided into five chambers: civil, criminal, administrative, social and military. There is also a special chamber consisting of the president of the Supreme Court, presidents of each chamber and 2 judges from each chamber. This chamber presides over special cases, such as the delegalisation of the Basque Herri Batasuna.[171] The highest public officials, such as the Prime Minister and

169 More: A. Benito Sánchez, *Poder Judicial, Accountability legal y transición a la democracia en España*, "Foro Internacional" 2009, vol. XLIX, no. 1, pp. 163–199.

170 More about the structure of the judiciary in Spain: T. Moładawa, *System konstytucyjny…*, op. cit., pp. 123–126.

171 On March 27, 2003 the Supreme Court delegalised Herri Batasuna, as a political branch of the ETA.

members of the government, are responsible before the Supreme Court. However, in the case of criminal responsibility connected with a crime against state security, they are prosecuted at a motion of the Congress of Deputies. The second court with nationwide jurisdiction is the aforementioned National Court, formed on 5 January 1977[172], and which consists of 3 chambers: criminal, administrative and social. The National Court presides over trials for crimes against the Crown and the highest state institutions, including drug smuggling, terrorism and money forging. The National Court also examines complaints against collective labor agreements or against acts of ministers and secretaries of state. What differentiates the Supreme Court and the National Court is their respective areas of specialisation. If we analyse the activity of both organs in the quantitative dimension, it turns out that the activity of the first organ is concentrated on administrative cases, while that of the second on criminal cases.[173]

Among professional judges there are three categories: lower instance judges, tribunal and court judges, and Supreme Court judges. What is important from the point of view of the checks and balances system is the method of appointment. The first category of judges is appointed by a resolution of the General Council of the Judiciary, which is a supervisory organ for the judiciary. The second and third are appointed on a motion of the same Council by a royal decree countersigned by the Minister of Justice. The Council was formed under the Constitution of 1978 as a kind of novelty in the history of Spanish constitutionalism. The Council's position within the judicial system was further specified in the Organic Act on Judicial Power (LOPJ) of 1 July 1985. The Council's authority include appointing members of the most important institutions of the justice system, including candidates for the President of the Supreme Court and two candidates for members of the Constitutional Court. The Council also nominates, by a decree, lower instance judges and presents Supreme Court judges for royal nomination, as well as presidents of tribunals and judges of higher courts. The council's duties also include providing opinions on draft bills and other normative acts regarding the judiciary, as well as oversight over the actions of tribunals and courts.

172 Royal Decree-Law por el que se crea la Audiencia Nacional no. 1/1977 of January 1977, B.O.E. no. 4.

173 Statistics regarding the activities of judicial organs can be found on the official website of the judicial branch: Poder Judicial, www.poderjudicial.es/cgpj/es/Temas/Estadistica_Judicial/Analisis_estadistico.

The Constitutional Court was formed under the 1978 Constitution, through the Organic Act on the Constitutional Court of 3 October 1979.[174] Unlike in the Polish Constitutional Tribunal, fewer entities are able to refer bills and other legal acts to the Constitutional Court. These entities are the Prime Minister, the Defender of the People, a group of 50 MPs or of 50 senators, collegial executive organs of the autonomous communities, and in some cases their parliamentary assemblies. The Constitutional Court also examines motions for the defence of constitutional rights and liberties if they are being violated (Art. 53(2)) in cases and in forms detailed in the act on the Constitutional Court. A complaint on the violation of rights can be made by any natural or legal person, the Defender of the People, and the Prosecutor's Office. The Constitutional Court also resolves conflicts of authority between the state and the autonomous communities, as well as between individual autonomous communities. Courts also can file a motion with the Supreme Court for an interpretation of the law, though the so-called prejudicial question[175].

The Prosecutor's Office was integrated with the judicial branch based on the Act of 30 December 1981, while retaining its autonomy.[176] Under Art. 124(1) of the Constitution, the duties of the Prosecutor's Office include supporting the activities of the justice system in the defence of legality, citizens' rights and the public interest defended by the acts of parliament. Another duty of the Prosecutor's Office is watching over the independence of courts and appearing before them on behalf of the public interest. Prosecutors can act both *ex officio* and at the motion of the interested parties. The Prosecutor's Office consists of the following organs: Prosecutor General (*Fiscal General del Estado*), the Prosecution Council (*Consejo Fiscal*), the Assembly of Prosecutors of the Chamber of the Supreme Court (*Junta de Fiscales Jefes de Sala del Tribunal Supremo*) together with the Assembly of Prosecutors of Autonomous Communities (*Junta de Fiscales de la Comunidades Autónomas*), Prosecution of the Supreme Court (*Fiscalía del Tribunal Supremo*), Prosecution of the National Court (*Fiscalía de la Audiencia Nacional*), Prosecution of the Court of Accounts (*Fiscalía del Tribunal de Cuentas*), Special Prosecutors' Offices (*Fiscalías Especiales*) including the Special Prosecutor's Office Against Drug Trafficking (*Fiscalía especial contra el Tráfico de Estupefacientes*), the Special Prosecutor's Office Against Corruption and Organized Crime (*Fiscalía*

174 Organic Law of 3 October May 1979 regarding the Constitutional Court, B.O.E. no. 239.

175 See: T. Mołdawa, *System konstytucyjny…*., op. cit., pp. 129–131.

176 Law 50/1981 of 30 December 1981 por la que se regula el Estatuto Orgánico del Ministerio Fiscal, , B.O.E. no. 11.

Especial contra la Corrupción y la Criminalidad Organizada), Territorial Prosecutors' Offices (*Fiscalías Territoriales*), including: Prosecution of the Autonomous Communities (*Fiscalía de las Comunidades Autónomas*), the Provincial Prosecutors' Offices (*Fiscaliás Provinciales*), and Local Prosecutors' Offices (*Fiscalías de Área*). The State Prosecutor General (*Fiscal General del Estado*) is appointed by the monarch at the motion of the government, after consultation with the General Council of the Judiciary. The General Prosecution Council is an advisory institution for the Prosecutor General. There are three categories of prosecutors: Prosecution Attorney (*Abogado Fiscal*), Prosecutor (*Fiscal*) and Supreme Court Prosecutor (*Fiscales de Sala del Tribunal Supremo*). Prosecutors enjoy a status comparable to judges.

The institution of the Defender of the People was formed based on the 1978 Constitution (Art. 54). In the Organic Act on the Defender of the People of 6 April 1981, its position in the government system was further specified.[177] The Defender is a high commissioner of the Cortes Generales, and is appointed by the parliament in order to defend the rights and liberties specified in the Constitution. As previously mentioned, the Defender can refer both constitutional complaints and ones regarding the defence of rights to the Constitutional Court. He or she can also motion for the Prosecution to take appropriate actions. Each legal and natural person can address the Defender of the People, citing a legal interest. The Defender of the People is obliged to present an annual report to the Cortes Generales. Additionally, in 1992, a Mixed Committee for contacts with the Defender of the People was formed, consisting of both MPs and senators.

The final institution described here is the Court of Accounts, which also has the status of a constitutional organ (Art. 136, 153). The Court of Accounts not only conducts control activities, but is also entitled to rule on actions taken by individuals responsible for the use of public resources. It can also award damages and impose fines.[178] The control function is of an external, continual character and consists of verifying whether the economic and financial activity of the public sector is conducted in accordance with the principles of legality, effectiveness and economy. The judicial function consists only of instituting proceedings regarding financial liability in connection with managing public property and goods. The Court of Accounts is a collegial organ and consists of financial auditors. The most important organs of the Court of Accounts are the Plenum (*Pleno*) and the

177 Organic Law of 7 May 1981 regarding the Defensor del Pueblo, BOE no. 109–937 with amendments.

178 Organic Law of 7 May 1981 regarding the Defensor del Pueblo, BOE no. 109–937 with amendments.

President (*Presidente del Tribunal de Cuentas*). The principles of independence, irremovability and incompatibility of multiple positions also refer to the President and financial auditors, who can only be removed through a disciplinary process. The Court presents the Cortes with an annual report, as well as around 30 separate reports on selected issues.

Table 10. The composition, method of selection and terms of the organs and institutions of judicial power in Spain (state for 2011)

Organ	Number of members selected by the executive branch	Number of members selected by the legislative branch	Number of members selected by the judicial branch	Term length
Supreme Court			**President of the Supreme Court**, like the other judges, are elected by the General Council of the Judiciary	5 years
National Court			**President of the National Court**, like the other judges, are elected by the General Council of the Judiciary	5 years
General Council of the Judiciary	**The Minister of Justice** is automatically a member of the Council	**8 members** of the Council are elected by the parliament from out of attorneys and lawyers (4 members by the Congress of Deputies and 4 by the Senate) through 3/5 majority vote. **12 members** are elected from a list proposed by professional associations of judges and by non-aligned judges (6 by the Congress of Deputies, 6 by the Senate) through 3/5 majority vote.	The President of the Supreme Court is the President of the Council	5 years without the right to re-election except the President of the Council

Organ	Number of members selected by the executive branch	Number of members selected by the legislative branch	Number of members selected by the judicial branch	Term length
Constitutional Court	**2 judges** appointed by the government	**4 judges** are elected by the Congress of Deputies through 3/5 majority vote **4 judges** are elected by the Senate through 3/5 majority vote based on the list of candidates proposed by the regional parliaments	**2 judges** appointed by the General Council of the Judiciary	9 years without the right to re-election
Prosecutor's Office	**The Prosecutor General** is appointed at the motion of the government			4 years without the right to re-election
Defender of the People		First elected by the Congress of Deputies through 3/5 majority vote, and then by the Senate also by 3/5 majority		5 years with the right to re-election
Court of Accounts		**6 members** (financial auditors) elected by the Congress of Deputies through 3/5 majority vote **6 members** (financial auditors) elected by the Senate through 3/5 majority vote based on the list of candidates proposed by the regional parliaments Members of the Court elect a **President** for a three-year term.		9 years with the right to re-election

Source: own work.

When analysing the composition, method of appointment and the terms of each organ of the judicial branch and institution of special mandate, it should be emphasised that to a much larger extent than in Poland, the legislative power influences the selection of members of individual organs and institutions. The procedure for the selection and appointment of judges to the main organs of judicial power is almost entirely in the hands of the General Council of the Judiciary, which is elected by the Cortes Generales. Among the 22 members of the Council, as many as 20 are elected by the parliament, of which 12 members are elected from a list proposed by the professional associations of judges and by judges not belonging to the Judicial Council, while 8 are proposed by members of parliament. Therefore, none of the members of the Council is elected by judges themselves. In the case of the Constitutional Court, the government appoints 2 judges, the Cortes Generales 8, and the General Council of the Judiciary appoints 2. Additionally, the Defender of the People and the Court of Accounts are selected by the Spanish Parliament. Only the Prosecutor General is appointed by the government. Therefore, what is symptomatic of the Spanish judicial branch is the strong influence of the legislature. What is especially worrying from the point of view of the separation of powers is the method by which members of the General Council of the Judiciary and the Court of Accounts are selected. It should, however, be emphasised that the requirement of a 3/5 majority in the vote leads to compromise between the governing majority and the opposition. This is a kind of safeguard, preventing the most important positions in the country from being filled by the winner of the election, which is especially important in Spain where, since 1982, only two parties have been in power – PSOE and PP.

4.2.2. Political practice

According to the law as of 2011, aside from the judiciary and the prosecutor's office, the composition of each of the institutions described here depended on the legislative or the executive branch. Because of the method of appointing members to the General Council of the Judiciary, the legislative branch also has an influence on the judicial branch. This is why the General Council of the Judiciary, which is the managerial organ of the judicial branch, is key from the perspective of horizontal accountability; it is this organ that renders it difficult to speak of an apolitical judiciary in Spain. How is it that one of the organs of the judicial branch decides about the politicisation of the entire system of justice? The Council, as already mentioned, has two kinds of competences. On the one hand, it selects members of the most important institutions of the justice system, including nominating the candidate for the President of the Supreme Court and nominating by a 3/5 majority candidates for members of the Constitutional Court; it also appoints judges in lower instance courts and proposes Supreme Court judges and presidents of tribunals and judges of higher courts for nomination by the crown. On the other hand, it is also responsible for writing opinions on draft bills and other normative acts regarding the judiciary and supervision of the activities of tribunals and courts. This is why, during the entire analysed period of 1982–2011, subsequent governments engaged in efforts to change the method in which members of the Council were appointed.

Until 1985, under the Organic Act on the General Council of the Judiciary, 12 of the body's 20 members were elected by judges adjudicating in courts of lower instance, from among those judges and tribunal/court justices. The other 8 were appointed by the parliament from among prestigious attorneys and lawyers. In 1985, the Felipe González government, having an absolute majority in the Cortes Generales, enacted the Judicial Branch Act (LOAPJ),[179] altering the method of appointing members to the Council. Each of the chambers was still to be elected by a 3/5 majority for 4 Council members each, from among prestigious attorneys and lawyers with at least 15 years of professional practice. However, the method of selecting the other 12 members of the Council was changed. From then on, each house would elect 6 members of the Council from among judges in courts of lower instance and tribunal and court justices. This change in the method of selecting Council members can be seen as an attempt by the González government at eliminating the influence of Francoist judges on the justice system. It is no secret that from the beginning the Council was controlled by judges from Asociación Profeisonal de la Magistratura, whose members were part of the Francoist establishment[180]. This is why deputies of the opposition party PP, something of the heir to Francoism, protested the LOAPJ before the Constitutional Court. However, the Constitutional Court determined that the act was not unconstitutional.[181]

After the PP came to power in 1996, work began on changing the method of appointing the Council's members. As a consequence, in 2001 a new amendment to the LOAPJ was enacted as the People's Party enjoyed an absolute majority in the Congress of Deputies. That said, the changes were mostly "cosmetic" – 8 members are still elected by the parliament from among attorneys and lawyers, while the other 12 are also elected by the parliament, with the difference that they come from a list proposed by professional associations of judges and by non-aligned justices. From among 36 candidates presented by the associations, the Congress of Deputies elects 6 judges. However, these modifications in the method

179 Organic Law of July 2 1985 on the Judiciary, BOE. no. 157.

180 Via R. Serra Cristóbal, *La elección de los meibros del Consejo General del Poder Judicial. Una propuesta de Consejo más ingrador e indepenciente*, "Tería y Realidad Constitucional" 2013, no. 31, pp. 277–322.

181 See.: Recurso de inconstitucionalidad no. 839/1985, B.O.E. no. 193 of 13 August 1986.

of electing Council members has not increased the organ's independence.[182] Although candidates are proposed by associations, in practice they have political affiliations, which in Spain's party system boils down to PSOE or PP. This is best illustrated by the data from Council elections following the changes in 2001. From among the 12 elected members, 9 were candidates of associations, while 3 were nonaligned. The associations account for slightly less than 50% of all judges.[183] In reality, neither of the two parties that have alternately ruled Spain for over 20 years is interested in losing influence on the justice system, which is clear in the character of the changes passed by the PP in 2001 when it had absolute majority in the Congress of Deputies.

When analyzing Chart 22, it can easily be observed that beginning from 2010 the Council has been viewed much less favourably by respondents. This is not, however, related to changes made by lawmakers, but is likely due to the loss of trust in public institutions that began with the start of the economic crisis in 2008. The Spanish institutional system started coming in for harsh criticism both in mass media and in scholarly publications. This is likely the explanation for the drastic increase in the prevalence of negative opinions on the Council.

Chart 22. General Council of the Judiciary

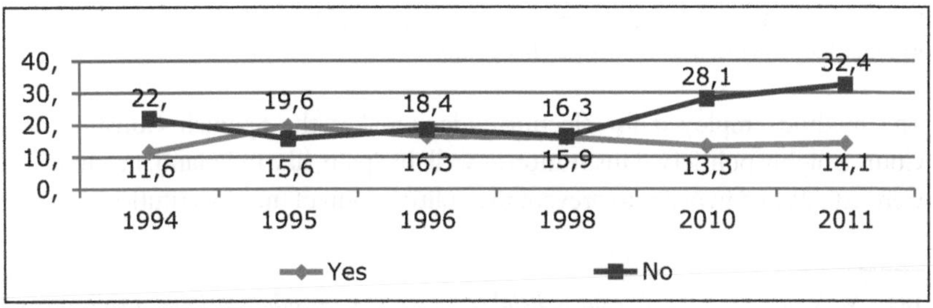

Source: own work based on the data on the website of Centro de Investigaciones Sociológica, datosbd.cis.es/ciswebconsultas/serieSearchLoad.htm#.

Not only is the activity of the Council viewed negatively by Spanish society. Opinions about the courts are poor, and trust towards them in Spain is weak. M. Villoria notes that in the case of the courts these opinions should not be associated

182 See: Ley Orgánica sobre composición del Consejo General del Poder Judicial por la que modifica la Ley Orgánica del Poder Judicial of 29 June 2001, B.O.E no. 155.

183 R. Blanco Valéz, *La politización de la justicia*, "Letras libres" 2009, October 2009, p. 43; R. Serra Cristóbal, *La elección de los…*, op. cit., p. 303.

with aspects regarding the independence of the judicial branch or corruption, but rather with the functioning of the judicial branch in terms of effectiveness, as relates to the personal experiences of citizens.[184] The level of trust was very low in 1996. This is the moment when, after 14 years of being in power and enveloped in multiple corruption scandals, PSOE lost power to the PP. The decline in trust that began in 2008 is likely connected with the start of the economic crisis, as previously mentioned in the case of the Council.

Chart 23. Evaluation of the functioning of courts and trust in them in Spain[185]

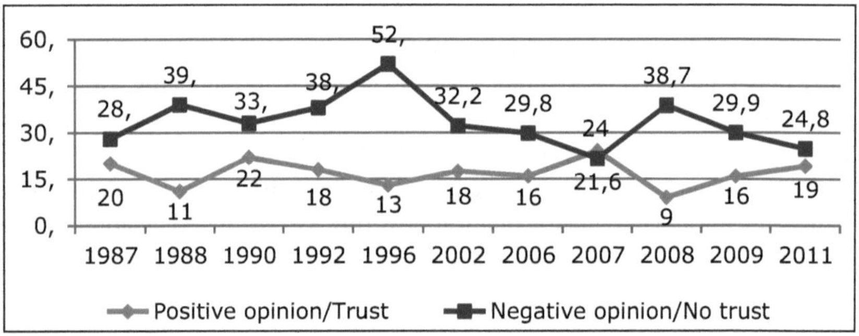

Source: own work based on the data on the website of Centro de Investigaciones Sociológica: http://datosbd.cis.es/ciswebconsultas/serieSearchLoad.htm#.

The method employed for electing judges makes the Spanish Constitutional Court a highly politicised institution as well. In Spain, like in Poland, mechanisms were established in order to prevent the politicisation of the Constitutional Court.

184 M. Villoria, *La corrupción judicial: razones de su estudio, variables explicativas e instrumentos de combate en España*, Paper presented at the VII Congreso Internacional del CLAD sobre la Reforma del Estado y de la Administración Pública, Lisboa, Portugal, 8–11 October 2000, unpan1.un.org/intradoc/groups/public/documents/CLAD/clad0044122.pdf, p. 20.

185 In Spain, polls regarding the activities of courts have not conducted regularly. Therefore, this chart shows the assessment of courts (1987–1992) and trust in courts (1996–2011). The scale for the assessment of courts has five grades, from very good, through good, neither good nor bad, to bad and very bad. On the chart, the "good" includes both very good and good, while "bad" includes both very bad and bad. In the case of trust, the scale has 10 grades, from 0 – no trust (0–1), through little trust (2–3), neither trust nor distrust (4-5-6), high trust (7–8) and very high trust (9–10). In the chart the categories of high and very high trust were added together, as was no trust and little trust.

The first is the requirement of a qualified majority: in both the Congress and in the Senate, the 8 Constitutional Court judges must be elected by a 3/5 majority in each of the houses. The second is the long term of office for Constitutional Court judges, 9 years. The third mechanism is partial renewal of the composition of the Constitutional Court, as every three years 1/3 of the members are appointed. However, these safeguards do not seem to be entirely effective, as practically since the beginning of its existence political parties have made attempts at taking over the Constitutional Court. Additionally, in Spain the mechanism of the so-called casting vote (*voto de calidad*) is employed when the same number of members of the Constitutional Court are for and against a given ruling. In that case, the President of the Constitutional Court can settle the tie. In the history of the Constitutional Court, the President of the Court has cast the decisive vote four times. This negatively influences the public perception of the court and leads to even higher politicisation of the election of its President.

The first Constitutional Court was elected in 1980, mostly on criteria of merit rather than party affiliation. This is evidenced be the election of Manuel García Pelayo as the President of the Constitutional Court, even though he was not the government's preferred candidate. However, the election of new judges in 1989 was conducted in a much different atmosphere. For the first time, the system of "party quotas" was used in the case of judges elected by the Congress of Deputies and the Senate. This meant that PSOE and PP settled the composition of the Court based on the number of seats in the Cortes Generales. Also in 1989, for the first time a judge who had been a senator was elected following nomination by the PP; this recurred in the case of both PP and PSOE. In 1992, the PP, now in the opposition, blocked the election of Constitutional Court judges not because it was against the quota system, but because it believed it was due more judges in the Constitutional Court. Finally, in 2001 the two largest parties decided to negotiate the election of new judges in a so called "package", together with new judges in the Court of Accounts, the previously described General Council of the Judiciary, and the National Energy Commission.[186] This allowed for political balance to be established, often at the cost of the composition of individual institutions. At the same time, substantive criteria became much less important. If we analyse the composition of the first Constitutional Court, we will see that as many as 8 judges are university professors of various legal disciplines. This changed significantly in 2002, when the appointees were individuals with the requisite legal

186 Fundación Alternativas*La estrategia de la crispación. Derrota, pero no fracaso*, Informe sobre la Democracia en España 2008, Madrid 2009, pp. 104–105.

background, but not authorities in any particular area of the law. It also became customary to appoint former Supreme Court judges to the Constitutional Court. In 2001, only 5 of the 12 judges were university professors. The case of the autonomous statute of Catalonia, which was referred to the Constitutional Court in 2007, is an example which clearly demonstrates the instrumentalisation of the Constitutional Court in political disputes. In order for Constitutional Court rulings to meet the expectations of the two major political powers, something assured by the composition of the Court at that time, its membership was not renewed for three years. In 2011, due to a delay in the selection of new judges 1/3 of them served longer than their official term limit (9 years). On the one hand it led to a situation in which the principle of gradual turnover was broken, while on the other it weakened the legitimacy of the Constitutional Court. Another scandal connected with the election of Constitutional Court judges was the fact that one judge withheld information about his membership in the PP.[187] According to the data displayed in Chart 24, the level of trust for the Constitutional Court is rather low. Also, the decline in trust started even earlier than in the case of other institutions, in 2006.

Chart 24. Level of trust in the Constitutional Court in Spain

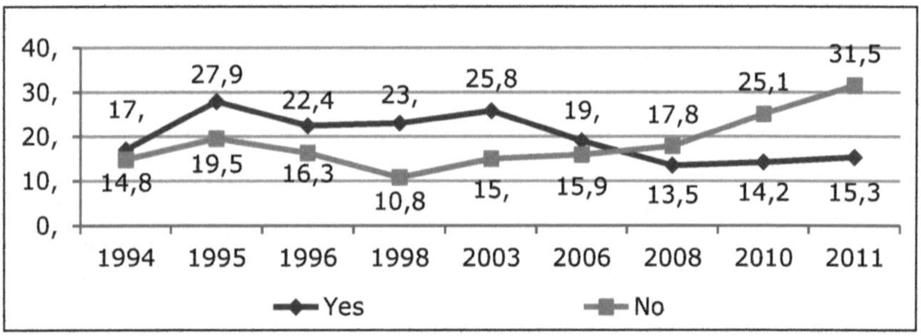

Source: own work based on the data on the website of Centro de Investigaciones Sociológica, datosbd.cis.es/ciswebconsultas/serieSearchLoad.htm#.

In the case of the Prosecutor's Office, it was in 2009 that the Organic Statute of the Prosecution was amended, introducing additional guarantees that strengthened the independence of the Prosecutor General. As a result of these changes, the

187 G. Sala, *La politización del Tribunal Constitucional: ¿Desde cuándo y hasta cuándo?*, "Eldiario.es" z 19.09.2013, www.eldiario.es/agendapublica/nueva-politica/politizacion-Tribunal-Constitucional_0_177082923.html.

office of Prosecutor General can be held by an individual of widely recognised prestige, with at least 15 years of experience. The Prosecutor General can be appointed only for a single 4-year term, and there is a closed catalogue of reasons for which he or she may be dismissed. The selection of the candidate must follow consultations with the General Council of the Judiciary, and the candidate must appear before Congress. Despite these changes, the election of the Prosecutor General, done along party lines, remains controversial. One of the recommendations of GRECO (Group of States Against Corruption), aside from amending the election procedure for members of the General Council of the Judiciary, is the depoliticisation of the office of Prosecutor General. GRECO notes that the politicised method of electing the members of the Council and the Prosecutor General leads to corruption.[188] In the case of the prosecution, there is a lack of polling data, which means we are not aware of how Spanish society rates this institution.

In Spain, the oversight institution is the Court of Accounts. The appointment of Court of Accounts members reflects the political composition of the parliament, and thus in this case as well the requirement of strong support for candidates to this court does not necessarily lead to their greater independence. The division of seats in the Court in the years 1982–2011 was dependent on the division of seats among each party in the Cortes Generales. In practice, this meant the division of seats in the court between the PSOE and PP. The only exception was Lluis Arntet, who represented the Catalan parties. The Court is also criticised for the age of some individuals holding the positions of financial auditors, like Juan Valverde, who has been a member of the Court since 1991, while Ubaldo Nieto has been one since 1982. In the press, the PSOE and PP are accused of a lack of interest in the effective functioning of this institution, which, among other things, controls the financing of political parties. Therefore the court has become a kind of "heritage park" for well-paid, distinguished politicians.[189] Centro de Investigaciones Sociológicas has only once asked about public opinion concerning the Court of Accounts. Among the respondents, 13.2% did place any trust in the Court, while 12.6% declared that they did trust the institution. What distinguishes this particular body is the fact that 44.2% of respondents did not have an opinion about it.[190]

188 Group of States against corruption (GRECO), *Corruption…*, op. cit.

189 D. Focada, *PP y PSOE convierten el Tribunal de Cuentas en un 'geriátrico dorado' a 112.000 € por consejero*, –politica.elpais.com/politica/2013/02/09/actualidad/1360438194_544177.html.

190 Estudio CIS 2309, December 1998, www.cis.es/cis/export/sites/default/-Archivos/Marginales/2300_2319/2309/e230900.html.

The most highly rated institution in Spain is the Defender of the People. This may also be associated with the fact that the Defender enjoys a guarantee of independence not only in the procedural dimension, but also in practice. This can be attested to by the fact that individual Defenders have not belonged to any political parties prior to being appointed. The only exception is Enrique Múgica Herzog, a distinguished PSOE activist, who was the only Defender out of the four holding the position in the years 1982–2011 to be appointed twice. For the first time he was appointed for a five-year term in 2000, when the PP had an absolute majority in the Congress of Deputies. The second time, he took office during the PSOE minority government, in 2005. However, the fact that a distinguished PSOE activist was appointed by a PP government is not in itself an indication of anything, as this was connected with the previously mentioned quota system. The Defender of the People comes in for praise concerning his/her independence of activities by such organisations as Transparency International.[191]

Chart 25. Trust in the Defender of the People

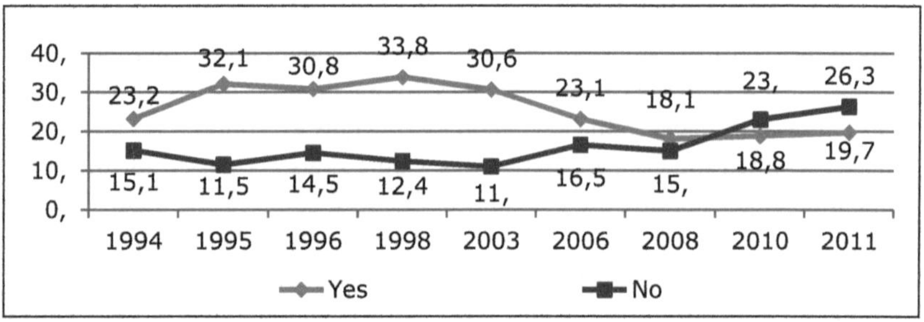

Source: own work na podstawie danych Centro de Investigaciones Sociológicas z lat 1994–2011, datosbd.cis.es/ciswebconsultas/serieSearchLoad.htm#.

In summary, what was to serve the consolidation of democracy has led over the years to deep politicisation of not only the justice system, but also mandate agencies. A statement attributed to Alfonso Guerra, Deputy Prime Minister in the years 1982–1986, which he made after the passage of LOAPJ in 1985 to the effect that "Montesquieu has died"[192] remains widely cited. Additionally, the introduction of party quotas has led to the "colonisation" of control organs, such as in the case of

191 Transparency International. España, *National Integrity System Assessment. Spain*, 28 September 2012, issuu.com/tispain/docs/spain_nis_en?e=6538824/2888443.

192 M. Agís Villa Verde, *Montesquieu ha muerto*, http://www.elcorreogallego.es/opinion/firmas/ecg/montesquieu-ha-muerto/idNoticia-342789/.

the Court of Accounts. The lack of a clear separation of powers in the state can lead to impunity for politicians as well as for officials of the justice system itself, and to corruption. This, in turn, leads to very low trust in the justice system on the part of citizens. The cited poll results would seem to confirm this. The most highly-rated institution is the Defender of the People, followed by the Constitutional Court, while the worst rated ones are courts and the General Council of the Judiciary.

***

When comparing the position of the judicial branch and mandate agencies in Poland and Spain within the system of accountability, it can easily be said that individual institutions and organs differ significantly in terms of composition and method of appointment (Table 9 and 10). In Poland, the procedure of selection and appointment of judges in individual organs of the judicial branch is almost entirely in the hands of the judiciary. In Spain, on the other hand, the legislative branch has influence to a greater extent than in Poland on the selection of members of individual organs and institutions. This is due to the General Council of the Judiciary, which selects and appoints judges to the main organs of the judicial branch, while the Council itself is elected by the Cortes Generales (out of 22 members of the Council, as many as 20 are chosen by the parliament). In the case of the Polish National Council of the Judiciary, as many as 15 out of 25 of its members are elected from among judges and by judges. Therefore, the influence of individual governments on the election of judges in Poland is minimal and is based on legal conditions, while in Spain it is highly politicised. Also, what differentiates the two countries is the method by which the Prosecutor General is appointed. In Poland, since 2010 this appointment has been reliant on the executive to a lesser extent than in Spain. According to the presented opinion poll results, both in Poland and in Spain courts are the lowest-rated institutions (this is also true of the Polish Prosecutor's Office, while no such data is available in the case of Spain). However, it is difficult to declare that this is caused in both countries by the influence of the executive and legislative branches on courts and prosecutors, which was discussed in Chapter 4.

However, when comparing the selection of members of the Constitutional Court, it can be observed that the situation is similar in both Poland and Spain – in both cases the other branches influence the composition of Tribunals. Despite the high level of politicisation affecting the method of selection for the Constitutional Tribunal, particularly in Poland this institution is very highly rated. The situation is radically different concerning the Central Anti-Corruption Bureau, which does not have a Spanish equivalent; in the case of this institution, the negative perception is likely caused by its lack of independence. The methods of electing the Commissioner for Human Rights and the Defender of the People are also similar, as they are appointed by their respective country's parliament. However, in the case of the Supreme Audit Office and the Court of Accounts, the Sejm appoints only the President of the Supreme Account Office, while in Spain the entire Court of Accounts is elected by the lower house of the parliament. The Supreme Audit Office and the Commissioner for Human Rights are the most highly-rated institutions in Poland, which may be associated with the weak influence of the other branches of power on their activities. The case of the Spanish Defender of the People is similar. As for the Court of Accounts, it is hard to draw any conclusions due to the lack of comprehensive research.

What differentiates Poland from Spain is the fact that in the former country candidates are in practice appointed by the parliamentary majority forming the government, while in the latter a 3/5 majority is required. In Spain this leads to the need to arrive at a compromise between the parliamentary majority and the opposition. However, in political practice over recent years it has not lead to the depoliticisation of the judicial branch and mandate agencies. The alternating PSOE and PP governments have resulted in the introduction of party quotas, and therefore a kind of "colonisation" of the institutions of the judiciary and control organs by the main political parties.

Therefore, the analysis presented in chapter four does not allow us to unambiguously confirm the first hypothesis: *In Poland and Spain, the independence of the judicial branch and mandate agencies is more dependent on procedural conditions than on the power configuration in the lower houses of parliament.* Even if one were to consider the correctness of the preceding hypothesis in the case of Poland, the party quotas introduced in Spain seem to counter it.

When analysing the influence of the support that the government enjoys in Poland and Spain on limiting the independence of the judicial branch and mandate agencies, the second hypothesis also cannot be confirmed: *The weaker and less stable the parliamentary support for a given government in Poland and Spain, the lower its ability to limit the independence of the judicial branch and mandate agencies.* The above relation only appears in Spain, while the changes occurring in Poland during the 2005–2007 term do not confirm it.

Similarly, the third hypothesis turned out to be unverified: *The longer the time elapsed from political transformation, the greater the independence of the judicial branch and mandate agencies in the system of accountability, and therefore in Spain it is stronger than in Poland.* The most telling evidence against it comes in the form of the aforementioned party quotas in Spain.

Part III. Vertical accountability

Chapter 5. Determinants of vertical accountability

Every election in Poland during the period 1997–2011, excepting the last, has led to a new party assuming power; meanwhile, in Spain we can distinguish periods in which the same political party succeeded in attaining a large enough advantage to form successive governments (PSOE in the years 1982–1996 and 2004–2011, PP in 1996–2004). Can we therefore assume that Polish voters more eagerly demonstrate their displeasure with the governing class, while Spanish society rewards those exercising power by re-electing them? As it turns out, when transferring the theoretical assumptions of the accountability conception to the empirical sphere, this dependency is quite difficult to prove. This comes as a consequence of difficulties in assessing the extent to which institutional factors serve to limit the application of vertical accountability on the one hand, while on the other it results from the problems that arise in the process of interpreting voters' behaviours.[193] This is also why the effect of institutional determinants will be the object of study in this chapter, while the next chapter will engage the issue of whether Poland and Spain do in fact display evidence of economic voting, itself the measure of vertical accountability.

The capturing of factors displaying of an institutional nature results from the conviction that an analysis of vertical accountability should encompass not only the determinants exerting influence at the individual voter level, but also the general nature of the system, as well as the contexts in which voters function. Indeed, the nature of systemic conditions has an impact on issues associated with assigning responsibility, which in turn hamper the functioning of vertical accountability. G.B. Powell says of this phenomenon that if the citizens of a democratic state are not able to establish responsibility for policies, they are equally unable to use elections as a tool for enforcing responsibility for the manner politics is conducted. When responsibility is unclear, politicians are also less motivated to understand and fulfil the expectations of citizens. Clarity in responsibility is thus an

193 As defined by Raciborski, electoral behaviours are defined as: "(…) the general collection of behaviours revealed in conjunction with the electoral process. This concept thus encompasses behaviours of various types: taking an electoral decision and its content, both voting and refraining from voting, interest in elections, participation in campaigns, and passivity". J. Raciborski, *Polityka polska. Szkice*, Warsaw 2003, p. 96.

important condition in the exercise by voters of their oversight.[194] This is also why factors of an institutional nature limiting the capacity of politicians being held to account, both in the procedural dimension and in respect of ultimate effects, will be the object of the investigations presented in this chapter. The procedural factors explored will include the type of electoral system and territorial structure of a country. Among the determinants from the second group, the studies will address the type of party system and type of government. The significance and role of each determinant in the system of horizontal accountability will be discussed in successive subchapters. It should also be mentioned here that analysis of the determinants impacting electoral accountability will not be comprehensive. Certain tendencies visible in the two political systems will be described. Organising the chapter in this manner will make it possible to find an answer to the main research question, which is: Do institutional factors disrupt the functioning of mechanisms of vertical accountability in Poland and Spain? Hypothesis: Both in Poland and in Spain we may speak of determinants of an institutional nature which disrupt the functioning of vertical accountability, which is a result of the institutional architecture adopted in both political situations, while the more time that has passed since the moment of systemic transformation, the lesser are the distortions of vertical accountability.

5.1. The electoral system

G.B. Powell and G.D. Whitten point to the influence of electoral systems on the capacity of citizens to exercise oversight of their government. The authors emphasise *inter alia* that in majority systems it is easier to assign responsibility to parties, whereas the picture becomes muddied under proportional systems.[195] This means that majority systems produce both victors and vanquished in absolute terms, while proportional systems generate relative winners and relative losers. Furthermore, the type of electoral system adopted has an influence on the capacity for formation of single- or multi-party governments, the latter of which make accountability more difficult.[196] To put it differently, majority systems generally

194 G.B. Powell, *Wybory…*, op. cit., p. 57.

195 G.B. Powell, G. D. Whitten, *A Cross-National…*, op. cit., pp. 391–414, G. B. Powell, *Wybory…*, op. cit.

196 For more on the subject of the polemic on the effects of electoral systems, see D. Nohlen, *Prawo wyborcze i system partyjny*, Warsaw 2004, pp. 404–423.

ensure one-party governments in which large parties rule independently, which in turn makes it easier to hold those governments to account.[197]

In conclusion, from the perspective of vertical accountability, the greater the proportionality of an electoral system, the more significant are the problems voters have with determining the accountability of governments. This is a result of the extensive party fragmentation and coalition governments that typically develop out of proportional electoral systems. In this portion of the book analysis will also be undertaken of the electoral systems in Poland and Spain, both of which are proportional; comparison will be made of both the degree of proportionality and of the stability of the electoral systems in the two countries, as it is precisely these two dimensions of the electoral system which would seem to be of significance when considering vertical accountability. In both cases only the lower house of parliament will be subjected to analysis. Measuring and comparison of the degree of proportionality exhibited by the two systems will be performed using indices that are applied in determining the disproportionality between electoral preferences and the ultimate party configuration. The lower the value of an index, the higher the level of proportionality; this means that electoral preferences are more faithfully reflected in the composition of particular terms of parliament. However, there is no consensus as to which of the existing indices is the most adequate in measuring disproportionality. None of them are universal in nature, as the fit of a given index is largely dependent on the electoral formula applied in a given system.[198] As argued by M. Gallagher, every method used in calculating disproportionality is inextricably bound up with the electoral formula in use, and every formula generates its own index.[199] Nevertheless, there are cases such as that of Poland in which the electoral formula has been changed

---

197 In proportional systems, power is frequently exercised jointly by various political parties, which leads to problems with assigning responsibility for the activities of the government. It should, however, be added that while in majoritarian systems the issue of responsibility is clear, the distance between the median voter and the government is also greater. This means that majoritarian institutions lead to governments being more distant from voters in the political sphere, while being easier to hold accountable. For more see: B. Manin, S. Przeworski, S. Stokes, *Elections and Representation*, S. Przeworski, S. Stokes, B. Manin, (eds.) *Democracy…*, op. cit., p. 47.

198 A. Lijphart, *Electoral Systems and Party Systems. A Study of Twenty-Seven Democracies, 1945–1990*, Oxford 1994, p. 57; G. W. Cox, M. S. Shugart, *Comment on Gallagher's Proportionality, Disproportionality and Electoral Systems*, "Electoral Studies" 1991, no. 10, pp. 348–352.

199 M. Gallagher, *Proportionality, Disproportionality and Electoral Systems*, "Electoral Studies" 1991, no. 10, pp. 33–51.

on multiple occasions in recent decades, and thus selecting one index for the applied electoral formula would not be the best solution. In addition, it would be difficult to make comparisons across states in which various electoral formulas have been used. This is why in the majority of comparative scholarly works the disproportionality index offered by M. Gallagher is applied, which many researchers feel to be the most useful in examining the level of proportionality in an electoral system. This work will also use the index proposed by that author as the primary measure of disproportionality, although by way of comparison other propositions for grading the proportionality of electoral systems: the Saint Laguë Index, the adjusted Rae's Index, the Loosemore and Handby Index, the d'Hondt Index and the Lijphart Index.

The starting point in this section of the book will be an analysis of the evolution of electoral law in the two countries as well as its potential significance for vertical accountability. As P. Bellucci has proven, changes in electoral systems can impact the use of economic voting, which is the gauge of vertical accountability. In that author's opinion, the stability of the party system in Italy through 1993 was associated with socio-political divisions of a primarily religious nature, which led to the failure of economic voting to emerge. However, the 1993 change in the electoral system from a proportional to a mixed one resulted in the weakening of party loyalties and growth in the importance of the carrot/stick mechanism when explaining electoral behaviours.[200] In other words, he proved that changes in the electoral system can be a factor that allows for the maintenance of strong ideological identifications as well as for their relaxation. While the objective of this portion of the book is not to explore the correlation between changes in the electoral system and the ideological self-identification of voters, the aforementioned studies do confirm the relationship between the stability of the law underpinning an electoral system and vertical accountability. In other words, frequent changes in the electoral system may lead to the use of economic voting.

5.1.1. Poland

In accordance with Art. 96(2) of the Polish Constitution, elections to the lower house of parliament are conducted under a proportional system with electoral districts uneven in respect of the number of mandates up for grabs. The primary elements of the present electoral law are: threshold of 5% for political parties and

200 P. Bellucci, *From class voting to economic voting – Patterns of individualization of electoral behavior in Italy*, in: H. Dorussen, M. Taylor (eds.), *Economic...op.cit.* pp. 261–283.

8% for electoral coalitions, 41 electoral districts (number of seats from 7 to 20), and the use of the d'Hondt formula to convert votes into seats. Voters employ a so-called preferential vote for a semi-open electoral slate. In practice this means that seats go in order to the candidates who receive the largest number of votes on a given list.

Characteristic of the Polish electoral system since 1989 is the absence of continuity. Since that year, which marks the beginning of atransition, through 2011, and thus until the moment the Electoral Code was adopted, there were four different electoral laws in place for the lower house of parliament. The first was adopted on 7 April 1989 and was to be in force for successive terms in 1989–1993.[201] Only 35% of MPs (136 seats) were to be selected in a fully democratic manner in free elections; their seats were to be filled under a majority electoral system. In this manner the so-called Contract Sejm was elected. That very Sejm adopted on 28 June 1991 a new electoral law in conjunction with snap elections. The new law was not only fully democratic, but also featured the most proportional electoral system in the history of democratic Poland[202]. It was characterised by the absence of a threshold; the only restriction was the necessity of collecting 5.000 signatures from voters in order to register an electoral committee. At the same time, in the event that a given committee gathered 50.000 signatures and/or registered its slates in at least 5 electoral districts, it could field candidates in all of the remaining electoral districts as well. For the first time a nationwide list was introduced (69 seats), which was designed to reinforce the position of the strongest parties. The lack of restrictions at the level of electoral thresholds and the invocation of one of the most proportional systems for counting votes (Hare-Niemeyer) combined with the 5% electoral threshold (the Sainte Laguë formula was applied to the nationwide list) gave the electoral law an extremely proportional character.

Elections were held in 1993 and 1997 under the electoral law passed on 28 May 1993.[203] Changes were made both to the electoral formula and to the requirements for registering electoral committees. Concerning the former, the Hare-Niemeyer system was discarded in favour of d'Hondt, while in respect of the latter the bar for registration of an electoral committee was lowered to just 3.000 signatures, but they had to be gathered in 26 electoral districts, *i.e.* half of the total number. One relaxation was the possibility of registering committees across the entire country without the necessity of gathering signatures in the case of groups which had at

201 The Act of 7 April 1989 on Elections to the Sejm of the Polish People's Republic of the 10th Term, for the years 1989–1993, OJ L1989 no. 19 item 102.
202 The Electoral Law of the Sejm of Poland of 28 June 1991, OJ L 1991 no. 59 item 252.
203 The Electoral Law of the Sejm of Poland of 28 June 1993, OJ L 1993 no. 45 item 205.

least 15 MPs during the previous term of office. An entirely new aspect was the introduction of electoral thresholds of 5% for political parties and 8% for electoral coalitions. However, the 69-mandate nationwide list was maintained, while the manner in which those seats were apportioned was altered and the d'Hondt formula adopted. This change in the electoral regime led to far-reaching changes in the party system.

The next amendment to the election law was enacted under the act of 12 June 2001.[204] Only the electoral thresholds remained unaltered. The electoral formula was again changed to that of Sainte Laguë, while the number of signatures required to register an electoral committee was increased to 5.000. Another significant change was the introduction of a new number of districts and of seats, which was associated both with the new administrative division of the country that had been enacted, as well as the elimination of the nationwide slate. The number of electoral districts was reduced to 41. Another change was the reintroduction of the d'Hondt formula, but the amendment of the electoral law passed on 25 July 2002 was limited only to a change in the manner in which votes were counted.[205] The last amendment to the electoral system was the adoption on 5 January 2011 of the Electoral Code, while from the perspective of elections to the lower house the sole significant change was the introduction of the requirement to allot at least 35% of the places on electoral lists to women.

Table 11. Changes in the Polish election system in the period 1991–2011

Election year	Number of electoral districts	System for apportioning seats	Electoral threshold
1991	37 districts (7–19) plus one nationwide electoral district (69)	Hare-Nimeyer modified Sainte Laguë	5% support (or winning seats in at least five districts as a condition of receiving seats from the nationwide list)
1993	52 districts (3–17) plus one nationwide electoral district (69)	d'Hondt	5% for electoral committees, 8% for electoral coalitions, 7% for the nationwide list

204 The Electoral Law of the Sejm and the Senate of Poland of 12 April 2001, OJ L 2001 no. 46 item 499.

205 The Act of 26 July 2002 on amendments to the Act on the Electoral Law of Commune Councils, County Councils and Provincial Assemblies, and on amendments to some other Acts, OJ L 2002 no. 127 item 1089.

Election year	Number of electoral districts	System for apportioning seats	Electoral threshold
1997	52 districts (3–17) plus one nationwide electoral district (69)	d'Hondt	5% for electoral committees, 8% for electoral coalitions, 7% for the nationwide list
2001	41 districts (7–19)	Modified Sainte Laguë	5% for electoral committees, 8% for electoral coalitions
2005	41 districts (7–19)	d'Hondt	5% for electoral committees, 8% for electoral coalitions
2007	41 districts (7–19)	d'Hondt	5% for electoral committees, 8% for electoral coalitions
2011	41 districts (7–19)	d'Hondt	5% for electoral committees, 8% for electoral coalitions

Source: M. Chmaj, W. Skrzydło, *System wyborczy w Rzeczypospolitej Polskiej*, Warsaw 2011, p. 65.

Frequent changes in the electoral system are not only a Polish specificity, as they have taken place in the majority of states in Central and Eastern Europe which engaged in a difficult systemic transformation at the beginning of the 1990s. The majority of them adopted a proportional electoral system in order to provide maximum representation of various electoral preferences. Later changes to electoral laws can, of course, be justified by the need to find a system that would combine the benefits of stability and representation, a difficult challenge in young democracies. There is no shortage of opinions, however, that frequent changes in electoral regulations – at least in the case of Poland – were associated with "electoral engineering" rather than the need to seek a compromise between stability and representation, particularly regarding those introduced into a consolidated political system.[206] This is the way J. Raciborski writes about the procedure: "In political practice, electoral law is rarely treated as a constitutional foundation of

206 R. Katz has classified the most common reasons why those in power decide to change the electoral rules that allowed them to achieve power. He distinguishes six: 1.The winners may believe that their continued victory is seriously threatened under the existing rules; 2. The winners are not entirely in control of the situation, and can have reforms imposed upon them; 3. There is division of interests among the members of the winning coalition; 4. Those able to adopt electoral reforms are overly optimistic about their own prospects under the new system, or misperceive its probable consequences; Parties may value long-term change in the competitive system over short-term electoral advantage; Parties may be willing to trade electoral advantage for other goals. From R. Katz, *Why Are There So Many (or So Few) Electoral Reforms?* in: M. Gallagher, P. Mitchell (eds.), *The Politics of Electoral Systems*, Oxford 2005, pp. 57–76.

the state. In Poland this amounts to one of our politicians' favourite toys, which they play with in the face of utter passivity on the part of the citizenry. This passive attitude is understandable, as electoral engineering and assessment of its effects require extensive expertise that cannot be expected of the general population."[207]

Setting aside the issue of what motivated the legislature at various times to make changes in Poland's electoral system, it should be emphasised that frequent changes in the electoral regime also impacted the level of proportionality in the system. That said, in Poland's case the previously mentioned problem with selection of the proper index emerged, owing to the frequent changes in the electoral formula. In this situation the selection of the Gallagher index would seem all the more justified. Referring to the calculations of J.R. Montero and P. Riera performed on the basis of 403 elections conducted in 32 democracies during the period, the average value of this index for proportional systems was 3.34, while for mixed systems it was 6.14, and for majority systems 10.21.[208] In Poland, during the period under study the average of this index oscillated around 6.90, which would indicate a mixed system under the calculations of the aforementioned authors. Nevertheless, it should be recalled that in the case of this index we are dealing with a distortion that results from the grouping together of all small parties, which makes the M. Gallager index a rather blunt instrument in spite of its widespread use.

The highest level of disproportionality in reference to the data from Table 12 was recorded during the 1997 elections, and while this most certainly may be associated with the use of the d'Hondt formula, it should also be kept in mind that as many as 23 of 52 electoral districts awarded no more than 7 seats, which reduces the impact of the d'Hondt formula as one effecting proportionality. In 2001 a new division of electoral districts was introduced, making them less numerous while giving them more seats. This most likely lead to reductions in disproportionality, something also attested to by the fact that, in spite of the use of the Sainte Laguë formula in 2005 and the retention of electoral districts' previous size, the data in the table indicate that this had no impact on reducing disproportionality in comparison to the year 2001. This is additionally attested to by the index from 2007, which dropped significantly in spite of the return to the d'Hondt

207 J. Raciborski, *Teoria demokracji a reguły wyborów*, „Nauka" 2006, no. 3, www.pan.poznan.pl/nauki/N_306_02_Raciborski.pdf, p. 30.

208 J.R. Montero, P. Riera, *El sistema electoral español: cuestiones de desproporcionalidad y de reforma*, "Anuario de la Facultad de Derecho de la Universidad Autónoma de Madrid" 2009, pp. 237–238.

formula. In 2011 it rose slightly. Thus, in accordance with the results displayed in Table 12, the correlation among individual indices is significant.

Table 12. Indices of disproportionality of the Polish electoral system in the years 1997–2011

Index %	1997	2001	2005	2007	2011	Average
Saint Laguë	21.27	10.60	14.08	5.71	7.06	11.74
Rae (corrected)	3.63	2.25	2.25	2.22	2.48	2.57
Lossemore&Handby	18.30	9.37	13.03	7.91	10.08	11.74
d'Hondt (Lijphart)	9.80	5.92	6.70	3.98	5.82	6.44
Lijphart	10.58	6.33	6.96	4.67	5.94	6.90
Gallagher	10.58	6.34	6.97	4.67	5.95	6.90

Source: own calculations on the basis of information given by www.pkw.gov.pl.

The changes described above in the electoral regime are also reflected in the values of indices referring not only to the electoral level, but the parliamentary one as well. Values of the fractionalisation index point to a decline in the diffusion of the Polish political scene in the years 1997–2011. An exception was the year 2005, but within the context of the period under study the years 2007 and 2011 also demonstrated visible declines. The hyperfractionalisation index turned out to be an even more sensitive instrument, as its deviation was even greater in 2005; it can clearly be seen that in the last two terms of office in the period being reviewed we are encountering the lowest level of fractionalisation. The total of votes received by the two largest parties and the number of seats also grew. In accordance with the figures displayed in Table 13, the value of the index of the sum of the two largest parties at the electoral level oscillated between 51.12% and 73.62%, while at the parliamentary level from 61.09% to 81.52%. As in the case of the previously mentioned fractionalisation index, there are also significant differences in respect of the sum of the two largest parties for the 2005–2007 term and that of 2007–2011.

Table 13. Indices of fragmentarisation, concentration, and the effective number of parties at the electoral and parliamentary level in Poland during the years 1997–2011

Index (%)	1997	2001	2005	2007	2011	Average
Rae Fragmentation Index (votes)	0.78	0.78	0.83	0.70	0.73	**0.76**
Rae Fragmentation Index (seats)	0.66	0.72	0.77	0.65	0.67	**0.69**

Index (%)	1997	2001	2005	2007	2011	Average
I Kesselman and Wildgen Hyperfractionalization Index (votes)	6.15	6.24	7.68	4.09	4.78	**5.80**
I Kesselman and Wildgen Hyperfractionalization Index (seats)	3.46	4.73	5.00	3.22	3.63	**4.01**
Sartori Competition Index (votes)	6.70	28.35	2.85	9.40	9.29	**11.32**
Sartori Competition Index (seats)	8.04	32.83	4.78	9.35	10.87	**13.17**
Laakso&Taagepera Effective Party Number Index (votes)	4.57	4.50	5.86	3.32	3.74	**4.40**
Laakso&Taagepera Effective Party Number Index (seats)	2.95	3.60	4.26	2.82	3.00	**3.33**

Source: own calculations on the basis of information given by www.pkw.gov.pl.

In summary, it should be said that the Polish electoral system during the analysed period was not at all an extremely proportional one. This undoubtedly leads to reduced limitations in the potential to employ the reward/punishment mechanism, although not exactly as in the case of majoritarian systems. However, what indisputably contributes to the use of economic voting, which is the measure of vertical accountability, is that the frequent changes in Polish political conditions associated with frequent changes in the electoral system make it more difficult to build lasting political affiliations among voters; in accordance with the theory of P. Bellucci, this could contribute to the use of the economic vote.

5.1.2. Spain

Similarly to the case of Poland, in Spain we encounter a bicameral system where the role of the Senate is essentially the chamber of the second reading. The electoral threshold has been set at 3%, at the level of the electoral district, which in Spain is equivalent to a province (52 electoral districts). The d'Hondt formula is employed to convert votes into seats. At the same time, closed electoral lists were introduced, and voters select a party without being able to change the order of candidates on the list. Another feature of the Spanish electoral system is that one may not vote for an independent candidate. A distinguishing element of the Spanish electoral system, universally emphasised by Spanish scholars, is its low proportionality. In the name of stability, representativity was sacrificed at the altar of the Spanish electoral system. By the same token, the low level of fractionalisation in the party system was also achieved at the cost of representativity. This type of system was implemented in 1977 with the Decree on the Electoral Rules.[209] The Decree served as the legal basis for the elections of both 1979 and 1982, in spite of its initially temporary character. It should also be added that the electoral system established in 1977 was the product of negotiations between various political forces; to a large extent it was a response to the guarantee of representation by the then-ruling UCD. That party desired to ensure electoral victory for itself by reinforcing the strength of conservative voters located in the central regions of Spain. This manoeuvre was to ensure the necessary parliamentary majority for UCD in the 1979 elections. On the one hand, constitutionalists sought to avoid electoral fragmentation, which was to facilitate the creation of stable governments; on the other hand, there was the intention to promote the interests of rural and conservative interests before those of urban and progressive groups. In practice, this meant promoting centre-right parties over left-wing ones.[210] Most likely, the fact that the same electoral law established under the 1977 Decree allowed PSOE to take power in 1982 led to the passage in 1985 of the Organic Law on the Electoral Regime (LOREG); this legislation replaced the earlier decree, but did not introduce any significant changes in the electoral system.[211]

Stability of the electoral system is an element of the Spanish political system that is subjected to criticism. A lively debate has lasted for years regarding the necessity of amending the electoral law. Since the eruption of the economic crisis in 2008 it is precisely this "calcification" of the party system, brought about by the majoritarian effects of the electoral system, which is pointed to as the primary cause of the Spanish political system's poor functioning. Regardless of whether it is really the electoral system that is "to blame" for the poor condition Spain has been in over recent years, it should be emphasised that the premium afforded to large parties is significant; this is indicated in the data contained in Table 14, in effect leading to a low level of proportionality and poor reflection of electoral preferences.

---

209 Royal Decree-Law on the Election Rules (RDLNE) 20/1977, 18 March 1977, B.O.E. no. 70.

210 J.R. Montero, F.J. Llera, M. Torcal, *Sistemas electorales en España: una recapitualción*, "Revista Española de Investigaciones Sociológicas" 1992, no. 58, pp. 7–56.

211 Organic Law of 12 May 1982 on the Court of Accounts, BOE no. 121 with amendments.

*Table 14. Difference between the number of votes and seats received in elections in Spain during the years 1982–2011**

Elections	PSOE	AP/PP	CDS	UCD	PCE/IU	UPiD	CiU	PNV
1982	+10.4	+4.7	-2.2	-3.1	-2.4		–0.2	+0.5
1986	+8.5	+3.9	-3.8	-	-2.7	-	+0.1	+0.2
1989	+10.4	+4.8	-3.9	-	-4.3	-	+0.1	+0.2
1993	+6.0	+5.5	-		-4.5	-	0	+0.2
1996	+2.8	+5.7	-		-4.6	-	0	+0.1
2000	+1.6	+7.8	-		-3.2	-	+0.1	+0.5
2004	+4.2	+4.6	-		-3.5	-	-0.4	+0.4
2008	+4.6	+3.6	-		-3.2	-0.9	-0.1	+0.5
2011	+2.6	+8.5	-	-	+3.7	-3.2	+0.1	+0.1

Source: own calculations based on José Ramón Montero, Pedro Riera, *Informe sobre la reforma del sistema electoral*, Presentado a la Comisión de Estudios del Consejo de Estado en Diciembre 2008, p. 24, and www.congreso.es/consti/elecciones/generales/index.htm.
*Plus sign indicates overrepresentation, minus sign represents underrepresentation.

It should be noted here that the primary cause for the quite low level of proportionality in the Spanish electoral system is not only the use of the d'Hondt formula to convert votes into seats, but rather its use in conjunction with a large number of districts having few seats. For example, in 2000 there were 30 districts with between 1 and 5 seats, while the proportional effects of the d'Hondt formula begin to emerge at a level of 7 seats. Those 30 electoral districts concentrated 25% of the population and 33% of the seats in the Congress of Deputies.[212] The situation has not significantly changed since 2000; in the 2011 elections, 35 of 52 electoral districts had no more than 5 seats.

Nevertheless, in analysing the data contained in Table 14 it should be said that the indices of disproportionality are not as high as could be expected on the basis of the public debate surrounding the electoral law, nor the conviction of a portion of Spanish scholars that there is a *de facto* majoritarian system in effect.[213] The average value of the Gallagher index comes in at 6.72, similarly to the

212 C. Moreno, P.Oñate, *Tamaño del distrito y voto estratégico en España*, "Revista Española de Investigaciones Sociológicas" 2004, no. 107, pp. 123–151.

213 Many Spanish scholars emphasize the majoritarian effects of the Spanish electoral system. The high level of disproportionality leads to the conclusion that the Spanish electoral system should be classified with majoritarian ones, rather than "imperfect" proportional systems. For more see: J.R. Montero, J.M. Vallés, *El debate sobre la reforma elctoral: ¿para que´las reformas?*, "Claves de Razón Práctica" 1992, no. 22,

situation in mixed systems. In spite of the absence of changes to the electoral law, on two occasions – 1989 and 2011 – we can observe an increase in the Gallagher index. This resulted from the appearance of new parties in the electoral arena. Therefore, in accordance with the results displayed in Table 14, the correlation between individual indices is high.

Table 15. Indices of disproportionality in the Spanish electoral system in the years 1982–2011

Index %	1982	1986	1989	1993	1996	2000	2004	2008	2011	average
Saint Laguë	12,67	11,28	13,72	10,61	5,69	7,65	5,99	7,01	11,04	9,86
Rae corrected	2,43	2,13	1,90	1,63	1,42	1,38	2,02	1,43	1,64	1,78
Lossemore&Handby	13,87	12,69	15,10	12,01	8,08	8,68	7,35	7,47	11,04	10,72
d'Hondt	9,38	8,24	10,12	6,33	5,40	7,09	4,18	3,44	6,55	7,16
Lijphart	8,14	7,32	8,95	6,80	5,32	5,70	4,59	4,42	6,15	6,70
Gallagher	8,17	7,35	8,97	6,82	5,33	5,72	4,61	4,44	6,18	6,72

Source: own calculations using Indelec software on the basis of information supplied by Boletín Oficial del Estado, www.boe.es.

What, therefore, drives the conviction that the electoral law in Spain produces majoritarian effects? This is most likely associated not as much with the so-called mechanical effects of the electoral system, but rather with the so-called psychological effects, pursuant to the distinction drawn by M. Duverger.[214] The psychological effect does not have a direct impact on the party system, but rather on political elites and voters. It entails adaptation of electoral behaviours and political strategies to the mechanical and reducing effects exerted by the electoral system on the party system. Such a situation demands from political elites that they enter into pre-election alliances in order to take advantage of the effect of a party's overrepresentation. However, in the case of voters, this may lead to a situation in which they do not vote for smaller parties in spite of their feeling that those parties best reflect their views and would protect their interests; they

pp. 2–11; J. R.Montero, *El debate sobre el sistema electoral: rendimientos, criterios y propuestas de reforma*, in: J. Montables (ed.), *El sistema electoral a debate*, Madrid 1998, p. 46; J.M. Vallés, A. Bosch, *Sistemas elecotrasles y gobierno represenativo*, Barcelona 1997; J.R. Montero, P. Riera, *El sistema…*, op. cit., pp. 225–270.

214 For more see: G. Cox, *Making Votes Count Strategic Coordination in the Word's Electoral Systems*, Cambridge 1997; I. Lago, *El voto estratégico en las elecciones generals en España (1997–2000). Efectos y mecanismos causales en la explicación del ocmpartambiento elctoral*, Madrid 2005.

do so in the knowledge that those parties will fail to win any seats. This is also why voters strategically adapt their preferences to the mechanical effects of the electoral system, to avoid wasting their vote. This type of behaviour is labelled strategic or useful voting, which, according to G. Sartori, leads to a constructive effect that occurs prior to voting and influences the distribution of votes.[215] Of course, these are processes of a reciprocal nature, *id est* the psychological effect is impacted by the mechanics of the electoral system, and vice versa. The use of strategic voting boosts electoral support for the two largest parties, while at the same time enhances the effect of the absence of proportionality.

This additionally has an influence on other indices in the electoral and party system. In spite of the existence of a large number of small parties in the Congress of Deputies, fragmentarisation is limited; its average in the period under review was 0.70 (votes) and 0.63 (seats). The hyperfractionalisation index would seem to be more sensitive to changes, yet it too records relatively low values with averages of 5.38 and 3.47. Nevertheless, the level of fractionalisation does not constitute any barrier at all to the performance of parliamentary tasks, as the sum of the two largest parties during the period under review went from 65.8 to 82.64 at the electoral level and 76% and 84.57% at the parliamentary level. The values of yet another index, that of the effective party number, were also very low, between 2.89 and 4.09 at the electoral level, while at the parliamentary level they were between 2.33 and 3.15. The preceding analysis of the values of indices at both the electoral and the parliamentary level indicates that we are faced to a larger degree with the majority effects of the electoral system rather than proportional effects. Furthermore, the studied period is distinguished by the high stability of those values and the absence of large deviations.

---

215 G. Sartorii, *Comparative Constitutional Engineering: An Inquiry into Structures, Incentives and Outcomes*, London 1994, pp. 32, 37, 40; I. Lago, S. Lago, *El sistema electoral español: Una cuantificación de sus efectos mecánico y psicológico*, "Revista de Estudios Políticos" 2000, no. 107, pp. 225–250.

Table 16. Indices of fragmentarisation, concentration, and effective number of parties at the electoral and parliamentary level in Spain in the period 1982–2011

Index (%)	1982	1986	1989	1993	1996	2000	2004	2008	2011	average
Fragmentarization (votes)	0.69	0.72	0.76	0.71	0.69	0.67	0.65	0.69	0.75	**0.70**
Fragmentarization (seats)	0.57	0.63	0.65	0.63	0.63	0.60	0.60	0.64	0.68	**0.63**
Hyperfractionalization (votes)	5.24	5.93	6.80	5.43	4.58	4.60	4.30	4.79	6.79	**5.38**
Hyperfractionalization (seats)	3.06	3.38	3.31	2.78	3.40	3.26	3.36	3.60	5.05	**3.47**
Sum of two largest parties (votes)	74.8	70.5	65.8	74.1	77.2	79.87	82.64	78.25	67.43	**74.51**
Sum of two largest parties (seats)	88.3	82.6	80.6	85.7	84.9	88	88.57	84.57	76	**84.36**
Sartori competition (votes)	21.86	18.20	13.90	4.05	1.17	10.52	5.56	2.16	16.63	**10.44**
Sartori competition (seats)	27.14	22.57	19.43	5.14	4.29	16.57	5.14	2.29	21.14	**12.82**
Effective party number (votes)	3.20	3.59	4.09	3.47	3.21	3.03	2.89	3.19	3.95	**3.40**
Effective party number (seats)	2.33	2.68	2.85	2.67	2.72	2.48	2.53	2.74	3.15	**2.68**

Source: own calculations using Indelec software on the basis of information supplied by Boletín Oficial del Estado, www.boe.es.

In summary, it should be said that while the Spanish electoral system is, like Poland's, nominally a proportional one, in practice it displays characteristics of a majoritarian system. This is associated not only with the institutional architecture of the electoral system, but also with psychological effects. From the perspective of vertical accountability this is a far more advantageous situation: as previously explained, low proportionality is correlated with greater electoral accountability. Nevertheless, the occurrence of strategic voting, which is an effect of so-called strong electoral systems, can have a negative impact on electoral accountability. If we assume that a voter is not satisfied with the activity of the political party holding the reins of power, but does not hold that party to account because the only alternative is a party that voter cannot identify with in the slightest, this leads to a distortion of the vertical accountability process. In multi-party systems this type of voter can cast a vote for a party that was not in power but is also ideologically palatable, as the number of parties on offer is far greater. However, in accordance with the results of studies on strategic voting in Spain, this type of voting occurs in electoral districts with small and average numbers of seats.[216] The stability of electoral regulations characteristic of the Spanish electoral system, in accordance with the theory of P. Bellucci, also contributes to ideological rather than economic voting, by the same token limiting the use of the reward/punishment mechanism through strengthening party and ideological ties.

5.2. The territorial structure of the country

Decentralisation is frequently viewed as a sort of panacea for all types of political and institutional problems. It is *inter alia* perceived as being associated with better oversight of those in power, as it leads to an increase in the number of decision centres and levels of participation. Decentralisation brings administration closer to the citizenry, which should contribute to greater transparency and responsibility of political actors. Nevertheless, in conditions of a decentralised state it is more difficult for citizens to assign responsibility, as it is not entirely clear which rung on the ladder of administration is responsible for a given policy. Does this therefore mean that in highly decentralised states we are faced with problems resulting from the impossibility of controlling those exercising power? In this case, are we in fact blessed by the wonders of decentralisation if there are problems with assigning responsibility? Undoubtedly, this problem affects Spain to a far greater extent than Poland, which is a result of the level of decentralisation of the two countries.

Poland is a unitary decentralised state, while Spain is nominally a regional state whose structure has evolved into that of a federal territorial one.[217] In the "Regional Authority Index", which is composed of many variables used as the basis for measuring various aspects of decentralisation and self-government levels among OECD countries, Poland scored 8 points while Spain scores 22.5[218]. It is precisely the degree of decentralisation which is of key significance when considering the

216 More on the subject of strategic voting: I. Lago Peñas, *El voto estratégico…*, op. cit.; C. Moreno, P.Oñate, *Tamaño del…*, op. cit.

217 For more see: A. Sroka, *Hiszpańska droga do federalizmu*, Wrocław 2008, pp. 87–119.

218 L. Hooghe, G. Marks, A. H. Schakel, *The rise of regional authority: a comparative study of 42 democracies*, New York 2010, pp. 171–186.

difficulties associated with assigning accountability, something that comes into particularly sharp focus in the case of federal states.[219]

Two types of studies can be distinguished regarding the association between decentralisation and accountability, although the number of comprehensive works addressing the subject is not impressive. In the first of them, individual data is used as the basis for measuring the capacity of citizens to assign competencies, and in consequence responsibility, to the appropriate level of administration. However, a problem occurring in this type of studies is the small number of polls in which citizens are asked directly about their knowledge regarding who is responsible for what.[220] The second type of study on the relationship between decentralisation and control of governments is concentrated around the dependency between the condition of the economy – in this case at both the national and the sub-national level – and re-election of governments at both levels. This involves examination of the extent to which re-election or the absence of it exerts influence on the condition of the economy at the subnational and national level. In this type of study, clarity in the assignment of liability is one of the factors that can serve to explain repeated re-election.[221]

---

219 For more see: F. Cutler, *Government Responsibility and Electoral Accountability in Federations*, "Publius. The Journal of Federalism" 2004, no. 2, pp. 19–38; W. Downs, *Accountability Payoffs in Federal Systems? Competing Logics and Evidence From Europe's Newest Federation*, "Publius. The Journal of Federalism" 1999, no. 29, pp. 87–110; S. León, *Who is Responsible for What? Clarity of Responsibilities in Multilevel States: The Case of Spain*, "European Journal of Political Research" 2007, no. 50, pp. 80–109.

220 C. Anderson *Economic Voting and Multilevel Governance: A Comparative Individual-Level Analysis*, "American Journal of Political Science" 2006, no. 50(2), pp. 449–463; C. Anderson, *Institutional Change, Economic Conditions and Confidence and Government: Evidence from Belgium*, "Acta Politica" 2009, no. 44, pp. 28–49, K. Arceneaux, *The Federal Face of Voting: Are Elected Officials Held Accountable for Functions Relevant to Their Office?*, "Political Psychology" 2006, no. 27, pp. 731–745; M. Peffley, *The Voter as Juror: Attributing Resposability for Economic Conditions*, "Political Behavior" 1984, no. 6(3), pp. 275–292; T. Rudolph, *Institutional Context and the Assignment of Political Responsibility*, "The Journal of Politics" 2003, no. 65 (1), pp. 190–215; T. Rudolph, *Who is…*, op. cit., pp. 698–713.

221 Among others: C. Anderson, Economic Voting, *Multilevel Governance and Economic Voting in Canada*, "Canadian Journal of Political Science" 2008, no. 41, pp. 328–354; F. Gélineau, E. Bélanger, *Electoral Accountability in a Federal System: National and Provincial Economic Voting in Canada*, "Publius. The Journal of Federalism" 2005, no. 35 (3), pp. 407–425; F. Gélineau, K. Remmer, *Political Decentralization and Electoral Accountability: the Argentine Experience, 1983–2001*, "British Journal of Political Science" 2006, no. 36 (1), pp. 133–157; K. Remmer, F. Gélineau, *Subnational Electoral*

The following subchapter will present individual data consistent with the first type of studies concerning dependencies between decentralisation and accountability. In the case of Poland, a problem is the lack of studies in which questions are asked directly about assignment of responsibility. This is why other polling research has been used which gives a partial understanding of the extent to which Poles can assign competences. In Spain such studies have been conducted, but they are not of a cyclical nature. In addition, with regard to Spain the results of studies based on economic voting have been invoked. It is worth adding that the results of studies in which economic voting is applied definitively show that in federal states, the dependency between economic results and accountability is far weaker than in unitary states.[222]

5.2.1. Poland

In Poland, from among the three levels of self-government, the most important role is played by the commune; this is visible *inter alia* in the division of funds allocated to various levels of administration.[223] Another indication is the number of people employed in communes, counties, and provinces.[224] Thus, as a result of the decentralisation process that began in the early 1990s, the level which is closest to the average citizen – the commune – has the strongest position in the country's territorial structure. This also has a positive impact on the assignment of responsibility, particularly following the introduction in 2002 of direct elections of prefects and mayors. This would also seem to find confirmation in the results of polls conducted among citizens of Poland. Studies carried out by CBOS indicate that the number of citizens who believe that they have an influence on matters in their commune is far greater than the number of those who feel they have an

Choice: Economic and Referendum Voting in Argentina, 1983–1999, "British Journal of Political Science" 2003, no. 36 (1), pp. 133–157; J. King, *Incumbent Popularity and Vote Choice in Gubernatorial Elections*, "Journal of Politics" 2001, no. 63(2), pp. 585–597.

222 C. Anderson, *Economic Voting and Multilevel…*, op. cit., pp. 449–463.

223 The 1990 Act on Communal Self-Government cemented the position of the commune at the local level. In 1998, legislation was introduced that altered the country's administrative structure, adding two levels: county and province. In 2002, direct elections of prefects and mayors at the local level were introduced.

224 Statistical Yearbook of Poland 2012, www.stat.gov.pl/gus/5840_2844_PLK_HTML.htm, p. 641; J. Bartkowski, *Samorząd terytorialny*, in: J. Raciborski, J. Bartkowski, B. Frątczak Rudnicka, J. Kilias, J.J. Wiatr (eds.), *Demokracja polska 1989–2003*, Warsaw 2002, pp. 147–176.

impact on national matters. These figures in 1992 were 16% and 7%, respectively, while in 2010 they were 52% and 36%.

Chart 26. Feeling of influence of Poles on public affairs (in %)

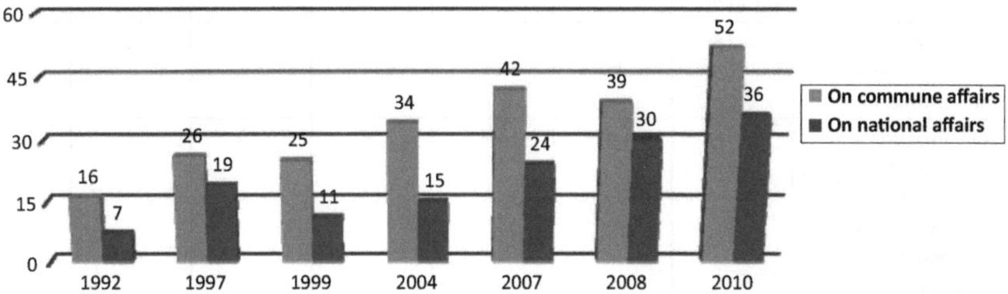

Source: CBOS, Samorządność w Polsce- bilans dwudziestolecia, Communique no. 4383 from CBOS study, BS/144/2010, Warsaw, October 2010.

The result of surveys concerning the role of self-governments and their powers would also seem to confirm the good condition of local democracy. The large majority of those polled is convinced that communal authorities should take responsibility for the majority of matters affecting local communities. As many as 45% of those surveyed felt that communes should be independent in their decisions, while 37% agree with the statement that only the most important decisions should be taken in consultation with central authorities, and only 9% feel that all decisions should be made in cooperation with higher authorities.[225] For this reason as well the answers of respondents to questions about assignment of responsibility should come as no surprise. In their eyes, it is precisely communes which should be responsible for the majority of matters affecting "little fatherlands". In the opinion of respondents, the commune should organise and oversee the majority of institutions. Exceptions are the matters of unemployment, entrepreneurship and the health service; in these cases, only one in four respondents felt that commune authorities are those who should bear responsibility for such matters.

225 CBOS, Samorządność w Polsce- bilans dwudziestolecia, Communique no. 4383 from CBOS research, BS/144/2010, Warsaw, October 2010.

*Table 17. Assigning responsibility to particular levels of administration in Poland (in %)**

	To borough/ neighbour authorities	To commune authorities	To county authorities	To provincial authorities	To central authorities	To EU authorities	Hard to say
Organization and oversight of social aid institutions	13	55	14	7	3	1	7
Organization and oversight of function of schools and other educational and behavioural institutions	6	47	18	13	8	1	7
Organization and oversight of health service institutions	3	28	20	23	17	2	8
Organization and oversight cultural institutions	7	46	18	14	7	0	7
Solving problems and supporting investments related to infrastructure growth	3	32	21	20	11	3	9
Solving problems of unemployment	2	26	22	17	26	2	6
Supporting entrepreneurship	3	27	20	19	19	3	9
Environmental protection	4	33	16	19	19	4	7
Ensuring public order and safety	8	36	20	12	18	1	6

Source: CBOS, Samorządność w Polsce- bilans dwudziestolecia, Communique no. 4383 from CBOS research, BS/144/2010, Warsaw, October 2010.

*In your opinion, authorities at which level bear primary responsibility for the following issues concerning the locality where you live? (in %)

In Poland, we lack detailed data concerning the knowledge of citizens regarding assignment of competences to particular levels of administration. However, it should be expected that Poles will not have any particular difficulty in doing so. This can be attested to both by the convictions of respondents that self-government, primarily at the local level, should take more responsibility on its shoulders, as well as indices of trust placed in self-government authorities by respondents.[226] Vertical accountability is the result of correct assignment of liability. In spite of the lack of comprehensive studies, it would seem that there is no problem with this in Poland. This is a consequence of the unitary structure of the country, and of the key role played by the commune among the three levels of administration. In this situation there is no problem with assigning responsibility; Polish voters, selecting the relevant authorities at the pools, would seem to have clarity regarding who should bear responsibility.

5.2.2. Spain

The level of decentralisation in Spain as measured by the Regional Authority Index is very close to that of federal states. Beginning in the 1980s, Spain has successively transferred powers to autonomous communities. Undoubtedly, the regions have been the primary beneficiaries of the decentralisation process in Spain, mainly at the expense of the central level, but the local level has been impacted as well. In highly decentralised countries we may distinguish two manners of assignment of powers, one of which is very clearly defined as in federal countries of the Anglo-Saxon tradition, such as the United States and Canada. The second type of federal state consists of those which do not feature such a clear division of powers, and many of them are shared, such as in the case of Germany and Austria. Spain, as a quasi-federal state, should be counted among the second type of strongly decentralised countries. In Spain, the distribution of power among particular levels of administration is not defined with precision, at least not to a degree that could result from theoretical models of federalism. We may very frequently encounter a situation where the same powers are exercised by various administrations.[227] The absence of clarity about responsibility leads to a weakening of the effectiveness of control over politicians, and by the same token leads to a weakening of the relations between the effects of implemented policies and holding politicians of the appropriate level of administration to account when voting. Additionally, politicians can take advantage of this muddling of responsibility by taking credit for successful policies that in fact fall outside their sphere of authority, or by accusing another level of administration for the

226 Ibid.

227 J. Rodden, *Hamilton's Paradox: The Promise and Peril of Fiscal Federalism*, Cambridge, 2006.

bad situation and poor governance even though they are the ones in fact responsible for it. Studies show that this is a quite common practice.[228]

Opinion polling conducted in 2010 by Instituto de Estudios Fiscales confirms the fact that Spaniards have difficulty assigning powers to the appropriate level of administration.[229] It turns out that in the Spanish state of autonomous communities, the perceptions of citizens concerning assignment of responsibility to local and central governments are largely consistent with reality; this is not, however, the case in respect of regions. It is the central government which is correctly assigned responsibility for old-age pensions and benefits for the unemployed, whereas communes are mentioned as responsible for managing public gardens and parks. The Spanish autonomous communities, for years the relevant authorities in matters of education, social welfare benefits and the health service, are not identified with those areas by respondents. In addition, studies have shown that this condition did not change significantly between 2005 and 2010; citizens still believe that the central government is responsible for those areas, while the fact is that for over ten years they have been matters for the regions.

*Table 18. Assignment of responsibility to particular levels of administration in Spain**

Areas of authority	Central	Autonomous communities	Communes	Shared	Don't know	Total
Health service (rescue and hospitals)	40.4	44.3	2.5	9.1	3.7	100
Infrastructure (roads, airports, etc.)	50.7	28.3	4.1	13.1	3.8	100
Transport	21.6	29.9	32.1	12.7	3.7	100
Libraries and museums	15.2	22.8	50.9	8.2	2.9	100
Education (schools and universities)	29.1	49.4	8.6	11	1.9	100
Old-age pensions	81.9	8.8	1.8	4.9	2.6	100
Primary social assistance (for the elderly and minors)	37	35.2	12.9	9.9	5	100
Benefits for the unemployed	78.8	10.6	2	6.1	2.5	100
Public gardens and parks	5.6	12.7	75.5	4.6	1.7	100
Disability benefits	74.1	12.6	2.7	7.8	2.7	100
Municipal waste management	7	13.3	69.8	5.7	4.2	

228 K.M. McGraw, *Avoiding Blame: An Experimental Investigation of Political Excuses and Justifications*, "British Journal of Political Science" 1990, no. 20(1), pp. 119–131; K.M. McGraw, R. Timpone, G. Bruck, *Justifying Controversial Political Decisions: Home Style n the Laboratory*, "Political Behavior" 1993, no. 15(13), pp. 289–308; R. Weaver, R.K., *The Politics of Blame Avoidance*, "Journal of Public Policy" 1986, no. 6(4), pp. 371–398.

229 *Opiniones y Actitudes Fiscales 2010, Instituto de Estudios Fiscales*, www.ief.es/documentos/recursos/publicaciones/documentos_trabajo/2011_09.pdf.

Source: Instituto de Estudios Fiscales, *Opiniones y Actitudes Fiscales 2010*, www.ief.es/documentos/recursos/publicaciones/documentos_trabajo/2011_09.pdf.
*In your opinion, which level of administration is responsible for addressing grievances: central, autonomous communities, commune, or is it joint responsibility?

The results of surveys conducted by CiS in 2010 demonstrate that problems with assignment of responsibility in Spain are a result of the specifics of the decentralisation process.[230] Studies were conducted in five autonomous communities, of which four – Andalusia, Galicia, Catalonia, and Basque Country – were granted a full range of powers under the so-called "regionalisation fast-track", while Castile and Leon received them following the so-called "regionalisation slow-track".[231] It should also be recalled that Basque Country enjoys a far greater scope of financial autonomy in comparison with the remaining regions of Spain.[232] Not being conducted in all autonomous communities, the studies were not comprehensive, but they do indicate certain dependencies. As it turns out, in the autonomous communities which received at the very beginning the full range of powers, respondents were more frequently able to correctly assign them to the appropriate levels of administration, whereas in Castile and Leon the responses were more frequently incorrect. Equally interesting is the fact that in the case of Basque Country, respondents assigned powers belonging to the central level, such as

230 *Atribución de responsabilidades*, Centro de Investigación Sociológica CIS no. 2734, 6.10.2007, www.cis.es/cis/opencm/ES/1_encuestas/estudios/ver.jsp?estudio=8900&cuestionario=11236.

231 The process of decentralisation in Spain was an asymmetrical one. Initially a division into regions was implemented, with the full range of powers granted under Art.151 of the Spanish Constitution of 1978, as a result of the so-called regionalisation fast-track. These regions were: Basque Country, Catalonia, Galicia, Andalusia. A similar scope of powers was granted to Valencia under Art. 143 and the Canary Islands under Art. 150.2, as well as Navarra pursuant to the First Additional Provision. The remaining autonomous communities, i.e. Asturias, Balearic Islands, La Rioja, Murcia, Aragon, Castile and Leon, Castile-La Mancha, Estremadura, Cantabria and Madrid received limited powers under Art. 143, following the slow track to regionalisation. For more see: A. Sroka, *Hiszpańska droga…*, op. cit., pp. 87–101.

232 Along with Basque Country, Navarra was also granted a special system of financing. Both communities collect the majority of taxes, and then remit a portion of revenue in the form of *cupo* and *aportación* to the state treasury as payment for the services and functions performed by the state. *Cupo* and *aprortacion* constitute about 11.1% of the two communities' revenue. As for the remaining autonomous communities, the state determines and manages the majority of taxation, and then transfers a portion of the tribute to a given autonomous community.

old-age pensions, to local authorities; this may be associated with the broad fiscal and financial freedom enjoyed by that autonomous community. Furthermore, it also results from the preceding studies that the longer powers remain in the hands of autonomous communities, the lesser the problems respondents have properly assigning responsibility. Additionally, the broader scale of financial autonomy has led to regional authorities being held responsible for powers delegated to the central government. This could point to a dependency under which the greater the scope of competencies granted to autonomous communities, the greater the requirements respondents make on regional authorities.

In summary, it should also be added that for decentralisation to lead to greater transparency and accountability, it would seem vital that elections at the sub-national level be linked to sub-national issues. Nevertheless, in many federal countries, elections at the local level are nationalised. One of the causes leading to regional elections becoming an arena for national politics is precisely the absence of clarity in matters of responsibility. An informational campaign in Spain could most certainly contribute to combatting this lack of definition. However, it would seem that politicians are not entirely interested in conducting a campaign that would allow citizens to understand who is responsible for what.

5.3. The party system

Doubtlessly there is a connection between the party system and electoral accountability. J.M. Maravall and A. Przeworski use studies on the impact of the economy on the popularity of the F. Gonzalez government in Spain during the period 1982–1996 to show that vertical accountability is stronger when political parties are weaker.[233] Other studies conducted in such countries as the United Kingdom have confirmed the hypothesis proposed by J.M. Maravall and A. Przeworski. H.D. Clarke, C. Marianne, and P.F. Whitley, among other researchers, have proven that the stronger voters' identification with the Conservatives or the Labour Party, the less heed they paid to their feelings about the condition of the state economy.[234]

The hypothesis proposed by J.M. Maravall and A. Przeworski would imply that of exceptional importance in the context of accountability, at least in young democracies, is one particular aspect of the party system, *id est* the degree of institutionalisation. As it turns out, the stronger the institutionalisation of the party

233 J.M. Maravall, A. Przeworski, *Political Reactions to the Economy: The Spanish Experience*, in: S. Stokes (ed.), *Public Support for Market Reforms in New Democracies*, Cambridge 2001, pp. 35–76.

234 H.D. Clarke, C. Marianne, P.F. Whitley, *Emotions…*, op. cit., pp. 235–260.

system, the more frequently we encounter ideological voting. This means that the economic vote is not applied.[235] There is thus a correlation between institutionalisation of the party system, the associated strong or weak rooting of political parties and vertical accountability. No less important is the institutionalisation of political parties themselves; however, in the context of vertical accountability, the institutionalisation of the party system would seem far more important as it is derived to an extent from the institutionalisation of political parties.[236] Pioneers of the operationalisation of this concept are S. Mainwaring and T. Scully. Both authors pointed to the fact that the level of institutionalisation of the party system is attested to by: The existence or absence of stable patterns of inter-party competition, weak or strong rooting of parties in society, legitimacy of the electoral process and its actors or lack thereof, and strong or weak organisational structure of parties. In addition, the cited authors emphasise the role of a strong party leader, which they feel can indicate a weakly institutionalised party system.[237] Many other scholars have made the effort to define and operationalise the concept of institutionalisation of the party system, among whom it is necessary to mention L. Morlino, V. Randall, and L. Svasand. What joins the cited authors, however, is the distinction of stability as a vital element in studying the extent of institutionalisation.[238]

An interesting control of analysis of the extent of party system institutionalisation is proposed by A. Antoszewski, who distinguishes three levels of institutionalisation of the party system. These are: electoral, parliamentary, and cabinet.

---

235 However, it should be added that in mature democracies as well we encounter weakened ideological identification, which can be interpreted in various ways, such as young voters' entry into the electoral process; these voters are more likely to employ the reward/punishment mechanism.

236 For more on the distinction of institutionalization of political parties and institutionalization of party systems, see: A. Rothert, *Rola instytucjonalizacji partii politycznych i systemów partyjnych na przykładzie doświadczeń państw postkomunistycznych*, Z. Kiełmiński, J. Szymanek (eds.), *Instytucje prawa konstytucyjnego w perspektywie politologicznej*, Warsaw 2013, pp. 136–154, F. Casal Bértoa, *Party System Institutionalization and the Quality of Democracy in Eastern Europe*, Working Paper Series, DISC WP/2009/7, pdc.ceu.hu/archive/00005498/01/fernando-paper-web_2.pdf.

237 S. Mainwaring, T. Scully, *Building Democratic Institutions: Party Systems in Latin America*, Stanford 1995; S. Mainwaring, *Party Systems in The Third Wave*, "Journal of Democracy" 1998, vol. 9, no. 3, pp. 67–81.

238 V. Randall, L. Svasand, *Party Institutionalization en New Democracies*, "Party Politics" 2002, vol. 8, no. 1, pp. 5–29; P. Mair, *Party Systems and Voter, The Freezing Hypothesis: an Evaluation*, in: L. Karvonen, S. Kuhnle (eds.), *Systems and Voter Alignments Revisited*, London 2001, L. Morlino, *Democracias y democratizaciones…*, op. cit.

In this author's opinion, a strongly institutionalised party system at the electoral level is characterised by: 1) the absence of doubt in the legitimacy of participants in the competition; 2) a decline in the number of splits and fusions; 3) support for the main political powers over the short term does not fluctuate radically; 4) the number of new parties declines, while the number of votes cast for them does not; 5) the number of votes cast for parties that do not enter parliament declines; 6) parties specify their political profile and capacity to create durable structures for competition; 7) the political attitudes of the electorate crystallise, electoral volatility declines and electoral cycles lengthen. At the parliamentary level, these are: 1) decline in fragmentation and growth in the effective number of parties; 2) decline in participation of new parties in parliament; 3) absence of anti-system parties (or their marginal role); 4) none of the leading political forces is permanently isolated; 5) it becomes more frequent that parties winning in previous elections maintain their position; 6) new parliamentary fractions become less common. As for the cabinet level, what distinguishes institutionalised party systems is: 1) the existence of repeatable patterns in the formation of cabinets; 2) shortening of the period of time needed to form a cabinet; 3) the appearance of new parties does not complicate the process of forming a new cabinet; 4) increased durability of cabinets; 5) smaller number of incidents involving the collapse of cabinet coalitions.[239]

Nevertheless, from the perspective of vertical accountability, the rooting of political parties, which is the most frequently measured index of electoral volatility, would seem to also be the most important. It should be kept in mind that, following the hypothesis of J.M. Maravall and A. Przeworski, weak rooting of political parties reinforces the use of reward/punishment mechanisms. As R. Markowski correctly points out, however, high electoral volatility is not necessarily a result of failure to develop political "electoral herds", but can also stem from an excess of cleverness among political elites.[240] The need for a broader analysis of the rooting of political parties is also attested to by the discussion concerning the correctness of employing the index of electoral volatility in weakly institutionalised party systems; this discussion is particularly lively within the Latin American states, where a similar phenomenon exists. It is increasingly emphasised that neither the classic measure of electoral volatility using the Pedersen index, neither volatility at the individual level are appropriate means of measuring the level of a party system's

239 A. Antoszewski, *System polityczny RP*, Warsaw 2012, p. 261.

240 For more see: R. Markowski, *System partyjny*, in: L. Kolarska-Babińska, J. Kucharczyk, J. Zbieranek (eds.), *Demokracja w Polsce 2005–2007*, Warsaw 2007, p. 155.

institutionalisation in "young" democracies. Electoral volatility need not result at all from the absence of stable electoral preferences, but rather from the offers presented to voters. This is why many scholars point out that a distinction should be introduced between fluidity and volatility, or that the volatility index should be pre-defined in such a manner that it be operative in countries with a low level of party system institutionalisation.[241]

This is why the following analysis of the influence of institutionalisation on vertical accountability will be performed in two dimensions of accountability, i.e. supply and demand. First, an analysis will be undertaken of the level to which Poland and Spain exhibit electoral volatility, both in the aggregate and individual spheres. Next, there will be an examination of the dependency between electoral volatility and fluidity of elites, at the electoral and the parliamentary level. It should be recalled that in a situation involving significant volatility of voters and political elites themselves, it is difficult to speak of effectively holding the latter to account. In particular, frequent transfers of politicians and changes in party names lead to those politicians responsible for bad governance avoiding the punishment of not being re-elected.

5.3.1. Poland

If we accept the year 1997 as the date marking the consolidation of the Polish political system, it should also be accepted that this consolidation became a fact of the party system at the same time. The values of the indices presented in the portion concerning the electoral system may attest to increased stability of the Polish party system in the years 1997–2011. However, if we look more closely at one of the most important indices measuring the degree of institutionalisation of the party system, *id est* electoral volatility, it turns out that stability is not one of the Polish party system's primary characteristics. In the period 1997–2011, both aggregate volatility (Pedersen index) and individual volatility measured in post-election polling were very high; the average global aggregate volatility measured during the examined period was 29.12%, and aggregate inter-bloc volatility 13.18%. In respect of individual inter-party volatility the average was 47.69%,

241 J. Toole, *Government formation and party system stabilization in East Central, Europe*, "Party Politics" 2000, vol. 6 no. 4, pp. 441–461; E. Powell, E. Neff, J. Tucker, *Rethinking Electoral Volatility in Post-Communist Countries: New Data, New Results and New Approaches*, "British Journal of Political Science", in: CJO 2013 doi:10.1017/S0007123412000531; A. Artiga González, *Fluidez y volatilidad en institucionalización de los sistemas de partidos*, "América Latina Hoy" 1998, no. 19, pp. 125–129.

while individual inter-bloc was 19.2%. Doubtlessly, these results point to a very low level of party system institutionalisation. However, taking the data from Chart 27, it can be said that the level of electoral volatility in Poland is systematically dropping. The highest values of aggregate inter-bloc volatility were recorded in 2005, at a level of 26.16%, while the lowest came in 2011, at 2.36%. There was also a clear drop in individual volatility. Similarly to the case of aggregate volatility, the highest values of individual inter-party volatility and inter-bloc volatility were recorded in 2005, at 62.64% and 27.69%, respectively. The lowest in respect of inter-party volatility came in 2011, at 23.12%, while for inter-bloc it was in 2007, at 15.36%.

It is held that a certain level of volatility is acceptable as vital for the proper functioning of electoral democracy, as it is associated with the freedom that voters possess to define their party preferences; it is also evidence of the existence of a deliberative society which takes into consideration assessment of the activities of the government when taking its electoral decision.[242] However, such high levels of electoral volatility in Poland at both the aggregate and individual levels attest to poor institutionalisation of the party system; they are rather not evidence confirming the proper condition of Polish democracy. Nevertheless, it should be clearly emphasised that in the last two terms of parliament, volatility levels have fallen. Both its types, aggregate and individual, should be correlated. That said, in the case of the Polish party system, interpretation of these values is quite problematic, which results from the fact of very frequent changes in the configuration of the dimensions of political competition. However, analysis of the two values taken separately (aggregate inter-bloc volatility and individual inter-bloc volatility) indicates that Polish political parties are weakly rooted. Comparing the global aggregate volatility with individual inter-party volatility, however, we can observe that they were not correlated in all periods. This was the case in 2005, which attests to the capture of electorates by parties belonging to the same family. Worthy of emphasis is the fact that the values of global aggregate volatility in the examined period fell dramatically, as much as 35.56%, which doubtlessly points to the institutionalisation of the Polish party system.

242 A. Drummond, *Electoral Volatility and Party Decline in Western Democracies: 1970–1995*, "Political Studies" 2006, no. 54, pp. 628–647.

Chart 27. Electoral volatility in the years 1997–2011 (in %)

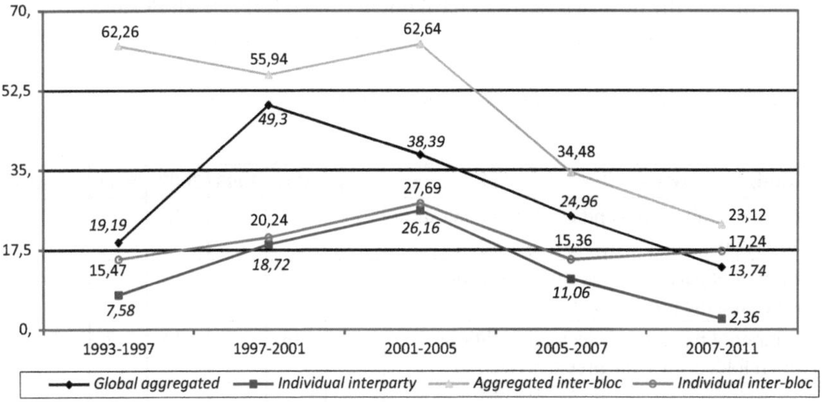

Source: R. Markowski, M. Cześnik, *Wybory parlamentarne w 2011 roku- kontynuacja i zmiana*, „Studia Polityczne" 2012, no. 29, p. 293.

The aforementioned values for indices of electoral volatility could indicate that Polish citizens have not been pleased with successive governments, and this is why they change their electoral preferences with such frequency. It should be remembered, however, that one source of influence on electoral volatility can be the "quality" of Polish political elites, as has been mentioned earlier. Thus electoral volatility itself need not necessarily be associated with the deliberate use of the reward/punishment mechanism by Polish voters, but rather with the problem of assigning responsibility that itself results from frequent changes in the electoral and parliamentary arena; these, in turn, are linked with the fluidity of political elites. At the electoral level, fluidity is depicted by the number of new parties starting in individual elections. The average number of parties participating in elections during the period was 15.8, and thus quite large; the average number of new parties was also high at 7.6. In addition, the average number of parties which ceased to exist from the previous elections was as high as 11.2. When we analyse the Polish party system more closely, it occurs that the only relevant political party whose roots are to be found in neither parties from the communist period (PZPR and ZSL), nor in the opposition which grew out of OKP and KPN, was Samoobrona, present in the Sejm in the years 2001–2007. The remaining new parties are so-called mutations, or even "mutated mutations". In 1997, the "almost new" groups with the capability to cross the electoral threshold were AWS and ROP. The particular case of AWS is interesting, as this formation not only crossed the electoral threshold, but even gained enough seats to become the primary coalition partner.

In 2001, however, three such parties belonged to that category: PO, PiS and LPR, while during the next two terms of parliament (2005–2011) both PO and PiS were the most relevant political parties in the Polish party system.

Table 19. Number of parties competing in the electoral and parliamentary arena in 1997–2011

Number of parties	1997	2001	2005	2007	2011	Average
Number of all parties and coalitions contesting the election	21	15	22	10	11	15.8
Number of parties and electoral coalitions not contesting the previous election	8	8	16	2	4	7.6
Number of parties and electoral coalitions which folded since the previous election	20	14	6	14	2	11.2
Number of parties which won seats in the Sejm	6	7	7	5	6	6.2
Number of new parties which won seats (number of entries)	3	4	0	0	1	1.6
Number of parties which did not win seats in the previous term (number of exits)	5	3	0	2	0	2.0

Source: own calculations based on election information, and ww.pkw.gov.pl.

Cleavages and divisions in political parties are visible not only in the electoral arena, but the parliamentary one as well. Table 20 contains the names of clubs and groups in individual terms of parliament, including those which were formed in the course of a term, as well as those which did not survive until the end of individual terms. Thus, during the 1997–2001 term there were four clubs which survived the entire term, although their compositions did change. In conjunction with the collapse of AWS, that club lost over 30% of its MPs, while the UW club saw almost 78% of its members leave. In the other two clubs created by SLD and PSL the changes were minimal. However, the number of unaffiliated MPs grew significantly. Two clubs and three groups were founded which lasted to the end of the term, as well as four groups which were founded and ceased their activities in the course of the term.

In the 2001–2005 term, a proportionally large number of seats were lost by LPR, around 50%. The Samoobrona parliamentary club also lost over 40% of its MPs. SLD, itself in power, was unable to avoid the split which led to the formation of such groups as SDPL, and lost 20% of its deputies. During the 2001–2005 term there were also significant splits among right-wing parties; although they did not involve the same large numbers of MPs, it is worth recalling that PO lost nearly 14% of its deputies. The only club that did not lose members during the term was PiS. In sum, during the term under discussion two new clubs and three deputies' groups were formed which later ceased functioning, while one new club and seven new groups survived until the end of the term. However, they gathered only a little over 15% of all MPs.

During the 2005–2007 term we could also observe the creation of new clubs and deputies' groups in the course of the term of parliament, but this affected mainly the right wing, and was not as extensive as during the two preceding terms. In total, six parliamentary clubs were founded that survived until the end of the term. Among them, the largest number of MPs departed from the clubs formed by Samoobrona and LPR 26% and almost 15%, respectively. In the case of the remaining clubs the changes were minimal, and the only club which remained entirely intact was SLD. During the term of parliament one club and two deputies' groups were founded which did not survive the entire term. The remaining two clubs which came about during the 2005–2007 term, *id est* RLCH-RLN and PR-prawica, functioned until the end of the term, but accounted for just under 3% of the statutory number of MPs.

At the beginning of the next term in the years 2007–2011, only four parliamentary clubs were formed, while only one club was affected by significant changes in the number of MPs belonging to it. This was PiS, which lost over 12% of its membership. The parliamentary clubs formed by SLD and PO also lost one deputy each. With respect to PiS, the loss of MPs was primarily associated with the creation of the new PJN party and that party's own club, which lasted until the end of the parliamentary term. Changes in the number of MPs also affected the left side of the political spectrum. However, in analysing the condition of membership in SLD at the beginning and the end of the term, we find no changes; it should also be added that during the term a coalition was established with members of SdPL, which failed to go the distance. Ultimately, PJN and SdPL were the only structures that were created in the course of the term and which subsequently survived until the end of it, unlike the LiD club and two deputies' groups, which began and ceased their operations during the 2007–2011 term of parliament. At the end of the term the number of MPs belonging to different clubs and groups than at the beginning did not exceed 2.5%.

*Table 20. Parliamentary clubs and deputies' groups in the period 1997–2011**

Clubs and groups – at the beginning and end of terms				
Parliamentary clubs and groups	**III Term 1997–1996**	**IV Term 2001–2005**	**V Term 2005–2007**	**VI Term 2007–2011**
AWS	20–134	-	-	-
UW	60–47	-	-	-
SLD	164–162	200–148	55–55	42–43
PSL	27–26	42–40	25–27	31–31
ROP	4–3	-	-	-
INDEPENDENT.	2–43	5–39	2–13	1–10
PO	-	65–56	133–131	209–208
PiS	-	44–45	155–151	166–146
Samoobrona	-	53–31	56–41	-
LPR	-	38–19	34–29	-
UP	-	16–11	-	-
Clubs and groups created during the course of the term and which functioned until its end				
Parliamentary clubs and groups	**III Term 1997–1996**	**IV Term 2001–2005**	**V Term 2005–2007**	**VI Term 2007–2011**
NK in PP	7–5	-	-	-
SKL	17–18	-	-	-
Alternatywa	6–4	-	-	-
PiS	18–18	-	-	-
SDPL	-	35–32	-	-
RKN	-	5–4	-	-
KL	-	7–5	-	-
SG	-	11–11	-	-
ROP	-	3–3	-	-
Dom Ojczysty	-	4–10	-	-
UP	-	14–11	-	-
RP	-	3–3	-	-
RLCh-RLN	-	-	7–7	-
PR - Prawica	-	-	6–6	-
PJN	-	-	-	15–15
SDPL	-	-	-	8–3

Clubs and groups which began and ceased their activity during the course of a term: state at the moment of creation and at the end of their existence				
Parliamentary clubs and groups	**III Term 1997–1996**	**IV Term 2001–2005**	**V Term 2005–2007**	**VI Term 2007–2011**
KPN-OP/ KPN-O	7–5	-	-	-
PPS-RLP	3–3	-	-	-
PRS	3–3	-	-	-
KdP	8–7	-	-	-
FKP	-	15–15	-	-
PSL-PBL	-	43–43	-	-
PBL	-	4–3	-	-
PRS	-	5–3	-	-
RP	-	3–3	-	-
RLN	-	-	15–15	-
NKP	-	-	7–5	-
KPB	-	-	4–3	-
LiD	-	-	-	53–53
Polska Plus	-	-	-	9–9

Source: Sejm of the Republic of Poland, Third Term. Information about parliamentary activity (20 October 1997–18 October 2001), Kancelaria Sejmu, Wydawnictwo Sejmowe, Warsaw 2002, p. 11; Sejm of the Republic of Poland, Fourth Term. Information about parliamentary activity (19 October 2001–18 October 2005), Kancelaria Sejmu, Wydawnictwo Sejmowe, Warsaw 2006, pp. 12–14, Sejm of the Republic of Poland, Fifth Term. Information about parliamentary activity (19 October 2005–4 October 2007), Kancelaria Sejmu, Wydawnictwo Sejmowe, Warsaw 2008, pp. 34–35, Sejm of the Republic of Poland, Sixth Term. Information about parliamentary activity (5 November 2007–7 November 2011), Kancelaria Sejmu, Wydawnictwo Sejmowe, Warsaw 2012, pp. 11–12.
*A table with a full legend of parliamentary clubs and deputies" groups by term of parliament is contained in the annex.

In summary, we may speak of a very high level of electoral volatility in Poland, which may attest to the weak rooting of political parties, and in consequence lead to the frequent use of the punishment/reward mechanism. Nevertheless, we also may observe fluidity, or even volatility of political elites, at both the electoral and parliamentary levels. When discussing volatility of political elites, it is associated with the transfer of politicians, whom we can separate into two groups: "political nomads" and "escapees".[243] The former meander form party to party as they see

243 E. Bakke, N. Sitter, *To Stay the Course or Cross the Floor: Members of Parliament, Parties and Party System Change in Central Europe*, Report 5/2005, www.bi.no/FellesFiles/05-5-CEEC.pdf; G. Shabad, K. Słomczynski, *Inter-party Mobility among Parliamentary Candidates in Post-communist East Central Europe*, "Party Politics" 2004, no. 10/2, pp. 151–176; D.M. Olson, *Party Formation and Party System*

better potential in a new formation to realise their own ambitions or political programme, while the latter are "jumping off sinking ships", counting on their presence in a new formation to enable them to achieve power. It is this second category of politicians who are the initiators of new or "almost new" political parties. This phenomenon affects practically all political parties; not even the post-communist formations avoided the tendency to fractionalize, although in large measure this procedure affects the Polish right wing. For this reason as well, determining in the Polish political system which parties are responsible for governments can be a difficult task considering the large number of splits and fusions; this renders it hard to determine which parties are, in fact, new ones. It is highly likely that such actions are associated with a strategy of avoiding responsibility. However, it should be emphasised that only two splinter parties, *id est* PO and PiS, succeeded in establishing themselves over the long term in the Polish political world.

5.3.2. Spain

As it turns out, the level of party system institutionalisation is associated with the time elapsed from the moment of transition. Spain is a clear example of how even a very young democracy can be characterised by a stable party system distinguished *inter alia* by a low level of electoral volatility.

In Spain, during the period 1982–2011 both global aggregate, inter-party and inter-bloc volatility were relatively low. The calculated average for each type of volatility in the analysed period was 12.82%, 8.83% and 3.99%, respectively. Doubtlessly, these results indicate a high level of institutionalisation in the Spanish party system. The highest level of global aggregate volatility was recorded in 1982, at 42.3%, while the lowest, at 4.3%, came in 2008. A similar dependency can be observed with inter-party volatility variables. In 1982 the highest such level was recorded at 35.6%, while the lowest came in 2008, at 2.4%. However, in respect of inter-bloc volatility, the highest number was registered in 2004 at 8.5%, while the lowest came in 1986, 1989 and 1993, at 1.7%.

Consolidation in the New Democracies of Central Europe, "Political Studies" 1998, no. 46/3, pp. 432–464.

Chart 28. Electoral volatility in the years 1982–2008 (in %)

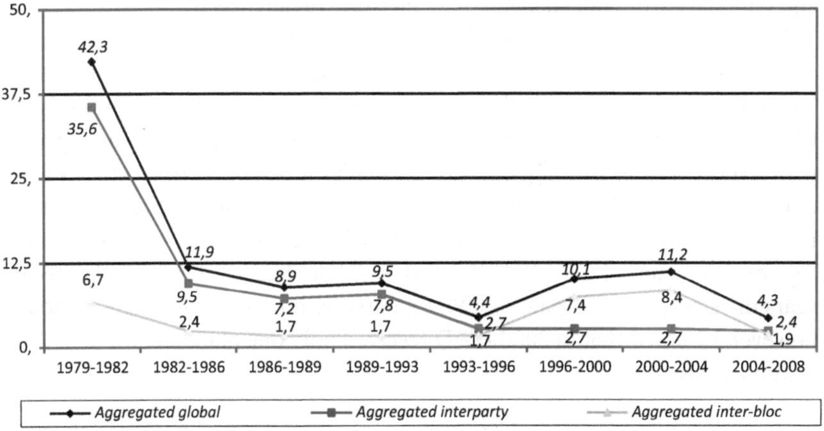

Source: J.R.Montero, I.Lago, Introducción: 2008, las décimas elecciones desde la restaruación de la democracia, w: J.R. Montero, I. Lago, Elecciones Generales 2008, Madrid 2010, p. 38.

Thus in Spain we can observe low levels of electoral volatility, whether global, inter-party or inter-bloc. The sole exception was 1982. Then, nearly half of Spanish voters adjusted their preferences. Nevertheless, in later years a low level of electoral volatility was noted, with minor fluctuations in 2000 and 2004. This state of affairs is likely associated with the fact that in Spain the electorate is very loyal. In accordance with the results of studies conducted using exit polls by J.R. Montero and I. Lago, loyal voters, meaning those who vote for the same party in two consecutive elections, were recorded in the following years at: 1982 – 48%, 1986 – 59%, 1989 – 62%, 1993 – 64%, 1996 – 72%, 2000 – 62%, 2004 – 70%, 2008 – 75%.[244] This is associated with the strong ideological divide existent in the Spanish political arena, which functions as a sort of "dyke" preventing higher levels of electoral volatility. Furthermore, the Spanish party system, referred to as "two-and-a-half parties", leads to the emergence of structural barriers which brake the growth of electoral volatility in an obvious manner. On the right side of the Spanish political spectrum there is no other relevant political party than PP. Meanwhile, PSOE occupies nearly all of the political space on the left side of the spectrum; from the moment of transition IU has never entirely succeeded in transforming into a relevant political formation. The strong divide in Spanish

244 J.R. Motero, I. Lago, *Introducción: 2008, las décimas elecciones desde la restaruación de la democracia*, in: J.R. Moneto, I. Lago, *Elecciones Generales 2008*, Madrid 2010, p. 40.

society between the centre and the periphery also leads to voters of nationalist and regional parties not changing their electoral preferences.

Nevertheless, as the data in Table 21 demonstrates, in Spain there is a rather significant number of parties participating in individual elections, as well as of "entries" and "exits" at the parliamentary level. However, in the case of the Spanish party system, save for 1982 the data depicting the number of new parties which succeeded in winning seats for particular terms of parliament, as well as that concerning political formations which failed to return to the Congress of Deputies, relates to small parties frequently of a regional character. The only exceptions were the failure of the group led by Adolfo Suarez in 1982, and in recent years the emergence in Spain of UPiD, a party with nationwide reach. It should, however, be noted that in 2008 UPiD received only one mandate, while in 2011 it won five seats.

Table 21. Number of parties competing in the electoral and parliamentary arena in 1982–2011

Number of parties	1982	1996	1989	1993	1996	2000	2004	2008	2011	Avg.
Number of all parties and coalitions contesting the election	29	30	30	23	19	26	21	27	25	25.56
Number of all parties winning seats in the Congress of Deputies	11	12	13	11	11	12	11	10	13	11.56
Number of new parties winning seats (number of entries)	1	4	2	1	2	1	1	1	0	1.56
Number of parties which failed to win seats in the previous term (number of exits)	2	2	1	2	2	2	1	2	3	2

Source: own calculations based on electoral committee information.

In Spain as well the issue of fluidity of political elites at the parliamentary level is not a problem. This does not mean, however, that the flow of deputies at the parliamentary level is not a topic of discussion, all the more so in light of the closed electoral lists characteristic of the lower chamber of the Spanish parliament. Furthermore, in Spain we are dealing with either single-party majority or minority governments, which will be addressed later in the chapter. In such a situation the loss of even a few seats in the Congress of Deputies can determine the fate of a government. This is also why the problem of *transfuguismo* has not only been broadly discussed, but has even landed on the docket of the Constitutional Tribunal. The Spanish Constitutional Tribunal, based on the classic concept of the unbound mandate, ruled that the use of any kind of sanctions against politicians who switch party loyalties in the course of a term of parliament would be in violation of the constitution.[245]

In analysing the data contained in Table 21, it is clear that in Spain we do not see significant fluidity of elites at the parliamentary level. One exception was the 1986–1989 term of parliament. This was primarily related to the disintegration of the People's Coalition. Initially, the People's Coalition consisted of AP - People's Covenant (69), PDP Democratic People's Party (21), PL-Liberal Party (12), and UPN – Navarra People's Union (2), CiG Galician Centrists (1). On the day after the election, DPL decided it would not enter the GP People's Coalition, but rather join the Mixed Group.[246] In September 1986, MPs from the PDP formed the Christian Democrats' Group within the Mixed Group. At the request of AP, in January 1987 the DPL also reinforced the ranks of the Mixed Group, thus creating the Liberal Group. For two years the People's Group was comprised only of MPs from AP, UPN, and CdG. However, in February 1989 the People's Covenant rechristened itself as the People's Party, joined by members of DC and PL. During the same term of parliament, PNV also lost two deputies, which was the result of the new party created by Eusko Alkartasun, whose loyalists joined the ranks of the Mixed Group.[247] PSOE also lost three deputies, as did IU. Additionally, MPs selected from the lists of HB refused to take up their seats, which *de facto* allowed PSOE to achieve a governing majority. Nevertheless, in accordance with the data contained in Table 22, it is clear that in later terms of parliament there is essentially zero fluidity of elites at the parliamentary level. It should be added, however, that in Spain there is a procedure known as "lending" deputies in order to constitute a parliamentary group.[248] Such a situation occurred *inter alia* in respect of the Canary Parliamentary Group during the V, VI, VII, and VIII terms of parliament.

245 Constitutional Tribunal rulings: 5/1983, 10/1983, 20/1983, 30/1983, 28/1984), hj.tribunalconstitucional.es.

246 The mixed group is composed of MPs from political groups which do not fulfil the requirements for establishing a separate parliamentary group. See footnote no. 63 for more.

247 A. Sroka, *Hiszpańska droga…*, op. cit., pp. 262–280.

248 Under Art. 25 of the Statute of the Congress of Deputies, the following is required for form a parliamentary group: a minimum of 5 MPs and 5% of votes, or 15% of

*Table 22. Parliamentary clubs and deputies' groups in the period 1982–2011**

Parliamentary groups (PG) – state as of the beginning and the end of the term	**II Term 1982–1986**	**III Term 1986–1989**	**IV Term 1989–1993**	**V Term 1993–1996**	**VI Term 1996–2000**	**VII Term 2000–2004**	**VIII Term 2004–2008**	**IX Term 2008–2011**
ePG Socialists	202–201	184–181	176–175	159–159	141–141	125–124	162–164	169–169
PG Popular	105–102	84–89	106–106	141–141	154–155	179–183	148–147	154–152
PG Catalonian Minority/ Catalonian Group (CiU)	12–12	18–19	18–18	17–17	16–16	14–15	10–10	10–10
PG Centrists	12–11	-	-	-	-	-	-	-
PG Basque (PNV)	8–8	6–4	5–5	5–5	5–5	6–7	7–7	6–6
PG Mixed	10–14	34–18	10–17	5–6	5–11	5–9	5–9	4–8
PG CDS	-	19–28	14–12	-	-	-	-	-
PG IU-IC/PG Federal IU/	-	-	17–17	18–18	21–16	8–8	5–5	7–5
PG Canary/PG-New Canary	-	-	-	5–4	6–4	7–4	5–2	-
PG ERC	-	-	-	-	-	8–8	8–8	-
Groups within the Mixed Group functioning from the beginning to the end of the term	**III Term 1982–1986**	**III Term 1986–1989**	**IV Term 1989–1993**	**V Term 1993–1996**	**VI Term 1996–2000**	**VII Term 2000–2004**	**VIII Term 2004–2008**	**IX Term 2008–2011**
PG Mixed – Group IU-IC/Group IU-IpC	-	7–6	-	-	-	-	-	-
Groups within the Mixed Group which ceased functioning in the course of a term	**III Term 1982–1986**	**III Term 1986–1989**	**IV Term 1989–1993**	**V Term 1993–1996**	**VI Term 1996–2000**	**VII Term 2000–2004**	**VIII Term 2004–2008**	**IX Term 2008–2011**
PG Mixed – Christian Democrats	-	20–21	-	-	-	-	-	-
GP Mixed – Liberal Party	-	10–7	-	-	-	-	-	-

Source: own work based on the website of the Congress of Deputies, www.congreso.es and www.historiaelectoral.com/.

* A table with a full legend of parliamentary clubs and deputies' groups by term of parliament is contained in the annex.

---

the votes in the electoral districts where candidates from a given political formation contested the election, www.congreso.es/portal/page/portal/Congreso/Congreso/Hist_Normas/Norm/reglam_congreso.pdf (or Moldavia).

In summary, Spain features a low level of electoral volatility, which may attest to strong rooting of political parties. The situation is similar in the case of fluidity and volatility of political elites. At the electoral and parliamentary level, such changes are insignificant. From the perspective of vertical accountability, such a situation generates two types of consequences. Firstly, the high level of institutionalisation present in the Spanish party system leads to a situation in which there is no problem to assign responsibility; the small number of changes at the electoral level and the parliamentary level means that the Spanish voter has no difficulty in determining which party is responsible for the present state of the economy and policy in the country. On the other hand, however, strong rooting of political parties may lead to limitations in the use of reward/punishment mechanisms, as in the Spanish party system there are practically no two parties with similar platforms that a dissatisfied voter could choose between, which has already been discussed in the context of the Spanish electoral system.

5.4. The type of government

Concentration of power impacts vertical accountability; the more power is concentrated, the clearer and more direct the relationship between the government and policies. This leads in turn to enhanced control of politicians by voters. Some authors feel that the presence of minority governments which do not enjoy a parliamentary majority, as well as of coalition governments consisting of more than one political party, hinder the assignment responsibility to such a degree that it is in fact entirely absent. This means that without certainty as to who should be evaluated, voters do not assign responsibility for the manner in which government operates.[249]

We frequently encounter situations in which political parties, in spite of giving their support to minority governments or entering coalition governments, attempt to avoid being sanctioned for policies pursued. In the event of poor results, they shift blame onto coalition partners or the parties which gave the support vital for forming minority governments, whilst in the case of good results they take credit for the positive things accomplished. Predicting how the voters will react in such

249 For more: G.B. Powell, G.D. Whitten, *A Cross-National…*, op. cit., pp. 391–414; P. Nannestad, M. Paldam, *The V-P Function. A Survey of the literature on vote and popularity functions after 25 years*, "Public Choice" 1994, vol. 79 no. 3–4, pp. 213–245; J. Font, *El pez…*, op. cit., p. 169; K. Leyden, S. Borrelli, *The Effect of State Economic Conditions on Gubernatorial Elections: Does Unified Government Made a Difference?*, "Political Research Quarterly" 1995, vol. 48, no. 2, pp. 275–290.

a situation, whether they will elect to assign blame to smaller coalition partners or parties giving support to minority governments, is a difficult exercise. The question thus arises if all parties are held to account to the same degree, or do some of them benefit more often from problems in assigning responsibility. It would seem that voters assign responsibility to the most visible parties in a given coalition. However, the visibility of those parties is associated with the size of the partner in the coalition itself; it would therefore seem logical to assume that voters assign greater responsibility to the parties which constitute the strongest coalition partners.

However, before proceeding to analyse the assignment of responsibility in Poland and in Spain in the context of type of government, we should decide as to the criteria based on which particular cabinets will be classified. K. Strom distinguishes four manners of "counting" governments: 1) after each election; 2) after each change of Prime Minister; 3) after each modification of the party composition of the government; 4) following partial elections which lead to a change in political status.[250] The following analysis works under the assumption consistent with the proposal of A. Antoszewski[251] and K. Zuba[252] that the basis for distinguishing the number of cabinets is the existence of the same configuration of the Council of Ministers led by the same Prime Minister,[253] not only a change of the person holding the office of PM, as proposed by the authors in such works as *Coalition Governments in the Third Polish Republic* [*Rządy koalicyjne w III RP*].[254] This means that in a situation where the number and/or type of parties comprising the coalition changes, the cabinet is reviewed separately in spite of the same individual holding the office of PM, and vice versa – if the number and type of parties constituting the government remains unchanged while a different person takes the post of Prime Minister, that government is analysed separately.

5.4.1. Poland

In respect of Poland, adoption of the aforementioned criteria means that in the period under examination, *id est* 1997–2010, the number of cabinets increases from 6 to 12. From among those governments, six constituted majority coalitions, five were single-party minority governments, and one a minority coalition.

---

250 K. Strom, *Monority government and majority rule*, Cambridge 1990.

251 A. Antoszewski, *System polityczny RP…*, op. cit., p. 204.

252 K. Zuba, *Polska scena…*, op. cit., pp. 132–141.

253 This criterion was also adopted by W. Wojtasik, see: W. Wojtasik, *Gabinety koalicyjne w Polsce w latach 1989–2005*, in: M. Mazur, M. Migalski, W. Wojtasik (eds.), *Polski system partyjny*, Warsaw, 2006, pp. 230–235.

254 M. Chmaj, *Rządy koalicyjne w III RP*, Olsztyn 2006.

Table 23. Types of government in Poland in the years 1997–2011

Government	Duration	Time in government (months)	Party composition	Status
Jerzy Buzek (AWS)	31.10.1997–06.06.2000	31	AWS, UW	Majority coalition
Jerzy Buzek (AWS)	06.06.2000–19.10.2001	16.5	AWS	Single-party minority
Leszek Miller (SLD)	19.10.2001–03.03.2003	16	SLD-UP, PSL	Majority coalition
Leszek Miller (SLD)	03.03.2003–02.05.2004	14	SLD-UP	Single-party minority
Marek Belka (no party affiliation)	02.05.2004–31.10.2005	18	SLD-UP	Single-party minority
Kazimierz Marcinkiewicz (PiS) I	31.10.2005–4.05.2006	5.5	PiS	Single-party minority
Kazimierz Marcinkiewicz (PiS) II	05.05.2006–10.07.2005	3	PiS, LPR, Samoobrona	Majority coalition
Jarosław Kaczyński (PiS) I	14.07.2006–21.09.2006	2	PiS, LPR, Samoobrona	Majority coalition
Jarosław Kaczyński (PiS) II	22.09.2006–17.10.2006	1	PiS, LPR	Coalition minority
Jarosław Kaczyński (PiS) III	18.10.2006–12.08.2007	9.5	PiS, LPR, Samoobrona	Majority coalition
Jarosław Kaczyński (PiS) IV	13.08.2007–16.11.2007	4.5	PiS	Single-party minority
Donald Tusk (PO)	17.11.2007–08.11.2007	48	PO, PSL	Majority coalition

Source: on the basis of K. Zuba, *Polska scena polityczna: ciągłość i zmiana*, Warsaw 2012, p. 338.

Doubtlessly, frequent changes in the nature of the government during the same term of parliament can hinder assignment of responsibility. Changes of majority coalitions into minority governments took place in 1997–2001 and 2001–2005, while during the 2005–2007 term the minority government also lost a coalition partner. Only during the 2007–2011 term did the governing coalition survive the full four-year period. From the data gathered in Table 23 it is difficult to draw conclusions concerning the extent to which voters in Poland hold all coalition parties to account, not only the primary coalition members. Essentially it is quite difficult to perceive any particular truisms. Most likely, both AWS and UW in 2001 were held to account at the ballot box; nevertheless, it should be remembered that on the right side of the political spectrum three new parties arose, PO, PiS and LPR, which could have swallowed the electorates of both of the parties comprising the government. In the 2005 elections, SLD, the party in power during the preceding term, experienced a crushing defeat. The coalition partner, PSL, also lost 2% of its electoral support, while UP failed even to cross the electoral threshold. An entirely different situation occurred in 2007, as the primary coalition partner PiS not only did not lose any portion of its voter base, but even improved on its previous result by 5.1%; meanwhile, the coalition parties of Samoobrona and LPR did not even enter the next parliament. However, it is rather unlikely that those parties were punished by the voters for their policies, as they had been part of the governing coalition. First, the coalition was of an ephemeral nature, and second, in such a situation PiS would likely also be punished. This is why it seems that other explanations should be sought. In 2011, as the main coalition partner PO lost a portion of its electoral base, although the decline was not so spectacular, while the junior partner in the coalition, PSL, not only retained its support but even managed to improve its showing at the polls.

*Table 24. Election results of parties comprising governing coalitions in the years 1997–2011 (in %)**

Government	Elections	Senior coalition partner				Junior governing or parliamentary coalition partner			
		AWS	SLD	PiS	PO	UW	S	LPR	PSL
AWS/UW 1997	2001	-28.2	-	-	-	-10	-	-	-
SLD-UP/PSL 2001	2005	-	-29.7	-	-	-	-	-	-2
PiS/LPR/"S" 2005	2007	-	-	5.1	-	-	-11.2	-6.6	-
PO/PSL 2007	2011	-	-	-	-2.3	-	-	-	0.6

Source: own calculations.

* Electoral results are calculated by the difference in votes received by the parties comprising governments in comparison with successive elections. Negative values indicate a loss of votes, while positive ones indicate votes gained in relation to previous elections.

It can only be suspected that assignment of responsibility in Poland can be problematic, as we are faced with coalition governments. Additional difficulty stems from the phenomenon of coalition partners exiting the coalition in the course of a term of parliament. This leads to continual changes in the nature of the government; the only exception is the 2007–2011 term. Nonetheless, the preceding analyses do not allow for a definitive determination of whether problems associated with assignment of responsibility, and thus *de facto* lack of knowledge, lead Polish voters to apply reward/punishment mechanisms to both governing parties and coalition partners. The data cited above allow only for the statement that

Polish voters do not display any consistency or pattern of behaviour. The empirical analysis performed in the next chapter concerning economic voting will go some way in clearing this up.

5.4.2. Spain

In the case of Spain, since 1977, and thus from the beginning of the political transformation, each government has been formed by only one party; this is unlike any other country in Europe.[255] During the period under analysis of 1982–2011, two parties constituted governments without interruption (1982–1993 PSOE,[256] 1996–2000 PP, 2004–2011 PSOE). In this time eight governments were formed, six of which were single-party majority governments, while two were single-party minority governments. None of them were composed of coalitions.

Table 25. Types of cabinets in Spain in 1982–2011

Government	Date of formation	Date of dissolution	Duration of government (months)	Party composition	Status
Felipe González (PSOE) I (II Term 1982–1986)	01.12.1982	23.06.1986	34	PSOE	Single-party majority
Felipe González (PSOE) II (III Term 1986–1989)	23.07.1986	30.10.1989	39	PSOE	Single-party majority
Felipe Gonzaléz (PSOE) III (IV Term 1989–1993)	05.12.1989	07.06.1993	42	PSOE	Single-party majority
Felipe González (PSOE) IV (V Term 1993–1996)	10.06.1993	04.03.1996	33	PSOE	Single-party minority
José María Aznar (PP) I (VI Term 1996–2000)	05.05.1996	18.01.2000	44	PP	Single-party minority
José María Aznar (PP) II (VII Term 2000–2004)	26.04.2000	17.03.2004	47	PP	Single-party majority

255 For more: J.E. Lane, S.O. Ersson, *Política europea: una introdución*, Madrid 1998, pp. 201–231.

256 PSOE succeeded in forming a government for the first time in 1982. It lasted 43 months, from 1.12.1982 until 23.06.1986. It was a single-party majority government. In the Congress of Deputies, PSOE had 201 seats at its disposal, while the remaining parties and parliamentary groups had 148 (PP – 102, UCD – 11, CiU – 12, Mixed – 15, PNV – 8).

Government	Date of formation	Date of dissolution	Duration of government (months)	Party composition	Status
José Luis Rodríguez Zapatero (PSOE) I (VIII Term 2004–2008)	17.04.2004	12.03.2008	47	PSOE	Single-party majority
José Luis Rodríguez Zapatero (PSOE) II (IX Term 2008–2011)	13.04.2008	23.11.2011	43	PSOE	Single-party majority

Source: own work based on: J.M. Reniu and Vilamala, *La formación de gobiernos minoritarios en España 1997–1996*, Madrid 2002, p. 122 and Boletín Oficial del Estado, www.boe.es/diario_boe/.

During the described period, parliamentary coalitions for minority governments were formed by two large nationwide parties – PSOE and PP – together with regional parties, save for IU during the 2004–2008 term. Excluding IU, it is precisely regional parties in the years 1993–2000 and 2004–2008, *id est* CiU, PNV, ERC, BNG and CC, which offered support to minority governments[257] at the national level. Regional parties provided the fourth government of Felipe González as well as the first governments of José María Aznar and José Luis Rodríguez Zapatero with stable parliamentary support. This support was negotiated in advance of the formation of the government, and was of a formal nature. Additionally, parties supporting particular governments expressly declared their will to maintain the parliamentary coalition beyond the investiture process. It is also established that both PSOE and PP in 1993–2000 wished to form coalition governments at the national level. Why, then, were minority governments formed instead of coalitions, in spite of the fact that regional party support was vital for PSOE and PP to govern?

The occurrence of minority governments is doubtlessly associated with the territorial structure of Spain, primarily the existence of party sub-systems; this, in turn, is linked with the existence of real power at the regional level, as well as the issue of

257 Governments from the years 1993–1996, 1996–2000 and 2000–2004 were not the first minority governments in the history of democratic Spain. In 1979–1982 there were minority governments, although they were significantly different from those formed in later years. The first years of democracy were a unique period during which political formation were sharply divided between those from the Francoist camp, and those from the opposition. The division between left and right led to UCD being unable to achieve a parliamentary majority and in turn a stable position, as the opposition was not capable of cooperating. At the same time, UCD itself was not very cohesive. For more: J.M. Reniu Vilamala, *La formación de gobiernos minoritarios en España 1997–1996*, Madrid 2002.

avoiding responsibility. Entering the government at the central level is simply not a beneficial move for regional parties. First, this is because there is frequently no congruence between the parties forming regional governments and those in power at the national level. It should also be mentioned that coalition governments are the norm at the regional level.[258] However, this argument may not seem entirely convincing when we consider that in the years 1996–2000, CiU and CC governed in their own regions in coalitions with PP. Furthermore, regional parties would not be able to engage in a strategy of making the central government responsible for both the situation in the country and the slow tempo of decentralisation. It is the problem of decentralisation which constituted the *leitmotif* of the election campaigns to regional parliaments, primarily in Catalonia and Basque Country.

The fact that regional parties, in spite of the absence of their representatives in the government of Spain, have, through participation in parliamentary coalitions, ensured they wield influence over the drafting of laws while remaining free from the obligation of being held to account, would seem to indicate they have adopted a strategy of avoiding responsibility. It should be added, however, that this dynamic was slightly different in the years 1993–2000 and 2004–2008. During the Gonzalez and Aznar government, the engagement of CiU, PNV and CC was not always at the same level. Only CiU maintained a firm understanding with the governments of Gonzalez and Aznar, which allowed it to influence the creation of law. Furthermore, it is CiU that provided the two governments with an absolute majority, whereas the impact of PNV and CC was not as great taking into consideration the number of seats involved.[259] As for the Basque party, it has traditionally maintained a low level of involvement in matters of the Spanish parliament. PNV displayed a rather passive attitude, neither openly objecting nor attempting to push through its own initiatives or changes to legislation. The incorporation of PNV into the parliamentary majority was in the interests of PSOE and PP, but not those of the Basque formation itself. The activity of CC was limited to matters concerning the Canary Islands, which is understandable considering the number of seats that party held during the period under study. In the middle of the 5th term CC even decided to leave the parliamentary coalition. However, it did offer its support in the 6th term. A slightly different situation occurred in the case of the third minority government during the 8th term. While the parliamentary situation was

258 For more see: A. Sroka, *Hiszpańska droga…*, op. cit., pp. 135–145, 326–329.

259 For more on the role of CiU in government coalitions at the national level from the perspective of the centre-periphery divide, see: K. Sobolewska-Myślik, *Partie i systemy partyjne na poziomie regionu. Przykład Szkocji i Karalonii*, Kraków 2012, pp. 163–173.

similar to that of the preceding term, the political strategy employed by PSOE to cement the government's stability was significantly different compared to previous periods. CiU alone could not guarantee a majority for PSOE in the Spanish parliament; additionally, in Catalonia the socialists had formed a government with ERC and ICV. The idea of a new statute for the Basque Country threatening the unity of Spain pushed by Juan José Ibarretxe, the leader of that autonomous community, made it impossible for PSOE to arrive at an understanding with PNV. This is also why Rodriguez Zapatero preferred to seek support among regional left-wing parties without the necessity of entering into covenants, which would entail coalitions at the parliamentary level with ERC, CC, BNG, ICV, CHA and IU. However, problems associated with the process of reforming the Catalonian statute weakened the ties between PSOE and ERC, which is also why, during the second half of the term of parliament, PSOE began to seek the support of CiU; this led to destabilisation of the coalition between PSC and ERC in Catalonia, and resulted in snap elections. This example highlights that the Spanish political system functions as a system of connected vessels, which results largely from the nature of the country's territorial structure. However, in parliamentary practice, the proceeding isolation of PP and polarisation in the Spanish parliament, CiU and PNV gave their support to the socialists in order to avoid comparisons with the PP.

*Table 26. Elections results of parties in power and parties offering them support in the investiture process (in %)**

Government	Elections	Parties forming government		Parties offering support**					
		PSOE	PP	CiU	PNV	CC	IU	BNG	ERC
PSOE 1982	1986	-4.0							
PSOE 1986	1989	-4.4	-	-	-	-	-	-	-
PSOE 1989	1993	- 0.1	-	-0.2	-+0	-	-	-	-
PSOE 1993	1996	-2	-	-0.3	-+0	+0	-	-	-
PP 1996	2000	-	+8	-0.3	+0.3	+0.2	-	-	-
PP 2000	2004	-	-7.4	-0.9	-	-0.2	-	-	-
PSOE 2004	2008	+3.2	-	-	-	-0.2	-0.6	+/-0	-1.4
PSOE 2008	2011	-17.3	-	-	-	-	-	-	-

Source: own work based on: www.congreso.es/consti/elecciones/generales/index.htm.

* Electoral results are calculated by the difference in votes received by the parties comprising governments in comparison with successive elections. Negative values indicate a loss of votes, while positive ones indicate votes gained in relation to previous elections.

** Parties which supported the government in the act of investiture; it should, however, be added that for particular votes in the case of majority governments, the party in power also concluded temporary alliances with opposition parties.

In summary, parliamentary coalitions allowed for formalisation of the relations between the parties constituting the government and the most important regional parties. Most likely, the reason for forming minority governments was precisely the strategy of avoiding responsibility employed by regional parties. It would seem that this strategy was very effective, something confirmed by the data in Table 26. Practically none of the parties supporting the government at the parliamentary level lost support in successive elections to the Congress of Deputies. This would mean that the voters, owing to these parties' decision to not enter government, do not assign responsibility to them for governing; rather, this blame is reserved for the parties constituting the government. This is one possible interpretation, as such a situation can also be linked with the issue of national identities, which has already been discussed while analysing the party system in Spain.

***

Comparing the impact of the first of the analysed institutional determinants, *id est* the type of electoral system, it turns out that the election laws adopted in Poland and Spain lead to similar average values for the most important indices (Tables 12, 13, 15, 16). Levels of disproportionality, fragmentarisation and competition are comparable. Although in the case of Poland the level of disproportionality and of fragmentation is slightly higher, in Spain the level of competition is greater. The values for the index of effective number of parties and the sum of the two largest parties exhibit greater differences, at both the level of votes and mandates. This data confirms that while the Spanish electoral system, similarly to the Polish one, is a proportional system, in practice it exhibits characteristics of a majoritarian system; in consequence, it leads to the formation of majority governments and facilitates vertical accountability. Therefore, in accordance with the adopted premise that the greater the proportionality of an electoral system, the more difficult it is for the voter in assigning responsibility for governments (as proportional systems generally lead to party fragmentarisation and coalition governments), it can be said that Poland exhibits greater levels of distortions in the functioning of vertical accountability than Spain. Nevertheless, when we take into account the use of strategic voting in Spain, the situation takes on a slightly different look as this type of voting exerts a negative impact on vertical accountability. Distinctly from Poland, in Spain we may speak of very stable electoral rules, which, in accordance with the thesis of P. Bellucci, contributes to the use of ideological rather than economic voting; by the same token, it limits the use of the reward/punishment mechanism through the reinforcement of party and ideological ties. We can therefore assume that there is greater distortion of vertical accountability in Spain than in Poland, and by the same token less use of economic voting. As for the time elapsed since the moment of systemic transformation, it would seem that, with time, the distortions of vertical accountability in Poland are increasingly smaller; this is reflected primarily in the values of indices from the last two terms of parliament (Tables 12 and 13). In Spain, these indices remained at a similar level throughout the entire analysed period (Table 15 and 16), which would point to the absence of the aforementioned dependency.

The impact of the next determinant, *id est* that of territorial structure on assignment of responsibility, is clearer. The results discussed in Chapter Five of public opinion surveys leave no doubt that it is more difficult in Spain for citizens to assign responsibility, as it is not entirely clear which level of administration is liable for policies pursued; this is associated with the decentralised territorial structure of that country. In spite of the fact that neither in Poland nor in Spain have there been comprehensive studies regarding citizens' knowledge about the assignment of competences to particular levels of administration, existing data can allow for the supposition that the time elapsed from the moment of consolidation has led to better assignment of responsibility. In Poland, this has been expressed *inter alia* by the growing confidence of respondents that self-government entities should take on greater responsibility, as well as rising indices of trust towards local self-government authorities. Survey research in Spain also shows that the longer particular powers are entrusted to autonomous communities, the lesser the problems respondents have with assigning responsibility. However, in Spain we undoubtedly face larger problems than in Poland with assigning competences, and therefore responsibility, which may limit the use of economic voting.

The next determinant of vertical accountability is the party system; more specifically, the degree of its institutionalisation. In accordance with the hypothesis advanced by J.M. Maravall and A. Przeworski, the stronger a party system is institutionalised, the more frequently we encounter ideological rather than economic voting. Thus vertical accountability, including the use of economic voting, is associated with strong or weak rooting of political parties. When comparing the data contained in Charts 27 and 28 on electoral volatility in Poland and Spain, one of the measures of the strength or weakness of political parties' rooting, it can easily be observed that Poland exhibits far greater electoral volatility; this can lead in consequence to more frequent use of the reward/punishment mechanism. Nevertheless, in Poland, unlike in Spain, we may observe fluidity and even volatility of political elites, at both the electoral and parliamentary level. This procedure affects all political options, but in general it affects the right wing to a greater extent. This is also why assigning responsibility in the Polish political system is far more difficult than in Spain, as a permanent feature of the Polish political scene is the frequent occurrence of splits and fusions of parties. Perhaps this is associated with a strategy of avoiding responsibility by politicians in successive elections. Undoubtedly in Spain there is no difficulty with assigning responsibility. Voters have no difficulty in determining which party is responsible for the present condition of the economy and politics; nevertheless, the strong rooting of political parties, in accordance with the hypothesis previously invoked, can lead to limitations on use of the reward/punishment mechanism. This is particularly the case when we take into consideration the fact that there are no relevant political parties with similar platforms that dissatisfied voters could shift their support to. Analysing the party system, it also turns out that the time which has elapsed from the moment of consolidation of democracy is significant in the case of Poland, whereas it is not in Spain. The Polish party system, as evidenced by the values of electoral volatility, is subjected to gradual institutionalisation; the example of Spain clearly demonstrates that young democracies as well can feature a stable party system.

Comparison of the last of the analysed determinants of vertical accountability, namely the type of government, also presents difficulties. The empirical data analysed in Chapter 5 show that both in Poland and in Spain there exist minority governments, while Poland also has minority coalitions. From among the 12 cabinets in Poland during the period under review, five of them were single-party minority governments, one was a minority coalition, and the remaining six were majority coalitions; in Spain, eight cabinets formed during the studied period featured four single-party minority governments and four single-party majority. Analysing the election results of parties comprising governing coalitions in the years 1997–2011 in Poland, it can only be said that there are no consistent patterns of behaviour among Polish voters. Votes were lost in successive elections by the main coalition partners in governments formed during the whole period, while in the 1997–2001 and 2005–2007 terms this also affected coalition partners. This is also why the analyses conducted in Chapter 5 do not allow for a definitive determination of whether problems experienced by Polish voters with assigning responsibility, and thus *de facto* ignorance, lead them to employ reward/punishment mechanisms to both senior and junior coalition partners (Table 24). However, in respect of Spain, both PP and PSOE concluded parliamentary coalitions with regional parties, which was vital to govern in conditions of minority cabinets. In accordance with the data presented in Table 26, only during the 2004–2008 term did this lead to the loss of votes by parties which had provided the support necessary for the creation of a minority government. It would therefore seem that in the Spanish case, voters generally hold the parties forming the government responsible, not those providing support in parliament. However, another interpretation is possible, associated with the existence of a strong division in Spain between the centre and the periphery. In both Poland and Spain the impact of time on reducing distortions in vertical accountability is difficult to assess unambiguously.

In summary, in both Poland and Spain we may observe problems with assigning responsibility. As a result, the answer to the question of whether institutional factors disrupt the functioning of mechanisms of vertical accountability in Poland and Spain must be affirmative. Nevertheless, the following tested hypothesis: "In both Poland and in Spain we are faced with determinants of an institutional nature which disrupt the functioning of vertical accountability; this is a consequence of the adopted institutional architecture in both political systems. The more time elapsed from the moment of consolidation of the political system, the lesser are the distortions to vertical accountability", has only been partially confirmed. The impact of the passage of time on the functioning of vertical accountability is not so definitive. Additionally, in the absence of quantitative data it is very difficult to determine in which of the two countries limitations on the use of economic voting result to a greater degree from the impact of the discussed determinants.

Chapter 6. Economic voting as an expression of vertical accountability

In this chapter, the question of to what extent voters in Poland and Spain are driven by the will to reward or punish the governing party will be examined. In other words, whether the retrospective economic vote is used in Poland and Spain. The research will use the multinomial logistic regression model. It should be noted, however, that studies grounded in rational choice theory are called into question. This is connected mostly with the fact that studies based on models of voter behaviour within the bounds of rational choice theory, from which economic voting is derived, are usually performed over a short period of time on a large number of countries. This has been noted *inter alia* by K. Jasiewcz, who analysed interpretations of voter behaviour in Central and Eastern European countries.[260]

The approach used here tries to address these problems, as in the case of Poland the research encompasses the years 1997–2011, and in the case of Spain 1982–2011. When analysing only election results in Poland, one could conclude that citizens' expectations towards their representatives are not being met, as every election in the years 1997–2007 resulted in a new governing coalition. Only once in the examined period, in 2011, were the parties forming the government in the years 2007–2011, i.e. PO and PSL, able to gain enough seats in the parliament to form a government for the second time. In Spain, there have been periods in which the same party gained enough seats to again form a government (PSOE in the years 1986–1993 and 2004–2012, PP in 1996–2004), which can be a sign of voters' expectations being met. However, an analysis that would amount to simply interpreting the differences in the number of votes gained by parties trying to get re-elected would not allow us to dispel doubts regarding whether changes of the governing parties in Poland and Spain were connected with voter accountability, or were rather a consequence of other determinants. Therefore, the main research question to be answered in this chapter is: does the retrospective economic vote, which is considered a measure of voter accountability, occur in Poland and Spain? The hypothesis tested in this chapter is: *Both in Poland and in Spain there exists electoral accountability; positive retrospective assessment of the economic situation in the country increases the likelihood of voting for the party vying for re-election.*

260 K. Jasiewicz, *Portfel czy różaniec? Wzory zachowań wyborczych Polaków w latach 1995–2001*, in: R. Markowski (ed.), *System partyjny i zachowania wyborcze. Dekada polskich doświadczeń*, Warsaw 2002, pp. 76–81.

6.1. Studies on vertical accountability in light of rational choice theory – operationalisation of economic voting

Already at the beginning of the 20th century scholars began wondering how the economy influences levels of government acceptance. In the 1930s, the first analyses regarding the effects of periods of prosperity and crisis on re-electability were published.[261] However, only in the 1970s did papers appear in which these relations were analysed in detail. The most important ones were articles by J.E. Mueller (1970),[262] C.A.E. Goodhart and R.J. Bhasala (1970),[263] and G.H. Kramer (1971).[264] These works helped drive the development of research regarding economic voting. J.E. Mueller was concerned with the function of the popularity of the U.S. president; his research was statistical, but conceptually very complex. G.H. Kramer examined the U.S. congressional elections in the years 1896–1964, while research by C.A.E. Goodhart and R.J. Bhasala was concerned with the popularity of political parties and their leaders in the United Kingdom in the years 1947–1968. After that, further analyses were undertaken in such countries as Germany, France, Japan, and Scandinavian countries. By the end of the 1980s a qualitative change had occurred in the creation of models. This was associated with the formation of a research group in Zurich that began studying the relations between the function of popularity and the reaction of citizens, joining them into one political-economical model: the closed and integrated B.S. Frey and F. Schneider model, in which almost all variables were endogenous.[265] At the same time, another research group was formed at Harvard University under the leadership of D.A. Hibbs, whose lasting effect on the development of research in this field consisted not in proposing a new approach or technique, but rather new methods and the use of a non-linear model. In this model, it is assumed that each government, at the beginning of its term, enjoys a credit of popularity that changes while it is in power, and the increase or decrease in popularity results from good or bad economic results.[266]

In the 1980s and early 1990s, researchers discussed the role and meaning of the conditioning of individual election behaviour. Despite agreement as to the validity of retrospective vote theory, according to which citizens rely on their experiences

261 V.O. Key Jr., *The responsible…*, op. cit.

262 J.E. Mueller, *Presidential Popularity…*, op. cit., pp. 18–34.

263 C.A.E. Goodhert, R.J. Bhansali, *Political Economy…*, op. cit., pp. 43–106.

264 G.H. Kramer, *Schort-term Fluctuations…*, op. cit., pp. 131–143.

265 B.S. Frey, F.Schneider, *A Politico-Economic Model…*, op. cit., pp. 243–253.

266 D.A. Hibbs, *The Mass Public…*, op. cit., pp. 705–731.

when forming their expectations regarding the future,[267] there was no consensus to what extent the economic situation of the voter and the general economic situation of the country are significant at the moment of voting. In other words, whether the vote is sociotopic or egotopic (the so-called "wallet vote"), D.R. Kinder and R.D. Kieweit defended the assumption that the voter decision is influenced by the economic situation of the country;[268] this was met with harsh criticism, although many researchers eventually came to the same conclusion. Among others, P. Nannestad and M. Padam have proven that electoral behaviour is comprised of both types of voting, and the predominance of one over the other is derived from social context.[269] One of the most important studies proving the importance of the sociotopic vote was conducted by M.S. Lewis-Beck, who compared the functions of popularity in five European countries and in the United States.[270]

Current studies on the function of popularity are much more varied. One of the main research trends concentrates on studying changes in the function of popularity depending on the social group to which a given voter belongs. Another one is concerned with so-called spatial voting, studying the extent to which functions of popularity change depending on the characteristics of the studied region.[271] In summary, it can be said that in recent years there have been attempts at generalising popularity functions in studies concerned with various countries, groups and situations; in all of these studies, the accountability function is assigned to elections.

In Poland, there is a lack of comprehensive studies using the economic vote model. Partial analyses have been done by P. Grzelak. However, they review only

267 M.P. Fiorina, *Retrospective Voting…*, op. cit.

268 D.R. Kinder, R.D. Kiewiet, *Sociotopic Politics…*, op. cit., pp. 129–161.

269 P. Nannestad, P.M. Paldam, *From the Pocketbook…*, op. cit., pp. 119–137.

270 M.S. Lewis-Beck, *Economics and Elections…*, op. cit.

271 More on the literature regarding the function of popularity and the economic vote: P. Nannestad, M. Paldam, *The VP-function: A Survey of the Literature…*, op. cit., pp. 213–245; A. Bosch; A. Diaz, C. Riba, *Las funciones de popularidad: estado de la cuestión y principales debates*, „Revista Española de Investigaciones Sociológicas" 1999, vol. 85 no. 1, pp. 171–197; A. Przeworski, S.C. Stokes, B. Manin (eds.) *Democracy…*, op. cit.; J.M. Maravall, *El control de los politicos*, Madrid 2003; J.A. Cheibub, A. Przeworski, *Democracy, Elections, and Accountability for Economic Outcomes*, w: A. Przeworski, S. Stokes, B. Manin (eds.), *Democracy, Accountability…*, op. cit,; M.S. Lewis-Beck, M. Stegmaier, *Economic determinants of electoral outcomes*, „Annual Review of Political Science" 2000, no. 3, pp. 183–219; M.S. Lewis-Beck, M. Celeste Ratto, *Economic voting…*, op. cit., pp. 489–493; M. Kanji, K. Tannahill, *What are the…*, op. cit., pp. 391–392; S. Weschle, *Two Types…*, op. cit.

the years 1997 and 2001.[272] In Spain, this field of research is much more developed. Among the most important studies regarding economic voting are the analyses of M. Fraile, in which the author studied economic voting in Spain over the last 20 years, based on both surveys and panels.[273] Although the models used by M. Fraile allow for comprehensive study of electoral accountability, due to the use of data available only in Spanish opinion polls and panel studies they cannot be easily transferred to Poland in the analysed time period.

There are two main approaches used in studies of economic voting. In the first one, the economic variable is measured through macroeconomic indicators. The second approach is based on citizens' individual perceptions of economic phenomena. They can be both aggregated retrospective and prospective assessment of the financial situation of individual citizens (wallet voting), and of the state of the country's economy. The complex endogenic randomness between these four subjective variables (prospective and retrospective sociotopic variable, prospective and retrospective egotropic variable) has led to a situation in which economic voting has been referred to as a "Pandora's box."[274]

The model of economic voting applied in this part of the study uses the second approach to studies of economic voting, based on individual perceptions of

272 P. Grzelak, *Głosowanie ekonomiczne w Polsce w wyborach parlamentarnych w 1997 i 2001 roku*, in: R. Markowski (ed.), *System partyjny i zachowania wyborcze. Dekada polskich doświadczeń (1989/1991–2001)*, Warszawa 2003, pp. 217–240; P. Grzelak, *Populizm w modelu głosowania ekonomicznego w Polsce 2001*, in: R. Markowski (ed.), *Populizm a demokracja*, Warsaw 2004, pp. 203–238.

273 M. Fraile, *Una comparación del voto económico en las elecciones de 1996 y 2000*, „Revista Española de Ciencia Política" 2002, no. 6, pp. 129–151; M. Fraile, *Cuando la economía entra en las urnas: el voto económico en España (1979–1996)*, Madrid 2005; M. Fraile, M.S. Lewis-Beck, *Economic voting in Spain: A 2000 panel test*, „Electoral Studies" 2010, no. 29, pp. 210–220; M. Fraile, M.S. Lewis-Beck, *Economics and Elections in Spain (1982–2008): Cross-Measures, Cross-Time*, „Electoral Studies" 2012, no. 31, pp. 485–490; M. Fraile, M.S. Lewis-Beck, *Economic Vote Instability: Endogeneity or Restricted Variance? Spanish Panel Evidence (2008 and 2011)*, „European Journal of Political Research" 2013, doi: 10,1111/1475-6765,12018; M. Fraile, S. Pardós-Prado, *Correspondence between the objective and the subjective economies: personal economic circumstances as a heuristic*, „Political Studies" 2013, doi: 10,1111/1467-9248,12055; M. Fraile, M.S. Lewis-Beck, *Multi-Dimensional Economic Voting in Spain: the 2008 Elections*, „Electoral Studies" 2013, in: dx.doi.org/10.1016/j.electstud.2013.05.027.

274 P. Nannestad, M. Paldam, *Into Pandora's Box of Economic Evaluations: a Study of the Danish Macro VP Function 1986–1997*, „Electoral Studies" 2000, no. 19, pp. 123–140; M. Padam, P. Nannestad, *What do voters know about the economy? A study of Danish data. 1990–1993*, „Electoral Studies" 2000, no. 19, pp. 363–391.

phenomena. To examine to which extent economic voting is used in Poland and Spain, and therefore whether the reward/punishment mechanism functions in both countries, three independent variables have been used: a retrospective assessment of the country's economic situation, prospective assessment of the country's economic situation, and retrospective assessment of the political situation. The use of these independent variables was based on the following factors: first, using only the sociotopic retrospective assessment of the economy with the exclusion of the egotropic assessment was dictated by, on one hand, the fact that it is highly problematic to determine the government's influence on the individual economic situation of citizens, as it can result from personal experiences and not from any decisions made by the government;[275] on the other hand, the results of studies done by P. Grzelak and M. Fraile prove that in both countries the so-called "wallet voting" is practically non-existent.[276]

Including in the model not only retrospective assessment of the state of the country's economy, but also prospective assessment is, in turn, a response to the common criticism of economic voting connected with a lack of realism in interpretations of voter behaviour. This criticism is connected with the fact that including only retrospective opinions on the economy would indicate a situation in which voters would not take into consideration the solutions proposed to various issues by political parties.[277] Therefore, in more recent literature it is assumed that elections also contain a prospective element and are not used only to punish or reward the ruling party, but also to elect a party offering the best political program. This model thus also includes a prospective assessment of the country's economy, which indicates the expectations of voters.

Adding also the retrospective assessment of the political situation results, in turn, from the fact that the relation between the state of the economy and the popularity of the parties forming the government is not so unambiguous. When analysing existing study results, it can be noted that periods of economic growth do not necessarily reward the ruling party and result in its re-election, and vice

275 For more see: G. Kramer, *The ecological fallacy revisited: Aggregate versus individual level findings on economic and elections, and sociotropic voting*, „American Political Science Review" 1983, no. 77, pp. 92–111.

276 M. Fraile, *Una comparación…*, op. cit.; M. Fraile, *Cuando la economía entra…*, op. cit.; P. Grzelak, *Głosowanie ekonomczne…*, op. cit.

277 For more, see: D.R. Kinder, R.D. Kiewiet, *Sociotropic…*, op. cit., pp. 129–141; H. Rattinger, *Unemployment and Elections in West Germany*, in: H. Norpoth, M.S. Lewis-Beck, J.-D. Lafay (eds.), *Economics and Politics: The Calculus of Support*, Ann Arbor, 1991, pp. 49–62.

versa – periods of economic recession need not result in punishing the government and the election of an opposition party. One explanation can be the relation empirically ascertained by M. Fraile based on the example of elections during the period 1979–1996 in Spain. The author proved that negative or positive assessments of the ruling party in time of crisis depends on whether it proposed compensation in the form of social policy to the voters. Therefore, the government is assessed based on not only the state of the economy, but also on its social policies.[278] This is why, when analysing the relationship between the state of the economy and public opinion, the political and social context should also be taken into consideration. Therefore, the model also includes retrospective assessment of the political situation. Additionally, as argued by P.C. Magalhães, L. Aguiar-Conraria, and M. Lewis-Beck, assessment of the political situation in the country can be used as an approximate indicator of the government's popularity – as emphasised by the authors, the aggregated level of correlation between opinions regarding the general political situation in the country and approval for the government is high.[279] Such an expanded model of economic voting allows for more comprehensive analysis of the connections between public opinion and the economy.

The model of multinomial logistic regression used in the study is expressed in the equation:[280]

Voter decision = $\beta_0 + \beta_1$ retrospective assessment of the economic situation + β_2 prospective assessment of the economic situation + β_3 retrospective assessment of the political situation $+\Sigma\beta_n$ control variables $+\varepsilon$

The dependent variable Y means the declared support for the current ruling parties or for opposition parties. Depending on the analysed elections, various party configurations existed, which will be described in detail later. It is worth noting here that because of the number of cases, it was not possible to consider

278 M. Fraile, *El voto económico en las elecciones de 1996 y 2000: una comparación*, „Revista Española de Ciencia Política" 2002, no. 6, pp. 129–151.

279 P.C. Magalhães, L. Aguiar-Conraria, M. Lewis-Beck investigated the level of correlation between opinions regarding the general political situation in the country and approval of the government. In the case of Spain in the years 1993–2009 it was $r = 0.81$. Source: P.C.Magalhães, L.Aguiar-Conraria, M.Lewis-Beck, *Forecating Spanish elections*, „International Journal of Forecasting" 2012, no. 28, p. 770.

280 Full equation: Voter decision = $\beta_0 + \beta_1$ retrospective assessment of the economic situation + β_2 prospective assessment of the economic situation + β_3 retrospective assessment of the political situation + β_4 political self-identification + β_5 age + β_6 gender + β_7 unemployed + β_8 homemaker + β_9 student + β_{10} retired + β_{11} vocational education + β_{12} secondary education + β_{13} higher education $+\varepsilon$.

all opposition parties separately, which is why some of them were placed in the "others" category.[281]

The main independent variables, i.e. retrospective economic assessment, prospective economic assessment, and retrospective political assessment, are of a dichotomic character. For people who thought that the economic/political situation had improved during the previous year, the value (1) was assigned; for people who thought that the situation had worsened or did not change, (0). Similarly, people who thought that in the next year the situation would improve were assigned (1), while people who thought that it would worsen or remain unchanged were assigned (0).

Additionally, 10 control variables were introduced, which are usually included in analyses regarding the determinants of voting on an individual level. The first was political self-identification on the left-right scale. In the case of the year 1982 in Spain, from 0 – left to 7 – right, and in other years from 0 – left to 10 – right. The inclusion of this variable allows us to determine whether the connection between assessment of the economic situation and voting is a result of rationalisation, which is a reflection of political views. Second, variables controlling the occupational situation of the respondents: unemployed, retired, student, homemaker[282], which can influence the assessment of the economic situation, were included. The other variables are concerned with the social and demographic status of respondents: Gender (men: (1), women: (0)); age, education (elementary, vocational, secondary, higher).

It should also be added that the model does not include respondents who did not participate in the election. Without any doubt, it cannot be ruled out that not voting may also be a kind of punishment for ruling parties, especially if we consider that in Poland the voter turnout level is one of the lowest in Europe, while turnout in Spain is high.[283] However, interpretation of the reasons of voter absence will not be analysed, as it exceeds the framework of this study.

---

281 The basis for selection was too few people declaring a vote for a given party or the existence of empty cells at the crossing of independent and dependent variables, which would make analysis of the multinominal regression impossible.

282 Dichotomic variables, reference category – workers.

283 The average voter turnout in Poland in the examined period, i.e. in the years 1997–2011 was 47.52%, while in Spain it was 73.46%. Based on the data from: www. pkw.gov.pl and www.congreso.es/consti/elecciones/generales/index.htm.

For the elections in Poland in the years 1997–2011, the post-election surveys performed by the Polskie Generalne Studium Wyborcze will be used.[284] Depending on the year, the following variables were taken into consideration:

Variables used in the model	**1997**	**2001**	**2005**	**2007**	**2011**
Survey study	PGSW 1997	PGSW 2001	PGSW 2005	PGSW 2007	PGSW 2011
Independent variables					
Retrospective assessment of the economic situation	x	x	x	x	x
Prospective assessment of the economic situation	x	x	x	x	x
Retrospective assessment of the political situation	x	x	x	x	x
Control variables					
Political self-identification	x	x	x	x	
Age	x	x	x	x	x
Gender	x	x	x	x	x
Unemployed	x	x	x	x	x
Homemaker	x	x	-	x	-
Student	-	x	x	x	x
Retired	x	x	x	x	x
Vocational education	x	x	x	x	x
Secondary education	x	x	x	x	x
Higher education	x	x	x	x	x

In the analysis of Spain, the data came from surveys performed by Centro de Investigaciones Sociológicas. Some of them, i.e. ones from the years 1982–1996, were based on polls done soon after the elections, while the 2000–2011 data was based on post-election barometers.[285]

284 Polskie Generalne Studium Wyborcze: http://www.isppan.waw.pl/subpage/pgsw/index.html.

285 Centro de Investigaciones Sociológicas, http//www.cis.es.

Variables used in the model	1982	1986	1989	1993	1996	2000	2004	2008	2011
CiS survey study no..	1341	1545	1845	2062	2215	2384	2559	2757	2920
Independent variables									
Retrospective assessment of the economic situation	x	x	x	x	x	x	x	x	x
Prospective assessment of the economic situation	x	x	x	x	x	x	x	x	x
Retrospective assessment of the political situation	-	x	x	x	x	x	x	x	x
Control variables									
Political self-identification	x	x	x	x	x	x	x	x	x
Age	x	x	x	x	x	x	x	x	x
Gender	x	x	x	x	x	x	x	x	x
Unemployed	x	x	x	x	x	x	x	x	x
Homemaker	x	x	x	x	x	x	x	x	x
Student	x	x	x	-	x	x	x	x	x
Retired	x	x	x	x	x	x	x	x	x
Vocational education	x	x	x	x	x	x	x	x	x
Secondary education	x	x	x	x	x	x	x	x	x
Higher education	x	x	x	x	x	x	x	x	x

In the case of both Poland and Spain each election was described separately, and each time the results indicate the influence of individual variables on the probability of voting for a given party compared to the probability of voting for a party running for re-election.

6.2. Poland – economic voting in the elections of:

In Poland, in the year 1997 the parties that fought for enough votes to form another government were SLD and PSL, while in 2001 they were AWS and UW, in 2005 SLD and PSL, in 2007 PiS, LPR and Samoobrona, and in 2011 PO and PSL. The opposition parties[286] in 1997 were UW, ROP, UP, and AWS, in 2001 PSL, PO, LPR, Samoobrona, PiS and SLD, in 2005 PSL, PO, LPR, Samoobrona, and PiS, in 2007 SLD, PSL, and PO, while in 2011 SLD, PSL, and PiS. Poll results are shown for the main coalition parties, not for government coalitions, as the results in both cases are rather similar, and this interpretation of the results seems clearer. However, the appendix includes results for government coalitions as well.

286 Other parties included in the analyses were placed in the "others" category.

The point of reference for the interpretation of results generated through the model used is the economic and political situation in the years 1997–2011. The political situation during these terms of parliament was described in Chapter 2. The main points of political conflicts and precise election results of individual political parties were described. Therefore, in this part only the economic situation in the years 1997–2011 will be characterised.

As the political situation in the years 1993–1997 was not analysed due to the time period adopted for discussion in this work, it is worth describing it briefly here, considering it serves as a point of reference for the results of the regression from 1997. The winning party in the 1993 election was SLD, which received 20.4% of the vote and 37% of seats in the Sejm. Its coalition partner was PSL, which received 15.4% of the votes and almost 29% of seats. For the first time since 1989, the same coalition formed a government for the entire parliamentary term. However, cooperation between the partners was stormy. In March 1995 a new Prime Minister was appointed, with Waldemar Pawlak from PSL replaced by Józef Oleksy from SLD; after the latter's resignation connected with accusations against him of cooperation with Russian intelligence, he himself resigned and was replaced by Włodzimierz Cimoszewicz in February 1996. When analysing the economic situation, it is worth adding that in the years 1993–1997, Poland experienced significant economic growth. GDP increased by 3.4%, unemployment decreased by 3.1%, and inflation by 10.7%. In summarising the 1993–1997 term of parliament, it should be stressed that despite tensions within the coalition, this period saw political stabilisation compared to the one before it, as well as a good economic situation.

During the 1997–2001 term of parliament, all macroeconomic indicators except inflation show a worsening economic situation. GDP decreased by 5.9% in 2001 compared to 1997, while unemployment rose by 7.4%. The only indicator that saw improvement was inflation, which fell by 16.4%. In the next parliamentary term of 2001–2005, GDP increased by 3.2% but the level of unemployment decreased only slightly, by 0.5%, and inflation rose by 0.9%. In the 2005–2007 term, all macroeconomic indicators except for inflation improved. GDP rose by as much as 3.2%, unemployment decreased by 8.2%, and inflation increased only slightly, by 1.4%. The 2007–2011 term, in turn, saw a decrease in GDP of 2.5%, a very slight increase in unemployment of 0.01%, and a decrease in inflation of 9%.

Table 27. Main macroeconomic indicators in Poland in the years 1997–2011

Years	GDP growth	Unemployment rate	Inflation rate
1993	3.7	14	30.6
1994	5.3	14.4	37.2
1995	7.0	13.2	28.0
1996	6.2	12.1	17.9
1997	7.1	10.9	19.9
1998	5.0	10.2	11.1
1999	4.5	13.4	6.0
2000	4.3	16.1	7.3
2001	1.2	18.3	3.5
2002	1.4	20.0	2.2
2003	3.9	19.7	0.4
2004	5.3	19.0	4.1
2005	3.6	17.8	2.6
2006	6.2	13.9	1.5
2007	6.8	9.6	4.0
2008	5.1	7.1	3.1
2009	1.6	8.2	3.7
2010	3.9	9.6	1.4
2011	4.3	9.7	3.1

Source: *Statistical Annex of European Economy, Attum* 2012, European Commission, 2012, pp. 35, 49, 77.

When summarising the results of macroeconomic indicators (Tab. 27) and their influence on voter behaviour, it should be added that a characteristic trait of the economy in the first years of the democratic transition occurring in Poland was dynamic economic growth. However, such growth did not necessarily result in conviction on the part of citizens that Poland's economic situation had improved, as the prior state of the Polish economy was very weak. The same increase in GDP in highly developed countries would be felt differently, as for citizens it would mean a major increase in wealth. GDP in the period 2007–2011 requires separate remarks. When analysing the small increase in GDP, it might be expected that the government ruling during that term of parliament will be blamed. However, it should be remembered that 2008 saw a global economic crisis, and therefore small growth was viewed not as a failure but as a major accomplishment. In studies regarding the retrospective economic vote, it has been proven that the largest factor influencing it comes from another indicator – the level of unemployment.

It can therefore be expected that in 2001 the retrospective economic vote should have been used, but not in 2005. Regarding inflation, in most of the studies no direct link between the increase or decrease in the frequency of economic voting and the level of inflation has been proven to exist. However, it seems that in the situation of countries such as Poland, which underwent a deep systemic transformation, including economic overhauls, levels of inflation cannot be compared with those recorded in highly developed countries. It can therefore be presumed that in periods during which inflation was very high, resulting in citizens' decreased purchasing power, this indicator can be positively correlated with the use of retrospective economic voting. Such a situation occurred in the periods 1993–1997 and 1997–2001. Both terms of parliament saw a spectacular decrease in inflation, which should reward ruling parties. The study results cited below will allow us to ascertain the level to which the economy entered the ballot box in the years 1997–2011, both in the retrospective and prospective aspects, and how important the role of assessment of the political situation was.

6.2.1. 1997

In the 1997 campaign, the party running for re-election was SLD (in the model it is the category of reference), which had ruled in a coalition with PSL during the 1993–1997 term. The analyses also include AWS, PSL, UW, ROP and UP. Other parties were included in the category "others". When analysing the most important variable from the perspective of accountability, i.e. retrospective assessment of the state of the country's economy, it should be emphasised that positive assessment of the state of economy increased the probability of voting for SLD and decreased the probability of voting for AWS – the main opposition party – which won the 1997 election. In other cases it was not statistically relevant. This means that the hypothesis of accountability in the case of the 1997 election was partially confirmed, as retrospective economic voting was employed. A negative assessment of the state of the economy decreased the probability of voting for the party running for re-election in relation to the probability of voting for AWS. The prospective economic vote was used to a larger extent, as aside from voting for AWS it was also important in voting for UW. Positive expectations regarding the country's economy in the future decreased the likelihood of voting for SLD (compared to AWS and UW). Retrospective assessment of the political situation was also important, as indicated by those voting for AWS, PSL and those voting for the "other" parties. Here the relation is similar to that in retrospective assessment of the economy, as a negative assessment of the political situation in the past decreased the likelihood of voting for SLD. The relationship indicated for

PSL should be noted, as this party was coalition partner with SLD for the entire length of the term of parliament, and therefore was partially responsible for the shape of Polish policies at that time.

In the case of political self-identification, it should be noted that it was statistically relevant for all parties save AWS. This means that ideology had a major influence on the likelihood of voting for all parties except for AWS when compared to the likelihood of voting for SLD. In the case of these parties' voters, the more they identified as right-wing on the left-right axis, the less likely they were to vote for SLD. Even though these results should not be surprising, the fact that the same was also the case for UP voters is quite interesting.

Table 28. Economic voting in the 1997 election in Poland[287]

Variables	**Vote for AWS *versus* SLD**	**Vote for PSL *versus* SLD**	**Vote for UW *versus* SLD**	**Vote for ROP *versus* SLD**	**Vote for UP *versus* SLD**	**Vote for others *versus* SLD**
Retrospective assessment of the economic situation	-0.45 (0.35)**	0.31 (0.41)	-0.32 (0.34)	-0.31 0.55)	0.01 (0.51)	-0.39 (0.40)
Prospective assessment of the economic situation	0.69 (0.30)***	0.44 (0.38)	0.64 (0.31)**	0.51 (0.44)	0.41 (0.48)	0.26 (0.40)
Retrospective assessment of the political situation	-1.21 (0.30)***	-1.5 (0.38)***	-0.47 (0.32)	-0.83 (0.44)	-0.33 (0.50)	-0.79 (0.39)*
Political self-identification	1.09 (0.08)	0.44 (0.08)***	0.69 (0.080)***	1.00 (0.11)***	0.44 (0.11)***	0.84 (0.00) ***
N...817						
Log probability..968.572						
LR Chi²(72) 690.39						
Prob >Ch² 0.000						
Pseudo- R²...0.262						

*p<05; **p<01; ***p<001; standard error given in parenthesis.

287 Data with all coefficients of the multinominal logistic regression and the full list of control variables is included in the appendix.

Therefore, we may hypothesise that SLD's loss in the election was due to retrospective economic voting, as voters for the main opposition party indicated thus. However, given the good economic results in the years 1993–1997, the use of the retrospective economic vote may be doubtful. One could try to explain it by invoking the positive correlation between SLD's failure to achieve re-election and negative assessment of the political situation, as well as the conviction that another party might deal with future challenges to the Polish economy better.

6.2.2. 2001

In the 2001 election, the party attempting to remain in power was AWS (in the model it is the category of reference), which ruled in the years 1997–2001 in a coalition with UW. The analyses also include SLD, PSL, PO, PiS, and Samoobrona. Other parties were included in the "others" category. According to the results in Table 29, in 2001 retrospective assessment of the economic situation did not influence the likelihood of voting for any of the parties. However, the prospective economic vote was important in the case of SLD, UW, and PO. This means that a positive assessment of the state of the economy in the future increased the likelihood of voting for SLD, UW, or PO in comparison to AWS. Yet retrospective assessment of the political situation in the case of all included parties was not statistically relevant, which means that it did not influence the likelihood of voting for a given political party. Additionally, in the 2001 election ideology was important to those voting for SLD, PSL, PO and Samoobrona. The relation should be interpreted in light of the results in Table 30 as voters being less likely to vote for AWS the more they identified as left-wing.

Table 29. Economic voting in the 2001 election in Poland

Variables	Vote for SLD *versus* AWS	Vote for PSL *versus* AWS	Vote for UW *versus* AWS	Vote for PO *versus* AWS	Vote for PiS *versus* AWS	Vote for Samoobrona *versus* AWS
Retrospective assessment of the economic situation	-0.70 (1.13)	1.10 (1.11)	0.57 (1.47)	0.99 (0.98)	1.00 (1.01)	0.75 (1.10)
Prospective assessment of the economic situation	1.86 (0.68)***	1.69 (0.71)	1.78 (0.85)**	1.45 (0.68)**	1.26 (0.70)	1.50 (0.69)
Retrospective assessment of the political situation	-0.80 (0.76)	-1.01 (0.84)	-2.29 (1.29)	-1.01 (0.72)	-1.29 (0.78))	-1.04 (0.81)
Ideological self-identification	-1.02 (0.11)***	-0.50 (0.11)***	-0.22 (0.14)	-0.22 (0.10)**	-0.13 (0.10)	-0.46 (0.10)***

Variables	Vote for SLD *versus* AWS	Vote for PSL *versus* AWS	Vote for UW *versus* AWS	Vote for PO *versus* AWS	Vote for PiS *versus* AWS	Vote for Samoobrona *versus* AWS
N......916						
Log probability......-1266.513						
LR Chi²(72)......525.31						
Prob >Ch²......0.000						
Pseudo- R^2......0.172						

*p<05; **p<01; ***p<001; standard error given in parenthesis.

As mentioned before, in previously conducted studies regarding economic voting there were situations in which, despite a worsening economic situation, voters did not punish the ruling parties by voting for the opposition; this could be associated with compensation in the form of social policy or a general positive assessment of the previous government in respect of other policies. However, with reference to the term of parliament analysed here, retrospective assessment of neither the economic nor political situation was statistically relevant. Nevertheless, it was a period in which the economic situation significantly deteriorated: among other issues, the unemployment rate rose, which is directly correlated with the responsibility hypothesis. Additionally, this term of parliament was also characterised by strong political conflict, which could also lead to a negative assessment of the government. This is why the results cited above may be viewed as doubtful. One explanation for this situation is the genesis of the newly-created parties: PO and PiS. As has already been mentioned in Chapter 5, the politicians forming these two groups were in the main members of AWS. After careful analysis of the survey data, it transpired that this fact disturbed the functioning of the model used, as the number of people declaring in the poll that they voted for AWS was very small (only 6% of respondents). It is most likely that these newly-formed parties took over the AWS electorate. This is why, in the case of 2001, additional calculations were made as a result of the appearance of new parties formed partly through the decomposition of the previous ruling party. PO and PiS were included alongside AWS as parties running for re-election.

Table 30. Economic voting in the 2001 election in Poland

Variables	Vote for SLD versus *AWS/* PO/PIS	Vote for PSL *versus* AWS/ PO/PIS	Vote for LPR *versus* AWS/PO/ PIS	Vote for Samoobrona *versus* AWS/ PO/PIS	Vote for UW *versus AWS/* PO/PIS
Retrospective assessment of the economic situation	-1.74 (0.70)***	0.12 (0.69)	-0.82 (0.87)	-0.22 (0.68)	-0.34 (1.19)
Prospective assessment of the economic situation	0.15 (0.49)**	-0.16 (0.60)	0.20 (0.61)	-0.17 (0.56)	-1.17 (1.16)
Retrospective assessment of the political situation	0.61 (0.26)	0.45 (0.33)	-0.11 (0.42)	0.26 (0.31)	0.53 (0.58)
Ideological self-identification	-0.85 (0.06)***	-0.32 (0.07)***	0.10 (0.07)	-0.29 (0.06)***	-0.08 (0.12)
N...775					
Log probability...836.812					
LR Chi²(55) 553.95					
Prob >Ch² 0.000					
Pseudo- R²...0.249					

*p<05; **p<01; ***p<001; standard error given in parenthesis.

The new composition of the category of parties running for re-election proves correct the hypothesis of responsibility in the case of the main opposition party, i.e. SLD: retrospective economic voting took place. This means that a negative opinion on the state of the economy made the probability of voting for AWS, PO and PiS lower than for SLD. In the case of SLD and other analysed parties, other dependent variables and the control variable were mostly unchanged in comparison with the results from the model in which the reference party was only AWS. In summary, based on the modified model of economic voting in 2001, it can be concluded that the mechanism of punishment/reward was used in the case of SLD. This likely explains the loss of both AWS, and of the parties created as a result of its breakdown, i.e. PO and PiS.

6.2.3. 2005

In 2005, the party seeking re-election was SLD (in the model it is the category of reference), which ruled in the years 2001–2005 in a coalition with PSL. The analysis also includes PiS, PSL, PO, LPR, and Samoobrona. The other parties were included in the category "others". When analysing the most important variable indicating vertical accountability, i.e. retrospective assessment of the economic situation, it should be stressed that in the case of support for PiS, LPR, and Samoobrona in comparison to SLD, it was statistically relevant. This means that a poor assessment of the existing economic situation reduced the likelihood of voting for SLD. The prospective assessment of the economy variable was also statistically relevant in the case of PiS and PO versus SLD. Therefore, a positive assessment of the state of the economy in the future reduced the likelihood of voting for the party running for re-election. Retrospective assessment of the political situation, however, was not statistically significant. Ideology also had a major influence on the likelihood of voting for PiS, PSL, PO, LPR and Samoobrona in relation to voting for SLD. The more to the right a voter was on the left-right axis, the lower the probability of voting for the party seeking re-election.

Table 31. Economic voting in the 2005 election in Poland

Variables	Vote for PIS *versus* SLD	Vote for PSL *versus* SLD	Vote for PO *versus* SLD	Vote for LPR *versus* SLD	Vote for Samoobrona *versus* SLD	Vote for others *versus* SLD
Retrospective assessment of the economic situation	-1.51 (0.41)***	-0.15 (0.49)	-0.55 (0.39)	-2.00 (0.67)***	-1.49 (0.54)***	-0.61 (0.44)
Prospective assessment of the economic situation	0.98 (0.36)***	-0.69 (0.51)	0.85 (0.36)**	0.38 (0.47)	-0.11 (0.43)	0.61 (0.42)
Retrospective assessment of the political situation	0.03 (0.56)	0.24 (0.67)	0.09 (0.55)	0.31 (0.77)	-0.16 (0.69)	-0.27 (0.67)
Ideological self-identification	0.94 (0.08)***	0.61 (0.09)***	0.83 (0.08)***	1.04 (0.11)***	0.67 (0.09)***	0.52 (0.08)***
N......916						
Log probability......-1266.513						
LR Chi²(72)......525.31						
Prob >Ch²......0.000						
Pseudo- R²......0.172						

*p<05; **p<01; ***p<001; standard error given in parenthesis.

In summary, it should be stressed that in the 2005 election the hypothesis of responsibility was partially confirmed, even though the economic situation did not worsen, but even slightly improved. In the case of the main opposition party, i.e. PiS, as well as LPR and Samoobrona, the economic vote was used. Expectations for the future were also not without importance in the probability of choosing a political party, in the case of PiS as well as PO, the party receiving the second-highest number of votes) in relation to SLD. In conclusion, the economic vote was relevant in the 2005 election, although expectations regarding the economic situation in the future also exercised a major influence on the voting decision.

6.2.4. 2007

Politically, the years 2005–2007 were tempestuous. The coalition formed by PiS (in the model it is the category of reference), LPR, and Samoobrona was very unstable. Given this, the analysis includes SLD, PSL, PO, PiS, and Samoobrona. Other parties were included in the category "others". The interpretation of the election results is similar to that of previous years; negative assessment of the economic situation reduces the likelihood of voting for PiS compared to the probability of voting for PO. Prospective assessment of the economy was statistically relevant in the case of PO, PSL, and SLD. Positive expectations regarding the economic situation in the future increased the probability of casting a vote for one of these groups. In addition, retrospective assessment of the political situation was relevant in the case of all opposition parties; in this case, negative assessment of the earlier political situation in the country reduced the likelihood of voting for PiS. Ideology was also important in 2007, increasing the probability of voting for all opposition parties except for PO. This result seems to confirm the opinion that at that point there was no major ideological gap between voters of PiS and PO: in this case, ideology did not influence the likelihood of voting for PiS or PO, and therefore did not differentiate the voters of those parties. In the case of the other parties, PSL and SLD, the more voters identified as left-wing, the more likely they were to vote for these parties.

Table 32. Economic voting in the 2007 election in Poland

Variables	Vote for PO *versus* PiS	Vote for PSL *versus* PiS	Vote for LiD *versus* PiS
Retrospective assessment of the economic situation	-0.64 (0.20)***	-0.58 (0.31)	0.17 (0.34)
Prospective assessment of the economic situation	1.99 (0.19)***	1.25 (0.28)***	1.05 (0.32)***
Retrospective assessment of the political situation	-0.86 (0.21)***	-1.25 (0.40)***	1.34 (0.47)***
Ideological self-identification	-0.28 (0.04)	-0.38 (0.07)***	-0.99 (0.08)***

Variables	Vote for PO *versus* PiS	Vote for PSL *versus* PiS	Vote for LiD *versus* PiS
N 1011			
Log probability .... -818.119			
LR $Chi^2(36)$ 601.77			
Prob $>Ch^2$ 0.000			
Pseudo- R^2 .... 0.270			

*p<0.5; **p<.01;***p<.001; standard error given in parenthesis.

When comparing the above results with the economic situation in the country in the years 2005–2007, the use of the retrospective economic vote in the case of PO is intriguing. During the parliamentary term in question practically all of the macroeconomic indicators displayed economic growth, including a major decrease in the unemployment rate. It thus transpires that in the case of PO, PSL and SLD, the voter decision was influenced by the political situation, one of very strong conflicts and confrontational politics during almost the entire term. Also, these voters decided that the perspective of another term with a PiS government would not be good for the economic situation in the country. In summary, one may wonder why the responsibility hypothesis is confirmed in respect of PO, the party that had the best election results in 2007. This may result from so-called total critique, the conviction that everything was bad during the passing parliamentary term, even though objective economic results do not confirm this view.

6.2.5. 2011

In 2011, the party running for re-election was PO (in the model it is the category of reference), which ruled in the period 2007–2011 in a coalition with PSL. The analyses also include SLD, PSL, and RP. Retrospective economic voting was not employed in the 2011 election. Therefore, the responsibility hypothesis was not confirmed. However, the situation was different in the case of the prospective economic vote. Prospective assessment of the economic situation turned out to be a statistically relevant variable in the case of PiS, PSL, and RP, with the only exception being SLD. A positive assessment of the state of the economy in the future increased the likelihood of voting for PO. Ideology also had a major influence on the likelihood of voting for all parties, except PSL, when PO is treated as the reference category. In the case of SLD and RP, the more to the left of the left-right axis voters identified themselves, the less likely they were to vote for these parties in relation to PO. In the case of PiS, exactly the opposite was true; the more to the right they were, the more likely they were to vote for PiS compared to PO.

Table 33. Economic voting in the 2011 election in Poland

Variables	Vote for PIS *versus* PO	Vote for PSL *versus* PO	Vote for SLD *versus* PO	Vote for RP *versus* PO
Retrospective assessment of the economic situation	-0.48 (0.30)	-0.69 (0.47)	-0.56 (0.50)	-0.37 (0.35)
Prospective assessment of the economic situation	-1.38 (0.28)***	-1.21 (0.43)***	0.03 (0.37)	-0.83 (0.32)***
Retrospective assessment of the political situation	-1.63 (0.35)***	-0.60 (0.44)	-0.85 (0.49)	0.31 (0.32)
Ideological self-identification	0.35 (0.05)***	-0.11 (0.06)	-0.54 (0.07)***	-0.21 (0.06)***
N	821			
Log probability	888.943			
LR $Chi^2(48)$	989.63			
Prob $>Ch^2$	0.000			
Pseudo- R^2	0.183			

***p<.001; **p<.01; *p<.05. Standard error given in parenthesis.

In summarising the results of multinomial regression of 2011, it should be stressed that the hypothesis of responsibility was not confirmed. Voters did not employ economic voting, despite a major deterioration in the economic situation. This may have occurred because of the government's informational campaign and constant comparisons to European Union countries that were undergoing economic recession. Compared to these, Poland seemed like a "green island", even though economic growth was halted. On the other hand, it should be noted that the main topic of the political campaign was not the economy, but attitudes towards the Smolensk airplane crash. Therefore, the competition between the two strongest political parties (PO and PiS) concentrated on issues other than the economy.

6.3. Spain – economic voting in the elections of:

During the analysed period in Spain, the parties that fought for enough votes to form another government were UCD in 1982, PSOE in 1986, 1993 and 1996, PP in 2000 and 2004, and PSOE again in 2008 and 2011. The parties in opposition were: in 1982: PSOE, PP, PCE; in 1986: PP, CDS, IU, CiU; in 1993: PP, IU, CiU; in

1996: PP, IU, CiU; in 2000: PSOE, IU; in 2004: PSOE, CiU; in 2008: PP, IU-ICV; in 2011: PP, IU-ICV, UPyD. In the case of each election the "others" category was included for parties for which no more than 50 respondents voted in a given survey.

As in the case of Poland, the points of reference for the interpretation of results acquired through the multinomial logistic regression model are the economic and political situations. The political situation and exact election results for the years 1982–2011 have been described in previous chapters. Therefore, here only the political and economic situation during the 1979–1982 term of parliament will be briefly described. In 1979, Adolfo Suarez, the leader of UCD, was elected Prime Minister for the second time. However, UCD won 34.74% of the vote, which meant 168 seats in the Congress of Deputies. The failure of coalition negotiations led to the creation of a minority government. The increasingly limited decision-making capabilities of the government caused by the departure of UCD deputies to other political parties, and by the decreasing potential of forming temporary alliances with opposition parties, led to Suarez's resignation in 1981. The new government was headed by Leopoldo Calvo-Sotelo, also of UCD, who managed to remain in his position until the end of the term despite a failed coup attempt in 1982. Spain's economic situation during that time was also not good, and the initial years of democratic transformation were painful. During the 1979–1982 parliamentary term GDP rose by 2.3% while inflation fell by 1.5%, but unemployment rose by 10.6%.

During the next term (1982–1986), all macroeconomic indicators showed an improved economic situation – economic growth indicated by an increase in GDP of 2.1%, a slight decrease in the unemployment rate of 1.4%, and a decrease in inflation of 2.7%. The situation was similar in the 1986–1989 term: GDP increased GDP by 1.5%, unemployment fell by 1.9%, and inflation dropped by 4%. The situation changed in the period 1989–993 (a clear economic recession in Spain). GDP fell drastically, by as much as 5.8%, while unemployment increased by 4.6%, and inflation fell by 2.7%. Although in 1993–1996 the situation improved and GDP grew by 3.4%, unemployment was still high (falling only by 0.09%), while inflation fell by 1.4%. The next term (1996–200) represented a major improvement in the condition of the Spanish economy. GDP rose by 2.6%, unemployment fell by as much as 7.4%, but inflation remained at the same level, rising 3.5% year-over-year. In the next term (2000–2004), GDP fell by 1.7%, the unemployment rate fell only slightly, by 0.8%, and inflation rose by only 0.5%. In the 2004–2008 parliamentary term, all macroeconomic indicators show a deterioration of the economic situation, expressed by a fall of GDP by 2.4%, a slight increase in unemployment by

0.4% and only inflation decreased by 1.6%. The 2008–2011 term is the period of the greatest crisis in the history of democratic Spain – this is confirmed especially by a drastic increase of unemployment rate – by as much as 10.4%, a drop in GDP of 0.5% and in inflation of 1.4%.

Table 34. Primary macroeconomic indicators in Spain in the years 1982–2011

Year	GDP growth	Unemployment rate	Inflation rate	Year	GDP growth	Unemployment rate	Inflation rate
1979/80	3.5	5.4	15.1	**1996**	2.4	19.1	3.5
1981	-0.1	14.2	12.3	**1997**	3.9	17.8	2.4
1982	1.2	16.0	13.6	**1998**	4.5	15.9	2.5
1983	1.8	14.3	11.9	**1999**	4.7	13.2	2.6
1984	1.8	16.7	10.9	**2000**	5.0	11.7	3.5
1985	2.3	17.8	8.6	**2001**	3.7	10.5	4.2
1986	3.3	17.4	10.9	**2002**	2.7	11.4	4.4
1987	5.5	18.5	5.9	**2003**	3.1	11.4	4.2
1988	5.1	17.5	5.9	**2004**	3.3	10.9	4.0
1989	4.8	15.5	6.9	**2005**	3.6	9.2	4.3
1990	3.8	14.4	7.3	**2006**	4.1	8.5	4.1
1991	2.5	14.5	6.9	**2007**	3.5	8.3	3.3
1992	0.9	16.3	6.7	**2008**	0.9	11.3	2.4
1993	-1.0	20.1	4.5	**2009**	-3.7	18	0.1
1994	2.4	21.3	3.9	**2010**	-0.3	20.1	0.4
1995	2.8	20.0	4.9	**2011**	0.4	21.7	1.0

Source: *Statistical Annex of European Economy: Attum 2012*, European Commission, October 19, 2012, pp. 34, 48, 76.

To summarise the economic situation in Spain based on the selected macroeconomic indicators, there have been several parliamentary terms when the economic situation was poor, and even significantly worsened. This was the case during the 1979–1982, 1989–1993, 1993–1996 and 2008–2011 terms of parliament. Therefore, when considering the responsibility hypothesis, during these terms the retrospective economic vote should have been used. Especially when we recall that unemployment is correlated with economic voting, and it should be noted that by the end of 1982 the unemployment rate was 17.4%, while in 1993 and 1996 it was 20.1% and 19.1% respectively, in 2011 reaching a level of 21.7%. Unemployment levels were more or less correlated with GDP. As for inflation, it should be expected that until 1986, when inflation was the highest, it could have also influenced the use of the retrospective economic vote. The parliamentary terms of

1986–1989, 1996–2000, and 2000–2004, on the other hand, are periods of relative prosperity in the Spanish economy, which should have rewarded parties running for re-election. The results of the study using the multinomial regression model shown below will allow us to determine to what extent in the period of 1982–2011 the economic vote was used in Spain, and to what extent the expectations of the voters regarding the state of the economy in the future and assessment of the political situation played a role.

6.3.1. 1982

In 1982, the party running for re-election was UCD (in the model it is the category of reference), which in the years 1979–1982 formed a minority government. The analysis also includes PSOE, PP, and PCE. The other parties were included in the category "others". When looking at the most important variable from the point of view of vertical accountability – retrospective assessment of the state of the country's economy – it should be noted that it did not lead to the failure of UCD to be re-elected, as it transpires that for voters choosing the opposition parties this variable was not relevant. The responsibility hypothesis, therefore, was not proven correct in the case of the 1982 election, and UCD being unsuccessful in achieving re-election was not based on a negative assessment of the economy. Therefore, the causes of the loss of Adolfo Suarez's party should be sought in reasons other than the economic policies of the 1979–1982 government. However, the results of the regression model given in Table 35 can provide a partial answer to the question of why UCD did not manage to win enough votes to form a government again. One explanation may be a positive relation between the vote and expectations for the future state of the economy. In the case of the main opposition party (PSOE), which won an absolute majority in the 1982 election, the conviction that the state of the Spanish economy would improve in the future turned out to be relevant. It means that the likelihood of voting for PSOE was higher than the likelihood of voting for UCD if a given voter assessed the future state of the economy positively. However, it seems that the prospective economic vote was not statistically significant for PP, PCE, and other parties in relation to support for UCD. Ideology also had a major influence on the likelihood of voting for all parties compared to voting for UCD. The more the voters self-identified as left-wing on the left-right axis, the more likely they were to vote for PSOE, PCE and CiU compared to UCD. The same was true for all other parties except for PP. In the case of PP, the less voters identified as right-wing, the more willing they were to vote for UCD.

Table 35. Economic voting in Spain in the 1982 election

Variables	Vote for PSOE versus UCD	Vote for PP versus UCD	Vote for PCE versus UCD	Vote for others versus UCD
Retrospective assessment of the economic situation	-0.01 (0.44)	-0.5 (0.52)	-0.90 (0.72)	-0.51 (0.55)
Prospective assessment of the economic situation	1.49 (0.26)***	-0.46 (0.29)	0.58 (0.45)	0.16 (0.30)
Ideological self-identification	-0.30 (0.06)***	0.17 (0.07)***	-1.78 (0.25)***	-0.16 (0.08)**
N............ 1329				
Log probability............ 1211.825				
LR Chi²(48)............ 553.42				
Prob >Ch²............ 0.000				
Pseudo- R^2............ 0.186				

*p<0.5, **p<0.1; ***p<0.01. Standard error given in parenthesis.

In summary, the hypothesis of economic voting in the 1982 election was not confirmed. Therefore it can be assumed that UCD lost the election for other reasons, unconnected with punishment for the economic recession that took place during the 1979–1982 term. Undoubtedly, in this situation the strong political conflicts occurring during nearly the entire term should be taken into consideration. Unfortunately, the lack of data regarding retrospective assessment of the political situation makes it impossible to confirm these suppositions. It is beyond doubt, however, that in 1982 the economy was not relevant at the ballot box.

6.3.2. 1986

The interpretation of the data in Table 36 is the same as in the case of the data presented in Table 35, with the difference being that from the beginning of 1986 the model includes an additional variable – retrospective assessment of the political situation, which was not included in the 1982 survey. In the 1982 contest the party running for re-election was PSOE (in the model it is the category of reference). The analyses also include PP, CDS, PCE, and CiU. Other parties were included in the category "others". The data in Table 36 indicates that in the 1986 election the responsibility hypothesis is only partially confirmed.

Retrospective economic voting was characteristic only in respect of IU and parties included in the "others" category. In this case, the more negatively voters assessed the existing economic situation in the country, the less likely they were to vote for PSOE. For PP, CDS, and CiU this variable is not significant. On the other hand, the prospective economic vote was significant also for the same parties, *id est* IU and the "others" category. In this case as well, the worse the assessment of the likelihood for improvement of the economic situation in the future, the less likely they were to vote for PSOE. However, retrospective assessment of the political situation was statistically significant for all parties except IU. In the case of PP, CDS, IU, CiU, and "others", a positive assessment of the previous political situation in the country reduced the likelihood of voting for these parties compared to PSOE. Political self-identification was relevant for PP, IU, and CiU. The further a voter was situated to the left, the more likely they were to vote for PSOE compared to PP and CiU. In the case of IU the situation was the opposite: the more to the right voters were, the more likely they were to vote for PSOE than for IU.

Table 36. Economic voting in Spain in the 1986 election

Variables	Vote for PP *versus* PSOE	Vote for CDS versus PSOE	Vote for IU *versus* PSOE	Vote for CiU *versus* PSOE	Vote for others *versus* PSOE
Retrospective assessment of the economic situation	-0.78 (0.43)	-0.16 (0.31)	-1.58 (0.42)***	-0.37 (0.52)	-0.75 (0.25)***
Prospective assessment of the economic situation	-0.65 (0.34)	-0.74 (0.28)***	-1.06 (0.32)***	0.03 (0.45)	-1.38 (0.22)***
Retrospective assessment of the political situation	-1.69 (0.38)***	-1.52 (0.29)***	-0.02 (0.31)	-1.59 (0.5)***	-1.45 (0.22)***
Ideological self-identification	1.89 (0.13)***	0.9 (0.1)	-0.8 (0.12)***	1.08 (0.16)***	-0.09 (0.07)
N............1315 Log probability............-1150.504 LR $Chi^2(65)$............1302.04 Prob >Ch^2............0.000 Pseudo- R^2............0.361					

*p<0.5; **p<0.1; ***p<0.01; standard error given in parenthesis.

In summary, the responsibility hypothesis is proven only partially true in the case of the 1986 election. It is not confirmed in the case of the main opposition party (PP), which received the largest percentage of votes among all opposition parties. This was undoubtedly related to the fairly good condition of the Spanish economy, as indicated by macroeconomic data. It should be added that while

PSOE again managed to achieve an absolute majority, it lost some votes in comparison with the 1982 election. This can most likely be explained to a large extent by the negative assessment of the political situation indicated by a number of respondents than by the voters' expectations regarding the state of the economy in the future.

6.3.3. 1989

The model used in 1989 is the same as in the previous election. Both in 1986 and in 1989 the party running for re-election was PSOE. The opposition parties were also PP, CDS, and IU. However, the number of voters who declared having voted for CiU did not exceed 50, and therefore people who voted for CiU were included in the "others" category.

When analysing the most important variable from the point of view of electoral accountability, i.e. retrospective assessment of the economic situation, it should be noted that in 1989, it was statistically significant in the case of all political parties except IU. A negative assessment of the previous economic situation reduced the likelihood of voting for PSOE. However, the prospective economic vote turned out to be insignificant, unlike the retrospective assessment of the political situation, which was statistically significant in the case of all political parties. Voters who positively assessed the previous political situation were less likely to vote for PP, CD, IU or others in comparison to PSOE. The self-identification of voters was also statistically important. The more voters identified as right-wing, the less likely they were to vote for PSOE compared to other parites with the only exception of IU. In the case of IU, the more to the left voters weref, the less likely they were to vote for the socialists.

Table 37. Economic voting in Spain in the 1989 election

Variables	Vote for PP *versus* PSOE	Vote for CDS *versus* PSOE	Vote for IU *versus* PSOE	Vote for others *versus* PSOE
Retrospective assessment of the economic situation	-1.00 (0.39)***	-0.80 (0.41)*	-0.31 (0.25)	-0.63 (0.27)**
Prospective assessment of the economic situation	-0.52 (0.36)	-0.03 (0.37)	-0.41 (0.25)	-0.37 (0.25)
Retrospective assessment of the political situation	-1.32 (0.37)***	-1.50 (0.41)***	-0.87 (0.23)***	-1.31 (0.25)***
Ideological self-identification	1.71 (0.13)***	0.82 (0.12)***	-0.64 (0.10)***	0.36 (0.09)***

Variables	Vote for PP *versus* PSOE	Vote for CDS *versus* PSOE	Vote for IU *versus* PSOE	Vote for others *versus* PSOE
N 1055				
Log probability .... -963.535				
LR $Chi^2(52)$ 956.83				
Prob $>Ch^2$ 0.000				
Pseudo- R^2 .... 0.332N				

*p<0.5; **p<0.1; ***p<0.01; standard error given in parenthesis.

In summary, in 1989 the economic vote was much more important than in previous terms with socialist governments. All respondents employed retrospective economic voting except IU. Also, retrospective assessment of the political situation was statistically significant in the case of all parties. This was definitely associated with the economic recession taking place, and most of all with a major increase in unemployment. Although PSOE was victorious in the election, it won with a much lower number of seats in the parliament, forcing them in turn to form a minority government.

6.3.4. 1993

The model used in 1993 does not differ from that of 1989. Nevertheless, the arrangement of Table 38 is different than the previous one, as alongside opposition parties such as PP, IU, and "others", CiU is again a separate category, like in 1986. As in the two previous terms, the party running for re-election was PSOE. In the 1993 election the responsibility hypothesis was not confirmed, as in respect of voters for neither party was the retrospective economic vote significant. The situation was different, however, in respect of the prospective economic vote, which was indicated in the case of all opposition parties. A negative assessment of the economy in the future reduced the likelihood of voting for PSOE. Retrospective assessment of the political situation was statistically significant only in the case of one party, *i.e.* CiU. In this case, negative assessment of the political situation reduced the likelihood of voting for PSOE. Again, political self-identification was statistically significant in the case of all voters. The relation with the type of identification and the likelihood of voting for PSOE was similar to that in previous years.

Table 38. Economic voting in Spain in the 1993 election

Variables	Vote for PP *versus* PSOE	Vote for IU *versus* PSOE	Vote for CIU *versus* PSOE	Vote for others *versus* PSOE
Retrospective assessment of the economic situation	-0.36 (0.43)	-0.46 (0.47)	-1.45 (1.06)	-0.45 (0.52)
Prospective assessment of the economic situation	-1.05 (0.22)***	-1.23 (0.23)***	-0.93 (0.33)***	-0.58 (0.24)**
Retrospective assessment of the political situation	-0.41 (0.33)	-0.59 (0.35)	-1.56 (0.75)**	-0.5 (0.38)
Ideological self-identification	1.39 (0.09)***	-0.56 (0.09)***	1.01 (0.11)***	0.57 (0.09)***
N......1186				
Log probability......1139.078				
LR $Chi^2(48)$......968.81				
Prob $>Ch^2$......0.000				
Pseudo- R^2......0.298				

*p<0.5; **p<0.1; ***p<0.01; standard error given in parenthesis.

In the 1993 election the responsibility hypothesis was not confirmed, which seems surprising given the high drop in the employment rate and GDP. However, for the opposition parties what was decisive was not the retrospective assessment of the state of the economy or politics (except for CiU), but expectations regarding the future of the Spanish economy. This last variable is what differentiated them from PSOE. It is likely that this explains the further loss of electoral support for PSOE, as the party was once again forced to form a minority government.

6.3.5. 1996

For the fourth time, in the 1996 election PSOE was running for re-election. The order of opposition parties included in Table 39 did not change compared to 1993, and neither did the model, remaining the same as in previous years.

The responsibility hypothesis was unconfirmed in both 1993 and 1996. Retrospective assessment of the state of the economy did not influence the loss of power by PSOE. This variable was not statistically significant for any of the parties. Therefore, one should look for the causes of the failure of Felipe González's party in reasons other than economic policy. This state of things is to some extent explained by the other two variables. One is prospective assessment of the economic situation, which was statistically significant for both PP and for parties in the "others" category. A positive opinion about the state of the economy in the future reduced the likelihood of voting for PSOE. Retrospective assessment of the political situation was significant for PP, which won the most seats in 1996. In the case of PP, a positive assessment of the political situation reduced the likelihood of voting for the party running for re-election (PSOE). Ideology also had a major influence on the likelihood of voting for all parties compared to the probability of voting for PSOE, except for the "others" category. As in previous years, the more the voters self-identified as left-wing, the more likely they were to vote for PSOE. Only in the case of IU the relation was the opposite – the more they identified as right-wing, the more likely they were to vote for PSOE.

Table 39. Economic voting in Spain in the 1996 election

Variables	**Vote for PP *versus* PSOE**	**Vote for IU *versus* PSOE**	**Vote for CIU *versus* PSOE**	**Vote for others *versus* PSOE**
Retrospective assessment of the economic situation	-0.30 (0.31)	-0.38 (0.33)	0.03 (0.40)	-0.67 (0.42)
Prospective assessment of the economic situation	1.01 (0.25)***	0.27 (0.25)	-0.03 (0.33)	0.72 (0.29)***
Retrospective assessment of the political situation	0.82 (0.26)***	0.39 (0.30)	0.05 (0.36)	-0.14 (0.37)
Ideological self-identification	1.84 (0.13)***	-0.51 (0.09)***	1.34 (0.14)***	0.03 (0.11)
N.........1117 Log probability.........990.492 LR $Chi^2(52)$.........1081.53 Prob $>Ch^2$.........0.000 Pseudo- R^2.........0.353				

*p<0.5; **p<0.1; ***p<0.01; standard error given in parenthesis.

The snap election called in 1996 was won by PP, and therefore PSOE lost power for the first time in 14 years. Despite the ongoing economic crisis, retrospective assessment of the economic situation was not the decisive factor. Undoubtedly, prospective assessment of the economy played the largest role. Voters expected that PSOE would not fulfil their expectations regarding the state of the Spanish economy in the future. In summary, despite PSOE failing to get re-elected, the responsibility hypothesis was not confirmed in the 1996 election. The decisive factors were prospective economic voting and retrospective assessment of the political situation. One explanation for this may be Spanish society's readiness for change and the loss of fear of power being gained by a party seen as an heir to Francoism. Without a doubt, the corruption scandals PSOE politicians were embroiled in, as well as the issue of GAL, the Spanish death squads formed by the Felipe González government, were not insignificant. Regardless, this scenario cannot be definitively confirmed, as questions regarding corruption were not included in the survey. Another explanation for this situation may be the introduction of complex social policy tools, which mitigated the extent to which the crisis was felt by Spanish citizens, an element proven in studies by the previously cited M. Freile.

6.3.6. 2000

In 2000, the party running for re-election was PP (in the model it is the category of reference). The analyses also included PSOE and IU. In 2000, the responsibility hypothesis was confirmed only in the case of PSOE. The likelihood of voting for PP compared to voting for PSOE was lower if voters assessed the state of the economy negatively. It turned out that prospective assessment of the economic situation also exerts a statistically significant influence on the likelihood of voting for all parties. Negative expectations regarding the economy reduced the likelihood of voting for PP. Retrospective assessment of the political situation influenced the likelihood of voting for PSOE and parties included in the "others" category. In both cases a negative assessment of the previous political situation was connected with the desire to punish the ruling party and vote for the other parties mentioned previously. Ideology also influenced the probability of voting for all parties compared to the probability of voting for PP. As with the previous term of parliament, the more the voters self-identified as left-wing, the greater their likelihood of voting for opposition parties.

Table 40. Economic voting in Spain in the 2000 election

Variables	Vote for PSOE *versus* PP	Vote for IU *versus* PP	Vote for others *versus* PSOE
Retrospective assessment of the economic situation	-0.70 (0.29)**	-0.13(0.43)	-0.35(0.30)
Prospective assessment of the economic situation	-0.89 (0.26)***	-0.15 (0.44)**	-0.91(0.27)***
Retrospective assessment of the political situation	-0.76 (0.31)***	-0.78(0.53)	-1.03(0.34)***
Ideological self-identification	-1.69 (0.11)***	-2.12 (0.15)***	-1.12 (0.1)***

Variables	Vote for PSOE *versus* PP	Vote for IU *versus* PP	Vote for others *versus* PSOE
N.. 1162			
Log probability.. 845.117			
LR $Chi^2(39)$.. 1010.59			
Prob >Ch^2 .... 0.000			
Pseudo- R^2.. 0.374			

*p<0.5; **p<0.1; ***p<0.01; standard error given in parenthesis.

In summary, retrospective economic voting was only partially used in the 2000 election, in the case of the main opposition party, *i.e.* PSOE. The responsibility hypothesis was thus confirmed, despite improvement in the economic situation felt by society. Regardless, the other two variables, *i.e.* retrospective assessment of the political situation and prospective economic voting, were statistically significant for all opposition parties, not only for PSOE. This situation can explain the fact that PP, having ruled in 1996–2000, managed to improve its election results in 2000 and achieve an absolute majority.

6.3.7. 2004

In 2004, the party running for re-election was again PP. The composition of Table 41, however, is different to that from 2000. Next to the main opposition party (PSOE), CiU was given a separate category, while IU was included with all other parties in the "others" category. A negative assessment of the previous state of the economy reduced the likelihood of voting for PP, both in the case of PSOE and parties in the "others" category. However, prospective economic voting was used only in the case of PSOE. They positively assessed the state of the economy in the future, so an optimistic view of the future economic situation increased the probability of voting for PSOE compared to voting for PP. Retrospective assessment of the political situation was statistically significant for all parties. Political self-identification was also important for all voters – the more voters self-identified as left-wing, the less likely they were to vote for PP.

Table 41. Economic voting in Spain in the 2004 election

Variables	Vote for PSOE *versus* PP	Vote for CiU *versus* PP	Vote for others *versus* PSOE
Retrospective assessment of the economic situation	-1.41 (0.30)***	-0.73 (0.50)	-1.06 (0.37)***
Prospective assessment of the economic situation	0.88 (0.26)***	0.11 (0.46)	0.28 (0.30)
Retrospective assessment of the political situation	1.03 (0.28)***	1.46 (0.41)***	1.23 (0.32)***
Ideological self-identification	-1.86 (0.13)***	-0.64 (0.16)***	-2.19 (0.14)***
N 1270			
Log probability............827.004			
LR $Chi^2(39)$............981.14			
Prob $>Ch^2$............0.000			
Pseudo- R^2............0.372			

*p<0.5; **p<0.1; ***p<0.01; standard error given in parenthesis.

In summary, it should be stressed that in 2004 the responsibility hypothesis was confirmed in the case of the main opposition party (PSOE) and for parties in the "others" category. However, taking into consideration the fact that in the 2000–2004 parliamentary term Spain was going through its greatest economic prosperity (as shown by all macroeconomic indicators), this situation may come as a surprise. Just like the positive retrospective assessment of the political situation in the light of the terrorist attack at the Atocha train station, committed three days before the election. However, among Spanish researchers there is no agreement regarding the extent of the terrorist attack's influence on election results.[288] Based on the pre-election polls, one can risk the hypothesis of a "technical draw" between PP and PSOE before the 2004 election. However, whether the

288 I. Lago, J.R. Montero, *Los mecanismos del cambio electoral. Del 11-M al 14-M*, „Claves de la Razón Práctica" 2005, no. 149, pp. 36–44; B. Barreiro, *14-M: elecciones a la sombra del terrorismo*, „Claves de Razón Práctica" 2004, no. 141, pp. 14–22; N. Michavila, *Guerra, terrorismo y elecciones: incidencia electoral de los atentados islamistas en Madrid*, „Documento de Trabajo" 2005, no. 13, Instituto Real Elcano, www.realinstitutoelcano.org/wps/portal/rielcano/contenido?WCM_GLOBAL_CONTEXT=/elcano/elcano_es/zonas_es/imagen+de+espana/dt13-2005; W.G. Gramacho, *El 14-M sin el 11-M: una estimación a partir de las. funciones de popularidad y voto*; Paper presented at the VII AECPA Congress, Madrid, September 21–23, 2005.

attack improved the result of PSOE by only 3.5% (as claimed by I. Lago and J.R. Montero) or whether it had a larger impact on the PSOE victory is debatable. It is, however, a fact that PSOE won with a 4.9% advantage over PP. Therefore, it is possible that given such a small difference, this was not reflected in the results of the multinomial logistic regression model employed.

6.3.8. 2008

The composition of the Table 42 in 2008 changed significantly compared to 2004, while the model remained the same. The party running for re-election in 2008 was PSOE. The second column of Table 42 includes the most important opposition party, PP, versus PSOE; the third contains IU-ICV versus PSOE; the fourth displays the other parties in the "others" category.

The responsibility hypothesis was not confirmed in 2008. On the other hand, prospective economic voting did occur in the case of PP and the "others" category. A negative assessment of the future of the country's economy reduced the probability of voting for PSOE in the case of voters from both categories. For PP as well, retrospective assessment of the political situation was statistically significant, although to a lesser extent than in the case of voting for "others" category. Therefore, a negative assessment of the political situation reduced the likelihood of voting for PSOE. Political self-identification was also important for voters for all political parties. The more to the right were voters, the more likely were to vote for PP or other in comparison to PSOE. The opposite was the case for IU-ICV – the more to the left, the more likely they were to vote for IU-ICV compared to PSOE.

Table 42. Economic voting in Spain in the 2008 election

Variables	Vote for PP *versus* PSOE	Vote for IU-ICV *versus* PSOE	Vote for others *versus* PSOE
Retrospective assessment of the economic situation	0.07 (0.39)	-0.51 (0.63)	-0.01 (0.41)
Prospective assessment of the economic situation	-1.55 (0.37)***	-0.71 (0.41)	-1.29 (0.39)***
Retrospective assessment of the political situation	-0.72 (0.34)**	-0.56 (0.39)	-1.11 (0.37)***
Ideological self-identification	1.79 (0.11)***	-0.62 (0.11)***	0.33 (0.08)***
N 1291			
Log probability 908.960			
LR $Chi^2(39)$ 1040.42			
Prob >Ch^2 .... 0.000			
Pseudo- R^2 .... 0.364			

*p<0.5; **p<.01; ***p<0.01; standard error given in parenthesis.

In summary, the responsibility hypothesis was not confirmed in the 2008 election. However, prospective economic voting was significant, as well as retrospective assessment of the political situation, to a lesser extent. Taking into account the mostly good economic results (although it should be added that the economic situation in Spain started to worsen), citizens' standard of living had not yet been affected. This situation explains to some extent PSOE's re-election; the 2004–2008 parliamentary term was also politically stable.

6.3.9. 2011

As in 2008, the party running for re-election was PSOE. For this reason, the composition of the table did not change extensively. The only difference is the appearance of a new party, UPyD. As in 2008, the second column contains data regarding the main opposition party (PP), the second concerns IU-ICV, the fourth UPyD, and the last column data regarding other parties.

In 2011 the responsibility hypothesis also went unconfirmed, which seems surprising given the fact that during the 2008–2011 term Spain underwent the most serious economic crisis since democratic transition. This does not mean that voters were uninterested in the economy – in fact, just the opposite was true. When reviewing the answers to CiS survey no. 2920, it turns out that the state of the economy constituted an important issue for voters of all political parties (*valence issues*), and the number of positive and negative assessments of the state of the economy in the previous term in the case of the electorate of the most important political parties was very close. Given this, the variable was not statistically significant, as it neither increased nor decreased the likelihood of voting for the party running for re-election. Practically all voters negatively assessed the state of the economy, even those who voted for PSOE again. Therefore, another variable seems of import – prospective assessment of the economy, which was statistically significant in the case of the most important opposition party, *i.e.* PP. Retrospective assessment of the political situation was not statistically significant in the case of any of the parties, which most likely indicates the political sphere being dominated by the economy. Traditionally, political self-identification was statistically significant. The relations were the same as in previous years. The more voters self-identified as right-wing, the less likely they were to vote for PSOE; in the case of IU-ICV the situation, however, was the opposite.

Table 43. Economic voting in Spain in the 2011 election

Variables	Vote for PP *versus* PSOE	Vote for IU-ICV *versus* PSOE	Vote for UPyD *versus* PSOE	Vote for others *versus* PSOE
Retrospective assessment of the economic situation	-0.62 (0.45)	-1.17 (0.67)	-0.44 (0.69)	-1.02 (0.58)
Prospective assessment of the economic situation	0.48 (0.24)*	-0.33 (0.33)	0.53 (0.38)	-0.35 (0.28)
Retrospective assessment of the political situation	0.58 (0.34)	-0.25 (0.50)	-1.57 (1.05)	0.14 (0.38)
Ideological self-identification	1.52 (0.09)***	-0.35 (0.08)***	0.80 (0.12)***	0.31 (0.07)***
N.. 1269				
Log probability........................ 1189.970				
LR $Chi^2(52)$........................ 1064.96				
Prob >Ch^2........................ 0.000				
Pseudo- R^2........................ 0.309				

*p<0.5; **p<0.1; ***p<0.01; standard error given in parenthesis.

To summarise the above analysis, it should be emphasised that the presented data contradicts the widespread opinion that Prime Minister Zapatero's election loss was caused by his ineffective economic policies. It turns out that the loss of power by PSOE was based on the voters' conviction that the opposition party would be better able to manage the economic crisis, as all voters negatively assessed the state of the economy; this did not determine PP's victory in the 2011 election.

***

When comparing the use of the economic vote in Poland and Spain, it can definitely be confirmed that in both countries the punishment/reward mechanism has been used. In Poland the retrospective economic vote was used in 1997, 2001 (modified model – the reference parties were AWS, PO and PiS), 2005 and 2007. This means that in four out of five elections the hypothesis of responsibility was confirmed. Each time the party running for re-election lost power. However, the use of retrospective economic voting was not always connected with an actual decline in the state of the economy. In Poland, such a situation took place in the 2005 and 2007 elections. Then, despite improvement in the economy, voters negatively assessed the economic situation and the party running for re-election did not win enough votes to form a government again. The opposite was the case in 2011. In

Spain, on the other hand, the mechanism of punishment/reward, and therefore electoral accountability, was used in the years 1982–2011, although not as often as might be expected. Retrospective economic voting was employed in the case of all opposition parties except IU in 1989, PSOE in 2000, and in 2004 in case of all opposition parties except for CiU. Negative assessment of the political situation in the past increases the likelihood of voting for the opposition parties three times: in 1989, 2000, and 2004. Out of these, only in 2004 did it lead to the loss of power by the governing party. Like in Poland, the use of retrospective economic voting was not always connected with an actual worsening in the state of the economy. It was used in the 2000 and 2004 elections in spite of the economic situation being objectively very good, but assessed negatively by voters. The opposite was the case in 1986 and 1993.

The acquired results were also confirmed through the use of an aggregated model of economic voting. This model, aside from the variables described in Chapter 6, also includes a control variable for Spain (which shows that Poland and Spain demonstrate statistically significant differences when it comes to the tested model). It also includes interactions between this variable and the key variables from the point of view of this study: retrospective assessment of the economic and political situation and prospective assessment of the economic situation. The results of the analyses are presented in Table 44.

Table 44. Economic voting – aggregated model. Detailed data Poland versus *Spain*

Country	Variables	Main opposition party	Other opposition parties ("others")
Poland	Retrospective assessment of the economic situation	-0.73 (0.10)***	-0.62 (0.09) ***
Spain	Retrospective assessment of the economic situation	-0.59 (0.13) ***	0.08 (0.12)
Poland	Prospective assessment of the economic situation	-0.31 (0.08) ***	-0.62 (0.08) ***
Spain	Prospective assessment of the economic situation	0.38 (0.10) ***	0.17 (0.10)
Poland	Retrospective assessment of the political situation	-0.37 (0.10) ***	-0.55 (0.09) ***
Spain	Retrospective assessment of the political situation	0.34 (0.12) ***	0.04 (0.11)
Spain	Spain	-1.10 (0.12) ***	-0.19 (0.11)
N............14539			
Log probability............-14226.69			
LR Chi²(36)............5087.95 3428.76			
Prob >Ch²............0.000			
Pseudo- R²............0.1075			

***p<.001; **p<.01; *p<.05. Standard error given in parenthesis.

Retrospective assessment of the economic situation, the most important variable from this study's perspective, turns out to generate a weaker influence on the likelihood of voting for the party running for re-election and the main opposition party in Poland than in Spain (the interaction is statistically significant, while the influence of the variable is stronger in Spain). It means that vertical accountability is present in both Poland and Spain. The influence of prospective assessment of the economic situation in Spain also differs in a statistically significant way from the influence of this variable in Poland (in Spain the influence of this variable is weaker, and the direction of its influence is the opposite of that in Poland). The influence of the retrospective assessment of the political situation also looks similar. In Poland, positive assessment of the political situation in the past increases the likelihood of voting for the party running for re-election. In Spain, the relation is the opposite in respect of the main opposition party, but much weaker.

However, based on the above results it can only be established that in both cases the independent variables are statistically significant, which means that they influence the election decision. The results of the study do not, however, allow us to answer the question to which extent they differ in Poland and Spain, and therefore in which country the economic vote, expectations for the future, and assessment of the political situation influence voters' preferences to larger extent. One of the ways of overcoming this is to introduce rules of statistical interference through the calculation of marginal effects: the change in the probability of voting for a given party with an increase in an independent variable by one unit while the other variables remain at an average level. An advantage of such calculations is comparability, although it should be remembered that this remains probability calculated for a limited number of cases. However, such an operation allows us to acquire additional information which helps us understand to a larger extent the influence of these variables on the choice of party forming the government in Poland and Spain.

Table 45. Economic voting in Poland and Spain – marginal effects

Variables with scale	Party running for re-election *(Poland)*	Main opposition party *(Poland)*	Other opposition parties *(Poland)*	Party running for re-election *(Spain)*	Main opposition party *(Spain)*	Other opposition parties *(Spain)*
Retrospective assessment of the economic situation: negative	0.35	0.34	0.31	0.37	0.34	0.29
Retrospective assessment of the economic situation: positive	0.51	0.24	0.25	0.43	0.22	0.36

Variables with scale	Party running for re-election *(Poland)*	Main opposition party *(Poland)*	Other opposition parties *(Poland)*	Party running for re-election *(Spain)*	Main opposition party *(Spain)*	Other opposition parties *(Spain)*
Difference (marginal effects)	**0.16**	**0.1**	**0.06**	**0.06**	**0.12**	**0.07**
Prospective assessment of the economic situation: negative	0.34	0.32	0.34	0.39	0.31	0.3
Prospective assessment of the economic situation: positive	0.45	0.31	0.24	0.33	0.38	0.3
Difference (marginal effects)	**0.11**	**0.01**	**0.1**	**0.06**	**0.07**	**0**
Retrospective assessment of the political situation: negative	0.35	0.33	0.32	0.39	0.31	0.3
Retrospective assessment of the political situation: positive	0.46	0.3	0.24	0.34	0.38	0.28
Difference (marginal effects)	**0.11**	**0.03**	**0.08**	**0.05**	**0.07**	**0.02**

All marginal effects are significant at the level of $p<0.001$. Standard error does not exceed 0.01 for Poland and 0.02 for Spain. Other variables are at an average level.

According to the results in Table 45, the probability that a voter who negatively assessed the economic situation would vote for the party seeking re-election in Poland was only 35%, while in the case of a positive assessment this probability was as high as 51%. On the other hand, in the case of the main opposition party and other parties it was 34% and 31%, respectively, (when negative) and 24% and 25% (when positive). In Spain, the probability that a voter who negatively assessed the economic situation would vote for a party running for re-election was 37%, while in the case of a positive assessment this probability was 43%. In the case of the main opposition party and other parties it was, respectively, 34% (when negative) and 22% (when positive). For other opposition parties it was 29% (when negative) and 36% (when positive). Therefore, in Poland a negative assessment of economic policy reduces the likelihood of voting for the ruling party while increasing the likelihood of voting for the opposition parties to a much larger extent than in Spain. This means that economic voting is more strongly rooted in Poland. More Spanish voters, ignoring the poor economic situation, decide to vote again for the ruling party. Additionally, Polish voters are not only more willing than Spanish ones to punish the ruling party for its policies by not supporting its re-election, but also more willing to reward the ruling party if they assess economic policy positively. However, we know from the results of the studies presented in Chapter 6 that positive assessments of economic policy in Poland are rare.

The differences between the strength of economic voting in Poland and Spain are even more visible when we take into consideration the gap between the likelihood of voting for the party seeking re-election in the case of positive and negative assessment. It should be noted that the differences in marginal effect reflect the "strength" of the variable. This means that the greater the difference, the more a positive assessment of the economy/politics influences the likelihood of voting for the party attempting to retain power. The situation is similar in the case of negative assessment – the larger the difference, the more the negative assessment of the economy/policy influences the likelihood of voting for the opposition parties. In Poland, the difference in marginal effects in the case of the party running for re-election is 16%, while in Spain it is 6%. In the case of the main opposition parties, it is 10% in Poland and 6% in Spain, while for other opposition parties it is 6% and 7%, respectively.

The influence of expectations regarding the future economic situation on the likelihood of re-electing the same party also distinguishes Poland from Spain. In Poland, when expectations regarding the future of the economy are pessimistic, the probability of voting for the ruling party is 34%, while in the case of positive assessment it is 45%. In the case of the main opposition party it is 32% (if the assessment is negative) and 31% (if positive). For other opposition parties, the probability reaches a level of 34% (if the assessment is negative) and 24% (if positive). In Spain, on the other hand, it is 39% (if the assessment is negative) and 33% (if positive) respectively in the case of the party running for re-election, while it is 31% (if the assessment is negative) and 38% (if positive) in the case of the main opposition party, and for other opposition parties it is 3% (if the assessment is negative) and 3% (if it is positive). Therefore, the difference between the likelihood of voting for the party seeking re-election in the case of positive and negative assessment of the prospective economic situation is 11% in Poland and 6% in Spain; in the case of the main opposition parties it is 1% in Poland and 7% in Spain; while for other parties it is 10% in Poland and 0% in Spain.

Retrospective assessment of the political situation, which can be interpreted as a measure of the government's popularity, as mentioned earlier, also differentiates the probability of voting for the party seeking re-election in Poland and Spain. According to the data in Table 45, in the case of negative assessment of the political situation in Poland, the likelihood of voting for the party running for re-election is only 35%, while in the case of positive assessment it is 45%. For the main opposition parties this figure is respectively 33% (if the assessment is negative) and 30% (if positive). In Spain, it is 39% (if the assessment is negative) and 34% (if positive), while for the main opposition parties 31% (if the assessment is negative) and 38% (if the assessment is positive); for other opposition parties it is 30% (if the assessment is negative) and 28% (if the assessment is positive). Therefore, the difference in the case of Poland for the party running for re-election is 11%, while in Spain it is 5%. In the case of the main opposition parties it is 3% in Poland and 7% in Spain, while for other opposition parties it is 8% in Poland and 2% in Spain.

In summary, the results of the empirical analysis confirmed that in both Poland and in Spain the punishment/reward mechanism is employed with effect, and in both countries accountability takes place. Therefore, the following hypothesis is confirmed: *Both in Poland and in Spain there exists electoral accountability; positive retrospective assessment of the economic situation in the country increases the likelihood of voting for the party vying for re-election.* Additionally, based on the data acquired, we also know that the frequency of using the economic vote differs in both countries. If we take into account the use of retrospective economic voting, we notice that the hypothesis of responsibility was confirmed in four out of five elections, while in Spain economic voting was used only thrice in the years 1982–2011. Additionally, the frequency with which the retrospective vote was used in Poland and in Spain was not always connected with an objective decline in the state of the economy. In Poland, economic voting was used twice despite an improvement in the economic situation, which led to a change of the ruling party. In Spain, such a situation took place only once. Additionally, differences in marginal effects indicated that the magnitude of the effect of the economic vote differs in Poland and Spain, that is, it is more significant in Poland.

Conclusion

The existence of this book is linked with the appearance of the new field of research that is quality of democracy. It is a testament to my journey in search of a conceptualisation and operationalisation of accountability, one of the most important elements present in the quality of democracy. The primary objective of the work was to explain at what moment and in which field such elements of changes are generated that in one country stimulate positive effects, while in another contribute to the emergence of multiple delays and increased numbers of negative post-transformation phenomena in the area of accountability.

In order to explain the aforementioned dependencies and for verification the hypothesis, I have developed a model of accountability. The creation of this model of accountability consisted firstly in defining the components, entities and instruments in the system of accountability. Next, I distinguished the determinants influencing the functioning of accountability. In line with the logic proposed by L. Morlino, the determinants were classified into the procedural dimension and the final result dimension (result of political practice). The final operation in the construction of a model of accountability was to define the manner of measuring the functioning of each entity distinguished within the system of accountability. Thus the achievement in the theoretical sphere was the development of a holistic model of accountability for studies on quality of democracy.I then applied the developed model to a study of accountability in Poland and in Spain, taking a comparative approach. This facilitated shifting the research from the theoretical to the empirical levelAnswers to more detailed research questions contained in successive chapters and the verification of partial hypotheses in turn facilitated delineation of differences and similarities in the scope of accountability in Poland and in Spain.

The data acquired from the conducted analyses provided confirmation of the hypotheses concerning the position of the executive branch in the accountability system. I was able to establish that the absence of cohabitation strengthened the position of the president in Poland as an active entity in the system of accountability, which undoubtedly reinforces the system of horizontal accountability. Confirmation was also achieved of the hypothesis regarding the impact of the support enjoyed by the government on its capacity to determine the legislative and decision agenda of parliament. It turned out that in both Poland and Spain, the smaller the support held by the government in parliament, the lesser its capacity to determine the parliament's legislative and decision agenda. However, this situation strengthens the parliament's position in the system of checks and balances, which, when considering the primary dependence between horizontal and vertical accountability consisting on the former's generation of information, seems of exceptional importance. Less certain are the results of research concerning the impact of procedural conditions and balance of powers in the lower houses of parliament on the dynamics of the use of accountability instruments. It is not possible to definitively determine which of the factors has a greater influence on the use of those instruments at the disposal of the lower chambers of parliament. Without a shade of a doubt, however, it can be said that the Congress of Deputies is more active than the Sejm in applying those tools. The further hypothesis, concerning the level of parliamentary support for the government on the potential to limit the independence of the judiciary and mandate agencies, was not fully confirmed in the empirical studies. It turned out that the assumption of weaker and less stable support enjoyed by the government leading to a reduction in its capacity to limit the independence of the judiciary and mandate agencies was untrue. What can be said unequivocally on the basis of the conducted analyses is that both the judiciary and mandate agencies are, in Spain, dependent primarily on the legislative branch to a greater extent than in Poland. This, in turn, has a very negative impact on the functioning of horizontal accountability.

As concerns vertical accountability, it can be stated definitively that in both countries we may speak of a problem with assigning responsibility. Both in Poland and in Spain, institutional factors disrupt the functioning of vertical accountability mechanisms. In Poland, the primary factor is the party system, while in Spain key significance would seem to be the influence of the existing territorial structure. Nevertheless, without quantitative studies it would seem exceptionally difficult to determine in which of the countries the workings of those determinants has a greater impact on limiting the use of economic voting, which is the measure of vertical accountability. However, as to the use of economic voting itself, it was invoked during the studied period in both Poland and Spain. In both countries the mechanisms of reward and punishment were applied, and in both cases a positive retrospective analysis of the economic situation in the country increased the chances of voting for the party attempting to retain power. The frequency with which the economic vote was used is different in the two countries: in Poland it was employed more frequently than in Spain. This would indicate that Polish voters much more frequently hold their politicians to account than Spanish ones during the act of voting.

An unusually interesting conclusion from the conducted analyses is the ambiguous impact of time on mechanisms of accountability, in spite of the natural expectation that the more time has passed since the moment of consolidation of the political system in the two countries, the greater mechanisms of accountability should strengthen. Some of the results of empirical analyses, however, would appear to run contrary to that assumption. The hypothesis concerning the strengthening of the government's position in the accountability system together with the passage of time was not confirmed. In respect of Spain, the hypothesis of the dependency between the time passed since the moment of consolidation of the political system and growing independence of the judicial branch and mandate agencies should also be rejected. Regarding determinants of vertical accountability, it was also not possible to prove that the greater the time elapsed from the moment of systemic consolidation, the lesser the distortions of vertical accountability. Only one of the hypotheses related to the passage of time was confirmed, that the control of the Congress of Deputies is institutionalised to a larger extent than that of the Sejm, which derives from the longer amount of time that has elapsed from the moment of consolidation of democracy.

On the basis of the conducted analyses it cannot, however, be stated definitively which country features a better accountability system, as one of the primary elements of quality of democracy. The only unambiguous research results are those concerning the use of economic voting; nevertheless, this is a product of the specifics of quantitative studies, as in this case the generation of unambiguous results stems from the fact of simplifying reality to a binary dynamic. Nevertheless, it is no problem to distinguish the weak aspects of accountability, such as the alarming condition of the judicial branch and mandate agencies in the Spanish accountability system. Another example is the lower effectiveness of accountability tools at the disposal of the Polish Sejm in comparison with the Congress of Deputies. However, neither in Poland nor in Spain may we speak of a so-called *democracia delegativa,* which is defined by G. O'Donnell as characterised by the illusory functioning of institutions and the absence of information about the activities of the government, which makes it impossible for voters to hold their politicians to account. In spite of the weakness of some instruments of horizontal accountability, both countries feature the appearance and subsequent publication of information. Generating and publishing information serves to counteract information asymmetry, which facilitates vertical accountability; this in spite of disruptions and limitations by institutional features, both in Poland and in Spain.

Although the proposed research strategy and the conducted analyses do not allow for a definitive answer to the question of which country features better functioning accountability mechanisms, the result of the work performed is the creation of a sort of map showing the weak points of accountability in both countries. Therefore, the preceding study may serve as a starting point for further and deeper analyses of accountability, not only in Poland and in Spain but in other countries as well.

Annex

Attachment 1

Party composition of governing coalitions and parliamentary opposition in Poland during the years 1997–2011*

Government	Composition of government and number of seats	Opposition parties and number of seats
Jerzy Buzek (AWS) I (III Term of the Sejm)*	AWS (201) UW (60) **TOTAL: 261**	SLD (164), PSL (27), ROP (4), Unaff. (2)
Jerzy Buzek (AWS) II (III Term of the Sejm)	AWS (186) **TOTAL: 186**	SLD (161), UW (59), PSL (26), PP (7), Unaff. (6), KPN (5), ROP (4), PRS (3), PPS-RLP (3)
Leszek Miller (SLD-UP) I (IV Term of the Sejm)	SLD (200), UP (16), PSL (42) **TOTAL: 258**	PO (65), Samoobrona (53), PiS (44), LPR (38), Unaff. (2)
Leszek Miller (SLD) II (IV Term of the Sejm)	SLD (193), UP (16) **TOTAL: 209**	PO (56), Samoobrona (37), PiS (43), PSL (39), LPR (28), Unaff. (15), PLD (9), SKL (8), PBL (5), RKN (5), PP (3), ROP (3)
Marek Belka (bezpartyjny) (IV Term of the Sejm)	SLD (157) **TOTAL: 157**	PO (55), Samoobrona (31), PiS (43), PSL (38), LPR (25), SDPL (33), Unaff. (19), FKP (17), UP (15), SKL (8), RKN (5), D. Ojczysty (4), PBL (3), PP (3), ROP (3)
Kazimierz Marcinkiewicz (PiS) I (V Term of the Sejm)	PIS (154) **TOTAL: 154**	PO (132), Samoobrona (56), SLD (55), LPR (32), PSL (25), Unaff. (6)
Kazimierz Marcinkiewicz (PiS) II (V Term of the Sejm)	PiS (154), Samoobrona (56), LPR (32) **TOTAL: 242**	PO (132), SLD (55), PSL (25), Unaff. (6) **TOTAL: 215**
Jarosław Kaczyński (PiS) I (V Term of the Sejm)	PiS (155), Samoobrona (55), LPR (29) **TOTAL: 245**	PO (131), SLD (55), PSL (25), Unaff. (5), NKP (5), RLN (7)

Government	Composition of government and number of seats	Opposition parties and number of seats
Jarosław Kaczyński (PiS) II (V Term of the Sejm)	PiS (154), LPR (29), RLN (15) **TOTAL: 198**	PO (131), SLD (55), Samoobrona (41), PSL (25), Unaff. (5), NKP (5)
Jarosław Kaczyński (PiS) III (V Term of the Sejm)	PiS (154), Samoobrona (41), LPR (29) **TOTAL: 224**	PO (131), SLD (55), PSL (27), Unaff. (12), NKP (5), PR (6)
Jarosław Kaczyński (PiS) IV (V Term of the Sejm)	PiS (151) **TOTAL: 151**	PO (131), Samoobrona (41), SLD (55), LPR (29), PSL (27), RLN (7), PR (6), Unaff. (13)
Donald Tusk (PO) (VI Term of the Sejm)	PO (209), PSL (31) **TOTAL: 240**	PiS (164), SLD (53), SDPL (3), Unaff. (3)

Source: own work on the basis of, www.sejm.gov.pl/Sejm7.nsf/page/archiwum.
*Number of seats at the beginning.

Attachment 2

Number of seats of individual political parties in the Congress of Deputies in the years 1986–2011*

Government	Party forming government	Parties supporting government	Opposition parties
Felipe González I (II Term 1982–1986)	PSOE[a](202)		AP-PDP (106), UCD (12), CiU (12), PNV (8), PCE (4), CDS (2), HB (2), EE (1), ERC (1) **TOTAL: 147**
Felipe González II (III Term 1986–1989)	PSOE[a](184)	-	PP (105), CDS (19), CiU (18), IU (7), PNV (6), HB (5), EE (2), UEC (1)CG (1), PAR (1), AIC (1), UV (1) **TOTAL: 166**
Felipe Gonzaléz III (IV Term 1989–1993)	PSOEb (175)	-	PP (101), CiU (18), IU (14), CDS (14)* EAJ-PNV (5), HB (4), IC (3), UPN-PP (3), PP-CG (3), PA (2), UV (2), EA (2), EE (2) PAR (1), AIC (1), **TOTAL: 175**

Government	Party forming government	Parties supporting government	Opposition parties
Felipe González IV (V Term 1993–1996)	PSOE[c] (159)	CiU (17), EAJ-PNV (5), CC (4) **TOTAL: 26**	PP (138)), IU (15), UPN-PP (3), IC (3), HB (2), ERC (1), PAR (1), UV (1), EA-EUE (1) **TOTAL: 165**
José María Aznar I (VI Term 1996–2000)	PP[d] (156)	CiU (16), EAJ-PNV (5), CC (4) **TOTAL: 25**	PSOEe (141) IU (19), IC-EV (2), BNG (2), HB (2), ERC (1), EA (1), UV (1) **TOTAL:169**
José María Aznar II (VII Term 2000–2004)	PP[f] (183)	CiU (15), CC (4) **TOTAL: 19**	PSOEg (125), IU (8), PNV (7), BNG (3), PA (1), ERC (1), IC-V (1), EA (1), ChA (1) **TOTAL: 148**
José Luis Rodríguez Zapatero I (VIII Term 2004–2008)	PSOE[h] (164)	CC (3), IUi (4), BNG (2), ERC (8) **TOTAL: 17**	PP (146), CiU (10), EAJ-PNV (7), UNP-PP (2), ChA (1), EA (1), Na-Bai (1), ENTENSA (1) **TOTAL: 169**
José Luis Rodríguez Zapatero II (IX Term 2008–2011)	PSOE[j] (169)	-	PP (152), CiU (10), EAJ-PNV (6), ERC (3), IU (2) BNG (2), CC-PNC (2), UPN-PP (2),UPyD (1), Na-Bai (1) **TOTAL: 181**
Mariano Rajoy (X Term 2011–)	PP (186)		PSOE (110), CiU (16), IU (11), Amaiur (7), UPyD (5), EAJ-PNV (5), ERC (3), BNG (2), CC-PNC (2), Compromis Q(1), Foro de Ciudadanos (1), Geroa Bai (1), **TOTAL: 164**

Source: own work based on website of Congress of Deputies, www.congreso.es.

* At the beginning of the term.

a. Number of seats held by PSOE[289] includes 21 acquired by PSC-PSOE.

b. Number of seats held by PSOE includes 20 acquired by PSC-PSOE.

c. Number of seats held by PSOE includes 18 acquired by PSC-PSOE

d. Number of seats held by PP includes 8 acquired by PP-PAR and 2 by UPN.

---

289 PSOE is a federal structure composed of regional branches. An exception is the Catalonian Partit Socialista de Catalunya (PSC-PSOE), which is registered as a separate party. Presently, PSC participates in essentially all internal activities, as do the other regional branches of PSOE; in addition, since 1982 it has composed together with PSOE a joint parliamentary club.

e. Number of seats held by PSOE includes 19 acquired by PSC-PSOE.
f. Number of seats held by PP includes 8 acquired by PP-PAR.
g. Number of seats held by PSOE includes 17 acquired by PSC-PSOE.
h. Number of seats held by PSOE includes 21 acquired by PSC-PSOE.
i. Number of seats held by IU includes 2 acquired by ICV-EUIA.
j. Number of seats held by PSOE includes 25 acquired by PSC-PSOE.

Attachment 3

Clubs and parliamentary groups in particular terms of parliament in the years 1997–2011

Term	Clubs and groups – at beginning and end of parliament term	Parliamentary clubs and groups which were formed and ceased their activity in the course of a term: state at the moment of formation and at the end of existence	Gropus and clubs formed in the course of the term and which functioned until the completion of it
Sejm III term (1997–2001)	AWS: 201–134 SLD: 164–162 UW: 60–47 PSL: 27–26 ROP: 4–3 INDEP.: 2–43	KPN-OP w KPN-O: 7–5[a] PPS-RLP: 3–3[b] PRS:⁻ 3–3[c] KdP: 8–7[d]	NK in PP: 7–5[e] SKL: 17–18[f] Alternatywa: 6–4[g] PiS:18–18[h]
Sejm IV term (2001–2005)	SLD: 200–148 PSL: 42–40 PO: 65–56 PiS: 44–45 Samoobrona:53–31 LPR: 38–19 UP: 16–11[i] INDEP.: 5–39	FKP:15–15j PSL-PBL: 43–43[k] PBL: 4–3[l] PRS:5–3[m] RP: 3–3[n]	SDPL: 35–32[o] KL: 7–5[p] RKN: 5–4[q] SG: 11–11[r] ROP: 3–3[s] PP: 3–3[t] Dom Ojczysty: 4–10[u] RP: 3–3[v]
Sejm V term (2005–2007)	PiS: 155–151 PO:133–131 Samoobrona:56–41 SLD: 55–55 LPR: 34–29 PSL:25–27 INDEP.: 2–13	RLN: 15–15[w] NKP: 7–5[x] RLN-KPB: 4–3[y]	RLCh -RLN: 7–7[z] PR – Prawica: 6–6[aa]

Term	Clubs and groups – at beginning and end of parliament term	Parliamentary clubs and groups which were formed and ceased their activity in the course of a term: state at the moment of formation and at the end of existence	Gropus and clubs formed in the course of the term and which functioned until the completion of it
Sejm VI term (2007-2011)	PO: 209–208 PiS: 166–146 SLD: 42–43 PSL: 31–31 INDEP. 1–10	LiD: 53–53[bb] Polska _XXI-Polska Plus: 9–9[cc] DKP-SD: 3–3 dd	PJN: 15–15[ee] SDPL: 8–3[ff]

Source: Sejm Rzeczypospolitej Polskiej, *III Kadencja. Informacja o działalności* (20 October 1997 –18 October 2001), Kancelaria Sejmu, Wydawnictwo Sejmowe, Warsaw 2002, p. 11; Sejm Rzeczypospolitej Polskiej, *IV Kadencja. Informacja o działalności* (19 October 2001–18 October 2005), Kancelaria Sejmu, Wydawnictwo Sejmowe, Warsaw 2006, pp. 12–14; Sejm Rzeczpospolitej Polskiej, *V Kadencja. Informacja o działalności* (19 October 2005 –4 November 2007), Kancelaria Sejmu, Wydawnictwo Sejmowe, Warsaw 2008, pp. 34–35; Sejm Rzeczypospolitej Polskiej, *VI Kadencja. Informacja o działalności* (5 November 2007–7 November 2011), Kancelaria Sejmu, Wydawnictwo Sejmowe, Warsaw 2012, pp. 11–12.

a. Parliamentary Group Koło Parlamentarne Konfederacja Polski Niepodległej–Obóz Patriotyczny (KPN-OP) was formed on 15.6.1998, 23.12.1999; changed name to Parliamentary Group Konfederacja Polski Niepodległej Ojczyzna (KPN-O); 12.12.2000 dissolved.
b. Parliamentary Group Polskiej Partii Socjalistycznej (PPS-RLP) formed on 4.11.1999, wound up 23.12.2000.
c. Member's Group Polskiej Racji Stanu (PRS) formed on 23.12.1999, wound up 12.07.2000.
d. Parliamentary Group Koalicja dla Polski (KdP) formed on 12.07.2000, wound up 2.04.2001.
e. Member's Group Nasze Koło (NK) formed on 9.09.1998, 13.11.1999 transformed into Member's Group Porozumienie Polskie (PP).
f. Parliamentary Club Stronnictwa Konserwatywno Ludowego (SKL) formed on 28.03.2001.
g. Parliamentary Group Alternatywa formed on 2.04.2001.
h. Parliamentary Club Prawo i Sprawiedliwość (PiS) formed on 7.07.2001.
i. Parliamentary Club Unii Pracy (UP) formed on 19.X.2001; like the remaining clubs formed at the beginning of the term, transformed on 16.02.2005 into Parliamentary Group Unii Pracy.
j. Federacyjny Klub Parlamentarny (FKP) formed on 24.01.2004, wound up 15.07.2004.
k. Parliamentary Club Polskiego Stronnictwa Ludowego – Polskiego Bloku Ludowego (PSL-PBL) formed on 18.03.2004 per an understanding between PSL and PBL; it lasted only a few months as on 02.04.2004 PBL left the coalition.
l. Parliamentary Group Polski Blok Ludowy (PBL) formed on 06.12.2002 following the exit of a few MPs from Samoobrona, wound up 16.01.2005.
m. Member's Group Polskiej Racji Stanu (PRS) formed on 16.09.2003, wound up 28.01.2004 r.
n. Member's Group Ruchu Patriotycznego (RP) formed on 1.07.2005 r., wound up 28.07.2005 r.
o. Parliamentary Club Socjaldemokracji Polskiej (SDPL) formed on 1.04.2004 r.

p. Member's Group Konserwatywno-Ludowe (KL) formed on 13.11.2001 r.
q. Member's Group Ruchu Katolicko-Narodowego (RKN) formed on 5.11.2002 r.
r. Member's Group Stronnictwa Gospodarczego (SG) formed on 17.03.2005 r.
s. Member's Group Ruchu Obudowy Polski (ROP) formed on 27.08.2002 r.
t. Member's Group Ruchu Porozumienia Polskiego (PP)formed on 15.01.2003 r.
u. Member's Group Dom Ojczysty formed on 21.04.2004 r.
v. Member's Group Ruchu Patriotycznego (RP) formed on 13.09.2005 r.
w. Member's Group Ruch Ludowo-Narodowy (RNL) formed on 22.09.2006, changed name on 03.10.2006 to Parliamentary Club Ruch-Ludowo-Narodowy, wound up 30.11.2006.
x. Narodowe Parliamentary Group (NKP) formed on 13.05.2006 r., wound up 21.09.2006.
y. Member's Group Ruch Ludowo-Narodowy (RLN) formed on 01.12.2006, changed name 25.04.2007 to Koło Posłów Bezpartyjnych (KPB), wound up 4.09.2007.
z. Member's Group Ruch ludowo-Chrześcijański (RLCh) formed on 18.12.2006, changed name 07.05.2007 to Koło Poselskie Ruch Ludowo-Narodowy (RLN).
aa. Member's Group Prawica Rzeczpospolitej (PR) formed on 27.04.2007, changed name on 07.12.2007 to Koło Poselskie Prawica Rzeczpospolitej (Prawica).
bb. Member's Group Lewica i Demokraci (LiD) formed on 05.11.2007, wound up 21.04.2008.
cc. Member's Group Polska XXI formed on 22.10.2008, changed name on 21.10.2009 to Parliamentary Group Polska Plus, wound up 30.09.2010.
dd. Demokratyczne Koło Poselskie (DKP) formed on 09.04.2008, changed name on 15.07.2009 to Demokratyczne Koło Poselskie Stronnictwa Demokratycznego (DKP_SD).
ee. Member's Club Polska jest Najważniejsza (PJN) formed on 23.11.2010, changed name on 18.08.2011 to Member's Group Polska jest Najważniejsza (PJN); wound up 30.08.2011, but one day later reformed as Member's Club Polska Jest Najważniejsza.
ff. Member's Club SDPL-Lewica Otwarta (SDPL-LO) formed on 22.04.2008, changed name on 23.04.2008 to Member's Group SDPL-Nowa Lewica(SDPL-NL), from 8.09.2009 Member's Group Socjaldemokracji Polskiej (SDPL).

Attachment 4

Number of seats held by particular parties in the Congress of Deputies in the years 1986–2011

Term	Parliamentary Groups (GP) – state at beginning and end of term
III Term1982–1986	GP Socialists 202–201[a] GP Popular 105–102[b] GP Catalonian Minority 12–12[c] GP Centre 12–11[d] GP Basque (PNV) 8–8 GP Mixed 10–14[e]
III Term 1986–1989 f	GP Socialists 184–181 GP Popular 84–89[g] GP CDS 19–28 GP Catalonian Minority 18–19 GP Basque (PNV) 6–4 GP Mixed 34–18[h]
	Party groups within the Mixed Group functioning from the beginning to the end of the term GP Mixed – IU-UEC Group/ IU-IpC Group/ 7–6[i]
	Party groups within the Mixed Group which wound up before the completion of the term GP Mixed – Liberal Party Group 10–7 GP Mixed – Christian Democrats Group 21–20
IV Term 1989–1993	GP Socialists 176–175[j] GP Popular 106–106[k] GP Catalonia (CiU) 18–18[l] GP IU-IC 17–17 GP CDS 14–12 GP Basque (PNV) 5–5 GP Mixed 10–17 HB[m]
V Term 1993–1996 n	GP Socialists 159–159 GP Popular 141–141 GP Federal IU 18–18 GP Catalonia (CiU) 17–17 GP Basque (PNV) 5–5 GP Canary Islands 5–4 GP Mixed 5–6

Term	Parliamentary Groups (GP) – state at beginning and end of term
VI Term 1996–2000	GP Popular 154–155 GP Socialists 141–141 GP Federal IU 21–16[o] GP Catalonia (CiU) 16–16 GP Basque (EAJ-PNV) 5–5 GP Canary Islands 6–4[p] GP Mixed 5–11
VII Term 2000–2004	GP Popular 179–183 GP Socialists 125–124 GP Catalonia (CiU) 14–15 GP Federal IU 8–8 GP ERC 8–8 GP Basque (EAJ-PNV) 6–7 GP Canary Islands 7–4[j] GP Mixed 5–9
VIII Term 2004–2008	GP Socialists 162–164 GP Popular 148–147 GP Catalonia (CiU) 10–10 GP ERC 8–8 GP Basque (EAJ-PNV) 7–7 GP IU-IC-V 5–5 GP Canary Islands-New Canary 5–2[k] GP Mixed 5–9
IX Term 2008–2011	GP Socialists 169–169 GP Popular 154–152 GP Catalonians (CiU) 10–10 GP Basque (EAJ-PNV) 6–6 GP IU- ICV 7–5 GP Mixed 4–8

Source: own work based on the webpage of the Congress of Deputies: www.congreso.es.

a. The Socialists' Parliamentary Group included representatives of the following federal socialist structures: PSOE, PSC, PSE, PAD.

b. The Popular Parliamentary Group included representatives of the following parties: AP, PDP, UP, PAR, UV.

c. The Catalonian Minority Parliamentary Group included representatives of the following parties: CDC and UDC.

d. In 1983 the Democratic Centre Union was dissoled, yet the Centre Parliamentary Group formed by it continued to function; initially only one politician transferred to the Popular Group. At the end of the term the Parliamentary Group presented itself thus: MIXED (3), PDP (2), CG (2), AP (2), PL (1), AIC (1).

e. At the beginning of the term, the composition of the Mixed Group presented itself thus: PCE (4), CDS (2), ERC (1), EE (1). At the end of the term, the number of MPs increased by 4 (PCE (3), CDS (2), HB (2), MUC (1), ERC (1), EE (1), MIXED (4).
f. MPs from HB were not captured in the table as they refused to take up their seats.
g. The Popular Coalition was comprised of AP – Popular Alliance(69), PDP – Democratic People's Party (21), PL-Liberal Party (12), UPN – Navarra People's Union (2), CiG – Galician Centrists (1). One day after the elections, DPL decided it would not enter the GP Populist's Coalition but rather the Mixed Group. On 16 September 1986, MPs from PDP within the Mixed Group formed the Christian Democrat Group. At the request of AP, DPL entered the Mixed Group on 29 January 1987, forming the Liberal Group (10). For two years, the Popular Group is composed only of MPs from AP, UPN, and CdG. In February 1989, Popular Alliance transformed into the Popular Party, drawing members from DC and PL as well. In conjunction with this, the Popular Group was reinforced with MPs from DC (14) and PL (5). During the same term the Popular Group was abandoned by MPs from AP transferring to the Mixed Group. At the end of the term, the Popular Coalition was composed of 89 MPs.
h. At the beginning of the term the Mixed Group was composed of EE (2), PAR (1), UV (1), AIC (1), CG (1). At the end, the number of MPs had increased from 6 to 18 (MPs joined from: EA (2), RD (1), PAM (1), MIXED (8).
i. IU-UEC was not initially allowed to form a separate parliamentary group as it had not received 5% of the vote, which is way on 23 September 1986 the United Left-Left Catalonia Group was formed as part of the Mixed Group. This group was composed of PCE (4), PCPE (1), FP (1), PSUC (1). In 1987 it changed its name to United Left-Initiative for Catalonia (IpC was composed of PSCU, PCC, ENE). In December 1987, one member of that group trasnferred to CDS.
j. The Socialists' Parliamentary Group was composed of representatives of the following parties: PSOE and PSC.
k. The Popular Parliamentary Group was composed of representatives of the following parties: PP, UPN, CdG.
l. The Catalonian Parliamentary Group was composed of representatives of the following parties: CDC and UDC.
m. In conjunction with the murder of Josu Maguruzu on 20 November 1989, and thus before accreditation, deputies of HB (4) did not enter any parliamentary group; in the summer of 1990 they joined the Mixed Group.
n. During the term, no MPs switched parliamentary groups. Nevertheless, one MP from PAR spent two days in the Canary Coalition Group in order for it to have the 5 members necessary for forming a group in accordance with the Regulation of the Congress of Deputies.
o. Three MPs from PDNI within the IU Parliamentary Group transferred to the Mixed Group, as did two MPs of IpC and Els Verds.
p. Two MPs from UPN joined the Canary Coalition Group in order for it to be founded.
J. Three MPs joined the Canary Coalition Group in order for it to be founded.
k. Two MPs from PSOE joined the Canary Coalition Group in order for it to be founded. In January 2005, a split occurrs in the Canary Islands Initiative party, leading to the founding of New Canary Islands, which as a consequence leads to the collapse of GP Canary-New Canary Islands.

Attachment 5

Tools of accountability used in the Spanish Senate, by parliamentary group

Tool	Term II	Term III	Term IV	Term V	Term VI	Term VII	Term VIII
Interpellations:	PSOE 0 PP 158 Mixed 17 CiU 8 PNV 0	PSOE 0 PP 107 CdiS 49 CiU 15 PNV 2 Mixed 54 ADC 30 APL 4	PSOE 0 PP 202 CiU 38 PNV 0 CdiS 59 Mixed142	PP 97 PSOE 0 CiU 15 PNV 9 CC 13 Mixed 26	PP 0 PSOE 100 CiU 18 PNV 12 Mixed 35	PP 0 PSOE 86 CiU 32 Entensa 33 PNV 11 CC 14 Mixed 51	PSOE 0 PP 90 CiU 42 ERC 39 PNV 16 IU-IpCV 41 CC 7 Mixed 85
Verbal queries (preguntas orales al gobierno pleno)	PSOE 45 PP 330 Mixed 100 CiU 15 PNV 1	PSOE 21 PP 296 CDiS 113 CiU 21 PNV 1 Mixed 112 ADC 88 APL 71	PSOE 333 PP 369 CiU 57 PNV 1 CdiS 62 Mixed 132	PP 256 PSOE 242 CiU 30 PNV6 CC 21 Mixed 32	PP 360 PSOE 362 CiU 80 PNV 33 Mixed 80	PP 420 PSOE 433 CiU 139 Entensa 112 PNV 82 CC 122 Mixed 158	PSOE 773 PP 872 CiU 96 ERC 99 PNV 88 IU-IpCV 121 CC 84 Mixed 94
Verbal queries Pregutnas orales en las comisiones	No data	No data	PSOE 1 PP 170 CiU 0 PNV 0 CdiS 4 Mixed 1	PP 23 PSOE 38 CiU 0 PNV 0 CC 5 Mixed 0	PP 141 PSOE 1415 CiU 36 PNV 37 Mixed 15	PP 16 PSOE 488 CiU 51 Entensa 54 PNV 17 CC 1 Mixed 96	PSOE 1051 PP 2217 CiU 117 ERC 123 PNV 11 IU-IpCV 21 CC 0 Mixed 107
Written queries (preguntas escritas al gobierno)	PSOE 311 PP 4826 Mixed 113 CiU 20 PNV 5	PSOE 220 PP 3534 CDiS 72 CiU 77 PNV 1 Mixed 420 ADC 1204 APL 183	PSOE 546 PP 10607 CiU 137 PNV 1 CdiS 13 Mixed 613	PP 9911 PSOE 1230 CiU 154 PNV 9 CC 989 Mixed 122	PP 3543 PSOE 27048 CiU 450 PNV379 Mixed 582	PP 2557 PSOE 22367 CiU 1527 Entensa 936 PNV 216 CC 1172 Mixed 466	PSOE 10924 PP 114780 CiU 5187 ERC 2504 PNV 51 IU-IpCV 2281 CC 244 Mixed 4293
Resolutions Mociones *	No data	PSOE 4 PP 49 CDiS 14 CiU 2 PNV 0 Mixed 16 ADC 14 APL 3	PSOE 13 (1)(2) PP 123 (1)(2) CiU 14 (1) PNV 1 (1) CdiS 20 (1) Mixed 41 (1) (2)	PP 79 (1)(2) PSOE 40 (1)(2) CiU 7 (1) PNV 6 (1) CC 33 (1)(2) Mixed 12 (1)(2)	PP 73 (1)(2)(3) PSOE73 (1)(5) CiU 55 (1)(2) (3)(4) (5) PNV 33 (1)(2) (3)(4)(5) Mixed 40 (1) (3)(5)	PP 152 (1)(2) PSOE85 (1)(3) CiU 56 (1)(2)(4) Entensa 49 (1) (3)(4) PNV 28 (1)(2) CC 52 (1) Mixed 10 (1)	PSOE 36 PP 29 CiU 36 ERC 29 PNV 14 IU-IpCV 30 CC 6 Mixed 36

Tool	Term II	Term III	Term IV	Term V	Term VI	Term VII	Term VIII
Resolutioins following interpellations Mocionoes consecuencia de la interpelacion	No data	No data	No data	PP 18 PSOE 0 CiU 3 PNV 5 CC 1 Mixed 5	PP 0 PSOE 67 CiU 6 PNV 2 Mixed 13	PP 0 PSOE 48 CiU 17 Entensa 22 PNV 7 CC 5 Mixed 20	PSOE PP CiU ERC PNV IU-IpCV CC Mixed
Resolutions in commissions **Mociones en comision**	No data	No data	No data	No data	PP 16 (6) PSOE 245(6) CiU 13 (6) PNV 45 (6) Mixed 9 (6)	PP 17 PSOE 159 CiU 39 Entensa 36 PNV 4 CC 9 Mixed 55	PSOE PP CiU ERC PNV IU-IpCV CC Mixed

Source: own work based on: Memoria de la II Legislatura del Senado (1982–1986), Secretaría General del Senado, Madrid 1987, pp. 491, 493, 497–498, 500, 502; Memoria de la III Legislatura del Senado (1986–1989), Secretaría General del Senado, Madrid 1990, pp. 480–481, 483–484; Memoria de la IV Legislatura del Senado (1989–1993), Secretaría General del Senado, Madrid 1995, p. 594; Memoria de la V Legislatura del Senado (1993–1996), Secretaría General del Senado, Madrid 1998, p. 752; Memoria de la VI Legislatura del Senado (1996–2000), vol. II, Secretaría General del Senado, Madrid 2001, p. 1097; Memoria de la VII Legislatura del Senado (2000–2004), Secretaría General del Senado, Madrid 2005, p. 916; Memoria de la VIII Legislatura del Senado (2004–2008), Secretaría General del Senado, Madrid 2011, pp. 418–421, 435–436.

*Term IV: (1) Resolutions submitted jointly by all parliamentary groups; (2) Resolutions submitted jointly by PP, PSOE, Mixed; Term V: (1) Resolutions submitted jointly by all parliamentary groups, (2) Resolutions submitted jointly by all parliamentary groups, (2) Resolutions submitted jountly by PSOE, PP, CC; Term VI: (1) Resolutions submitted jointly by Mixed Group, AGC (Agrupación Democrática Cristiana), APL (Agrupación Partido Liberal) – 1, (2) Resolutions submitted jointly by all parliamentary groups – 9, (3) Resolutions submitted jointly by PP, CiU, PNV – 3, (4) Resolutions submitted jointly by CiU, PNV – 2, (5) Resolutions submitted jointly by PSOE, CIU, PNV, Mixed Group – 1, (6) Resolutions submitted jointly by all parliamentary groups – 1; Term VII: (1) Resolutions submitted jointly by all parliamentary groups – 20, (2) Resolutions submitted jointly by CiU, PP, PNV – 1, (3) Resolutions submitted jointly by PSOE and Entensa – 1, (4) Resolutions submitted jointly by Entensa and CiU – 1.

Attachment 6

Economic voting in Poland in elections of 1997 (reference party – SLD)

Vote for SLD versus	**Independent variables**	**B**	**Z**	**P>z**	**95% Conf,**	**Interval**
AWS	Fixed	-3.80 (0.82)	-4.63	0.00	-5.00	-2.19
	Retrospective assessment of economic situation	-0.45 (0.35)	-1.30	0.20	-1.13	0.23
	Prospective assessment of economic situation	0.69 (0.30)	2.28	0.02	0.10	1.28
	Retrospective assessment of political situation	-1.21 (0.30)	-4.01	0.00	-1.80	-0.62
	Political identification	1.09 (0.08)	13.8	0.00	0.93	1.24
	Age	-0.01 (0.01)	-0.57	0.57	-0.03	0.02
	Gender	-0.17 (0.29)	-0.59	0.56	-0.73	0.39
	Unemployed	0.85 (0.58)	1.46	0.15	-0.29	1.99
	Housemaker	0.95 (0.72)	1.33	0.19	-0.45	2.36
	Retired	-0.06 (0.42)	-0.15	0.88	-0.89	0.77
	Vocational education	-0.38 (0.44)	-0.85	0.39	-1.25	0.49
	Secondary education	-1.15 (0.38)	-3.06	0.00	-1.89	-0.41
	Tertiary education	-0.62 (0.50)	-1.25	0.21	-1.60	0.35
PSL	Fixed	-2.22 (0.97)	-2.30	0.02	-4.12	-0.33
	Retrospective assessment of economic situation	0.31 (0.41)	0.76	0.45	-0.49	1.11
	Prospective assessment of economic situation	0.44 (0.38)	1.16	0.25	-0.31	1.19
	Retrospective assessment of political situation	-1.5 (0.38)	-3.97	0.00	-2.24	-0.76
	Political identification	0.44 (0.08)	5.21	0.00	0.27	0.60
	Age	0.02 (0.02)	1.41	0.16	-0.01	0.05
	Gender	0.02 (0.35)	0.05	0.96	-0.68	0.71
	Unemployed	-0.16 (0.76)	-0.21	0.83	-1.66	1.33
	Housemaker	-0.9 (1.16)	-0.77	0.44	-3.17	1.38
	Retired	-1.31 (0.53)	-2.48	0.01	-2.35	-0.27
	Vocational education	-0.66 (0.52)	-1.26	0.21	-1.69	0.37
	Secondary education	-1.19 (0.45)	-2.63	0.01	-2.08	-0.30
	Tertiary education	-0.86 (0.61)	-1.41	0.16	-2.06	0.34

Vote for SLD versus	Independent variables	B	Z	P>z	95% Conf,	Interval
UW	Fixed	-2.93 0.85)	-3.44	0.00	-4.59	-1.26
	Retrospective assessment of economic situation	-0.32 (0.34)	-0.93	0.35	-0.99	0.36
	Prospective assessment of economic situation	0.64 (0.31)	2.06	0.04	0.03	1.24
	Retrospective assessment of political situation	-0.47 (0.32)	-1.46	0.14	-1.09	0.16
	Political identification	0.69 (0.080)	9.14	0.00	0.54	0.84
	Age	-0.01 (0.010)	-0.62	0.54	-0.03	0.02
	Gender	-0.52 (0.29)	-1.79	0.07	-1.10	0.05
	Unemployed	0.38 (0.63)	0.6	0.55	-0.86	1.63
	Housemaker	0.28 (0.74)	0.38	0.70	-1.17	1.74
	Retired	-0.12 (0.44)	-0.27	0.79	-0.99	0.75
	Vocational education	0.05 (0.51)	0.10	0.92	-0.94	1.05
	Secondary education	-0.12 (0.42)	-0.29	0.77	-0.95	0.70
	Tertiary education	1.35 (0.5)	2.73	0.01	0.38	2.32
ROP	Fixed	-6.55 (1.33)	-4.93	0.00	-9.16	-3.95
	Retrospective assessment of economic situation	-0.31 0.55)	-0.57	0.57	-1.38	0.76
	Prospective assessment of economic situation	0.51 (0.44)	1.17	0.24	-0.35	1.36
	Retrospective assessment of political situation	-0.83 (0.44)	-1.91	0.06	-1.69	0.02
	Political identification	1.00 (0.11)	9.19	0.00	0.79	1.22
	Age	0.00 (0.02)	0.16	0.87	-0.03	0.04
	Gender	0.19 (0.44)	0.44	0.66	-0.66	1.04
	Unemployed	-0.32 (1.16)	-0.27	0.78	-2.58	1.95
	Housemaker	0.36 (1.22)	0.29	0.77	-2.04	2.75
	Retired	-0.53 (0.65)	-0.82	0.41	-1.81	0.74
	Vocational education	0.64 (0.69)	0.93	0.36	-0.72	2.00
	Secondary education	-0.27 (0.65)	-0.42	0.68	-1.53	1.00
	Tertiary education	0.24 (0.80)	0.31	0.76	-1.32	1.80

Vote for SLD versus	Independent variables	B	Z	P>z	95% Conf,	Interval
UP	Fixed	-2.47(1.27)	-1.95	0.05	-4.96	0.01
	Retrospective assessment of economic situation	0.01 (0.51)	0.03	0.98	-0.99	1.02
	Prospective assessment of economic situation	0.41 (0.48)	0.86	0.39	-0.53	1.35
	Retrospective assessment of political situation	-0.33 (0.50)	-0.65	0.52	-1.32	0.66
	Political identification	0.44 (0.11)	4.20	0.00	0.24	0.65
	Age	-0.01 (0.02)	-0.68	0.50	-0.06	0.03
	Gender	-0.67 (0.46)	-1.45	0.15	-1.57	0.23
	Unemployed	0.35 (0.88)	0.40	0.69	-1.37	2.08
	Housemaker	-0.02 (1.15)	-0.02	0.99	-2.28	2.24
	Retired	-0.1 (0.70)	-0.14	0.89	-1.47	1.27
	Vocational education	-0.06 (0.74)	-0.08	0.93	-1.52	1.40
	Secondary education	-0.33 (0.62)	-0.53	0.59	-1.54	0.88
	Tertiary education	0.02 (0.83)	0.02	0.99	-1.6	1.64
other	Fixed	-2.87 (1.05)	-2.74	0.01	-4.92	-0.82
	Retrospective assessment of economic situation	-0.39 (0.40)	-0.81	0.42	-1.35	0.56
	Prospective assessment of economic situation	0.26 (0.40)	0.65	0.52	-0.53	1.05
	Retrospective assessment of political situation	-0.79 (0.39)	-2	0.05	-1.56	-0.02
	Political identification	0.84 (0.00)	8.96	0	0.65	1.02
	Age	-0.03 (0.02)	-1.77	0.08	-0.06	0
	Gender	-0.18 (0.38)	-0.48	0.63	-0.92	0.56
	Unemployed	0.40 (0.90)	0.44	0.66	-1.37	2.17
	Housemaker	0.34 (1.20)	0.28	0.78	-2.01	2.69
	Retired	1.22 (0.57)	2.14	0.03	0.1	2.33
	Vocational education	-1.17 (0.59)	-1.99	0.05	-2.32	-0.02
	Secondary education	-1.59 (0.48)	-3.31	0	-2.53	-0.65
	Tertiary education	-0.83 (0.66)	-1.26	0.21	-2.12	0.46

N...817
Log likelihood 968.572
LR $Chi^2(72)$ 690.39
Prob >Ch^2 ....0.000
Pseudo- R^2..0.262

*p<05; **p<01; ***p<001; standard error given in parenthesis.

Attachment 7

Economic voting in Poland in elections of 1997 (reference party – SLD/PSL)

Vote for SLD-PSL versus	Independent variables	B	Z	P>z	95% Conf.	Interval
AWS	Fixed	-3.81 (0.80)	-4.78	0	-5.37	-2.25
	Retrospective assessment of economic situation	-0.54 (0.32)	-1.7	0.09	-1.17	0.08
	Prospective assessment of economic situation	0.53 (0. 27)	1.99	0.05	0.01	1.05
	Retrospective assessment of political situation	-0.66 (0.26)	-2.55	0.01	-1.16	-0.15
	Political identification	0.94 (0.07)	13.59	0	0.8	1.07
	Age	-0.02 (0.01)	-1.29	0.2	-0.04	0.01
	Gender	-0.18 (0.25)	-0.71	0.48	-0.68	0.32
	Unemployed	0.94 (0.52)	1.8	0.07	-0.08	1.95
	Housemaker	1.14 (0.65)	1.74	0.08	-0.14	2.41
	Student	-0.11 (0.70)	-0.15	0.88	-1.49	1.27
	Retired	0.39 (0.38)	1.03	0.3	-0.35	1.14
	Vocational education	-0.13 (0.39)	-0.34	0.74	-0.9	0.64
	Secondary education	-0.69 (0.34)	-2.03	0.04	-1.35	-0.02
	Tertiary education	-0.35 (0.45)	-0.77	0.44	-1.23	0.53
UW	Fixed	-3.73 (0.86)	-4.35	0	-5.41	-2.05
	Retrospective assessment of economic situation	-0.43 (0.32)	-1.32	0.19	-1.06	0.21
	Prospective assessment of economic situation	0.49 (0.28)	1.76	0.08	-0.05	1.04
	Retrospective assessment of political situation	0.01 (0.28)	0.05	0.96	-0.54	0.57
	Political identification	0.55 (0.07)	8.33	0	0.42	0.68
	Age	0.00 (0.01)	-0.19	0.85	-0.03	0.02
	Gender	-0.58 (0.27)	-2.16	0.03	-1.11	-0.05
	Unemployed	0.66 (0.59)	1.11	0.27	-0.5	1.81
	Housemaker	0.49 (0.70)	0.7	0.48	-0.88	1.86
	Student	1.40 (0.66)	2.13	0.03	0.11	2.68
	Retired	0.11 (0.42)	0.27	0.79	-0.7	0.92
	Vocational education	0.46 (0.47)	0.97	0.33	-0.47	1.38
	Secondary education	0.34 (0.39)	0.86	0.39	-0.43	1.11
	Tertiary education	1.77 (0.46)	3.86	0	0.87	2.66

Vote for SLD-PSL versus	Independent variables	B	Z	P>z	95% Conf.	Interval
ROP	Fixed	-6.52 (1.35)	-4.84	0	-9.16	-3.88
	Retrospective assessment of economic situation	-0.40 (0.53)	-0.76	0.45	-1.44	0.64
	Prospective assessment of economic situation	0.35 (0.41)	0.86	0.39	-0.45	1.16
	Retrospective assessment of political situation	-0.28 (0.41)	-0.69	0.49	-1.08	0.52
	Political identification	0.85 (0.10)	8.4	0	0.65	1.05
	Age	-0.01 (0.02)	-0.37	0.72	-0.05	0.03
	Gender	0.19 (0.42)	0.45	0.65	-0.63	1.01
	Unemployed	-0.24 (1.13)	-0.21	0.83	-2.45	1.97
	Housemaker	0.54 (1.19)	0.45	0.65	-1.79	2.86
	Student	-0.35 (1.24)	-0.28	0.78	-2.77	2.08
	Retired	-0.06 (0.63)	-0.09	0.92	-1.29	1.17
	Vocational education	0.86 (0.67)	1.29	0.2	-0.44	2.17
	Secondary education	0.19 (0.62)	0.31	0.76	-1.03	1.42
	Tertiary education	0.50 (0.77)	0.65	0.52	-1.01	2.01
UP	Fixed	-2.98 (1.37)	-2.17	0.03	-5.66	-0.29
	Retrospective assessment of economic situation	-0.07 (0.50)	-0.15	0.88	-1.05	0.91
	Prospective assessment of economic situation	0.29 (0.46)	0.63	0.53	-0.62	1.2
	Retrospective assessment of political situation	0.13 (0.49)	0.26	0.79	-0.83	1.09
	Political identification	0.33 (0.10)	3.3	0	0.13	0.52
	Age	-0.01 (0.02)	-0.65	0.52	-0.06	0.03
	Gender	-0.69 (0.45)	-1.55	0.12	-1.57	0.18
	Unemployed	0.52 (0.86)	0.6	0.55	-1.17	2.21
	Housemaker	0.14 (1.14)	0.12	0.9	-2.09	2.36
	Student	0.70 (1.01)	0.69	0.49	-1.28	2.67
	Retired	0.17 (0.69)	0.24	0.81	-1.19	1.52
	Vocational education	0.20 (0.73)	0.28	0.78	-1.23	1.64
	Secondary education	0.06 (0.61)	0.1	0.92	-1.13	1.25
	Tertiary education	0.29 (0.82)	0.36	0.72	-1.32	1.9

Vote for SLD-PSL versus	Independent variables	B	Z	P>z	95% Conf.	Interval
other	Fixed	-4.04 (1.12)	-3.62	0	-6.23	-1.86
	Retrospective assessment of economic situation	-0.52 (0.47)	-1.11	0.27	-1.44	0.4
	Prospective assessment of economic situation	0.13 (0.38)	0.35	0.73	-0.61	0.87
	Retrospective assessment of political situation	-0.33 (0.37)	-0.91	0.37	-1.05	0.39
	Political identification	0.69 (0.09)	8.08	0	0.52	0.86
	Age	-0.02 (0.02)	-1.05	0.3	-0.06	0.02
	Gender	-0.21 (0.36)	-0.59	0.55	-0.91	0.49
	Unemployed	0.84 (0.88)	0.95	0.34	-0.89	2.56
	Housemaker	0.71 (1.17)	0.61	0.54	-1.58	3.01
	Student	1.87 (0.82)	2.27	0.02	0.25	3.48
	Retired	1.55 (0.56)	2.78	0.01	0.46	2.65
	Vocational education	-0.62 (0.56)	-1.11	0.27	-1.71	0.48
	Secondary education	-1.10 (0.45)	-2.43	0.02	-1.99	-0.21
	Tertiary education	-0.29 (0.63)	-0.45	0.65	-1.52	0.95
N......817						
Log likelihood......863.040						
LR $Chi^2(65)$......627.13						
Prob >Ch^2......0.000						
Pseudo- R^2......0.267						

*p<05; **p<01; ***p<001; standard error given in parenthesis.

Attachment 8

Economic voting in Poland in elections of 2001 (reference party – AWS)

Vote for versus AWS	Independent variables	B	Z	P>z	95% Conf.	Interval
SLD	Fixed	9.36 (1.49)	6.29	0	6.45	12.28
	Retrospective assessment of economic situation	-0.70 (1.13)	-0.62	0.54	-2.91	1.51
	Prospective assessment of economic situation	1.86 (0.68)	2.74	0.01	0.53	3.19
	Retrospective assessment of political situation	-0.80 (0.76)	-1.05	0.3	-2.29	0.69
	Political identification	-1.02 (0.11)	-9.52	0	-1.23	-0.81
	Age	-0.03 (0. 02)	-1.16	0.25	-0.07	0.02
	Gender	0.40 (0.45)	0.9	0.37	-0.48	1.28
	Unemployed	-0.27 (0.82)	-0.32	0.75	-1.88	1.34
	Student	-0.70 (1.08)	-0.65	0.52	-2.81	1.42
	Retired	-0.71 (0.71)	-1	0.32	-2.09	0.68
	Vocational education	-0.78 (0.74)	-1.06	0.29	-2.23	0.67
	Secondary education	-1.18 (0.64)	-1.84	0.07	-2.43	0.08
	Tertiary education	-0.37 (0.79)	-0.47	0.64	-1.91	1.17
PSL	Fixed	6.59 (1.58)	4.16	0	3.49	9.7
	Retrospective assessment of economic situation	1.10 (1.11)	0.99	0.32	-1.08	3.28
	Prospective assessment of economic situation	1.69 (0.71)	2.39	0.02	0.31	3.07
	Retrospective assessment of political situation	-1.01 (0.84)	-1.2	0.23	-2.65	0.64
	Political identification	-0.50 (0.11)	-4.6	0	-0.71	-0.28
	Age	-0.04 (0.02)	-1.56	0.12	-0.09	0.01
	Gender	0.92 (0.49)	1.88	0.06	-0.04	1.87
	Unemployed	-1.21 (0.92)	-1.31	0.19	-3.02	0.6
	Student	-1.42 (1.17)	-1.21	0.23	-3.72	0.88
	Retired	-0.61 (0.76)	-0.81	0.42	-2.1	0.88
	Vocational education	-1.02 (0.77)	-1.34	0.18	-2.53	0.48
	Secondary education	-1.52 (0.68)	-2.25	0.02	-2.85	-0.2
	Tertiary education	-2.55 (0.97)	-2.63	0.01	-4.45	-0.65

Vote for versus AWS	Independent variables	B	Z	P>z	95% Conf.	Interval
PO	Fixed	4.29 (1.47)	2.91	0	1.4	7.18
	Retrospective assessment of economic situation	0.99 (0.98)	1	0.32	-0.94	2.92
	Prospective assessment of economic situation	1.45 (0.68)	2.12	0.03	0.11	2.79
	Retrospective assessment of political situation	-1.01 (0.72)	-1.41	0.16	-2.41	0.39
	Political identification	-0.22 (0.10)	-2.25	0.02	-0.42	-0.03
	Age	-0.02 (0.02)	-0.85	0.39	-0.06	0.02
	Gender	0.43 (0.44)	0.97	0.33	-0.44	1.3
	Unemployed	-1.54 (0.88)	-1.75	0.08	-3.27	0.18
	Student	-0.91 (1.04)	-0.88	0.38	-2.96	1.13
	Retired	-1.22 (0.71)	-1.72	0.09	-2.61	0.17
	Vocational education	-0.70 (0.76)	-0.92	0.36	-2.18	0.79
	Secondary education	-0.48 (0.65)	-0.74	0.46	-1.74	0.79
	Tertiary education	-0.08 (0.79)	-0.1	0.92	-1.62	1.47
Samoobrona	Fixed	7.49 (1.53)	4.89	0	4.49	10.49
	Retrospective assessment of economic situation	0.75 (1.10)	0.68	0.5	-1.41	2.91
	Prospective assessment of economic situation	1.50 (0.69)	2.16	0.03	0.14	2.85
	Retrospective assessment of political situation	-1.04 (0.81)	-1.29	0.2	-2.62	0.54
	Political identification	-0.46 (0.10)	-4.41	0	-0.66	-0.25
	Age	-0.04 (0.02)	-1.82	0.07	-0.09	0
	Gender	0.44 (0.46)	0.95	0.34	-0.47	1.35
	Unemployed	-1.27 (0.89)	-1.43	0.15	-3.01	0.47
	Student	-1.14 (1.10)	-1.04	0.3	-3.3	1.02
	Retired	-0.44 (0.73)	-0.6	0.55	-1.87	1
	Vocational education	-1.33 (0.74)	-1.81	0.07	-2.77	0.11
	Secondary education	-2.06 (0.65)	-3.18	0	-3.33	-0.79
	Tertiary education	-2.86 (0.91)	-3.16	0	-4.64	-1.08

Vote for versus AWS	Independent variables	B	Z	P>z	95% Conf.	Interval
UW	Fixed	0.39 (2.24)	0.17	0.86	-4	4.78
	Retrospective assessment of economic situation	0.57 (1.47)	0.39	0.7	-2.31	3.45
	Prospective assessment of economic situation	1.78 (0.85)	2.08	0.04	0.1	3.45
	Retrospective assessment of political situation	-2.29 (1.29)	-1.77	0.08	-4.82	0.24
	Political identification	-0.22 (0.14)	-1.55	0.12	-0.51	0.06
	Age	0.00 (0.03)	0.09	0.93	-0.06	0.06
	Gender	0.49 (0.64)	0.77	0.44	-0.75	1.74
	Unemployed	-0.49 (1.31)	-0.37	0.71	-3.05	2.07
	Student	-0.06 (1.55)	-0.04	0.97	-3.1	2.98
	Retired	-1.51 (1.03)	-1.46	0.14	-3.54	0.52
	Vocational education	-0.77 (1.60)	-0.48	0.63	-3.9	2.36
	Secondary education	0.29 (1.27)	0.23	0.82	-2.19	2.77
	Tertiary education	2.01 (1.31)	1.53	0.13	-0.56	4.59
PiS	Fixed	2.36 (1.54)	1.53	0.13	-0.66	5.37
	Retrospective assessment of economic situation	1.00 (1.01)	0.98	0.33	-0.99	2.98
	Prospective assessment of economic situation	1.26 (0.70)	1.81	0.07	-0.11	2.64
	Retrospective assessment of political situation	-1.29 (0.78))	-1.65	0.1	-2.82	0.24
	Political identification	-0.13 (0.10)	-1.29	0.2	-0.33	0.07
	Age	-0.02 (0.02)	-0.95	0.34	-0.07	0.02
	Gender	0.42 (0.46)	0.91	0.37	-0.49	1.32
	Unemployed	-0.60 (0.85)	-0.7	0.48	-2.27	1.08
	Student	-0.76 (1.08)	-0.7	0.48	-2.88	1.36
	Retired	-0.17 (0.73)	-0.23	0.82	-1.6	1.26
	Vocational education	0.18 (0.81)	0.23	0.82	-1.4	1.76
	Secondary education	0.52 (0.69)	0.76	0.45	-0.83	1.88
	Tertiary education	0.44 (0.85)	0.51	0.61	-1.23	2.11

N...725
Log likelihood 875.801
LR $Chi^2(72)$ 519.00
Prob >Ch^2 ....0.000
Pseudo- R^2..0.229

*p<05; **p<01; ***p<001; standard error given in parenthesis.

Economic voting in Poland in elections of 2001 (reference party – AWS/UW)

Vote for AWS-UW versus	Independent variables	B	Z	P>z	95% Conf.	Interval
SLD	Fixed	8.36 (1.22)	6.84	0.00	5.96	10.75
	Retrospective assessment of economic situation	-1.03 (0.96)	-1.07	0.28	-2.91	0.85
	Prospective assessment of economic situation	0.99 (0.45)	2.19	0.03	0.10	1.88
	Retrospective assessment of political situation	0.07 (0.68)	0.11	0.92	-1.26	1.41
	Political identification	-0.93 (0.09)	-10.42	0.00	-1.10	-0.75
	Age	-0.03 (0.02)	-1.58	0.11	-0.06	0.01
	Gender	0.16 (0.36)	0.45	0.65	-0.55	0.88
	Unemployed	-0.04 (0.70)	-0.06	0.95	-1.41	1.32
	Student	-0.63 (0.91)	-0.69	0.49	-2.40	1.15
	Retired	-0.11 (0.57)	-0.19	0.85	-1.23	1.01
	Vocational education	-0.50 (0.67)	-0.74	0.46	-1.81	0.82
	Secondary education	-1.20 (0.58)	-2.08	0.04	-2.32	-0.07
	Tertiary education	-1.26 (0.63)	-1.99	0.05	-2.50	-0.02
PSL	Fixed	5.59 (1.35)	4.15	0.00	2.95	8.23
	Retrospective assessment of economic situation	0.77 (0.95)	0.80	0.42	-1.10	2.64
	Prospective assessment of economic situation	0.84 (0.50)	1.68	0.09	-0.14	1.81
	Retrospective assessment of political situation	-0.16 (0.77)	-0.21	0.83	-1.68	1.35
	Political identification	-0.41 (0.09)	-4.46	0.00	-0.58	-0.23
	Age	-0.04 (0.02)	-1.97	0.05	-0.08	0.00
	Gender	0.68 (0.41)	1.65	0.10	-0.13	1.49
	Unemployed	-0.99 (0.82)	-1.21	0.23	-2.6	0.61
	Student	-1.35 (1.02)	-1.32	0.19	-3.35	0.65
	Retired	-0.03 (0.64)	-0.05	0.96	-1.30	1.23
	Vocational education	-0.75 (0.70)	-1.07	0.29	-2.12	0.63
	Secondary education	-1.55 (0.62)	-2.50	0.01	-2.76	-0.33
	Tertiary education	-3.42 (0.85)	-4.01	0.00	-5.09	-1.75

Vote for AWS-UW versus	Independent variables	B	Z	P>z	95% Conf.	Interval
PO	Fixed	3.28 (1.21)	2.70	0.01	0.90	5.66
	Retrospective assessment of economic situation	0.65 (0.80)	0.82	0.42	-0.91	2.21
	Prospective assessment of economic situation	0.60 (0.47)	1.29	0.20	-0.31	1.51
	Retrospective assessment of political situation	-0.14 (0.63)	-0.23	0.82	-1.37	1.09
	Political identification	-0.13 (0.08)	-1.63	0.10	-0.29	0.03
	Age	-0.02 (0.02)	-1.20	0.23	-0.06	0.01
	Gender	0.20 (0.36)	0.55	0.58	-0.51	0.91
	Unemployed	-1.34 (0.78)	-1.72	0.09	-2.86	0.19
	Student	-0.84 (0.87)	-0.97	0.33	-2.55	0.86
	Retired	-0.64 (0.58)	-1.11	0.27	-1.78	0.49
	Vocational education	-0.42 (0.70)	-0.61	0.55	-1.78	0.94
	Secondary education	-0.49 (0.59)	-0.84	0.40	-1.65	0.66
	Tertiary education	-0.92 (0.64)	-1.44	0.15	-2.18	0.33
Samoobrona	Fixed	6.49 (1.29)	5.05	0.00	3.97	9.02
	Retrospective assessment of economic situation	0.41 (0.95)	0.44	0.66	-1.44	2.27
	Prospective assessment of economic situation	0.65 (0.48)	1.35	0.18	-0.29	1.59
	Retrospective assessment of political situation	-0.20 (0.74)	-0.27	0.78	-1.66	1.25
	Political identification	-0.37 (0.09)	-4.27	0.00	-0.53	-0.20
	Age	-0.05 (0.02)	-2.31	0.02	-0.08	-0.01
	Gender	021 (0.39)	0.54	0.59	-0.55	0.97
	Unemployed	-1.05 (0.78)	-1.35	0.18	-2.59	0.48
	Student	-1.07 0.94)	-1.14	0.26	-2.92	0.77
	Retired	0.14 (0.62)	0.23	0.82	-1.07	1.34
	Vocational education	-1.05 (0.67)	-1.57	0.12	-2.36	0.26
	Secondary education	-2.08 (0.59)	-3.54	0.00	-3.24	-0.93
	Tertiary education	-3.73 (0.78)	-4.77	0.00	-5.26	-2.19
PiS	Fixed	1.38 (1.31)	1.06	0.29	-1.18	3.95
	Retrospective assessment of economic situation	0.66 (0.86)	0.77	0.44	-1.02	2.33
	Prospective assessment of economic situation	0.43 (0.50)	0.88	0.38	-0.54	1.40
	Retrospective assessment of political situation	-0.46 (0.71)	-0.65	0.52	-1.85	0.93

Vote for AWS-UW versus	Independent variables	B	Z	P>z	95% Conf.	Interval
PiS	Political identification	-0.04 (0.08)	-0.51	0.61	-0.21	0.12
	Age	-0.02 (0.02)	-1.27	0.20	-0.06	0.01
	Gender	0.19 (0.39)	0.48	0.63	-0.57	0.95
	Unemployed	-0.39 (0.75)	-0.52	0.61	-1.86	1.08
	Student	-0.69 (0.92)	-0.75	0.46	-2.49	1.12
	Retired	0.40 (0.61)	0.65	0.51	-0.80	1.60
	Vocational education	0.45 (0.75)	0.59	0.55	-1.03	1.93
	Secondary education	0.49 (0.64)	0.77	0.44	-0.77	1.76
	Tertiary education	-0.39 (0.72)	-0.54	0.59	-1.82	1.030

N..725
Log likelihood 854.994
LR $Chi^2(60)$ 495.28
Prob >Ch^2 ....0.000
Pseudo- R^2..0.262

*p<05; **p<01; ***p<001; standard error given in parenthesis.

Attachment 9

Economic voting in Poland in elections of 2001 (reference party – AWS/PO/PIS)

Vote for AWS/ PO/PIS versus	Independent variables	B	Z	P>z	95% Conf.	Interval
PSL	Fixed	2.23 (0.90)	2.47	0.01	0.46	4.00
	Retrospective assessment of economic situation	0.12 (0.69)	0.18	0.86	-1.23	1.48
	Prospective assessment of economic situation	-0.16 (0.60)	-0.28	0.78	-1.33	1.00
	Retrospective assessment of political situation	0.45 (0.33)	1.35	0.18	-0.20	1.10
	Political identification	-0.32 (0.07)	-4.86	0.00	-0.46	-0.19
	Age	-0.02 (0.01)	-1.25	0.21	-0.04	0.01
	Gender	0.54 (0.31)	1.73	0.08	-0.07	1.15
	Student	-0.03 (0.65)	-0.04	0.97	-1.30	1.24
	Retired	0.12 (0.47)	0.25	0.80	-0.81	1.05
	Vocational education	-0.72 (0.47)	-1.54	0.12	-1.64	0.19
	Secondary education	-1.45 (0.44)	-3.27	0.00	-2.31	-0.58
	Tertiary education	-2.55 (0.71)	-3.59	0.00	-3.94	-1.16
LPR	Fixed	-2.10 (1.07)	-1.95	0.05	-4.20	0.01
	Retrospective assessment of economic situation	-0.82 (0.87)	-0.95	0.34	-2.53	0.88
	Prospective assessment of economic situation	0.20 (0.61)	0.32	0.75	-1.00	1.39
	Retrospective assessment of political situation	-0.11 (0.42)	-0.27	0.79	-0.93	0.70
	Political identification	0.10 (0.07)	1.33	0.19	-0.05	0.24
	Age	0.02 (0.02)	0.95	0.34	-0.02	0.05
	Gender	-0.90 (0.36)	-2.50	0.01	-1.60	-0.20
	Unemployed	-0.02 (0.70)	-0.03	0.98	-1.40	1.36
	Retired	-0.27 (0.53)	-0.51	0.61	-1.30	0.76
	Vocational education	0.56 (0.54)	1.04	0.30	-0.50	1.61
	Secondary education	-0.91 (0.53)	-1.73	0.08	-1.95	0.12
	Tertiary education	-0.32 (0.57)	-0.55	0.58	-1.44	0.81

Vote for AWS/ PO/PIS versus	Independent variables	B	Z	P>z	95% Conf.	Interval
„S"	Fixed	3.25 (0.82)	3.96	0.00	1.64	4.85
	Retrospective assessment of economic situation	-0.22 (0.68)	-0.32	0.75	-1.56	1.12
	Prospective assessment of economic situation	-0.17 (0.56)	-0.30	0.76	-1.25	0.92
	Retrospective assessment of political situation	0.26 (0.31)	0.85	0.40	-0.34	0.86
	Political identification	-0.29 (0.06)	-4.77	0.00	-0.40	-0.17
	Age	-0.02 (0.01)	-1.95	0.05	-0.05	0.00
	Gender	0.08 (0.28)	0.28	0.78	-0.47	0.62
	Unemployed	-0.12 (0.60)	-0.20	0.84	-1.30	1.06
	Retired	0.33 (0.43)	0.77	0.44	-0.51	1.18
	Vocational education	-1.03 (0.42)	-2.46	0.01	-1.85	-0.21
	Secondary education	-1.98 (0.40)	-4.94	0.00	-2.77	-1.20
	Tertiary education	-2.88 (0.62)	-4.63	0.00	-4.10	-1.66
UW	Fixed	-3.34 (1.80)	-1.86	0.06	-6.87	0.18
	Retrospective assessment of economic situation	-0.34 (1.19)	-0.29	0.78	-2.68	2.00
	Prospective assessment of economic situation	-1.17 (1.16)	-1.01	0.31	-3.45	1.11
	Retrospective assessment of political situation	0.53 (0.58)	0.92	0.36	-0.61	1.67
	Political identification	-0.08 (0.12)	-0.66	0.51	-0.30	0.15
	Age	0.02 (0.02)	0.67	0.51	-0.03	0.06
	Gender	0.10 (0.51)	0.20	0.84	-0.91	1.11
	Unemployed	0.48 (1.13)	0.43	0.67	-1.72	2.69
	Retired	-0.78 (0.86)	-0.91	0.36	-2.46	0.90
	Vocational education	-0.49 (1.48)	-0.33	0.74	-3.39	2.41
	Secondary education	0.37 (1.15)	0.32	0.75	-1.89	2.63
	Tertiary education	1.82 (1.13)	1.60	0.11	-0.41	4.04

Vote for AWS/ PO/PIS versus	Independent variables	B	Z	P>z	95% Conf.	Interval
SLD	Fixed	5.22 (0.74)	7.06	0.00	3.77	6.67
	Retrospective assessment of economic situation	-1.74 (0.70)	-2.47	0.01	-3.11	-0.36
	Prospective assessment of economic situation	0.15 (0.49)	0.32	0.75	-0.80	1.11
	Retrospective assessment of political situation	0.61 (0.26)	2.32	0.02	0.10	1.13
	Political identification	-0.85 (0.06)	-13.35	0.00	-0.97	-0.72
	Age	-0.01 (0.01)	-0.92	0.36	-0.03	0.01
	Gender	0.02 (0.24)	0.10	0.92	-0.45	0.49
	Unemployed	0.92 (0.49)	1.88	0.06	-0.04	1.88
	Retired	0.10 (0.37)	0.26	0.79	-0.63	0.83
	Vocational education	-0.53 (0.42)	-1.28	0.20	-1.35	0.28
	Secondary education	-1.06 (0.38)	-2.80	0.01	-1.80	-0.32
	Tertiary education	-0.40 (0.43)	-0.95	0.34	-1.24	0.43

N..775
Log likelihood 836.812
LR Chi²(55) 553.95
Prob >Ch² 0.000
Pseudo- R²..0.249

*p<05; **p<01; ***p<001; standard error given in parenthesis.

Attachment 10

Economic voting in Poland in elections of 2005 (reference party – SLD)

Vote for SLD versus	Independent variables	B	Z	P>z	95% Conf.	Interval
PiS	Fixed	-1.74 (0.97)	-1.79	0.07	-3.65	34.6
	Retrospective assessment of economic situation	-1.51 (0.41)	-3.70	0.00	-2.30	31.41
	Prospective assessment of economic situation	0.98 (0.36)	2.67	0.01	0.26	29.49
	Retrospective assessment of political situation	0.03 (0.56)	0.06	0.96	-1.07	32.54
	Political identification	0.94 (0.08)	11.70	0.00	0.78	30.58
	Age	-0.03 (0.02)	-1.79	0.07	-0.06	32.54
	Gender	0.50 (0.33)	1.54	0.12	-0.14	31.72
	Unemployed	-0.65 (0.59)	-1.11	0.27	-1.81	33.04
	Student	0.85 (0.93)	0.92	0.36	-0.97	34.39
	Retired	0.53 (0.45)	1.19	0.24	-0.35	34.46
	Vocational education	-0.88 (0.56)	-1.57	0.12	-1.98	34.61
	Secondary education	-1.03 (0.52)	-2.00	0.05	-2.05	34.44
	Tertiary education	-0.77 (0.64)	-1.2	0.23	-2.02	35.09
PSL	Fixed	-1.52 (1.24)	-1.22	0.22	-3.96	6.15
	Retrospective assessment of economic situation	-0.15 (0.49)	-0.31	0.76	-1.12	0.82
	Prospective assessment of economic situation	-0.69 (0.51)	-1.33	0.18	-1.70	0.32
	Retrospective assessment of political situation	0.24 (0.67)	0.36	0.72	-1.08	2.39
	Political identification	0.61 (0.09)	6.44	0.00	0.42	1.11
	Age	-0.03 (0.02)	-1.36	0.17	-0.06	2.40
	Gender	0.56 (0.42)	1.31	0.19	-0.27	2.50
	Unemployed	-0.84 (0.81)	-1.04	0.30	-2.42	3.14
	Student	-0.18 (1.18)	-0.15	0.88	-2.50	4.63
	Retired	0.13 (0.57)	0.23	0.82	-0.99	4.38
	Vocational education	-0.38 (0.71)	-0.53	0.59	-1.78	5.65
	Secondary education	-0.47 (0.67)	-0.70	0.49	-1.79	5.23
	Tertiary education	-1.24 (0.93)	-1.33	0.19	-3.07	6.24

Vote for SLD versus	Independent variables	B	Z	P>z	95% Conf.	Interval
PO	Fixed	-1.69 (0.98)	-1.73	0.08	-3.61	10.61
	Retrospective assessment of economic situation	-0.55 (0.39)	-1.42	0.16	-1.31	6.45
	Prospective assessment of economic situation	0.85 (0.36)	2.34	0.02	0.14	7.71
	Retrospective assessment of political situation	0.09 (0.55)	0.16	0.87	-0.98	7.61
	Political identification	0.83 (0.08)	10.43	0.00	0.67	8.69
	Age	-0.03 (0.01)	-2.24	0.03	-0.06	7.61
	Gender	0.62 (0.33)	1.91	0.06	-0.02	9.95
	Unemployed	-0.14 (0.58)	-0.24	0.81	-1.27	8.60
	Student	1.33 (0.91)	1.46	0.15	-0.46	13.06
	Retired	0.22 (0.46)	0.49	0.63	-0.67	9.72
	Vocational education	-0.48 (0.58)	-0.83	0.41	-1.62	13.71
	Secondary education	-0.37 (0.53)	-0.69	0.49	-1.41	10.39
	Tertiary education	0.25 (0.64)	0.39	0.69	-1.01	15.22
LPR	Fixed	-3.10 (1.29)	-2.4	0.02	-5.63	18.56
	Retrospective assessment of economic situation	-2.00 (0.67)	-2.97	0.00	-3.32	14.54
	Prospective assessment of economic situation	0.38 (0.47)	0.81	0.42	-0.54	11.91
	Retrospective assessment of political situation	0.31 (0.77)	0.41	0.69	-1.20	16.36
	Political identification	1.04 (0.11)	9.83	0.00	0.83	13.15
	Age	-0.04 (0.02)	-2.17	0.03	-0.08	16.36
	Gender	0.52 (0.43)	1.20	0.23	-0.33	14.51
	Unemployed	-1.06 (0.84)	-1.26	0.21	-2.71	16.95
	Student	-1.08 (1.41)	-0.76	0.45	-3.85	16.20
	Retired	0.92 (0.61)	1.51	0.13	-0.27	19.07
	Vocational education	-1.41 (0.70)	-2.02	0.04	-2.77	16.16
	Secondary education	-1.19 (0.64)	-1.87	0.06	-2.44	19.13
	Tertiary education	-1.02 (0.82)	-1.25	0.21	-2.62	16.74

Vote for SLD versus	Independent variables	B	Z	P>z	95% Conf.	Interval
"S"	Fixed	-0.11 (1.07)	-0.10	0.92	-2.21	20.38
	Retrospective assessment of economic situation	-1.49 (0.54)	-2.79	0.01	-2.55	16.30
	Prospective assessment of economic situation	-0.11 (0.43)	-0.25	0.80	-0.96	19.30
	Retrospective assessment of political situation	-0.16 (0.69)	-0.24	0.81	-1.51	17.48
	Political identification	0.67 (0.09)	7.74	0.00	0.50	20.14
	Age	-0.03 (0.02)	-1.98	0.05	-0.07	17.48
	Gender	0.75 (0.37)	2.01	0.05	0.02	21.62
	Unemployed	-0.78 (0.66)	-1.18	0.24	-2.07	17.99
	Student	-0.14 (1.06)	-0.13	0.89	-2.23	23.56
	Retired	-0.06 (0.51)	-0.13	0.90	-1.07	18.93
	Vocational education	-0.83 (0.59)	-1.41	0.16	-1.99	23.89
	Secondary education	-1.65 (0.57)	-2.91	0.00	-2.76	18.39
	Tertiary education	-3.59 (1.19)	-3.03	0.00	-5.92	22.62
other	Fixed	-2.56 (1.18)	-2.16	0.03	-4.88	27.80
	Retrospective assessment of economic situation	-0.61 (0.44)	-1.38	0.17	-1.48	22.88
	Prospective assessment of economic situation	0.61 (0.42)	1.47	0.14	-0.21	21.81
	Retrospective assessment of political situation	-0.27 (0.67)	-0.41	0.68	-1.58	23.91
	Political identification	0.52 (0.08)	6.13	0.00	0.35	22.50
	Age	-0.02 (0.02)	-1.02	0.31	-0.05	23.93
	Gender	0.59 (0.38)	1.58	0.12	-0.14	23.83
	Unemployed	-0.68 (0.79)	-0.86	0.39	-2.23	24.8
	Student	1.35 (1.02)	1.33	0.19	-0.65	27.17
	Retired	0.55 (0.53)	1.04	0.30	-0.49	26.39
	Vocational education	0.39 (0.76)	0.51	0.61	-1.10	29.05
	Secondary education	0.26(0.71)	0.36	0.72	-1.13	28.04
	Tertiary education	1.53 (0.79)	1.95	0.05	-0.01	32.12

N..916
Log likelihood ....-1266.513
LR Chi²(72) 525.31
Prob >Ch² 0.000
Pseudo- R²...0.172

*p<05; **p<01; ***p<001; standard error given in parenthesis.

Attachment 11

Economic voting in Poland in elections of 2007 (reference party – PiS)

Vote for PiS versus	Independent variables	B	Z	P>z	95% Conf.	Interval
PO	Fixed	2.75 (0.53)	5.22	0.00	1.72	3.79
	Retrospective assessment of economic situation	-0.64 (0.20)	-3.26	0.00	-1.03	-0.26
	Prospective assessment of economic situation	1.99 (0.19)	10.73	0.00	1.63	2.36
	Retrospective assessment of political situation	-0.86 (0.21)	-4.11	0.00	-1.27	-0.45
	Political identification	-0.28 (0.04)	-6.40	0.00	-0.37	-0.19
	Age	-0.01 (0.01)	-1.33	0.18	-0.03	0.01
	Gender	-0.06 (0.18)	-0.34	0.74	-0.42	0.29
	Unemployed	0.40 (0.42)	0.93	0.35	-0.43	1.22
	Student	0.33 (0.63)	0.52	0.60	-0.91	1.57
	Retired	-0.06 (0.26)	-0.24	0.81	-0.58	0.45
	Vocational education	-0.81 (0.24)	-3.42	0.00	-1.28	-0.35
	Secondary education	0.26 (0.25)	1.04	0.30	-0.23	0.75
	Tertiary education	0.72 (0.28)	2.59	0.01	0.18	1.26
PSL	Fixed	1.36 (0.80)	1.69	0.09	-0.21	2.93
	Retrospective assessment of economic situation	-0.58 (0.31)	-1.89	0.06	-1.18	0.02
	Prospective assessment of economic situation	1.25 (0.28)	4.42	0.00	0.70	1.81
	Retrospective assessment of political situation	-1.25 (0.40)	-3.15	0.00	-2.02	-0.47
	Political identification	-0.38 (0.07)	-5.83	0.00	-0.51	-0.25
	Age	0.00 (0.01)	0.11	0.91	-0.02	0.03
	Gender	0.76 (0.28)	2.72	0.01	0.21	1.31
	Unemployed	-0.82 (0.82)	-1.00	0.32	-2.42	0.78
	Student	-0.06 (0.98)	-0.06	0.95	-1.97	1.85
	Retired	-0.41 (0.40)	-1.02	0.31	-1.20	0.38
	Vocational education	-0.49 (0.33)	-1.48	0.14	-1.14	0.16
	Secondary education	-0.14 (0.39)	-0.36	0.72	-0.91	0.63
	Tertiary education	-1.45 (0.66)	-2.21	0.03	-2.73	-0.16

LiD	Fixed	4.00 (0.88)	4.52	0.00	2.26	5.73
	Retrospective assessment of economic situation	0.17 (0.34)	0.50	0.62	-0.50	0.84
	Prospective assessment of economic situation	1.05 (0.32)	3.25	0.00	0.42	1.69
	Retrospective assessment of political situation	1.34 (0.47)	-2.85	0.00	-2.26	-0.42
	Political identification	-0.99 (0.08)	-12.79	0.00	-1.15	-0.84
	Age	-0.01 (0.02)	-0.53	0.60	-0.04	0.02
	Gender	0.50 (0.32)	1.57	0.12	-0.13	1.13
	Unemployed	-0.12 (0.82)	-0.15	0.88	-1.74	1.49
	Student	0.50 (0.91)	0.55	0.58	-1.28	2.27
	Retired	-0.02 (0.47)	-0.04	0.97	-0.93	0.90
	Vocational education	-0.61 (0.44)	-1.38	0.17	-1.48	0.26
	Secondary education	0.31 (0.45)	0.70	0.49	-0.57	1.19
	Tertiary education	0.94 (0.44)	2.15	0.03	0.08	1.79

N..1011
Log likelihood ....-818.119
LR $Chi^2(36)$ 601.77
Prob >Ch^2 ....0.000
Pseudo- R^2...0.270

*p<0.5; **p<0.1;***p<0.01; w nawiasie podano błąd standardowy.

Attachment 12

Economic voting in Poland in elections of 2007 (reference party –PiS/Samo./LPR)

Vote for PiS, Samoobrona, LPR versus	Independent variables	B	Z	P>z	95% Conf.	Interval
PO	Fixed	2.75 (0.53)	5.22	0.00	1.72	3.79
	Retrospective assessment of economic situation	-0.64 (0.20)	-3.26	0.00	-1.03	-0.26
	Prospective assessment of economic situation	1.99 (0.19)	10.73	0.00	1.63	2.36
	Retrospective assessment of political situation	-0.86 (0.21)	-4.11	0.00	-1.27	-0.45
	Political identification	-0.28 (0.04)	-6.4	0.00	-0.37	-0.19
	Age	-0.01 (0.01)	-1.33	0.18	-0.03	0.01
	Gender	-0.06 (0.18)	-0.34	0.74	-0.42	0.29
	Unemployed	0.40 (0.42)	0.93	0.35	-0.43	1.22
	Student	0.33 (0.63)	0.52	0.60	-0.91	1.57
	Retired	-0.06 (0.26)	-0.24	0.81	-0.58	0.45
	Vocational education	-0.81 (0.24)	-3.42	0.00	-1.28	-0.35
	Secondary education	0.26 (0.25)	1.04	0.30	-0.23	0.75
	Tertiary education	0.72 (0.28)	2.59	0.01	0.18	1.26
PSL	Fixed	1.36 (0.80)	1.69	0.09	-0.21	2.93
	Retrospective assessment of economic situation	-0.58 (0.31)	-1.89	0.06	-1.18	0.02
	Prospective assessment of economic situation	1.25 (0.28)	4.42	0.00	0.70	1.81
	Retrospective assessment of political situation	-1.25 (0.40)	-3.15	0.00	-2.02	-0.47
	Political identification	0.38 (0.07)	-5.83	0.00	-0.51	-0.25
	Age	0.00 (0.01)	0.11	0.91	-0.02	0.03
	Gender	0.76 (0.28)	2.72	0.01	0.21	1.31
	Unemployed	-0.82 (0.82)	-1.00	0.32	-2.42	0.78
	Student	-0.06 (0.98)	-0.06	0.95	-1.97	1.85
	Retired	-0.41 (0.40)	-1.02	0.31	-1.20	0.38
	Vocational education	-0.49 (0.33)	-1.48	0.14	-1.14	0.16
	Secondary education	-0.14 (0.39)	-0.36	0.72	-0.91	0.63
	Tertiary education	-1.45 (0.66)	-2.21	0.03	-2.73	-0.16

Vote for PiS, Samoobrona, LPR versus	Independent variables	B	Z	P>z	95% Conf.	Interval
LiD	Fixed	4.00 (0.88)	4.52	0.00	2.26	5.73
	Retrospective assessment of economic situation	0.17 (0.34)	0.50	0.62	-0.50	0.84
	Prospective assessment of economic situation	1.05 (0.32)	3.25	0.00	0.42	1.69
	Retrospective assessment of political situation	-1.34 (0.47)	-2.85	0.00	-2.26	-0.42
	Political identification	-0.99 (0.08)	-12.79	0.00	-1.15	-0.84
	Age	-0.01 (0.02)	-0.53	0.60	-0.04	0.02
	Gender	0.50 (0.32)	1.57	0.12	-0.13	1.13
	Unemployed	-0.12 (0.82)	-0.15	0.88	-1.74	1.49
	Student	0.50 (0.91)	0.55	0.58	-1.28	2.27
	Retired	-0.02 (0.47)	-0.04	0.97	-0.93	0.90
	Vocational education	-0.61 (0.44)	-1.38	0.17	-1.48	0.26
	Secondary education	0.31 (0.45)	0.70	0.49	-0.57	1.19
	Tertiary education	0.94 (0.44)	2.15	0.03	0.08	1.79

N...601.77
Log likelihood 820.159
LR Chi²(36) 601.77
Prob >Ch² 0.000
Pseudo- R²..0.268

*p<05; **p<01; ***p<001; standard error given in parenthesis.

Attachment 13

Economic voting in Poland in elections of 2011 (reference party – PO)

Vote for PO versus	Independent variables	B	Z	P>z	95% Conf,	Interval
PiS	Fixed	-1.87 (0.60)	-3.14	0.00	-3.04	-0.70
	Retrospective assessment of economic situation	-0.48 (0.30)	-1.61	0.11	-1.07	0.11
	Prospective assessment of economic situation	-1.38 (0.28)	-4.92	0.00	-1.93	-0.83
	Retrospective assessment of political situation	-1.63 (0.35)	-4.60	0.00	-2.32	-0.94
	Political identification	0.35 (0.05)	7.75	0.00	0.26	0.44
	Age	0.00 (0.01)	-0.24	0.81	-0.02	0.02
	Gender	-0.24 (0.19)	-1.22	0.22	-0.62	0.14
	Unemployed	0.04 (0.39)	0.10	0.92	-0.73	0.81
	Student	0.62 (0.47)	1.31	0.19	-0.31	1.55
	Retired	0.16 (0.29)	0.53	0.59	-0.42	0.74
	Vocational education	-0.20 (0.30)	-0.67	0.51	-0.80	0.39
	Secondary education	-0.37 (0.28)	-1.30	0.19	-0.92	0.18
	Tertiary education	-0.61 (0.34)	-1.78	0.08	-1.27	0.06
PSL	Fixed	1.24 (0.81)	1.52	0.13	-0.36	2.84
	Retrospective assessment of economic situation	-0.69 (0.47)	-1.47	0.14	-1.61	0.23
	Prospective assessment of economic situation	-1.21 (0.43)	-2.79	0.01	-2.06	-0.36
	Retrospective assessment of political situation	-0.60 (0.44)	-1.35	0.18	-1.47	0.27
	Political identification	-0.11 (0.06)	-1.72	0.09	-0.23	0.02
	Age	-0.02 (0.01)	-1.50	0.13	-0.04	0.01
	Gender	-0.27 (0.29)	-0.94	0.35	-0.83	0.29
	Unemployed	-0.85 (0.65)	-1.29	0.20	-2.13	0.44
	Student	-1.05 (0.85)	-1.24	0.21	-2.71	0.61
	Retired	-0.49 (0.44)	-1.10	0.27	-1.35	0.38
	Vocational education	-0.11 (0.44)	-0.26	0.80	-0.97	0.74
	Secondary education	-0.94 (0.44)	-2.13	0.03	-1.81	-0.07
	Tertiary education	-1.50 (0.53)	-2.83	0.01	-2.54	-0.46

Vote for PO versus	Independent variables	B	Z	P>z	95% Conf,	Interval
SLD	Fixed	1.66 (0.90)	1.86	0.06	-0.09	3.42
	Retrospective assessment of economic situation	-0.56 (0.50)	-1.12	0.26	-1.53	0.41
	Prospective assessment of economic situation	0.03 (0.37)	0.07	0.94	-0.70	0.76
	Retrospective assessment of political situation	-0.85 (0.49)	-1.72	0.09	-1.81	0.12
	Political identification	-0.54 (0.07)	-7.57	0.00	-0.69	-0.40
	Age	0.00 (0.01)	-0.10	0.92	-0.03	0.03
	Gender	0.01 (0.32)	0.03	0.98	-0.62	0.64
	Unemployed	0.03 (0.65)	0.05	0.96	-1.24	1.30
	Student	-0.26 (0.88)	-0.30	0.77	-1.98	1.46
	Retired	0.18 (0.47)	0.38	0.70	-0.74	1.10
	Vocational education	-0.70 (0.50)	-1.40	0.16	-1.69	0.28
	Secondary education	-1.15 (0.46)	-2.48	0.01	-2.06	-0.24
	Tertiary education	-0.81 (0.52)	-1.57	0.12	-1.82	0.20
RP	Fixed	0.94 (0.74)	1.26	0.21	-0.52	2.40
	Retrospective assessment of economic situation	-0.37 (0.35)	-1.06	0.29	-1.04	0.31
	Prospective assessment of economic situation	-0.83 (0.32)	-2.58	0.01	-1.45	-0.2
	Retrospective assessment of political situation	0.31 (0.32)	0.96	0.34	-0.32	0.94
	Political identification	-0.21 (0.06)	-3.67	0.00	-0.32	-0.1
	Age	-0.02 (0.01)	-2.06	0.04	-0.05	0.00
	Gender	0.34 (0.26)	1.31	0.19	-0.17	0.85
	Unemployed	0.42 (0.48)	0.88	0.38	-0.52	1.37
	Student	0.75 (0.49)	1.53	0.13	-0.21	1.71
	Retired	0.47 (0.43)	1.10	0.27	-0.37	1.31
	Vocational education	-0.72 (0.45)	-1.58	0.11	-1.61	0.17
	Secondary education	-0.54 (0.39)	-1.40	0.16	-1.29	0.22
	Tertiary education	-0.37 (0.43)	-0.86	0.39	-1.21	0.47

N..821
Log likelihood 888.943
LR $Chi^2(48)$ 989.63
Prob $>Ch^2$ 0.000
Pseudo- R^2...0.183

*p<0.5; **p<0.1;***p<0.01; w nawiasie podano błąd standardowy.

Attachment 14

Economic voting in Poland in elections of 2011 (reference party – PO/PSL)

Vote for PO-PSL versus	Independent variables	B	Z	P>z	95% Conf.	Interval
PiS	Fixed	-2.54 (0.57)	-4.44	0.00	-3.66	-1.42
	Retrospective assessment of economic situation	-0.40 (0.30)	-1.35	0.18	-0.98	0.18
	Prospective assessment of economic situation	-1.25 (0.28)	-4.50	0.00	-1.80	-0.71
	Retrospective assessment of political situation	-1.57 (0.35)	-4.46	0.00	-2.27	-0.88
	Political identification	0.37 (0.04)	8.38	0.00	0.28	0.46
	Age	0.00 (0.01)	0.08	0.93	-0.02	0.02
	Gender	-0.19 (0.19)	-1.03	0.30	-0.56	0.18
	Unemployed	0.18 (0.38)	0.47	0.64	-0.57	0.93
	Student	0.79 (0.46)	1.71	0.09	-0.12	1.69
	Retired	0.24 (0.29)	0.82	0.41	-0.32	0.80
	Vocational education	-0.20 (0.29)	-0.68	0.50	-0.76	0.37
	Secondary education	-0.21 (0.27)	-0.79	0.43	-0.74	0.32
	Tertiary education	-0.37 (0.33)	-1.12	0.27	-1.01	0.28
SLD	Fixed	0.97 (0.87)	1.11	0.27	-0.74	2.68
	Retrospective assessment of economic situation	-0.48 (0.50)	-0.97	0.33	-1.46	0.49
	Prospective assessment of economic situation	0.19 (0.37)	0.50	0.62	-0.54	0.91
	Retrospective assessment of political situation	-0.79 (0.49)	-1.61	0.11	-1.75	0.17
	Political identification	-0.52 (0.07)	-7.41	0.00	-0.66	-0.39
	Age	0.00 (0.01)	0.11	0.91	-0.03	0.03
	Gender	0.05 (0.32)	0.16	0.87	-0.57	0.67
	Unemployed	0.18 (0.64)	0.28	0.78	-1.08	1.44
	Student	-0.09 (0.87)	-0.11	0.92	-1.80	1.61
	Retired	0.26 (0.46)	0.57	0.57	-0.65	1.17
	Vocational education	-0.70 (0.49)	-1.41	0.16	-1.66	0.27
	Secondary education	-0.99 (0.46)	-2.17	0.03	-1.88	-0.09
	Tertiary education	-0.56 (0.51)	-1.11	0.27	-1.55	0.43

Vote for PO-PSL versus	Independent variables	B	Z	P>z	95% Conf.	Interval
RP	Fixed	0.29 (0.72)	0.41	0.68	-1.12	1.71
	Retrospective assessment of economic situation	-0.30 (0.34)	-0.88	0.38	-0.98	0.37
	Prospective assessment of economic situation	-0.70 (0.32)	-2.19	0.03	-1.33	-0.07
	Retrospective assessment of political situation	0.38 (0.32)	1.18	0.24	-0.25	1.01
	Political identification	-0.19 (0.06)	-3.41	0.00	-0.30	-0.08
	Age	-0.02 (0.01)	-1.86	0.06	-0.04	0.00
	Gender	0.38 (0.26)	1.48	0.14	-0.12	0.88
	Unemployed	0.56 (0.48)	1.17	0.24	-0.37	1.49
	Student	0.91 (0.48)	1.89	0.06	-0.03	1.85
	Retired	0.54 (0.42)	1.27	0.20	-0.29	1.36
	Vocational education	-0.72 (0.44)	-1.62	0.11	-1.59	0.15
	Secondary education	-0.39 (0.38)	-1.03	0.30	-1.13	0.35
	Tertiary education	-0.14 (0.42)	-0.33	0.74	-0.96	0.68

N...821
Log likelihood 729.231
LR Chi²(36) 349.67
Prob >Ch² 0.000
Pseudo- R²..0.193

*p<05; **p<01; ***p<001; standard error given in parenthesis.

Attachment 15

Economic voting in Spain in elections of 1982 (reference party – UCD)

Vote for UCD versus	Independent variables	B	Z	P>z	95% Conf.	Interval
PSOE	Fixed	4.33 (0.63)	6.83	0.00	3.09	5.58
	Retrospective assessment of economic situation	-0.01 (0.44)	-0.02	0.99	-0.86	0.85
	Retrospective assessment of economic situation	1.49 (0.26)	5.62	0.00	0.97	2.00
	Political identification	-0.30 (0.06)	-4.86	0.00	-0.43	-0.18
	Age	-0.04 (0.01)	-4.13	0.00	-0.06	-0.02
	Gender	0.5 (0.34)	1.45	0.15	-0.18	1.17
	Unemployed	0.18 (0.57)	0.32	0.75	-0.93	1.29
	Housemaker	0.24 (0.37)	0.63	0.53	-0.49	0.97
	Student	1.07 (1.07)	1.00	0.32	-1.03	3.18
	Retired	0.83 (0.50)	1.65	0.10	-0.15	1.81
	Vocational education	0.08 (0.76)	0.11	0.91	-1.41	1.57
	Secondary education	-1.09 (0.45)	-2.41	0.02	-1.98	-0.20
	Tertiary education	-0.11 (0.51)	-0.21	0.83	-1.11	0.89
PP	Fixed	0.57 (0.69)	0.83	0.41	-0.78	1.92
	Retrospective assessment of economic situation	-0.5 (0.52)	-0.96	0.34	-1.51	0.52
	Retrospective assessment of economic situation	-0.46 (0.29)	-1.60	0.11	-1.02	0.10
	Political identification	0.17 (0.07)	2.59	0.01	0.04	0.30
	Age	-0.02 (0.01)	-1.41	0.16	-0.04	0.01
	Gender	0.65 (0.37)	1.75	0.08	-0.08	1.37
	Unemployed	-0.16 (0.62)	-0.26	0.79	-1.39	1.06
	Housemaker	0.41 (0.40)	1.03	0.30	-0.37	1.20
	Student	1.15 (1.10)	1.04	0.30	-1.01	3.31
	Retired	0.35 (0.54)	0.65	0.52	-0.70	1.40
	Vocational education	0.6 (0.80)	0.75	0.46	-0.97	2.17
	Secondary education	0.19 (0.47)	0.41	0.68	-0.72	1.10
	Tertiary education	0.83 (0.53)	1.55	0.12	-0.22	1.87

Vote for UCD versus	Independent variables	B	Z	P>z	95% Conf.	Interval
PCE	Fixed	5.01 (1.25)	4.02	0.00	2.56	7.45
	Retrospective assessment of economic situation	-0.90 (0.72)	-1.25	0.21	-2.31	0.51
	Retrospective assessment of economic situation	0.58 (0.45)	1.29	0.20	-0.31	1.47
	Political identification	-1.78 (0.25)	-7.02	0.00	-2.28	-1.28
	Age	-0.04 (0.02)	-2.43	0.02	-0.08	-0.01
	Gender	1.81 (0.65)	2.77	0.01	0.53	3.09
	Unemployed	0.63 (0.74)	0.85	0.39	-0.81	2.07
	Housemaker	1.00 (0.83)	1.21	0.23	-0.62	2.62
	Student	0.90 (1.28)	0.71	0.48	-1.60	3.41
	Retired	1.33 (0.82)	1.62	0.11	-0.28	2.93
	Vocational education	-1.55 (1.34)	-1.16	0.25	-4.17	1.07
	Secondary education	-0.06 (0.67)	-0.09	0.93	-1.38	1.25
	Tertiary education	0.23 (0.7)	0.33	0.74	-1.15	1.61
Other*	Fixed	1.89 (0.74)	2.55	0.01	0.44	3.33
	Retrospective assessment of economic situation	-0.51 (0.55)	-0.92	0.36	-1.59	0.57
	Retrospective assessment of economic situation	0.16 (0.30)	0.53	0.59	-0.43	0.76
	Political identification	-0.16 (0.08)	-2.09	0.04	-0.31	-0.01
	Age	-0.03 (0.01)	-2.31	0.02	-0.05	0.00
	Gender	0.40 (0.39)	1.04	0.3	-0.35	1.16
	Unemployed	-0.32 (0.65)	-0.50	0.62	-1.61	0.96
	Housemaker	0.16 (0.44)	0.36	0.72	-0.70	1.01
	Student	0.96 (1.11)	0.87	0.39	-1.21	3.13
	Retired	0.94 (0.58)	1.63	0.10	-0.19	2.08
	Vocational education	1.66 (0.78)	2.12	0.03	0.12	3.19
	Secondary education	0.28 (0.49)	0.57	0.57	-0.68	1.25
	Tertiary education	1.51 (0.54)	2.83	0.01	0.46	2.56

N.. 1329
Log likelihood 1211.825
LR $Chi^2(48)$ 553.42
Prob $>Ch^2$ 0.000
Pseudo - R^2... 0.186

*p<05; **p<01; ***p<001; standard error given in parenthesis.

Attachment 16

Economic voting in Spain in elections of 1986 (reference party – PSOE)

Vote for PSOE versus	Independent variables	B	Z	P>z	95% Conf.	Interval
PP	Fixed	-10.21 (0.90)	-11.31	0.00	-11.98	-8.44
	Retrospective assessment of economic situation	-0.78 (0.43)	-1.81	0.07	-1.63	0.07
	Prospective assessment of economic situation	-0.65 (0.34)	-1.89	0.06	-1.33	0.02
	Retrospective assessment of political situation	-1.69 (0.38)	-4.47	0.00	-2.43	-0.95
	Political identification	1.89 (0.13)	14.44	0.00	1.64	2.15
	Age	-0.01 (0.01)	-0.56	0.57	-0.03	0.02
	Gender	-0.04 (0.37)	-0.1	0.92	-0.76	0.68
	Unemployed	-0.25(0.55)	-0.46	0.65	-1.32	0.82
	Housemaker	0.00 (0.43)	0.01	1.00	-0.84	0.85
	Student	0.35 (0.69)	0.52	0.61	-0.99	1.70
	Retired	-0.51 (0.53)	-0.97	0.33	-1.55	0.52
	Vocational education	0.27 (0.54)	0.5	0.62	-0.78	1.32
	Secondary education	1.01 (0.49)	2.05	0.04	0.05	1.98
	Tertiary education	1.55 (0.43)	3.57	0.00	0.7	2.40
CDS	Fixed	-4.35 (0.65)	-6.67	0.00	-5.63	-3.07
	Retrospective assessment of economic situation	-0.16 (0.31)	-0.52	0.60	-0.77	0.44
	Prospective assessment of economic situation	-0.74 (0.28)	-2.67	0.01	-1.29	-0.20
	Retrospective assessment of political situation	-1.52 (0.29)	-5.32	0.00	-2.09	-0.96
	Political identification	0.9 (0.1)	8.93	0.00	0.7	1.10
	Age	-0.01 (0.01)	-0.72	0.47	-0.03	0.01
	Gender	-0.03 (0.30)	-0.09	0.93	-0.62	0.57
	Unemployed	-0.53 (0.42)	-1.26	0.21	-1.36	0.29
	Housemaker	-0.33 (0.36)	-0.91	0.36	-1.05	0.38
	Student	0.11 (0.63)	0.17	0.86	-1.12	1.34
	Retired	-0.47 (0.45)	-1.05	0.29	-1.34	0.40
	Vocational education	0.47 (0.39)	1.21	0.23	-0.3	1.24
	Secondary education	0.22 (0.48)	0.46	0.64	-0.72	1.17
	Tertiary education	0.51 (0.42)	1.22	0.22	-0.31	1.33

Vote for PSOE versus	Independent variables	B	Z	P>z	95% Conf.	Interval
IU	Fixed	0.64 (0.7)	0.93	0.35	-0.72	2.01
	Retrospective assessment of economic situation	-1.58 (0.42)	-3.76	0.00	-2.41	-0.76
	Prospective assessment of economic situation	-1.06 (0.32)	-3.26	0.00	-1.69	-0.42
	Retrospective assessment of political situation	-0.02 (0.31)	-0.07	0.94	-0.63	0.59
	Political identification	-0.8 (0.12)	-6.58	0.00	-1.04	-0.56
	Age	0.00 (0.01)	-0.26	0.79	-0.03	0.02
	Gender	1.00 (0.39)	2.60	0.01	0.25	1.76
	Unemployed	-0.28 (0.39)	-0.71	0.48	-1.04	0.48
	Housemaker	-0.7 (0.62)	-1.13	0.26	-1.91	0.52
	Student	0.59 (0.58)	1.02	0.31	-0.54	1.72
	Retired	-0.49 (0.56)	-0.88	0.38	-1.58	0.60
	Vocational education	0.04 (0.5)	0.08	0.94	-0.93	1.01
	Secondary education	0.05 (0.56)	0.09	0.93	-1.05	1.15
	Tertiary education	1.29 (0.39)	3.29	0.00	0.52	2.06
CiU	Fixed	-5.87 (1.04)	-5.64	0.00	-7.91	-3.83
	Retrospective assessment of economic situation	-0.37 (0.52)	-0.71	0.48	-1.38	0.65
	Prospective assessment of economic situation	0.03 (0.45)	0.07	0.95	-0.85	0.91
	Retrospective assessment of political situation	-1.59 (0.5)	-3.18	0	-2.57	-0.61
	Political identification	1.08 (0.16)	6.87	0	0.77	1.38
	Age	-0.02 (0.02)	-1.08	0.28	-0.05	0.01
	Gender	-1.28 (0.45)	-2.84	0.01	-2.16	-0.40
	Unemployed	-0.69 (0.69)	-1.01	0.31	-2.04	0.66
	Housemaker	-0.99(0.54)	-1.82	0.07	-2.05	0.08
	Student	-1.11 (1.14)	-0.97	0.33	-3.34	1.13
	Retired	0.37 (0.71)	0.52	0.6	-1.02	1.76
	Vocational education	1.14 (0.6)	1.91	0.06	-0.03	2.32
	Secondary education	0.91 (0.67)	1.37	0.17	-0.39	2.22
	Tertiary education	1.23 (0.59)	2.08	0.04	0.07	2.39

Vote for PSOE versus	Independent variables	B	Z	P>z	95% Conf.	Interval
Other*	Fixed	-0.69 (0.47)	-1.47	0.14	-1.61	0.23
	Retrospective assessment of economic situation	-0.75 (0.25)	-2.96	0	-1.25	-0.25
	Prospective assessment of economic situation	-1.38 (0.22)	-6.21	0	-1.82	-0.95
	Retrospective assessment of political situation	-1.45 (0.22)	-6.68	0	-1.87	-1.02
	Political identification	-0.09 (0.07)	-1.24	0.21	-0.23	0.05
	Age	0.01 (0.01)	1.29	0.2	-0.01	0.02
	Gender	0.68 (0.25)	2.75	0.01	0.2	1.16
	Unemployed	-0.1 (0.28)	-0.37	0.71	-0.65	0.44
	Housemaker	-0.06 (0.33)	-0.18	0.85	-0.71	0.59
	Student	0.56 (0.42)	1.35	0.18	-0.26	1.38
	Retired	-0.68 (0.36)	-1.89	0.06	-1.39	0.02
	Vocational education	0.79 (0.31)	2.52	0.01	0.17	1.40
	Secondary education	1.22 (0.34)	3.55	0	0.55	1.90
	Tertiary education	1.91 (0.28)	6.76	0	1.36	2.47

N..1315
Log likelihood ....-1150.504
LR $Chi^2(65)$ 1302.04
Prob >Ch^2 ....0.000
Pseudo- R^2..0.361

*p<05; **p<01; ***p<001; standard error given in parenthesis.

Attachment 17

Economic voting in Spain in elections of 1989 (reference party – PSOE)

Vote for PSOE versus	Independent variables	B	Z	P>z	95% Conf.	Interval
PP	Fixed	-10.91 (1.03)	-10.6	0.00	-12.92	-8.89
	Retrospective assessment of economic situation	-1.00 (0.39)	-2.56	0.01	-1.77	-0.23
	Prospective assessment of economic situation	-0.52 (0.36)	-1.46	0.14	-1.23	0.18
	Retrospective assessment of political situation	-1.32 (0.37)	-3.60	0.00	-2.03	-0.60
	Political identification	1.71 (0.13)	13.32	0.00	1.46	1.96
	Age	0.03 (0.01)	2.09	0.04	0.00	0.05
	Gender	0.30 (0.36)	0.85	0.40	-0.39	1.00
	Unemployed	0.03 (0.63)	0.05	0.96	-1.20	1.26
	Housemaker	0.29 (0.44)	0.65	0.51	-0.58	1.15
	Student	1.21 (0.70)	1.72	0.09	-0.17	2.58
	Retired	-0.19 (0.56)	-0.34	0.73	-1.28	0.90
	Vocational education	-0.53 (0.65)	-0.83	0.41	-1.80	0.73
	Secondary education	1.39 (0.54)	2.58	0.01	0.33	2.45
	Tertiary education	1.63 (0.46)	3.56	0.00	0.73	2.52
CDS	Fixed	-6.29 (0.91)	-6.89	0.00	-8.08	-4.50
	Retrospective assessment of economic situation	-0.80 (0.41)	-1.93	0.05	-1.60	0.01
	Prospective assessment of economic situation	-0.03 (0.37)	-0.07	0.94	-0.75	0.70
	Retrospective assessment of political situation	-1.50 (0.41)	-3.70	0.00	-2.30	-0.70
	Political identification	0.82 (0.12)	6.83	0.00	0.59	1.06
	Age	0.02 (0.01)	1.86	0.06	0.00	0.05
	Gender	-0.45 (0.38)	-1.18	0.24	-1.19	0.30
	Unemployed	-0.29 (0.64)	-0.46	0.65	-1.54	0.95
	Housemaker	0.06 (0.45)	0.14	0.89	-0.82	0.95
	Student	0.51 (0.74)	0.69	0.49	-0.94	1.95
	Retired	-1.59 (0.85)	-1.86	0.06	-3.26	0.09
	Vocational education	1.11 (0.52)	2.15	0.03	0.10	2.13
	Secondary education	1.69 (0.51)	3.3	0.00	0.69	2.68
	Tertiary education	1.62 (0.49)	3.33	0.00	0.67	2.57

Vote for PSOE versus	Independent variables	B	Z	P>z	95% Conf.	Interval
IU	Fixed	1.73 (0.54)	3.23	0.00	0.68	2.78
	Retrospective assessment of economic situation	-0.31 (0.25)	-1.21	0.23	-0.80	0.19
	Prospective assessment of economic situation	-0.41 (0.25)	-1.68	0.09	-0.90	0.07
	Retrospective assessment of political situation	-0.87 (0.23)	-3.81	0.00	-1.32	-0.42
	Political identification	-0.64 (0.10)	-6.66	0.00	-0.83	-0.45
	Age	-0.01 (0.01)	-0.96	0.34	-0.03	0.01
	Gender	0.04 (0.25)	0.17	0.87	-0.45	0.53
	Unemployed	0.00 (0.33)	0.00	1.00	-0.65	0.65
	Housemaker	-0.49 (0.37)	-1.33	0.19	-1.21	0.23
	Student	0.14 (0.42)	0.32	0.75	-0.7	0.97
	Retired	-0.93 (0.62)	-1.49	0.14	-2.14	0.29
	Vocational education	0.52 (0.33)	1.57	0.12	-0.13	1.18
	Secondary education	0.61 (0.35)	1.76	0.08	-0.07	1.29
	Tertiary education	1.60 (0.31)	5.24	0.00	1.00	2.20
Other*	Fixed	-2.08 (0.56)	-3.69	0.00	-3.19	-0.98
	Retrospective assessment of economic situation	-0.63 (0.27)	-2.35	0.02	-1.16	-0.11
	Prospective assessment of economic situation	-0.37 (0.25)	-1.46	0.14	-0.86	0.13
	Retrospective assessment of political situation	-1.31 (0.25)	-5.30	0.00	-1.80	-0.83
	Political identification	0.36 (0.09)	4.12	0.00	0.19	0.53
	Age	0.00 (0.01)	0.16	0.87	-0.02	0.02
	Gender	-0.05 (0.25)	-0.19	0.85	-0.54	0.45
	Unemployed	-0.18 (0.38)	-0.48	0.63	-0.94	0.57
	Housemaker	-0.33 (0.34)	-0.96	0.34	-0.99	0.34
	Student	1.03 (0.42)	2.48	0.01	0.22	1.85
	Retired	-0.65 (0.50)	-1.31	0.19	-1.62	0.32
	Vocational education	0.33 (0.37)	0.89	0.37	-0.40	1.07
	Secondary education	0.76 (0.35)	2.17	0.03	0.07	1.45
	Tertiary education	1.23 (0.33)	3.71	0.00	0.58	1.88

Vote for PSOE versus	Independent variables	B	Z	P>z	95% Conf.	Interval
N...1055						
Log likelihood ....-963.535						
LR $Chi^2(52)$ 956.83						
Prob >Ch^2 ....0.000						
Pseudo- R^2..0.332						

*p<05; **p<01; ***p<001; standard error given in parenthesis.

Attachment 18

Economic voting in Spain in elections of 1993 (reference party – PSOE)

Vote for PSOE versus	Independent variables	B	Z	P>z	95% Conf.	Interval
PP	Fixed	-7.75 (0.63)	-12.34	0	-8.98	-6.52
	Retrospective assessment of economic situation	-0.36 (0.43)	-0.83	0.41	-1.2	0.48
	Prospective assessment of economic situation	-1.05 (0.22)	-4.74	0.00	-1.48	-0.62
	Retrospective assessment of economic situation	-0.41 (0.33)	-1.24	0.22	-1.05	0.24
	Political identification	1.39 (0.09)	15.95	0.00	1.22	1.56
	Age	0.01 (0.01)	0.88	0.38	-0.01	0.02
	Gender	0.39 (0.2)	1.93	0.05	-0.01	0.79
	Unemployed	-0.21 (0.35)	-0.61	0.54	-0.89	0.47
	Housemaker	Brak	Brak	Brak	Brak	Brak
	Student	0.43 (0.46)	0.94	0.35	-0.47	1.33
	Retired	-0.41 (0.36)	-1.15	0.25	-1.11	0.29
	Vocational education	1.00 (0.46)	2.18	0.03	0.10	1.90
	Secondary education	1.15 (0.35)	3.26	0.00	0.46	1.83
	Tertiary education	1.07 (0.29)	3.73	0.00	0.51	1.63
IU	Fixed	0.93 (0.53)	1.75	0.08	-0.11	1.97
	Retrospective assessment of economic situation	-0.46 (0.47)	-0.98	0.33	-1.38	0.46
	Prospective assessment of economic situation	-1.23 (0.23)	-5.27	0.00	-1.69	-0.77
	Retrospective assessment of economic situation	-0.59 (0.35)	-1.70	0.09	-1.27	0.09
	Political identification	-0.56 (0.09)	-6.32	0.00	-0.73	-0.39
	Age	0.00 (0.01)	-0.52	0.61	-0.02	0.01
	Gender	0.39 (0.22)	1.79	0.07	-0.04	0.81
	Unemployed	0.15 (0.29)	0.52	0.60	-0.42	0.73
	Housemaker	Brak	Brak	Brak	Brak	Brak
	Student	-0.47 (0.46)	-1.02	0.31	-1.36	0.43
	Retired	-0.43 (0.44)	-0.97	0.33	-1.29	0.44
	Vocational education	0.57 (0.49)	1.16	0.25	-0.39	1.53
	Secondary education	1.04 (0.32)	3.24	0.00	0.41	1.67
	Tertiary education	0.77 (0.30)	2.60	0.01	0.19	1.34

Vote for PSOE versus	Independent variables	B	Z	P>z	95% Conf.	Interval
CiU	Fixed	-7.74 (0.84)	-9.20	0.00	-9.39	-6.09
	Retrospective assessment of economic situation	-1.45 (1.06)	-1.37	0.17	-3.52	0.62
	Prospective assessment of economic situation	-0.93 (0.33)	-2.84	0.01	-1.58	-0.29
	Retrospective assessment of economic situation	-1.56 (0.75)	-2.07	0.04	-3.03	-0.08
	Political identification	1.01 (0.11)	9.58	0.00	0.80	1.22
	Age	0.03 (0.01)	2.29	0.02	0.00	0.05
	Gender	0.46 (0.29)	1.60	0.11	-0.10	1.02
	Unemployed	-0.03 (0.47)	-0.06	0.96	-0.95	0.90
	Housemaker	Brak	Brak	Brak	Brak	Brak
	Student	-0.5 (0.85)	-0.64	0.53	-2.22	1.13
	Retired	-1.01 (0.50)	-2.00	0.05	-1.99	-0.02
	Vocational education	1.03 (0.64)	1.61	0.11	-0.23	2.28
	Secondary education	1.32 (0.47)	2.82	0.01	0.40	2.23
	Tertiary education	0.69 (0.42)	1.64	0.10	-0.14	1.52
Other*	Fixed	-3.66 (0.63)	-5.78	0.00	-4.90	-2.41
	Retrospective assessment of economic situation	-0.45 (0.52)	-0.87	0.38	-1.46	0.56
	Prospective assessment of economic situation	-0.58 (0.24)	-2.43	0.02	-1.06	-0.11
	Retrospective assessment of economic situation	-0.5 (0.38)	-1.32	0.19	-1.24	0.24
	Political identification	0.57 (0.09)	6.40	0.00	0.39	0.74
	Age	-0.01 (0.01)	-0.54	0.59	-0.03	0.01
	Gender	-0.05 (0.23)	-0.22	0.82	-0.50	0.40
	Unemployed	-0.13 (0.38)	-0.34	0.73	-0.87	0.61
	Housemaker	Brak	Brak	Brak	Brak	Brak
	Student	0.54 (0.47)	1.16	0.24	-0.37	1.46
	Retired	0.06 (0.42)	0.14	0.89	-0.77	0.89
	Vocational education	0.87 (0.48)	1.79	0.07	-0.08	1.82
	Secondary education	0.70 (0.40)	1.78	0.08	-0.07	1.48
	Tertiary education	0.81 (0.32)	2.51	0.01	0.18	1.45

N.. 1186
Log likelihood 1139.078
LR Chi^2(48).. 968.81
Prob >Ch^2 .... 0.000
Pseudo-R^2 .... 0.298

*p<05; **p<01; ***p<001; standard error given in parenthesis.

Attachment 19

Economic voting in Spain in elections of 1996 (reference party – PSOE)

Vote for PSOE versus	Independent variables	B	Z	P>z	95% Conf.	Interval
PP	Fixed	-10.43 (0.83)	-12.61	0.00	-12.05	-8.8
	Retrospective assessment of economic situation	-0.30 (0.31)	-0.97	0.33	-0.9	0.31
	Prospective assessment of economic situation	1.01 (0.25)	4.12	0.00	0.53	1.50
	Retrospective assessment of economic situation	0.82 (0.26)	3.08	0.00	0.30	1.33
	Political identification	1.84 (0.13)	14.25	0.00	1.59	2.09
	Age	0.00 (0.01)	0.28	0.78	-0.02	0.02
	Gender	0.31 (0.27)	1.13	0.26	-0.23	0.84
	Unemployed	-0.07 (0.39)	-0.19	0.85	-0.83	0.69
	Housemaker	0.85 (0.39)	2.19	0.03	0.09	1.60
	Student	0.51 (0.50)	1.01	0.31	-0.48	1.49
	Retired	0.16 (0.43)	0.38	0.70	-0.68	1.01
	Vocational education	-0.55 (0.61)	-0.91	0.36	-1.74	0.64
	Secondary education	0.28 (0.37)	0.75	0.45	-0.45	1.00
	Tertiary education	0.65 (0.31)	2.07	0.04	0.04	1.26
IU	Fixed	0.65 (0.52)	1.25	0.21	-0.37	1.66
	Retrospective assessment of economic situation	-0.38 (0.33)	-1.15	0.25	-1.02	0.27
	Prospective assessment of economic situation	0.27 (0.25)	1.08	0.28	-0.22	0.76
	Retrospective assessment of economic situation	0.39 (0.30)	1.30	0.19	-0.20	0.98
	Political identification	-0.51 (0.09)	-5.68	0.00	-0.68	-0.33
	Age	0.00 (0.01)	0.50	0.62	-0.01	0.02
	Gender	-0.36 (0.23)	-1.55	0.12	-0.81	0.09
	Unemployed	-0.36 (0.28)	-1.28	0.20	-0.92	0.19
	Housemaker	-0.6 (0.38)	-1.57	0.12	-1.35	0.15
	Student	0.39 (0.45)	0.88	0.38	-0.49	1.27
	Retired	-1.06 (0.45)	-2.34	0.02	-1.94	-0.17
	Vocational education	1.32 (0.42)	3.17	0.00	0.51	2.14
	Secondary education	0.77 (0.31)	2.46	0.01	0.16	1.38
	Tertiary education	0.59 (0.28)	2.13	0.03	0.05	1.14

Vote for PSOE versus	Independent variables	B	Z	P>z	95% Conf.	Interval
CiU	Fixed	-9.15 (0.96)	-9.48	0.00	-11.04	-7.25
	Retrospective assessment of economic situation	0.03 (0.40)	0.08	0.94	-0.75	0.81
	Prospective assessment of economic situation	-0.03 (0.33)	-0.09	0.93	-0.67	0.61
	Retrospective assessment of economic situation	0.05 (0.36)	0.13	0.90	-0.66	0.75
	Political identification	1.34 (0.14)	9.55	0.00	1.06	1.61
	Age	0.02 (0.01)	1.65	0.10	0.00	0.05
	Gender	0.12 (0.34)	0.36	0.72	-0.54	0.78
	Unemployed	-0.06 (0.48)	-0.14	0.89	-1.00	0.87
	Housemaker	0.12 (0.50)	0.24	0.81	-0.85	1.09
	Student	1.12 (0.56)	1.99	0.05	0.02	2.23
	Retired	-0.95 (0.60)	-1.57	0.12	-2.13	0.24
	Vocational education	0.77 (0.65)	1.18	0.24	-0.51	2.06
	Secondary education	0.87 (0.45)	1.92	0.06	-0.02	1.76
	Tertiary education	1.13 (0.39)	2.92	0.00	0.37	1.89
Other*	Fixed	-2.39 (0.69)	-3.44	0.00	-3.75	-1.03
	Retrospective assessment of economic situation	-0.67 (0.42)	-1.57	0.12	-1.49	0.16
	Prospective assessment of economic situation	0.72 (0.29)	2.48	0.01	0.15	1.29
	Retrospective assessment of economic situation	-0.14 (0.37)	-0.39	0.70	-0.87	0.58
	Political identification	0.03 (0.11)	0.27	0.79	-0.18	0.24
	Age	0.01 (0.01)	0.80	0.42	-0.01	0.03
	Gender	-0.05 (0.29)	-0.16	0.87	-0.61	0.52
	Unemployed	-0.43 (0.40)	-1.09	0.28	-1.21	0.35
	Housemaker	-0.42 (0.50)	-0.83	0.41	-1.40	0.57
	Student	0.66 (0.52)	1.26	0.21	-0.37	1.68
	Retired	-0.63 (0.54)	-1.17	0.24	-1.69	0.43
	Vocational education	0.76 (0.62)	1.23	0.22	-0.45	1.97
	Secondary education	0.87 (0.40)	2.18	0.03	0.09	1.65
	Tertiary education	1.00 (0.34)	2.93	0.00	0.33	1.67
N..........1117						
Log likelihood..........990.492						
LR $Chi^2(52)$..........1081.53						
Prob $>Ch^2$..........0.000						
Pseudo- R^2..........0.353						

*p<05; **p<01; ***p<001; standard error given in parenthesis.

Attachment 20

Economic voting in Spain in elections of 2000 (reference party – PP)

Vote for PP versus	Independent variables	B	Z	P>z	95% Conf.	Interval
PSOE	Fixed	8.25 (0.77)	10.66	0.00	6.74	9.77
	Retrospective assessment of economic situation	-0.70 (0.29)	-2.42	0.02	-1.27	-0.13
	Prospective assessment of economic situation	-0.89 (0.26)	-3.47	0.00	-1.39	-0.39
	Retrospective assessment of economic situation	-0.76 (0.31)	-2.46	0.01	-1.36	-0.15
	Political identification	-1.69 (0.11)	-15.44	0.00	-1.90	-1.47
	Age	0.01 (0.01)	0.79	0.43	-0.01	0.03
	Gender	-0.11 (0.24)	-0.48	0.63	-0.58	0.35
	Unemployed	-0.30 (0.41)	-0.73	0.47	-1.11	0.51
	Housemaker	0.17 (0.35)	0.50	0.62	-0.52	0.87
	Student	-0.11 (0.48)	-0.24	0.81	-1.05	0.82
	Retired	-0.61 (0.39)	-1.55	0.12	-1.39	0.16
	Vocational education	-0.73 (0.42)	-1.75	0.08	-1.55	0.09
	Secondary education	-0.24 (0.30)	-0.79	0.43	-0.82	0.35
	Tertiary education	-0.27 (0.36)	-0.74	0.46	-0.98	0.44
IU	Fixed	7.64 (1.07)	0.07	7.12	5.54	9.75
	Retrospective assessment of economic situation	-0.13 (0.43)	-0.32	0.75	0.97	0.70
	Prospective assessment of economic situation	-0.15 (0.44)	-2.64	0.01	-2.00	-0.29
	Retrospective assessment of economic situation	-0.78 (0.53)	-1.46	0.14	-1.82	0.27
	Political identification	-2.12 (0.15)	-14.44	0.00	-2.41	-1.84
	Age	0.01 (0.02)	0.56	0.57	-0.02	0.04
	Gender	-0.42 (0.33)	-1.26	-1.21	-1.06	0.23
	Unemployed	0.18 (0.50)	0.35	0.72	-0.81	1.16
	Housemaker	-0.88 (0.62)	-1.41	0.16	-2.11	0.34
	Student	0.94 (0.56)	1.67	0.10	-0.16	2.04
	Retired	-1.38 (0.73)	-1.91	0.06	-2.81	0.04
	Vocational education	0.71 (0.62)	1.15	0.25	-0.50	1.92
	Secondary education	0.63 (0.52)	1.22	0.22	-0.38	1.64
	Tertiary education	1.25 (0.55)	2.26	0.02	0.17	2.34

Vote for PP versus	Independent variables	B	Z	P>z	95% Conf.	Interval
Other*	Fixed	4.87 (0.78)	6.23	0.00	3.34	6.40
	Retrospective assessment of economic situation	0.35 (0.30)	-1.17	0.24	-0.92	0.23
	Prospective assessment of economic situation	-0.91 (0.27)	-3.34	0.00	-1.45	-0.38
	Retrospective assessment of economic situation	-1.03 (0.34)	-3.01	0.0	-1.71	-036
	Political identification	-1.12 (0.10)	-10.75	0.00	-1.32	-0.92
	Age	0.01 (0.01)	0.52	0.61	-0.02	0.03
	Gender	0.14 (0.25)	0.58	0.56	-0.34	0.63
	Unemployed	-0.99 (0.49)	-2.03	0.04	-1.94	-0.04
	Housemaker	-0.44 (0.41)	-1.08	0.28	-1.24	0.36
	Student	0.10 (0.45)	0.23	0.82	-0.78	0.99
	Retired	-0.80 (0.44)	-1.82	0.07	-1.65	0.06
	Vocational education	0.33 (0.42)	0.78	0.44	-0.50	1.15
	Secondary education	0.19 (0.33)	0.57	0.57	-0.46	0.83
	Tertiary education	0.88 (0.36)	2.44	0.02	0.17	1.59
N.........1162						
Log likelihood.........845.117						
LR $Chi^2(39)$.........1010.59						
Prob $>Ch^2$.........0.000						
Pseudo- R^2.........0.374						

*p<05; **p<01; ***p<001; standard error given in parenthesis.

Attachment 21

Economic voting in Spain in elections of 2004 (reference party – PP)

Vote for PP versus	Independent variables	B	Z	P>z	95% Conf.	Interval
PSOE	Fixed	10.09 (0.83)	12.19	0.00	8.46	11.71
	Retrospective assessment of economic situation	-1.41 (0.30)	-4.65	0.00	-2.01	-0.82
	Prospective assessment of economic situation	0.88 (0.26)	3.39	0.00	0.37	1.40
	Retrospective assessment of economic situation	1.03 (0.28)	3.71	0.00	0.48	1.57
	Political identification	-1.86 (0.13)	-14.71	0.00	-2.10	-1.61
	Age	-0.01 (0.01)	-0.84	0.40	-0.03	0.01
	Gender	0.10 (0.26)	0.40	0.69	-0.40	0.61
	Unemployed	-0.22 (0.41)	-0.53	0.60	-1.02	0.59
	Housemaker	0.30 (0.38)	0.78	0.44	-0.45	1.05
	Student	0.22 (0.56)	0.39	0.70	-0.87	1.31
	Retired	0.54 (0.42)	1.29	0.20	-0.28	1.36
	Vocational education	0.35 (0.39)	0.90	0.37	-0.41	1.10
	Secondary education	-0.45 (0.35)	-1.29	0.20	-1.13	0.23
	Tertiary education	0.19 (0.32)	0.59	0.55	-0.44	0.83
CiU	Fixed	0.34 (1.25)	0.27	0.79	-2.12	2.79
	Retrospective assessment of economic situation	-0.73 (0.50)	-1.45	0.15	-1.72	0.26
	Prospective assessment of economic situation	0.11 (0.46)	0.23	0.82	-0.80	1.01
	Retrospective assessment of economic situation	1.46 (0.41)	3.57	0.00	0.66	2.26
	Political identification	-0.64 (0.16)	-4.06	0.00	-0.95	-0.33
	Age	0.02 (0.02)	1.06	0.29	-0.02	0.05
	Gender	0.02 (0.43)	0.04	0.97	-0.83	0.87
	Unemployed	-0.31 (0.83)	-0.37	0.71	-1.93	1.32
	Housemaker	-0.08 (0.67)	-0.11	0.91	-1.38	1.23
	Student	0.22 (0.92)	0.24	0.81	-1.58	2.02
	Retired	0.29 (0.66)	0.44	0.66	-1.00	1.58
	Vocational education	0.20 (0.71)	0.28	0.78	-1.20	1.60
	Secondary education	0.34 (0.53)	0.65	0.52	-0.70	1.39
	Tertiary education	-0.05 (0.58)	-0.09	0.93	-1.19	1.08

Vote for PP versus	Independent variables	B	Z	P>z	95% Conf.	Interval
Other*	Fixed	10.21 (0.93)	10.96	0.00	8.39	12.04
	Retrospective assessment of economic situation	-1.06 (0.37)	-2.85	0.00	-1.79	-0.33
	Prospective assessment of economic situation	0.28 (0.30)	0.91	0.36	-0.32	0.88
	Retrospective assessment of economic situation	1.23 (0.32)	3.90	0.00	0.61	1.85
	Political identification	-2.19 (0.14)	-15.22	0.00	-2.48	-1.91
	Age	-0.02 (0.01)	-1.74	0.08	-0.05	0.00
	Gender	0.29 (0.30)	0.97	0.33	-0.30	0.89
	Unemployed	-0.55 (0.50)	-1.10	0.27	-1.54	0.43
	Housemaker	-0.15 (0.51)	-0.30	0.77	-1.15	0.84
	Student	-0.62 (0.68)	-0.92	0.36	-1.95	0.71
	Retired	0.51 (0.53)	0.98	0.33	-0.52	1.55
	Vocational education	0.90 (0.45)	2.02	0.04	0.03	1.77
	Secondary education	0.10 (0.41)	0.25	0.80	-0.71	0.92
	Tertiary education	0.95 (0.38)	2.52	0.01	0.21	1.69
N....................1270 Log likelihood ....827.004 LR $Chi^2(39)$ ....981.14 Prob >Ch^2 ....0.000 Pseudo- R^2....................0.372						

*p<05; **p<01; ***p<001; standard error given in parenthesis.

Attachment 22

Economic voting in Spain in elections of 2008 (reference party – PSOE)

Vote for PSOE versus	Independent variables	B	Z	P>z	95% Conf.	Interval
PP	Fixed	-9.93 (0.72)	-13.81	0.00	-11.34	-8.52
	Retrospective assessment of economic situation	0.07 (0.39)	0.17	0.87	-0.71	0.84
	Prospective assessment of economic situation	-1.55 (0.37)	-4.21	0.00	-2.27	-0.83
	Retrospective assessment of economic situation	-0.72 (0.34)	-2.11	0.04	-1.39	-0.05
	Political identification	1.79 (0.11)	16.56	0.00	1.58	2.01
	Age	0.00 (0.01)	0.53	0.60	-0.01	0.02
	Gender	0.16 (0.21)	0.74	0.46	-0.26	0.57
	Unemployed	0.34 (0.37)	0.93	0.35	-0.38	1.07
	Housemaker	0.32 (0.38)	0.86	0.39	-0.41	1.06
	Student	-0.03 (0.52)	-0.05	0.96	-1.05	1.00
	Retired	0.35 (0.36)	0.96	0.34	-0.37	1.06
	Vocational education	0.38 (0.28)	1.34	0.18	-0.18	0.93
	Secondary education	0.56 (0.30)	1.85	0.07	-0.03	1.15
	Tertiary education	0.84 (0.27)	3.05	0.00	0.30	1.38
IU-ICV	Fixed	-0.24 (0.69)	-0.35	0.73	-1.59	1.11
	Retrospective assessment of economic situation	-0.51 (0.63)	-0.80	0.42	-1.74	0.73
	Prospective assessment of economic situation	-0.71 (0.41)	-1.76	0.08	-1.51	0.08
	Retrospective assessment of economic situation	-0.56 (0.39)	-1.44	0.15	-1.32	0.20
	Political identification	-0.62 (0.11)	-5.74	0.00	-0.84	-0.41
	Age	-0.01 (0.01)	-0.54	0.59	-0.03	0.02
	Gender	0.33 (0.28)	1.21	0.23	-0.21	0.88
	Unemployed	0.14 (0.43)	0.32	0.75	-0.71	0.99
	Housemaker	-0.31 (0.60)	-0.52	0.6	-1.48	0.86
	Student	-0.74 (0.79)	-0.94	0.35	-2.28	0.80
	Retired	-0.23 (0.57)	-0.40	0.69	-1.35	0.89
	Vocational education	0.89 (0.38)	2.37	0.02	0.15	1.64
	Secondary education	0.98 (0.40)	2.44	0.02	0.19	1.78
	Tertiary education	0.55 (0.38)	1.45	0.15	-0.19	1.28

Vote for PSOE versus	Independent variables	B	Z	P>z	95% Conf.	Interval
Other*	Fixed	-4.01 (0.59)	-6.77	0.00	-5.16	-2.85
	Retrospective assessment of economic situation	-0.01 (0.41)	-0.02	0.98	-0.81	0.80
	Prospective assessment of economic situation	-1.29 (0.39)	-3.35	0.00	-2.05	-0.54
	Retrospective assessment of economic situation	-1.11 (0.37)	-3.00	0.00	-1.83	-0.38
	Political identification	0.33 (0.08)	3.94	0.00	0.17	0.50
	Age	0.02 (0.01)	2.31	0.02	0.00	0.04
	Gender	0.22 (0.21)	1.06	0.29	-0.19	0.63
	Unemployed	0.00 (0.35)	0.00	1.00	-0.69	0.69
	Housemaker	-1.18 (0.52)	-2.28	0.02	-2.20	-0.17
	Student	0.15 (0.47)	0.31	0.75	-0.78	1.08
	Retired	-0.77 (0.39)	-1.95	0.05	-1.53	0.00
	Vocational education	0.92 (0.29)	3.21	0.00	0.36	1.48
	Secondary education	0.7 (0.32)	2.21	0.03	0.08	1.32
	Tertiary education	0.87 (0.28)	3.13	0.00	0.33	1.42

N...1291
Log likelihood 908.960
LR Chi^2(39) 1040.42
Prob >Ch^2 ....0.000
Pseudo- R^2..0.364

*p<05; **p<01; ***p<001; standard error given in parenthesis.

Attachment 23

Economic voting in Spain in elections of 2011 (reference party – PSOE)

Vote for PSOE versus	Independent variables	B	Z	P>z	95% Conf.	Interval
PP	Fixed	-7.34 (0.66)	-11.14	0.00	-8.64	-6.05
	Retrospective assessment of economic situation	-0.62 (0.45)	-1.38	0.17	-1.51	0.26
	Prospective assessment of economic situation	0.48 (0.24)	1.99	0.05	0.01	0.95
	Retrospective assessment of economic situation	0.58 (0.34)	1.71	0.09	-0.08	1.24
	Political identification	1.52 (0.09)	16.57	0.00	1.34	1.70
	Age	0.00 (0.01)	-0.12	0.91	-0.02	0.02
	Gender	0.10 (0.20)	0.48	0.63	-0.30	0.49
	Unemployed	0.20 (0.26)	0.79	0.43	-0.30	0.71
	Housemaker	-0.21 (0.42)	-0.50	0.62	-1.02	0.61
	Student	-0.21 (0.52)	-0.40	0.69	-1.23	0.82
	Retired	0.04 (0.36)	0.11	0.92	-0.67	0.75
	Vocational education	0.06 (0.29)	0.22	0.83	-0.51	0.63
	Secondary education	0.14 (0.32)	0.45	0.66	-0.49	0.78
	Tertiary education	-0.10 (0.26)	-0.40	0.69	-0.62	0.41
IU-ICV	Fixed	0.83 (0.58)	1.43	0.15	-0.31	1.97
	Retrospective assessment of economic situation	-1.17 (0.67)	-1.75	0.08	-2.48	0.14
	Prospective assessment of economic situation	-0.33 (0.33)	-1.00	0.32	-0.97	0.32
	Retrospective assessment of economic situation	-0.25 (0.50)	-0.50	0.61	-1.22	0.72
	Political identification	-0.35 (0.08)	-4.55	0.00	-0.50	-0.20
	Age	-0.02 (0.01)	-2.21	0.03	-0.04	0.00
	Gender	0.16 (0.22)	0.75	0.45	-0.26	0.59
	Unemployed	0.27 (0.26)	1.04	0.30	-0.24	0.79
	Housemaker	-0.32 (0.60)	-0.52	0.60	-1.50	0.87
	Student	0.23 (0.46)	0.49	0.62	-0.67	1.13
	Retired	-0.13 (0.42)	-0.31	0.76	-0.94	0.69
	Vocational education	0.28 (0.31)	0.92	0.36	-0.32	0.89
	Secondary education	0.37 (0.34)	1.11	0.27	-0.29	1.03
	Tertiary education	0.57 (0.28)	2.01	0.05	0.01	1.12

Vote for PSOE versus	Independent variables	B	Z	P>z	95% Conf.	Interval
UPyD	Fixed	-5.10 (1.01)	-5.03	0.00	-7.09	-3.11
	Retrospective assessment of economic situation	-0.44 (0.69)	-0.63	0.53	-1.8	0.92
	Prospective assessment of economic situation	0.53 (0.38)	1.40	0.16	-0.21	1.27
	Retrospective assessment of economic situation	-1.57 (1.05)	-1.49	0.14	-3.63	0.50
	Political identification	0.80 (0.12)	6.51	0.00	0.56	1.03
	Age	-0.03 (0.02)	-1.56	0.12	-0.06	0.01
	Gender	0.02 (0.33)	0.06	0.95	-0.62	0.66
	Unemployed	-0.08 (0.40)	-0.20	0.84	-0.87	0.71
	Housemaker	-1.06 (1.10)	-0.96	0.34	-3.21	1.09
	Student	-0.44 (0.76)	-0.58	0.56	-1.93	1.05
	Retired	-0.38 (0.77)	-0.50	0.62	-1.89	1.13
	Vocational education	1.15 (0.52)	2.21	0.03	0.13	2.17
	Secondary education	1.12 (0.56)	1.99	0.05	0.02	2.22
	Tertiary education	1.41 (0.47)	3.04	0.00	0.50	2.32
Other*	Fixed	-1.91 (0.57)	-3.36	0.00	-3.02	-0.8
	Retrospective assessment of economic situation	-1.02 (0.58)	-1.78	0.08	-2.15	0.11
	Prospective assessment of economic situation	-0.35 (0.28)	-1.24	0.22	-0.91	0.21
	Retrospective assessment of economic situation	0.14 (0.38)	0.36	0.72	-0.60	0.88
	Political identification	0.31 (0.07)	4.45	0.00	0.18	0.45
	Age	-0.01 (0.01)	-0.54	0.59	-0.02	0.01
	Gender	-0.17 (0.20)	-0.83	0.41	-0.56	0.22
	Unemployed	-0.08 (0.25)	-0.33	0.74	-0.57	0.41
	Housemaker	-0.72 (0.48)	-1.48	0.14	-1.67	0.23
	Student	-0.13 (0.49)	-0.26	0.80	-1.08	0.83
	Retired	-0.5 (0.38)	-1.30	0.19	-1.25	0.25
	Vocational education	0.95 (0.28)	3.40	0.00	0.40	1.49
	Secondary education	0.48 (0.33)	1.44	0.15	-0.17	1.13
	Tertiary education	0.80 (0.26)	3.05	0.00	0.29	1.32

N...1269
Log likelihood 1189.970
LR $Chi^2(52)$ 1064.96
Prob >Ch^2 ....0.000
Pseudo- R^2...0.309

*p<05; **p<01; ***p<001; standard error given in parenthesis.

Attachment 24

Economic voting - aggregated model. Detailed data Poland versus Spain

Party running for re-election versus	Variables	B	Z	P>z	95% Conf.	Interval
Main opposition party	Fixed	-0.85 (0.14)	-5.91	0.00	-1.13	-0.57
	Retrospective assessment of economic situation	-0.73 (0.10)	-7.40	0.00	-0.92	-0.53
	Retrospective assessment of economic situation **ES**	-0.59 (0.13)	-4.69	0.00	-0.84	-0.34
	Prospective assessment of economic situation	-0.31 (0.08)	-3.87	0.00	-0.47	-0.15
	Prospective assessment of economic situation **ES**	0.38 (0.10)	3.84	0.00	0.19	0.58
	Retrospective assessment of political situation	-0.37 (0.10)	-3.83	0.00	-0.56	-0.18
	Retrospective assessment of political situation **ES**	0.34 (0.12)	2.91	0.00	0.11	0.56
	Political identification	0.17 (0.01)	11.56	0.00	0.14	0.20
	Political identification **ES**	0.20 (0.02)	10.19	0.00	0.16	0.24
	Age	0.00 (0.00)	1.66	0.10	0.00	0.01
	Gender	0.04 (0.05)	0.88	0.38	-0.05	0.13
	Unemployed	0.04 (0.08)	0.58	0.57	-0.11	0.19
	Housemaker	0.03 (0.08)	0.44	0.66	-0.12	0.19
	Student	0.20 (0.11)	1.89	0.06	-0.01	0.41
	Retired	0.09 (0.07)	1.25	0.21	-0.05	0.23
	Vocational education	0.40 (0.07)	5.78	0.00	0.27	0.54
	Secondary education	0.25 (0.06)	4.05	0.00	0.13	0.37
	Tertiary education	0.28 (0.06)	4.46	0.00	0.16	0.41
	ES	-1.10 (0.14)	-8.98	0.00	-1.34	-0.86

Other opposition parties	Fixed	0.55 (0.14)	4.02	0.00	0.28	0.82
	Retrospective assessment of economic situation PL	-0.62 (0.09)	-6.78	0.00	-0.79	-0.44
	Retrospective assessment of economic situation **ES**	0.08 (0.12)	0.63	0.53	-0.16	0.31
	Prospective assessment of economic situation PL	-0.62 (0.08)	-8.16	0.00	-0.77	-0.47
	Prospective assessment of economic situation **ES**	0.17 (0.10)	1.67	0.10	-0.03	0.36
	Retrospective assessment of political situation PL	-0.55 (0.09)	-6.05	0.00	-0.73	-0.37
	Retrospective assessment of political situation **ES**	0.04 (0.11)	0.36	0.72	-0.18	0.27
	Political identification PL	0.08 (0.01)	5.64	0.00	0.05	0.10
	Political identification **ES**	-0.22 (0.02)	-11.08	0.00	-0.26	-0.18
	Age	-0.01 (0.00)	-2.83	0.01	-0.01	0.00
	Gender	0.13 (0.05)	2.87	0.0	0.04	0.22
	Unemployed	0.00 (0.07)	-0.01	0.99	-0.14	0.14
	Housemaker	-0.22 (0.09)	-2.52	0.01	-0.39	-0.05
	Student	0.34 (0.10)	3.42	0.00	0.14	0.53
	Retired	-0.19 (0.08)	-2.53	0.01	-0.34	-0.04
	Vocational education	0.52 (0.07)	7.67	0.00	0.39	0.65
	Secondary education	0.30 (0.06)	4.81	0.00	0.17	0.42
	Tertiary education	0.49 (0.06)	7.88	0.00	0.37	0.62
	ES	-0.19 (0.11)	-1.72	0.09	-0.40	0.03
N.........14539						
Log likelihood.........13398.926						
LR Chi^2(36).........5087.95						
Prob >Ch^2.........0.000						
Pseudo- R^2.........0.160						

*p<05; **p<01; ***p<001; standard error given in parenthesis.

References

I. Works cited

Agís Villa Verde M., *Montesquieu ha muerto*, http://www.elcorreogallego.es/opinion/firmas/ecg/montesquieu-ha-muerto/idNoticia-342789/.

Aguillar P., Sánchez-Cuenca I., *Performance or Representation? The Determinants of Voting in Complex Political Contexts*, in: J.M. Maravall, I. Sánchez-Cuenca (eds.), *Controlling Governments: Voters, Institutions and Accountability*, Cambridge 2008.

Alberski R., *Trybunał Konstytucyjny w polskich systemach Politycznych*, Wroclaw 2010.

Altman D., Pérez-Liñán A., *Assessing the Quality of Democracy: Freedom, Competiveness and Participation in Eighteen Latin American Countries*, "Democratization" 2002, vol. 9 no. 2.

Anderson C., *Economic Voting and Multilevel Governance: A Comparative Individual-Level Analysis*, "American Journal of Political Science" 2006, no. 50(2).

Anderson C., *Economic Voting, Multilevel Governance and Economic Voting in Canada*, „Canadian Journal of Political Science" 2008, no. 41.

Anderson C., *Institutional Change, Economic Conditions and Confidence and Government: Evidence from Belgium*, „Acta Politica" 2009, no. 44.

Anderson C.J., *The end of economic voting? Contingency dilemmas and the limits of democratic accountability*, „Annual Review of Political Science" 2007, no. 10.

Antoszewski A., *System polityczny RP*, Warsaw 2012.

Aragón Reyes M., *El control parlamentario como contol político*, „RDP" 1986, no. 23.

Arceneaux K., *The Federal Face of Voting: Are Elected Officials Held Accountable for Functions Relevant to Their Office?*, „Political Psychology" 2006, no. 27.

Artiga González A., *Fluidez y volatilidad en institucionalización de los sistemas de partidos*, „América Latina Hoy" 1998, no. 19.

Bagieńska-Masiota A., *Sejmowa komisja śledcza w systemie politycznym Rzeczpospolitej Polskiej*, Warsaw 2010.

Bakke E., Sitter N., *To Stay the Course or Cross the Floor: Members of Parliament, Parties and Party System Change in Central Europe*, Report 5/2005, www.bi.no/FellesFiles/05-5-CEEC.pdf.

Barreiro B., *14-M: elecciones a la sombra del terrorismo*, „Claves de Razón Práctica" 2004, no. 141.

Bartkowski J., Samorząd terytorialny, in: J. Raciborski, J. Bartkowski, B. Frątczak Rudnicka, J. Kilias, J.J. Wiatr (eds.), *Demokracja polska 1989–2003*, Warsaw 2002.

Bellucci P., *From class voting to economic voting – Patterns of individualization of electoral behavior in Italy*, in: H. Dorussen, M. Taylor (eds.), *Economic Voting*, New York 2002.

Benito Sánchez A., *Poder Judicial, Accountability legal y transición a la democracia en España*, "Foro Internacional" 2009, vol. XLIX, no. 1.

Bergman T., Müller W.C., Strom K., Blomgren M., *Democratic Delegation and Accountability: Cross-national Patterns*, in: K. Strom, W.C. Müller, T. Bergman (eds.), *Delegation and Accountability in Parliamentary Democracies*, Oxford 2003.

Binder A., *Introducción al libro Imagen de la justicia: independencia y asociacionismo en el sector judicial nicaragüense*, Managua 2001.

Blanco Valéz R., *La politización de la justicia*, „Letras libres" 2009.

Bosch A., Diaz A., Riba C., *Las funciones de popularidad (1): estado de la cuestión y principales debates*, „Revista Española de Investigaciones Sociológicas" 1999, vol. 85 no. 1.

Bovens M., *New Forms of Accountability and EU-Governance*, „Comparative European Politics" 2007, no. 5.

Bühlmann M., Merkel W., Müller L., Wessels B., *The Democracy Barometer: A New instrument to Measure the Quality of Democracy and tis Potential for Comparative Research*, in: European Political Science 2011, www.democracybarometer.org/Papers/eps201146_AOP.pdf.

Bühlmann M., Merkel W., Müller L., Wessels B., *The Quality of Democracy: Democracy Barometer for Established Democracies*, NCCR Democracy, University of Zurich Social Science Research Center Berlin (WZB), 2008, www.hertieschool.org/fileadmin/images/Downloads/working_papers/22.pdf.

Camp Keith L., *Writing Constitutions that Protects against Human Rights Abuse. How Important Are Provisions for Judicial Independence and Judicial Review?*, 1999, www.artsci.wustl.edu/~polisci/epstein/conference/archive99/Keith.pdf.

Cansino C., *Entre la democracia real y democracia ideal. Consideraciones críticas*, „Metapolítica" January/February 2005.

Cappelletti M., *La responsabilidad de los jueces*, La Plata 1999.

Carrillo Flórez F., *Instituciones democráticas de rendición de cuentas en América Latina: diseño legal y desempeño real*, in: J.M. Payene, D. G. Zovatto, M. Mateo

Díaz (eds.), *La politica importa. Democracia y desarrollo en América Latina*, Washington 2006.

Casal Bértoa F., *Party System Institutionalization and the Quality of Democracy in Eastern Europe*, Working Paper Series, DISC WP/2009/7, pdc.ceu.hu/archive/00005498/01/fernando-paper-web_2.pdf.

Cheibub J.A., *Presidentialism, Parliamentarism, and Democracy*, Cambridge 2007.

Cheibub J.A., Przeworski A., *Democracy, Elections, and Accountability for Economic Outcomes*, in: A. Przeworski, S. Stokes, B. Manin (eds.), *Democracy, Accountability and Representation*, Cambridge 1999.

Chmaj M., *Rządy koalicyjne w III RP*, Olsztyn 2006.

Chmaj M., Skrzydło W., *System wyborczy w Rzeczypospolitej Polskiej*, Warsaw 2011.

Clarke H.D., Marianne C., Whitley P.F., *Emotions, expectations and the dynamics of party support in Britain*, in: H. Dorussen, M. Taylor (eds.), *Economic Voting*, London 2002.

Cox G., *Making Votes Count Strategic Coordination in the Word´s Electoral Systems*, Cambridge 1997.

Cox G.W., Shugart M. S., *Comment on Gallagher's Proportionality, Disproportionality and Electoral Systems*, „Electoral Studies" 1991, no. 10.

Cutler F., *Government Responsibility and Electoral Accountability in Federations*, „Publius. The Journal of Federalism" 2004, vol. 34, no. 2.

Beetham D., *Democracy Ander Blair. A democratic audit of the United Kingdom*, London 2002.

R. Dahl, *Polyarchy: participation and opposition*, New Haven 1971.

Deschouwer K., *Political Parties as multi-level organizations*, in: R.S. Katz, W. Crotty (eds.), *Handbook of party politics*, London 2006.

Diamond L., *Is the Third Wave Over?*, „Journal of Democracy" 1996, no. 7.

Diamond L., Morlino L. (eds.), *Assessing the quality of democracy*, Baltimore 2005.

Dorussen H., Palmer H., *The context of economic voting*, in: H. Dorussen, M. Taylor (eds.), *Economic Voting*, New York 2002.

Dorussen H., Taylor M., *Group economic voting A comparison of the Netherlands and Germany*, in: H. Dorussen, M. Taylor (eds.) *Economic Voting*, New York 2002.

Downs A., *An Economic Theory of Democracy*, New York 1957.

Downs W., *Accountability Payoffs in Federal Systems? Competing Logics and Evidence From Europe's Newest Federation*, „Publius. The Journal of Federalism" 1999, no. 29.

Drummond A., *Electoral Volatility and Party Decline in Western Democracies: 1970–1995*, "Political Studies" 2006, no. 54.

Duch R.M., Stevenson R.T., *The Economic Vote: How Political and Economic Institutions Condition Election Results*, Cambridge 2008.

Dunn D., *Mixing Elected and Nonelected Officials in Democratic Policy Making: Fundamentals of Accountability and Responsibility*, in: A. Przeworski, S. Stokes, B. Manin (eds.), *Democracy, Accountability and Representation*, Cambridge 1999.

Fearon J., *Electoral Accountability and the Control of Politicians: Selecting Good Types versus Sanctioning Poor Performance*, in: B. Bernard, A. Przeworski, S.C. Stokes (eds.), *Democracy, Accountability and Representation*, Cambridge 1999.

Feld L., Voigt S., Economic Growth and Judicial Independence: Cross Country Evidence Using a New Set of Indicators, 2002, in: http://www.wirtschaft.uni-kassel.de/Voigt/PDF/Groningeno.evstv.pdf.

Fernández-Miranda Campoamor A., *Sobre la forma de gobierno:¿un exeso de racionalización?*, in: J.Garcia Roca, E.Albertí (eds.), *Treinta años de Constitución, Congreso Extraordinacio de Consititucionalistas de España*, Valencia 2010.

Fiorina M.P., *Retrospective Voting in American National Elections*, New Haven 1981.

Focada D., *PP y PSOE convierten el Tribunal de Cuentas en un 'geriátrico dorado' a 112.000 € por consejero*, www.politica.elpais.com/politica/2013/02/09/actualidad/1360438194_544177.html.

Font J., *El pez grande se come al chico: las consecuencias electorales de gobernar en las CC.AA. y municipios españoles*, „Revsita española de Investigaciones Sociológicas" 1999, no. 87.

Foryś G., *Wielokierunkowa opozycja parlamentarna w okresie rządów Kazimierza Marcinkiewicza i Jarosława Kaczyńskiego (2005-2007)*, in: K. Łabędź (ed.), *Opozycja parlamentarna w Polsce w latach 1997–2010*, Cracow 2012.

Fraile M., *El voto económico en las elecciones de 1996 y 2000: una comparación*, „Revista Española de Ciencia Política" 2002, no. 6.

Fraile M., *Cuando la economía entra en las urnas: el voto económico en España (1979–1996)*, Madrid 2005.

Fraile M., Lewis-Beck M.S., *Economics and Elections in Spain (1982-2008): Cross-Measures, Cross-Time*, „Electoral Studies" 2012, no. 31.

Fraile M., Lewis-Beck M., *Economic Vote Instability: Endogeneity or Restricted Variance? Spanish Panel Evidence (2008 and 2011)*, „European Journal of Political Research" 2013, doi: 10,1111/1475-6765,12018.

Fraile M., Lewis-Beck M.S., *Economic voting in Spain: A 2000 panel test*, „Electoral Studies" 2010, no. 29.

Fraile M., Lewis-Beck M., *Multi-Dimensional Economic Voting in Spain: the 2008 Elections*", „Electoral Studies" 2013, "http://dx.doi.org/10.1016/j.electstud.2013.05.027.

Fraile M., Pardós-Prado S., *Correspondence between the objective and the subjective economies: personal economic circumstances as a heuristic*, „Political Studies" 2013, doi: 10,1111/1467-9248,12055.

Fraile M., *Una comparación del voto económico en las elecciones de 1996 y 2000*, „Revista Española de Ciencia Política" 2002, no. 6.

Frey B.S., Schneider F., *A Politico-Economic Model of the United Kingdom*, „Economic Journal" 1978, no. 88.

Gallagher M., *Proportionality, Disproportionality and Electoral Systems*, „Electoral Studies" 1991, no. 10.

Gélineau F., Bélanger E., *Electoral Accountability in a Federal System: National and Provincial Economic Voting in Canada*, „Publius. The Journal of Federalism" 2005, vol. 35 no. 3.

Gélineau F., Remmer K., *Political Decentralization and Electoral Accountability: he Argentine Experience, 1983–2001*, „British Journal of Political Science" 2006, vol. 36 no. 1.

Giménez Sánchez I.M., *Balance de 30 años entre el Gobierno y Cortes Generales en la materia presupestaria*, in: *Treinta años de Constitución, Congreso Extraordinacio de Consititucionalistas de España*, Valencia 2010.

Goodhert C.A.E., Bhansali R.J., *Political Economy*, „Political Studies" 1970, no. 18.

Gramacho W.G., *El 14-M sin el 11-M: una estimación a partir de las funciones de popularidad y voto*; Paper presented at the VII AECPA Congress, Madrid, September 21–23, 2005.

Grant R.W., Koehane R., *Accountability and Abuses of Power in World Politics*, „American Political Science Review" 2005, vol. 99 no. 1.

Grzelak P., *Populizm w modelu głosowania ekonomicznego w Polsce 2001*, in: R. Markowski (ed.), *Populizm a demokracja*, Warsaw 2004.

Grzelak P.: *Głosowanie ekonomiczne w Polsce w wyborach parlamentarnych w 1997 i 2001 roku*, in: R. Markowski (ed.) System partyjny i zachowania wyborcze. Dekada polskich doświadczeń (1989/1991–2001), Warsaw 2003.

Guerrero E., *Responsabilidad y rendición de cuentas del gobierno*, in: A. Martínez (ed.), *Representación y caliad de la Democracia en España*, Madrid 2006.

Gurtowski M., *Rzecznik Praw Obywatelskich*, in: A. Kobylińska, G. Makowski, M. Solana-Lipiński (eds.), *Mechanizmy przeciwdziałania korupcji w Polsce. Raport z monitoringu*, Transparency International, Warsaw 2012.

Hallin D., Mancini P., *Comparing Media Systems: Three Models of Media and Politics*, Cambridge 2004.

Hammergen L., *Diagnosing Judicial Performance: toward a tool to help guide judicial reform programs*, 2001.

Hanssen F.A., *Is there a Politically Optimal Level of Judicial Independence?*, 2002, www.2.montana.edu/ahanssen/Papers/optimal%20level.pdf.

Henisz W., *The Institutional Environment for Economic Growth*, Economics and Politics" 2000, vol. 12 no. 1.

Heywood P., *Governing a new democracy: the power of the prime minister in Spain*, „Western European Politics" 1997, no. 2.

Herron E., Randazzo K., *Judicial Institutions and the Evolution of Independent Courts in New Democracies*, 2002, www.isp.msu.edu/CERS/randazz.htm.

Hibbs D.A., *The Mass Public and Macroeconomic Performance: The Dynamics of Public Opinion Toward Unemployment and inflation*, „American Journal of Political Science" 1979, no. 23.

Hopkin J., *Metody porównawcze*, in: D. Marsh, G. Stoker (eds.) *Teorie i metody w naukach politycznych*, Cracow 2006.

Jasiewicz K., *Portfel czy różaniec? Wzory zachowań wyborczych Polaków w latach 1995–2001*, in: R. Markowski (ed.) *System partyjny i zachowania wyborcze. Dekada polskich doświadczeń*, Warsaw 2002.

Jednaka W., *Gabinety koalicyjne w III RP*, Wroclaw 2004.

Kanji M., Tannahill K., *What are the current preoccupations of economic voting research?*, „Electoral Studies" 2013, vol. 32 no. 3.

Karlan P., *Two Concepts of Judicial Independence*, 1992, www.usc.edu/dept/law/symposia/judicial/pdf/karlan.pdf.

Katz R., *Why Are There So Many (or So Few) Electoral Reforms?*, in: M. Gallagher, P. Mitchell (eds.) *The Politics of Electoral Systems*, Oxford 2005.

Key V.O. Jr, *The responsible electorate: Rationality in presidential voting, 1936–1960*, New York 1968.

Kinder D.R., Kiewiet R.D., *Sociotopic Politics: The American Case*, „British Journal of Political Science" 1981, vol. 11 no. 2.

King A., *Modes of Executive-Legislative Relations: Great Britain, France and West Germany*, Legislative Studies Quarterly" 1976, vol. 1 no. 1.

King J., *Incumbent Popularity and Vote Choice in Gubernatorial Elections*, „Journal of Politics" 2001, no. 63(2).

Kramer G.H., *Schort-term Fluctuations in U.S. Voting Behavior, 1896–1964*, „American Political Science Review" 1971, no. 65.

Kramer G., *The ecological fallacy revisited: Aggregate versus individual level findings on economic and elections, and sociotropic voting*, „American Political Science Review" 1983, no. 77.

Kruk M., *Funkcja kontrolna sejmu*, Warsaw 2008.

Kruk M., *Wprowadzenie: prawa i wolności – przedmiotem ochrony prawnej*, in: M. Kruk (ed.), *System ochrony prawnej w Polsce*, Warsaw 2008.

La Porta R., López de Silanes F., Pop-Eleches C., Shleifer A., *The Guarantees of Freedom*, 2002, post.economics.harvard.edu/faculty/laporta/papers/freedom.pdf.

Lago I., *El voto estratégico en las elecciones generales en España (1977–2000). Efecots y mecanismos causales en la explicación del comportamiento electoral*, Madrid 2005.

Lago I., Lago S., *El sistema electoral español: Una cuantificación de sus efectos mecánico y psicológico*, „Revista de Estudios Políticos" 2000, no. 107.

Lago I., Montero J.R., *Los mecanismos del cambio electoral. Del 11-M al 14-M*, „Claves de la Razón Práctica" 2005, no. 149.

Lane J.E., Ersson S.O., *Política europea: una introdución*, Madrid 1998.

Larkins Ch., *Judicial independence and Democratization: A Theoretical and Conceptual Analysis*, „The American Journal of Comparative Law" 1996, no. XLIV.

León S., *Who is Responsible for What? Clarity of Responsibilities in Multilevel States: The Case of Spain*, "European Journal of Political Research" 2007, no. 50.

Levine D, Molina J., *Measuring the Quality of Democracy*, in: D. Levine, J Molina (eds.), *The Quality of Democracy in Latin America*, Boulder 2011.

Levine D., Molina J., *The Quality of Democracy: Strengths and Weaknesses in Latin America*, in: D. Levine, J Molina (eds.), The Quality of Democracy in Latin America, Boulder 2011.

Levine D., Molina J., *Evaluating the Quality of Democracy in Latin America*, in: D. Levine J. Molina (eds.), *The Quality of Democracy in Latin America*, Boulder 2011.

Lewis-Beck M.S., Celeste Ratto M., *Economic voting in Latin America: A general model*, „Electoral Studies" 2013, vol. 32, no. 3.

Lewis-Beck M.S., *Economics and Elections: The Major Western Democracies*, Ann Arbor 1988.

Lewis-Beck M.S., Stegmaier M., *Economic determinants of electoral outcomes*, „Annual Review of Political Science" 2000, no. 3.

Leyden K., Borrelli S., *The Efect of State Economic Conditions on Gubernatorial Elections: Does Unified Government Made a Difference?*, „Political Research Quarterly" 1995, vol. 48, no. 2.

Łabędź K., *Funkcjonowanie opozycji w VI kadencji Sejmu (2007-2010)*, in: K. Łabędź (ed.), *Opozycja parlamentarna w Polsce w latach 1997–2010*, Cracow 2012.

Lijphart A., *Electoral Systems and Party Systems. A Study of Twenty-Seven Democracies, 1945–1990*, Oxford 1994.

Lijphart A., *Patterns of Democracy: Government Forms and Performances in Thirty Six Countries*, New Haven, CT Yale University, 1999.

Lopez Nieto L., *El parlamento*, in: M. Alcantara, A. Martinez (eds.), *Política y Gobierno en España*, Valencia 1999.

López-Pintor R., *Para que la democracia crezca. Diagnosticao z propuesta*, in: *La sociedad: teoría e investigación empírica. Libro haomenaje a José Jiménez Blanco*, Madrid 2002.

Lowndes V., *Instytucjonalizm*, in: D. Marsh, G. Stoker (eds.) *Teorie i metody w naukach politycznych*, Cracow 2006.

Magalhães P.C., Aguiar-Cono.aria L., Lewis-Beck M., *Forecasting Spanish elections*, „International Journal of Forecasting" 2012, no. 1.

Mainwaring S., *Party Systems in The Third Wave*, „Journal of Democracy 1998, vol. 9, no. 3.

Mainwaring S., Scully T., *Building Democratic Institutions: Party Systems in Latin America*, Stanford University Press, Stanford 1995.

Mair P., *Party Systems and Voter, The Freezing Hypothesis: an Evaluation*, in: L. Karvonen, S. Kuhnle (eds.), *Systems and Voter Alignments Revisited*, London 2001.

Manin B., Przeworski A., Stokes S.C., *Introduction*, in: B. Manin, A. Przeworski, S.C. Stokes (eds.), *Democracy, Accountability and Representation*, Cambridge 1999.

Manin B., *Los principios del gobierno representativo*, Alianza, Madrid 1998.

Manin B., Przeworski, Stokes S., Elections and Representation, in: A. Przeworski, S. Stokes, B. Manin, (eds.), *Democracy, Accountability and Representation*, Cambridge 1999.

Maravall J.M., *El control de los politicos*, Madrid 2003.

Maravall J.M., Przeworski A., *Political Reactions to the Economy: The Spanish Experience*, in: S. Stokes (ed.), *Public Support for Market Reforms in New Democracies*, Cambridge 2001.

Maravall J.M., *Surviving Accountabilty*, in: A. Przeworski, S. Stokes, B. Manin (eds.), *Democracy, Accountability and Representation*, Cambridge 1999.

Markowski R., *System partyjny*, in: L. Kolarska-Babińska, J. Kucharczyk, J. Zbieranek (eds.), *Demokracja w Polsce 2005–2007*, Warsaw 2007.

Markowski R., Cześnik M., *Wybory parlamentarne w 2011 roku- kontynuacja i zmiana*, „Studia Polityczne" 2012, no. 29.

McCubbins M., Schwartz T., *Congressional Oversight Overlooked: Police Patrols versus Fire Alarms*, „American Journal of Political Science 1984, no. 28.

McGraw K.M., *Avoiding Blame: An Experimental Investigation of Political Excuses and Justifications*, „British Journal of Political Science 1990, no. 20(1).

McGraw K.M., Timpone R., Bruck G., *Justifying Controversial Political Decisions: Home Style in the Laboratory*, „Political Behavior" 1993, no. 15(13).

Mellado Prado P., *La responsabilidad política del gobierno*, „Revista de Derecho Político" 1992, no. 37.

Méndez J. E., *Legislatures, judiciaries and innovations in horizontal accountability*, wystapienie na konferencji pt. *Accountability, and Democratic Governance in Latin America*, Kellog Institute, Notre Dame 2000.

Michavila N., *Guerra, terrorismo y elecciones: incidencia electoral de los atentados islamistas en Madrid*, Documento de Trabajo no. 13/2005–10/03/2005, Instituto Real Elcano, www.realinstitutoelcano.org/wps/portal/rielcano/contenido?WCM_GLOBAL_CONTEXT=/elcano/elcano_es/zonas_es/imagen+de+espana/dt13–2005.

Montero G., Lago I., *The 2004 Election in Spain: Terrorism, Accountability, and Voting*, Working paper 253, Insitut de Ciénces Polítiques I Socials, Barcelona 2006.

Montero J.R., *El debate sobre el sistema electoral: rendimientos, criterios y propuestas de reforma*, in: J.Montables (ed.), *El sistema electoral a debate*, Madrid 1998.

Montero J. R., I.Lago, *Introducción: 2008, las décimas elecciones desde la restaruación de la democracia*, in: J.R. Montero, I. Lago, *Elecciones Generales 2008*, Madrid 2010.

Montero J.R., Llera F J., Torcal M., *Sistemas electorales en España: una recapitualción*, „Revista Española de Investigaciones Sociológicas" 1992, no. 58.

Montero J.R., Vallés J.M., *El debate sobre la reforma elctoral: ¿para que´las reformas?*, „Claves de Razón Práctica" 1992, no. 22.

Montero J.R., Riera P., *El sistema electoral español: cuestiones de desproporcionalidad y de reforma*, „Anuario de la Facultad de Derecho de la Universidad Autónoma de Madrid", Madrid 2009.

Montero J.R., Lago I., *Introducción: 2008, las décimas elecciones desde la restaruación de la democracia*, in: J.R.Moneto, I.Lago (eds.), *Elecciones Generales 2008*, Madrid 2010.

Moreno C., Oñate P., *Tamaño del distrito y voto estratégico en España*, „Revista Española de Investigaciones Sociológicas" 2004, no. 107.

Morlino L., *Calidad democrática entre líderes y partidos*, Florencja 2008, www.democraciaenamericalatina.org/articulos/seminarios/sem_partidos/morlino.pdf.

Morlino L., *Changes for Democracy: Actors, Structures, Processes*, Oxford University Press 2011.

Morlino L., *Qualities of democracy: how to analyze them*, 2009, indicatorsinfo.pbworks.com/f/Morlino+Qualities+of+Democracy.pdf.

Morlino L., *Democracias y democratizaciones*, Madrid 2009.

Morlino L., *Democracy Between Consolidation and Crisis: Parties, Groups, and Citizens in Southern Europe*, Oxford 1998.

Morlino L., *'Good' and 'Bad' Democracies: How to Conduct Research into the Quality of Democracy*, „Journal of Communist Studies and Transition Politics", vol. 20, no. 1 2004.

Mueller J.E., *Presidential Popularity from Truman to Johnson*, „American Political Science Review" 1970, no. 64.

Munck G., Verkuilen J., *Conceptualizing and Measuring Democracy: Evaluating Alternative Indices*, „Comparative Political Studies" 2002, vol. 35 no. 1.

Nannestad P., Paldam M., *Into Pandora's Box of Economic Evaluations: a Study of the Danish Macro VP Function 1986–1997*, „Electoral Studies" 2000, no. 19.

Nannestad P., Paldam M., *The V-P Function. A Survey of the literature on vote and popularity functions after 25 years*, „Public Choice" 1994, vol. 79, no. 3–4.

Niżnik J., Ryabinska N. (eds.), *Political Accountability. Conceptual, Theoretical and Empirical Dimensions*, Warsaw 2007.

Nannestad P., Paldam P.M., *From the Pocketbook of the Welfare Man: A Pooled Cross-Section Study of Economic Voting in Denmark, 1986–92*, „British Journal of Political Science" 1997, no. 27.

Nohlen D., *Prawo wyborcze i system partyjny*, Warsaw 2004.

Negretto G., Ungar M., *Independencia del poder judicial y Estado de derecho en América Latina: los casos de Argentina y Venezuela*, „Política y gobierno" 1997, no. IV.

O'Donnell G., *Further Thoughts on Horizontal Accountability"*, Conference on Institutions Accountability and Democratic Governance in Latin America, Notre Dame: Kellogg Institute for International Studies, 2000.

O'Donnell G., *Rendición de cuentas horizontal y neuvas poliarquías*, „Nueva Sociedad" 1997 (152).

O'Donnell G., Iazzetta O., Vargas-Cullell J., *The quality of democracy: theory and applications*, Notre Dame 2004.

O'Donnell G., *Accountability horizontal:la institucionalización legal de la desconfianza política*, „Revista Española de Ciencia Política" 2004, no. 11.

Olarieta Alberdi J.M., *El origen de la Audiencia Nacional*, „Jueces para la Democracia. Información y debate" 1997, no. 29.

Olson D.M., *Party Formation and Party System Consolidation in the New Democracies of Central Europe*, „Political Studies" 1998, no. 46/3.

Padam M., Nannestad P., *What do voters know about the economy? A study of Danish data 1990–1993*, „Electoral Studies" 2000, no. 19.

Peffley M., *The Voter as Juror: Attributing Responsibility for Economic Conditions*, „Political Behavior" 1984, no. 6(3).

Peters B. G., *El nuevo institucionalismo: Teoría institucional en ciencias políticas*, Barcelona 2003,

Peters B. G., *Institutional theory: problems and prospects*, in: J. Pierre, B. G. Peters, G. Stoker (eds.) *Debating Institutionalism*, Manchester 2013.

Peruzzotti E., *Rendición de cuentas, participación ciudadana y agencias de control en America Latina*, Paper presented at the at the 17th Asamblea General Ordinaria OLACEFS, 1–6 October 2007, Santo Domingo, in: www.acij.org.ar/wp-content/uploads/2010/12/peruzzotti-rendicion-de-cuentas-participacion-ciudadana-y-agencias-de-control-en-america-latina.pdf.

Pitkin H., *El conepto de representación polítca*, Madrid 1985.

Powell E., Neff E., Tucker J., *Rethinking Electoral Volatility in Post-Communist Countries: New Data, New Results and New Approaches*, „British Journal of Political Science", CJO 2013 doi:10.1017/S0007123412000531.

Powell G.B., Whitten G.D., *A Cross-National Analysis of Economic Voting: Taking Account of the Political Context*, „American Journal of Political Science" 1993, no. 37(2).

Powell G.B., *Wybory jako narządzie demokracji. Koncepcje większościowe i proporcjonalne*, Warsaw 2006.

Raciborski J., *Teoria demokracji a reguły wyborów*, „Nauka", 3/2006, www.pan.poznan.pl/nauki/N_306_02_Raciborski.pdf.

Raciborski R., *Polityka polska. Szkice*, Warsaw 2003.

Randall V., Svasand L., *Party Institutionalization en New Democracies*, „Party Politics" 2002, vol. 8, no. 1.

Rattinger H., *Unemployment and Elections in West Germany*, in: H. Norpoth, M.S. Lewis-Beck, J.D. Lafay (eds.), *Economics and Politics: The Calculus of Support*, Ann Arbor 1991.

Remmer K.F., Gélineau, F., *Subnational Electoral Choice: Economic and Referendum Voting in Argentina, 1983–1999*, „British Journal of Political Science" 2003, no. 36 (1).

Reniu Vilamala J.M., *La formación de gobiernos minoritarios en España 1997–1996*, Madrid 2002.

Rico J.M., Salas L., *Independencia judicial en América Latina, replanteamiento de un tema tradicional*, Florida 1989.

Roberts A., *The quality of democracy in Eastern Europe: public preferences and policy reforms*, New York 2009.

Rodden, J., *Hamilton's Paradox: The Promise and Peril of Fiscal Federalism*, Cambridge 2006.

Rose-Ackerman S., *Od wyborów do demokracji. Budowa państwa odpowiedzialnego przed społeczeństwem*, Warsaw 2008.

Rothert A., *Rola instytucjonalizacji partii politycznych i systemów partyjnych na przykładzie doświadczeń państw postkomunistycznych*, in: Z. Kiełmiński, J. Szymanek (eds.), *Instytucje prawa konstytucyjnego w perspektywie politologicznej*, Warsaw 2013.

Rudolph T., *Institutional Context and the Assignment of Political Responsibility*, „The Journal of Politics" 2003, 65 (1).

Rudolph T., *Who is Responsible for the Economy? The Formation and Consequences of Responsibility Attributions*, „American Journal of Political Science" 2003, vol 47, no. 4.

Rydlewski G., *Rządzenie koalicyjne w Polsce*, Warsaw 2000.

Rydlewski G., *Rząd Marka Belki (2 V 2004–31 X 2005)*, in: M. Chmaj (ed.), *Rządy koalicyjne w III RP*, Olsztyn 2006.

Sala G., *La politización del Tribunal Constitucional: ¿Desde cuándo y hasta cuándo?*, „Eldiario.es" z 19.09.2013, www.eldiario.es/agendapublica/nueva-politica/politizacion-Tribunal-Constitucional_0_177082923.html.

Salzberger E. M., *The Independence of the Judiciary an Economic Analysis of Law Perspective*, Budapest 2001, www.ceu.hu/legal/Salzberger.htm.

Sánchez de Dios M., La accountability democrática en Europa: el trabajo de los parlamentos, Paper presented at the X Congreso de la Asociación Española de Ciencia Política (AECPA), 7–9 September 2011, Murcia.

Sánchez de Dios M., *La moción de censura. Un estudio comparado*, Madrid 1992.

Sartori G., *Comparative Constitutional Engineering: An Inquiry Into Structures, Incentives and Outcomes*, New York 1994.

Sartori G., *Comparative Constitutional Engineering: An Inquiry into Structures, Incentives and Outcomes*, London 1994.

Schedler A., *Conceptualizing Accountability*, in: A. Schedler, L. Diamond, M. Plattner (eds.), *The selfrestraining state: power and accountability in new Democracies*, Boulder 1999.

Schmitter P., Karl T., *Czym jest demokracja i czym nie jest*, in: J. Szczupaczyński (ed.) *Władza i społeczeństwo: antologia tekstów z zakresu socjologii polityki*, Warsaw 1995.

Schumpetera J., Capitalism, Socialism and Democracy, London, 1976.

Serra Cristóbal R., *La elección de los meibros del Consejo General del Poder Judicial. Una propuesta de Consejo más ingrador e indepenciente*, „Tería y Realidad Constitucional" 2013, no. 31.

Shabad G., Słomczynski K., *Inter-party Mobility among Parliamentary Candidates in Post-communist East Central Europe*, „Party Politics" 2004, no. 10/2.

Sharman J., *Ética judicial: independencia, imparcialidad e integridad*, Washington 1996.

Skąpska G., Bryda G., *Apolityczność czy sprawiedliwość proceduralna? Zaufanie do sądowego wymiaru sprawiedliwości na tle innych instytucji publicznych w Polsce*, „Studia Socjologiczne" 2013, no. 1(208).

Simlat M., *Struktura i funkcjonowanie opozycji w IV kadencji Sejmu (2001–2005)*, in: K. Łabędź (ed.), *Opozycja parlamentarna w Polsce w latach 1997–2010*, Cracow 2012.

Smithey Sh., Ishyama J., *Judicious Choices: Designing Courts in Post-Communist Politics*, „Communist and Post-Communist Studies" 2002, no. 33.

Smulovitz C., Peruzzotti E., *Societal accountability in Latin America*, „Journal of Democracy" 2000, vol. 11, no. 14; C. Smulovitz, E. Peruzzotti, *Controlando la política.Ciudadanos y medios en las nuevas democracias*, Buenos Aires 2002.

Sobolewska-Myślik K., *Partie i systemy partyjne na poziomie regionu. Przykład Szkocji i Karalonii*, Cracow 2012.

Sobolwska-Myślik K., Kasprowicz D., *Opozycja parlamentarna w III kadencji Sejmu (1997–2001)*, in: K. Łabędź (ed.), *Opozycja parlamentarna w Polsce w latach 1997–2010*, Cracow 2012.

Sroka A., *Hiszpańska droga do federalizmu*, Wroclaw 2008.

Stokes S., *Public Opinion and Market Reforms: The limits of Economic Voting*, „Comparative Political Studies" 1996, no. 29.

Strom K, *Parliamentary Democracy and Delegation*, in: K. Strom, W. Mueller, T. Bergman (eds.), *Delegation and Accountability in Parliamentary Democracies*, Oxford 2003.

Strom K., *Minority government and majority rule*, Cambridge 1990.

Szewczak W., *Jak zmierzyć demokrację? Skale pomiaru demokracji politycznej stosowane w politologii porównawczej*, „Przegląd Politologiczny", no. 1/2011.

Toharia J.J., *La independencia judicial y la buena Justicia*, Justicia y Sociedad, PNUD 1999, no. 3.

Toole J., *Government formation and party system stabilization in East Central, Europe*, „Party Politics" 2000, vol. 6 no. 4.

Ugalde L.C., *Rendición de cuentas y democracia. El caso de México*, Mexico 2002.

Urquizu I., *Gobiernos de coalición y gobirnos unipartidista: ¿es posible la asignación de responsabilidades?* Paper presented at the VI Congreso de la Asociación Española de Ciencias Política y de la Administración (AECPA), Barcelona 18–20 September 2003.

Vallés J.M., Bosch A., *Sistemas elecotrasles y gobierno represenativo*, Barcelona 1997.

Villoria M., *La corrupción judicial: razones de su estudio, variables explicativas e instrumentos de combate en España*, Paper presented at the VII Congreso Internacional del CLAD sobre la Reforma del Estado y de la Administración Pública, VII Congreso Internacional del CLAD sobre la Reforma del Estado y de la Administración Pública, Lisboa, Portugal, 8–11 October 2000, unpan1.un.org/intradoc/groups/public/documents/CLAD/clad0044122.pdf.

www.transparency.org/iacc/9th_iacc/papers/day4/ws1/d4ws1_lhammergren.html.

Weaver, R.K., *The Politics of Blame Avoidance*, „Journal of Public Policy" 1986, no. 6(4).

Weschle S., *Two Types of Economic Voting: How Economic Conditions Jointly Affect Vote Choice and Turnout*, Electoral Studies, available online from 7 November 2013.

Winczorek P., *Wstęp do nauki o państwie*, Warsaw 1996.

Wojtasik W., *Gabinety koalicyjne w Polsce w latach 1989–2005*, in: M. Mazur, M. Migalski, W. Wojtasik (eds.), *Polski system partyjny*, Warsaw 2006.

Zuba K., *Polska scena polityczna: ciągłość i zmiana*, Warsaw 2012.

II. Reports, analyses, public opinion polling

Biuletyn Programu Spraw Precedensowych Helsińskiej Fundacji Praw Człowieka, February 2009.

Estudio CIS 2309, Decmber 1998, www.cis.es/cis/export/sites/default/-Archivos/Marginales/2300_2319/2309/e230900.html.

Centralne Biuro Antykorupcyjne, *Informacja o wynikach działalności Centralnego Biura Antykorupcyjnego w 2011 roku*, Warsaw 2012.

Centro de Investigación Sociológica CIS, *Atribución de responsabilidades*, no. 2734, 6.10.2007,ww.cis.es/cis/opencm/ES/1_encuestas/estudios/ver.jsp?estudio=8900&cuestionario=11236.

CBOS, Opinia publiczna o korupcji i lobbingu w Polsce, Communique no. 4302 z badań CBOS BS/63/2010, Warsaw, May 2010.

CBOS, Opinie o działalności instytucji publicznych. Communique no. 3013 from CBOS study, BS/167/2003, Warsaw, October 2003.

CBOS, Opinie o działalności instytucji publicznych. Communique no. 3083 from CBOS study, BS/36/2004, Warsaw February 2004.

CBOS, Opinie o działalności instytucji publicznych. Communique no. 3285 from CBOS study, BS/35/2005, Warsaw, February 2005.

CBOS, Opinie o działalności instytucji publicznych. Communique no. 3488 from CBOS study, BS/32/2006/B, Warsaw, February 2006.

CBOS, Opinie o działalności instytucji publicznych. Communique no. 3672 from CBOS study, BS/17/2007, Warsaw, February 2007.

CBOS, Opinie o działalności instytucji publicznych. Communique no. 3866 from CBOS study, BS/16/2008, Warsaw, January 2008.

CBOS, Instytucje publiczne w opinii społecznej. Communique no. 2361 from CBOS study, BS/104/2000, Warsaw, July 2000.

CBOS, Instytucje publiczne w opinii społecznej. Communique no. 2629 from CBOS study, BS/6/2002,Warsaw, January 2002.

CBOS, Ocena działalności wybranych instytucji politycznych. Communique no. 2026 from CBOS study,S/157/157/98 Warsaw, November 1998.

CBOS, Oceny działalności instytucji publicznej. Communique no. 22–80 from CBOS study, BS/23/2000, Warsaw, February 2000.

CBOS, Oceny instytucji publicznych. Communique no. 4107 from CBOS study, BS/42/2009, Warsaw, March 2009.

CBOS, Oceny instytucji publicznych. Communique no. 4278 from CBOS study, BS/39/2010, Warsaw, March 2010.

CBOS, Oceny instytucji publicznych. Communique no. 4442 from CBOS study, BS/30/2011, Warsaw, March 2011.

CBOS, Oceny instytucji publicznych. Communique no. 4619 from CBOS study, BS/39/201, Warsaw, March 2012.

CBOS, Samorządność w Polsce- bilans dwudziestolecia, Communique no. 4383 from CBOS study, BS/144/2010, Warsaw, October 2010.

European Commission, Statistical Annex of European Economy, Attum 2012.

Fundación Alternativas, *La estrategia de la crispación. Derrota, pero no fracaso*, Informe sobre la Democracia en España 2008, Madrid 2009.

Group of States Against Corruption (GRECO), *Corruption prevention in respect of members of parliament, judges and prosecutor. Evaluation Report Poland,* 25 January 2013, www.coe.int/t/dghl/monitoring/greco/evaluations/round4/GrecoEval4%282012%294_Poland_EN.pdf.

Group of States against corruption (GRECO), *Corruption prevention in respect of members of parliament, judges and prosecutor. Evaluation Report Spain*, 15 January 2014 r. www.coe.int/t/dghl/monitoring/greco/evaluations/round4/GrecoEval4%282013%295_Spain_EN.pdf.

Instituto de Estudios Fiscales, *Opiniones y Actitudes Fiscales 2010,* www.ief.es/documentos/recursos/publicaciones/documentos_trabajo/2011_09.pdf.

Kckic L., The Economist Intelligence Unit's index of democracy, „The Economist" 2006, no. specjalny: The World in 2007, www.economist.com/media/pdf/DEMOCRACY_INDEX_2007_v3.pdf.

Konrad Adenauer, Stiftung, *Índice de Desarrollo Democrático*, www.idd-lat.org/2013/. *Index of Democracy 2008*, „The Economist" 2008, no. specjalny: Democracy index 2010. Democracy in retreat, graphics.eiu.com/PDF/Democracy%20Index%202008.pdf.

Memoria de la II Legislatura del Senado (1982–1986), Secretaría General del Senado, Madrid 1987.

Memoria de la III Legislatura del Senado (1986–1989), Secretaría General del Senado, Madrid 1990.

Memoria de la IV Legislatura del Senado (1989–1993), Secretaría General del Senado, Madrid 1995.

Memoria de la V Legislatura del Senado (1993–1996), Secretaría General del Senado, Madrid 1998.

Memoria de la VI Legislatura del Senado (1996–2000), vol. II, Secretaría General del Senado, Madrid 2001.

Memoria de la VII Legislatura del Senado (2000–2004), Secretaría General del Senado, Madrid 2005.

Memoria de la VIII Legislatura del Senado (2004–2008), Secretaría General del Senado, Madrid 2011.

Montero J. M., Riera P., *Informe sobre la reforma del sistema electoral*, Madrid 2008.

Polity IV Project: Political Regime Characteristics and Transitions, 1800–2012, http://www.systemicpeace.org/polity/polity4.htm.

Projekt OMX TK, www.inpris.pl/wazne/omx-monitoring/omx-tk-poprzednie-wybory/.

Statistical Yearbook of Poland 2012, www.stat.gov.pl/gus/5840_2844_PLK_HTML.htm.

The Economist Intelligence Unit s Index of Democracy 2008, „The Economist" 2008, no. specjalny: The World in 2009, graphics.eiu.com/PDF/Democracy%20Index%202008.pdf; The Economist Intelligence Unit.

Transparency International. España, *National Integrity System Assessment. Spain*, 28 September 2012, issuu.com/tispain/docs/spain_nis_en?e=6538824/2888443.

Trybunał Konstytucyjny, *Informacja o istotnych problemach wynikających z działalności i orzecznictwa Trybunału Konstytucyjnego w 2012 roku*, Warsaw 2013.

Sejm Rzeczypospolitej Polskiej, *III Kadencja. Informacja o działalności (20 października 1997 r.–18 października 2001 r,)*, Kancelaria Sejmu, Wydawnictwo Sejmowe, Warsaw 2002.

Sejm Rzeczypospolitej Polskiej, *IV Kadencja. Informacja o działalności (19 października 2001 r.–18 października 2005 r,)*, Kancelaria Sejmu, Wydawnictwo Sejmowe, Warsaw 2006.

Sejm Rzeczypospolitej Polskiej, *V Kadencja. Informacja o działalności (19 października 2005 r.–4 listopada 2007 r.)*, Kancelaria Sejmu, Wydawnictwo Sejmowe, Warsaw 2008.

Sejm Rzeczypospolitej Polskiej, *VI Kadencja. Informacja o działalności (5 listopada 2007 r.–7 listopada 2011 r.)*, Kancelaria Sejmu, Wydawnictwo Sejmowe, Warsaw 2012.

III. Legal acts

Act of 1 August 1997 on the Constitutional Tribunal, OJ L no. 102, item 643 with amendments.

Act of 15 July 1987 on the Commissioner for Human Rights, OJ L 1987 no. 21 item 123 with amendments.

Act of 18 August 2011 on the System of Common Courts, OJ L 2001 no. 203 item 1192 with amendments.

Act of 20 December 1989 on the National Council of the Judiciary, OJ L no. 73, item 435.

Act of 20 June 1985 on the Prosecutorial Service of the People's Republic of Poland, OJ L no. 102, item 643 with amendments.

Act of 21 January 1999 on the Sejm Investigative Commisson, OJ L 2010 no. 182, item 1228 with amedments.

Act of 23 December 1994 on the Supreme Audit Office, OJ L 1995 no. 13 item 59 with amendments.

Act of 23 November 2002 on the Supreme Court, OJ L 2002 no. 240 item 2052 with amendments.

Act of 25 July 2002: Law of the System of Administrative Courts, OJ L no. 153, item 1269 with amendments.

Act of 26 July 2002 on amendments to the Act on the Electoral Law of Commune Councils, County Councils and Provincial Assemblies, and on amendments to some other Acts, OJ L 2002 no. 127 item 1089.

Act of 27 July 2001 on the National Council of the Judiciary, OJ L 2001 no. 100 item 1082 with amendments.

Act of 27 July 2001: Law of the System of Common Courts, OJ L 2001 no. 98 item 1070 with amendments.

Act of 30 August 2002: Law on Proceedings before Administrative Courts, OJ L 02.153.1270 with amendments.

Act of 9 June 2006 on the Central Anti-Corruption Bureau, OJ L no. 104 item 708.

Decisions of the Spanish Constitutional Court: 5/1983, 10/1983, 20/1983, 30/1983, 28/1984), www.tribunalconstitucional.es.

Law 50/1981 of 30 December 1981 por la que se regula el Estatuto Orgánico del Ministerio Fiscal, B.O.E. no. 11.

Law 50/1981 of 30 December 1981 *por la que se regula el Estatuto Orgánico del Ministerio Fiscal*, , B.O.E. no. 11.

Law Decree of 29 June 2001 sobre composición del Consejo General del Poder Judicial por la que modifica la Ley Orgánica del Poder Judicial of 29 June 2001, B.O.E no. 155.

Organic Law from General Electoral Regime (LOREG) 5/1985, 19 June 1985, B.O.E. no. 147.

Organic Law of 12 May 1982 on the Court of Accounts, BOE no. 121 with amendments.

Organic Law of 12 May 1982 on the Court of Accounts, BOE no. 121 with amendments.

Organic Law of 3 October May 1979 regarding the Constitutional Court, B.O.E. no. 239.

Organic Law of 7 May 1981 regarding the Defensor del Pueblo, BOE no. 109–937 with amendments.

Organic Law of July 2 1985 on the Judiciary, BOE. no. 157.

Reglamento del Congreso de los Diputados, www.congreso.es/portal/page/portal/Congreso/Congreso/Hist_Normas/Norm/reglam_congreso.pdf.

Reglamento del Senado, www.senado.es/web/conocersenado/normas/reglamentootrasnormassenado/index.html.

Regulamin Sejmu Rzeczpospolitej Polskiej, www.sejm.gov.pl/prawo/regulamin/kon7.htm.

Royal Decree-Law on the Election Rules (RDLNE) 20/1977, 18 March 1977, B.O.E. no. 70.

Royal Decree-Law por el que se crea la Audiencia Nacional no. 1/1977 of January 1977, B.O.E. no. 4.

Spanish Constitution from of 27th of December 1978, http://www.congreso.es/portal/page/portal/Congreso/Congreso/Hist_Normas/Norm/const_espa_texto_ingles_0.pdflibr.sejm.gov.pl/tek01/txt/konst/hiszpania2008.html.

The Act of 7 April 1989 on Elections to the Sejm of the Polish People's Republic of the 10th Term, for the years 1989–1993, OJ L1989 no. 19 item102.

The Constitution of the Republic of Poland of 2nd April 1997, http://www.sejm.gov.pl/prawo/konst/polski/kon1.htm.

The Electoral Law of the Sejm and the Senate of Poland of 12 April 2001, OJ L 2001 no. 46 item 499.

The Electoral Law of the Sejm of Poland of 28 June 1991, OJ L 1991 no. 59 item 252.

The Electoral Law of the Sejm of Poland of 28 June 1993, OJ L 1993 no. 45 item 205.

Uchwała Sejmu Rzeczypospolitej Polskiej z dnia 19 grudnia 2008 r. w sprawie zmiany Regulaminu Sejmu Rzeczypospolitej Polskiej, "Monitor Polski" 2009, no. 2, item 9.

Uchwała Sejmu Rzeczypospolitej Polskiej z dnia 28 października 1997 r. w sprawie zmiany Regulaminu Sejmu Rzeczypospolitej Polskiej, "Monitor Polski" no. 80 item 779.

Index of Tables

Index of Charts

Index of Figures

Index of Names

Studies in Politics, Security and Society

Edited by Stanisław Sulowski

Vol. 1 Robert Wiszniowski (ed.): Challenges to Representative Democracy. A European Perspective. 2015.

Vol. 2 Jarosław Szymanek: Theory of Political Representation. 2015.

Vol. 3 Alojzy Z. Nowak (ed.): Global Financial Turbulence in the Euro Area. Polish Perspective. 2015.

Vol. 4 Jolanta Itrich-Drabarek: The Civil Service in Poland. Theory and Experience. 2015.

Vol. 5 Agnieszka Rothert: Power of Imagination. Education, Innovations and Democracy. 2016.

Vol. 6 Zbysław Dobrowolski: Combating Corruption and Other Organizational Pathologies. 2017.

Vol. 7 Vito Breda: The Objectivity of Judicial Decisions. A Comparative Analysis of Nine Jurisdictions. 2017.

Vol. 8 Anna Sroka: Accountability and democracy in Poland and Spain. 2017.

Vol. 9 Anna Sroka / Fanny Castro-Rial Garrone / Rubén Darío Torres Kumbrián (eds.): Radicalism and Terrorism in the 21st Century. Implications for Security. 2017.

www.peterlang.com